GLOBAL INTERNET LAW
IN A NUTSHELL®

SIXTH EDITION

MICHAEL L. RUSTAD
Thomas F. Lambert Jr. Professor of Law &
Co-Director Intellectual Property
Law Concentration
Suffolk University Law School

WEST ACADEMIC

860 Blue Gentian Road, Suite 350
Eagan, MN 55121
1-877-888-1330

Published in the United States of America

ISBN: 979-8-31770-926-6

Dedicated to

Janice Marilyn Knowles, R.N. (1924–2013)

Wonderful Mother, Mother-in-Law,
Grandmother, and Lover of All
Creatures Great and Small

PREFACE

Global Internet Law is a succinct exposition of global Internet jurisdictional, contract, tort, privacy, criminal law, content regulation, and each branch of intellectual property law: copyrights, trademarks, trade secrets, and patents. Every chapter also illustrates global developments. The goal is to provide the reader with a succinct exposition of basic concepts and methods for each procedural and substantive branch of law in a global perspective.

This Sixth Edition of the *Global Internet Nutshell* covers rapidly evolving Internet-related developments such as cloud computing, social media liability, Artificial Intelligence, Machine Learning, Bitcoins, The Internet of Things, 3D Products Liability, and Products Liability Developments for Driverless Cars.

The Global Internet in a Nutshell is comprehensive in its coverage of global Internet issues that practitioners and students will encounter but will also serve as a useful introduction for non-lawyers and graduate as well as undergraduate students in diverse disciplines such as computer science, business, nursing, sociology, law and society and criminology. My purpose in updating Global Internet is to create a state of the art and comprehensive guide to the legal issues arising from the global Internet.

MICHAEL L. RUSTAD

August 1, 2026

ACKNOWLEDGMENTS (SIXTH EDITION)

Many thanks are due to Suffolk University Law School's reference librarians Diane D'Angelo and Rick Buckingham. I greatly appreciate the editorial and research contribution of my Suffolk University Law School faculty assistant Seth Markley.

Finally, as always, I appreciate the editorial work and good company of my wife, Chryss J. Knowles. Our dear grandsons, Dylan and Colin Ferreira, joyfully offer the perspective of youth, which energizes my each and every endeavor!

OUTLINE

Chapter 7. Internet-Related Privacy 327

TABLE OF CASES

References are to Pages

TABLE OF STATUTES

References are to Pages

TABLE OF AUTHORITIES

References are to Pages

Bloomberg BNA, Electronic Commerce & Law Report, Keeping Up With the Domain Name Explosion (Dec. 28, 2012), 608

Boyle, James, Foucault in Cyberspace: Surveillance, Sovereignty and Hardwired Censors, 66 U. Cinc. L. Rev. 177 (1997), 53

Brennan, Jason, Libertarianism: What Everyone Needs to Know (New York, New York: Oxford University Press, 2012), 48

Brexit Update—Changes To Loan Documentation, Mondaq (Mar. 1, 2021), 125

Bridy, Annemarie, The Evolution of Authorship: Work Made by Code, 39 Colum. J.L. & Arts 395 (2016), 541

Brooks, David, 'Deepfake' Tech Echoes Old N.H. Ruling on 'Morphed' Child Porn Pictures, Granite Geek Blog (June 26, 2019), 403

Bucher, Anne, Vizio Smart TV Data Privacy Class Actions Grouped in California, Top Class Actions (April 14, 2016), 226

Budaly, Najiyya, Financial Firms Warned To Watch Risks of Cloud Services, Law360 (Dec. 18, 2020), 185

Butler, Alan, Election Cybersecurity amid a Global Pandemic, 45 Hum. Rts. 9 (2020), 393

California SB-446 Data Breaches: Customer Notification (2025–2026), 361

Camillo, Nicholas, Fortnite Sparks a Battle Royale Over the Right to Use Dance Moves, Finnegan (Feb. 11, 2019), 295

Campagna, Mark V., Understanding Patent Reforms in the Context of Litigation (2009), 656

CCRI Cyber Civil Rights Initiative, 2017 Nationwide Online Study of Nonconsensual Porn Victimization (June 2017), 402

CCRI Statement on the Passage of the TAKE IT DOWN Act (S. 146) (April 28, 2025), 402

CCSI, What Is Edge Computing? (2019), 186

Cerf, Vint, et al., Brief History of the Internet, Internet Society (1997), 12

Cheriyan, Jithin, et al., Norm Violation in Online Communities—A Study of Stack Overflow Comments (Cornell University Computer Science Department 2020), 70

Internet Society (ISOC), The Internet Is For Everyone (2019), 22

Internet Society (ISOC), Top Ten Recommendations for the Future of the Internet (2019), 24

INTERPOL, INTERPOL Report Shows Alarming Rate of Cyberattacks During COVID-19 (Aug. 4, 2020), 390, 438

Investigators from Guangdong University of Technology Have Reported New Data on Telecommunication, Telecommunications Daily (Mar. 5, 2021), 24

IoT Device Statistics By Market Share And Trends (2026), Bayelsa Watch (Mar. 5, 2026), 353

IoT Hacking Statistics 2026, Global Trends and Key Insights, Malware News (Mar. 10, 2026), 355

Jobson, Guinevere, and Armen Nercessian, Developments Related to the Safe Harbors Under the Digital Millennium Copyright Act, 73 Bus. Law. 243 (2017–2018), 529

Johnson, David R. & David Post, Law and Borders—The Rise of Law in Cyberspace, 48 Stan. L. Rev. 1367 (1996), 52

Jourová, Věra, Directorate-General for Justice and Consumers, How Will the Data Protection Reform Help Fight International Crime?, European Commission (Fact Sheet 2016), 381

Judgments in Civil and Commercial Matters: Brussels I Regulation, European Justice (2021), 122

Jux Law Firm, Scandalous or Immoral, Disparaging, or Deceptive Marks: Can They Be Registered? (2014), 561

Kappos, David, Under Secretary of Commerce for IP & Director of the USPTO, An Examination of Software Patents, Keynote Address: Center for American Progress (November 12, 2012), 657

Key Mobile App Statistics for 2026: App Usage, Revenue & Success Factors, Itransition (Feb. 10, 2026), 4

Koenig, Thomas H. & Michael L. Rustad, Fundamentally Unfair: An Empirical Analysis of Social Media Arbitration Clauses, 65 Case W. Res. L. Rev. 341 (2014), 148

Koenig, Thomas H. & Michael L. Rustad, Global Information Technologies: Ethics and the Law (2d ed. 2023), 246, 443

Kollick, Alli, et al., Countries Without First Amendment Rights (Ames Iowa: Iowa State University, 2012), 479
Komaitis, Konstantinos, Trump Ends Americas Leadership on Internet Freedom, Tech Policy Press (Jan 8, 2026), 57
Kramer, Alexis, Trade Secret Cases Surge as Race for New Tech, Top Talent Heats Up, Electronic Commerce & Law Report (May 17, 2017), 643
Kurduban, Vitaly, Principal Product Manager, Digi International. Edge Computing Trends in Industrial and Enterprise Applications (Mar. 30, 2026), 186
Kwall, Roberta, John T. Cross et al., Global Issues in Intellectual Property Law 127 (2010), 540
Lessig, Lawrence, Architecting for Control: Version 1.0, Keynote given at the Internet, Cambridge Review of International Affairs, UK (May 11, 2000), 55, 60
Lessig, Lawrence, Code and Other Laws of Cyberspace (1999), 42, 63
Lessig, Lawrence, Code and Other Laws of Cyberspace, About the Project (2010), 54
Lessig, Lawrence, Code and Other Laws of Cyberspace, Version 2.0 (2006), 42, 54
Lessig, Lawrence, Code Is Law: On Liberty in Cyberspace, Harvard Magazine (Jan. 1, 2000), 62, 63
Lessig, Lawrence, The Laws of Cyberspace (1998), 61
Lessig, Lawrence, The New Chicago School, 27 J. Leg. Stud. 661 (1998), 44
Letter of April 2001 to Oklahoma Attorney General Drew Edmundson (1999), 154
Levin, Daniel, Building Social Norms on the Internet, 4 Yale J. L. & Tech. 99 (2002), 64
Lohstroh, Marten, & Edward A. Lee, An Interface Theory for the Internet of Things in Radu Calinescu & Bernhard Rumpe, An Interface Theory for the Internet of Things (2015), 43
Maayan, Gilad David, The IoT Rundown For 2020: Stats, Risks, and Solutions: Weak Passwords, Insecure Network Services and a Lack of Secure Update?, Security Today (Jan. 13, 2020), 6
Madrigal, Alexis C., The End of Cyberspace: Internet Theorists and Companies Once Declared Themselves

U.S. Department of Justice, U.S. Citizens and Chinese Nationals Arrested for Exporting Artificial Intelligence Technology to China (Nov. 30, 2025), 646
U.S. Department of Justice, United States Attorney's Office for the District of Massachusetts, Serial Cyberstalker Who Terrorized Women for 16 Years Sentenced to Nine Years in Prison (July 25, 2025), 259
U.S. Department of Justice's Review of Section 230 of the Communications Decency Act of 1996 (2020), 35
U.S. House of Representatives, Economic Espionage Prevention Act (May 6, 2025), 644
U.S. Senate, S. Rep. No. 105–190 (1998), 523
Ubata, Danica, What Is ICANN & What Do They Do?, Network solutions (Aug. 23, 2025), 21
UDRP Commentaries, Safe Harbor Under the ACPA: Reasonable Grounds for Believing Use Not Unlawful (Mar. 12, 2013), 594
United Nations, Internet Governance Forum, About Us, (2026), 20
United Nations, Why the Convention against Cybercrime Matters (Dec. 24, 2024), 435
United States Trademark & Patent Office, Patent Subject Matter Eligibility (2012), 663
University of Melbourne, Norms in Online Communities: Introduction and Problem 1 (2020), 69
USPTO, Trademark FAQs, What Are the Benefits of Federal Trademark Registration?, 555
USPTO, What Is a Trademark or Service Mark and How Do They Differ From Patents and Copyrights? (2021), 557
Vint Cerf—'Father of the Internet', Stanford University Engineering Department (2026), 11
Wade, Christine, Consumer Enforcers Clean Up Web in Worldwide Sweeps, Office of Fair Trading, Hermes Database (Oct. 8, 2004), 480
Watner, Carl, Computers and Privacy: National Identification Revisited from a Voluntarist Perspective, 190 Voluntarist 1 (July 1, 2021), 249
Watson & Band Law Office, Internet+ Legal Issues in Cross-Border Import E-Businesses (Sept. 10, 2015), 198
We Must Do More to Stop the Trolls, MENA (Aug. 22, 2020), 434

GLOBAL INTERNET LAW

IN A NUTSHELL®

SIXTH EDITION

CHAPTER 1
AN OVERVIEW OF THE GLOBAL INTERNET

§ 1-1. The Internet & Society

The Internet is essentially a network of computer networks. It grew out of work conducted by two relatively small groups of research-oriented governmental, academic, and corporate entities. The Internet has only been widely used by the general public for approximately three decades. This chapter is divided into four sections.

Section 1-1 is an overview of the Internet and society, while Section 1-2 covers Internet technologies. Section 1-3 explains how Internet standards are set through voluntary organizations such as the Open Systems Initiative (OSI). Finally, Section 1-4 predicts the future of the global Internet.

In June 1995, only 14% of Americans used the Internet. In 1995, only about 1% of the world's population used the Internet, around 45 million persons. By 2026, the number of Chinese Internet users alone was 1.125 billion. The number of Internet users in India reached 1 billion. There are over 300 million Internet users in the United States. As of early 2026, six billion people use the Internet. Nearly 75% of the world's population uses the Internet.

A 1970 Monsanto advertisement claimed, "Without chemicals, life itself would be impossible." In 2026, American households are reliant on the

Internet for streaming cloud services, instantly accessing information on flights, security systems, social media sites, and communication platforms.

In the last three decades, we have come to take the World Wide Web for granted as the most important instrumentality for: booking flights, communicating with each other, connecting with family and friends, purchasing e-books, shopping in virtual bookstores, listening to music, and exploring trending videos.

"Access to the Internet is one of the basic commodities of life these days. Its significance is no lesser than water, electricity, smartphone, landline, [and] gas connections." *What is The Impact of the Internet in Our Daily Life?,* DONCAPRIO.COM (Nov. 21, 2019). The following 2026 statistics demonstrate the centrality of the Internet in everyday life:

- There are 6 billion Internet users worldwide.
- Most Americans subscribe to home broadband internet and own a smartphone.
- There are 5 billion active social media identities.
- Google users do 40,000 queries a second or 1.2 trillion searches per year.
- On average, there are 56.8 exabytes of mobile traffic every month.
- 42.73 petabytes of that monthly traffic comes from video.

- In the U.S., the average adult spends an average of 4 hours 1 minute on mobile internet every day.

Lyndon Seitz, *Internet Statistics In 2026: Global Usage, Mobile Trends, Social Media, And Google*, BROADBAND SEARCH, (Feb. 13, 2026). I teach Suffolk University Law School courses on Zoom enabled by cloud applications:

> Cloud computing is the delivery of computing services—including servers, storage, databases, networking, software, analytics, and intelligence—over the Internet (the cloud) to offer faster innovation, flexible resources, and economies of scale.

Smartphones have become ubiquitous as judged by the following 2026 statistics.

- There are 8.9 billion mobile subscriptions globally, and the number is projected to exceed 9.4 billion by 2030.
- In December 2025, 54% of consumers globally and 53% in North America used mobile devices to access the Internet.
- 5G networks carried 43% of mobile data traffic by the end of 2025 and are expected to cover 80% of the total mobile data traffic by 2030.
- The global mobile application market size is estimated to reach $378 billion in 2026.

- The smartphone market is predicted to reach $1.2 trillion by 2035 with an annual growth rate of 14.04%.

Key Mobile App Statistics for 2026: App Usage, Revenue & Success Factors, ITRANSITION (Feb. 10, 2026).

The role of smartphones in everyday life is illustrated by the following statistics:

- Americans check their phones 186 times per day (11.6 times per hour).
- 72.2% use their phone at work.
- 87.4% use their phone while watching TV.
- 56.4% use their phone while eating dinner.
- 67.9% use their phone on the toilet.
- 60.7% have texted someone in the same room.
- 49.6% sleep with their phone at night.

Trevor Wheelwright, *Cell Phone Usage Stats 2026* (Jan. 1, 2025), https://www.reviews.org/mobile/cell-phone-addiction/.

X, formerly known as Twitter, produces an enormous amount of digital data:

- X has approximately 570 million monthly active users worldwide as of early 2026.
- There are between 557 and 610 million total users, though X is now a private company and official numbers are shared less frequently.

- Around 259 million people use X daily. This represents a 6.6% increase year-on-year, suggesting some stabilization in daily engagement despite broader controversies.
- The United States leads the world in the number of X users with an estimated 104 million. The U.S. accounts for almost a quarter of global X traffic.

Nic Dunn, CEO, Charle Agency, *55+ X (Formerly Twitter) Statistics You Need to Know in 2026* (Feb. 7, 2026).

The amount of data on the Internet was around 40 trillion gigabytes of data. By 2026, big data on the Internet is expanding:

- The amount of data will reach 230–240 ZB in 2026.
- By 2029, that number is expected to reach 527.5 ZB, about a 3.0× increase.
- 2025: 173 ZB/year ≈ 0.474 ZB/day ≈ ~474 million TB/day.
- 2028: 394 ZB/year ≈ 1.08 ZB/day ≈ ~1.08 billion TB/day.

Marija Naumovska, *How Much Data Is Created Every Day: 40 Key Figures and Insights*, DESIGNRUSH (June 27, 2025).

Given the scale of human participation on the Internet and the amount of data produced, contemporary society has taken the unfathomable scale of the Internet and its effects on our daily routines for granted.

How expansive is the Internet? Due to its decentralized architecture, it is difficult, if not impossible, to determine the Internet's precise dimensions at a specific point in time. The exact size of the Internet is unknown and unknowable, as the Worldwide Web is continuously expanding.

A world without Twitter (2006), Skype (2003), Pinterest (2010), Instagram (2010), YouTube (2005), LinkedIn (2002), or Facebook (2004) is difficult to imagine, but these Internet-based inventions have all been launched since the new millennium.

The most dramatic evidence of the importance of the Internet is the rise of the Internet of Things (IoT). IoT technology is an umbrella term that refers to connected physical and digital components. IoT components can transmit data without the assistance of human mediators.

Gilad David Maayan, *The IoT Rundown For 2020: Stats, Risks, and Solutions: Weak Passwords, Insecure Network Services and a Lack of Secure Update?*, SECURITY TODAY (Jan. 13, 2020).

The importance of smart homes and their rapid evolution is illustrated by the following statistics:

- The U.S. smart home market is projected to reach USD 35.28 billion by 2026.
- "The total number of smart homes in the U.S. is expected to reach USD 35.28 billion by

2026. Furthermore, household penetration is expected to grow 39% by 2027."

- "North America held a major share of the smart home market, with the market size reaching USD 56.29 billion in 2026 owing to the presence of major players, including Honeywell International Ltd, Snap One LLC, SmartRent LLC, Creston Corporation, and others."

Smart Home Market Size, Share & Industry Analysis, By Application (Retrofit and New Construction), By Protocol (Wired and Wireless), By Device Type (Safety & Security Access Control, Home Appliances, HVAC, Lighting Control, Smart Entertainment Devices, Smart Kitchen Appliances, and Others), and Regional Forecast, 2026–2034 (Feb. 16, 2026).

Carl Sagan famously said, "We live in a society exquisitely dependent on science and technology, in which hardly anyone knows anything about science and technology." The increase in access to the Internet over the last four decades demonstrates our dependence on the Internet. The following statistics illustrate the extent of commercialization of the Internet:

- 2.77 billion people worldwide shop online as of 2025.

- 78% of online shopping traffic comes from mobile users.

- Online consumer spending is projected to grow 6.79% per year through 2030.
- Online shopping represents 19.9% of all retail sales worldwide as of 2024.
- American online spending totaled $1.34 trillion in 2024; projections indicate that online spending will exceed *$2.5* trillion in 2030.

Online Shopping Statistics, CAPITOL ONE (Last updated: March 2, 2026).

The following global E-Commerce issues reveal the growth of online sales and services:

- The global E-Commerce growth rate is projected to be 8.4% in 2024, to reach $6.09 trillion.
- E-Commerce sales growth rates are expected to decelerate from 2023 to 2028, hitting $8.09 trillion in total sales by 2028.
- The growth rate of E-Commerce consistently outpaces that of total retail sales, indicating a continued shift in consumer preference toward online shopping over traditional retail channels.
- The global E-Commerce growth rate is projected to be 8.4% in 2024, to reach $6.09 trillion.
- E-Commerce sales growth rates are expected to decelerate from 2023 to 2028, hitting $8.09 trillion in total sales by 2028.

- The growth rate of E-Commerce consistently outpaces that of total retail sales, indicating a continued shift in consumer preference toward online shopping over traditional retail channels.

Global E-Commerce Sales Growth (2022–2028), OBERLO (March 5, 2026).

§ 1-2. The Technologies of the Internet

(A) INTRODUCTION TO THE INTERNET

The Internet runs on the *Internet Protocol Suite*, the standard communications protocol used by every computer on the Internet. Every computer connected to the Internet has an Internet Protocol Address or IP address, which is the unique number assigned to every computer connected to the Internet.

The TCP/IP protocol works by breaking data into packets at the source, routing them across networks, and reassembling them at the destination using protocols like TCP for reliability and IP for addressing. A router is a networking device that controls how data moves between different networks by checking destination IP addresses and choosing the best path.

The process of routing involves choosing the most efficient path in the network of computers; each packet has routing information that enables it to reach its ultimate destination.

When the packets leave a personal computer, smartphone or other computing device connected to the computer, they are transmitted through the network and may start "off in different directions taking the least busy path at that instant", but they are all on the most efficient path.

Teach, ICT, *What is Packet Switching?,* ICT.COM (2021).

"The router assigns a local IP address to each device on your network and directs the flow of data. This means your devices can talk to each other so you can share files, print wirelessly, and more. Finally, the router provides security protections such as firewalls and parental settings, allowing some degree of control over data access." *Id.*

> The higher layer, Transmission Control Protocol, manages the assembling of a message or file into smaller packets that are transmitted over the internet and received by a TCP layer that reassembles the packets into the original message. The lower layer, Internet Protocol, handles the address part of each packet so that it gets to the right destination.

Margaret Rouse, *TCP/IP*, TECHTARGET.COM (2015).

Vinton (Vin) Cerf and Robert Kahn of the U.S. Defense Department's Advanced Research Projects Agency (DARPA) created the Transmission Control Protocol (TCP), which determines how packets of data travel via the Internet.

Today, TCP Internet Protocol (TCP/IP) is the foundation for all data traffic on the Internet, and

Cerf and Kahn have been christened "the fathers of the Internet."

Vint Cerf—'Father of the Internet', STANFORD UNIVERSITY ENGINEERING DEPARTMENT (2026).

Cerf's TCP/IP "protocol transformed the Internet into a worldwide network. Throughout the 1980s, researchers and scientists used it to send files and data from one computer to another." *The Invention of the Internet*, HISTORY.COM (Oct. 28, 2019). Some basic approaches emerged from this collaboration between Robert Kahn and Vint Cerf:

- Communication between two processes would logically consist of a very long stream of bytes (they called them octets). The position of any octet in the stream would be used to identify it.

- Flow control would be done by using sliding windows and acknowledgments (acks). The *destination* could select when to acknowledge and each ack returned would be cumulative for all packets received to that point.

- It was left open as to exactly how the source and destination would agree on the parameters of the windowing to be used. Defaults were used initially.

- Although Ethernet was under development at Xerox PARC at that time, the proliferation of LANs were not envisioned at the time, much less PCs and workstations. The original model was national level networks like ARPANET of

> which only a relatively small number were expected to exist. Thus, a 32-bit IP address was used of which the first 8 bits signified the network and the remaining 24 bits designated the host on that network. This assumption that 256 networks would be sufficient for the foreseeable future, was clearly in need of reconsideration when LANs began to appear in the late 1970s.

Vint Cerf et al., *Brief History of the Internet*, INTERNET SOCIETY (1997).

Cerf's TCP/IP model is a four-layered framework that describes how data is transmitted across networks:

> With hybrid cloud environments, IoT expansion, and increased remote work, understanding how data moves through these layers helps you troubleshoot issues faster, secure networks more effectively, and design resilient infrastructure.

CP/IP Model Layers and Protocols You Must Know in 2026: Explained Simply, SKILLS FOR EVERYONE (Feb. 14, 2026).

Tim Berners-Lee developed its URL structure, hyperlinks, and in 1992, invented the first web browser. URLs and user-friendly browsers are features of the accessible World Wide Web. He developed the first "Graphic User Interface" (GUI) browser, named the "World Wide Web" and launched the first web page on August 6, 1991.

(B) U.S. GOVERNMENT'S ROLE

The Internet was first conceptualized by the U.S. Department of Defense's Advanced Research Projects Agency Network (ARPANET) fifty-seven years ago in 1969 The ARPANET received its primary support from the Department of Defense and defense-related agencies. ARPANET was the first wide-area packet-switching network and prefigured the modern Internet. This early governmental Internet connected research computers at different locations, with the first message sent from UCLA to SRI in 1969.

A communication network developed by the U.S. Department of Defense's Advanced Research Projects Agency (ARPA) preceded today's dynamic World Wide Web. President Dwight Eisenhower proposed the Advanced Research Projects Agency Network (ARPANET) in 1958 as a network of connected computers that could survive a nuclear war. ARPA had primary responsibility for the ARPANET and oversaw its evolution into the modern Internet.

> In December 1969, ARPANET connected four computer network nodes at the University of California, Los Angeles (U.C.L.A.), the Stanford Research Institute (S.R.I.) in Menlo Park, Calif., The University of California Santa Barbara (UCSB), and the University of Utah. The goal was to create an interconnected system of computers across the United States.

Early Sketch of ARPAnet's First Four Nodes, SCIENTIFIC AMERICAN (2009).

> On October 29, 1969, ARPAnet delivered its first message: a 'node-to-node' communication from one computer to another. (The first computer was located in a research lab at UCLA and the second was at Stanford; each one was the size of a small house.) The message—'LOGIN'—was short and simple, but it crashed the fledgling ARPA network anyway: the Stanford computer only received the note's first two letters.

Evan Andrews, *Who Invented the Internet?*, HISTORY.COM (Oct. 28, 2019).

ARPANET created a methodology for each entity connected to it (e.g., computer, router, network, etc.) to communicate with each other through a unique numeric "address." A unique identifier is required to enable one connected computer or network to identify and send information to another connected computer or network.

Those unique addresses are known as Internet Protocol Addresses or "IP addresses." Initially, IP addresses were assigned, and the master address list was maintained, by Dr. Jon Postel, of the University of Southern California's Information Sciences Institute. Dr. Postel performed this service as part of his work on the ARPANET project.

ARPANET was decommissioned in 1990, replaced by the National Science Foundation Network (NSFNET). NSFNET launched in 1986, created the backbone for the Internet connecting academic researchers to supercomputer centers.

This service evolved into the Internet Assigned Numbers Authority, which administered allocation of IP addresses. In November of 1998, the Internet Corporation for Assigned Names and Numbers (ICANN), a private, non-profit corporation was formed and designated as the governing body responsible for IP address allocation.

A New Hampshire federal district court described the early history of the Internet that led to the domain name system:

> IP addresses function much like Social Security numbers or telephone numbers: each IP address is unique and corresponds to a specific entity connected to the Internet. Because number strings can be cumbersome and difficult to remember, the Domain Name System ("DNS") was developed to allow users to link a unique (and easier to remember) domain name with a numeric (and more difficult to remember) IP address, thereby making it more convenient for users to access particular addresses on the Internet. So, for example, a user wishing to access the website maintained by International Business Machines need only remember the domain name "IBM.com," rather than the elaborate numerical IP address of the computer on which information relating to IBM's website is maintained (for example, a typical IP address might be something like: 192.168.0.10).

National A-1 Adver. v. Network Solutions, Inc., 121 F. Supp. 2d 156, 159 (D. N.H. 2000).

The National Science Foundation Network (NSFNET), sponsored by the National Science Foundation (NSF) from 1985 to 1995, promoted advanced research and education networking in the United States. NSFNET replaced ARPANET giving computer scientists at most universities access to the Internet for the first time.

Computer scientists at the University of Minnesota created "Gopher," the first user-friendly interface in 1991. The Gopher search engine enabled users to search, distribute, and retrieve documents from the Internet, prefiguring the World Wide Web's friendly user interfaces. In 1993, the National Center for Supercomputing Applications at the University of Illinois launched Mosaic, which was the first graphical web browser.

Intranets and Extranets need a greater connection to the Internet. "For larger businesses or high bandwidth applications, a T3 line at 45 Mbps is appropriate." *T3 Dedicated Business Internet,* DS3 TODAY (Apr. 2, 2021).

The privatization of the Internet began in the early 1990s when the NSF opened the Internet to businesses thus beginning the process of commercializing the Internet. "The U.S. government created the internet and has sole authority over the domain name system. . . . The current IP system is Version 4 (IPv4), which makes available over four billion IP addresses but the IPv4 addresses are depleted." *Internet Protocol Version 6: IPv6 for Consumers* (2019).

§ 1-3. Setting Standards Through Voluntary Organizations

(A) IETF

The Internet Engineering Task Force (IETF) is a voluntary international standards organization whose member are a "community of computer network designers and operators that writes the Internet's basic software code. . ." Organized into 118 working groups, the roughly 4,000 volunteers cooperate, debate, and vote using e-mail.

10 Quiet but Powerful International Bodies, NATIONAL JOURNAL (Nov. 20, 1999).

The IETF publishes its technical standards in the following way:

> The IETF publishes its technical documentation as RFCs, an acronym for their historical title Requests for Comments. They describe the Internet's technical foundations, such as addressing, routing, and transport technologies. RFCs also specify protocols like TLS 1.3, QUIC, and WebRTC that are used to deliver services used by billions of people every day, such as real-time collaboration, email, and the domain name system.
>
> Software developers, hardware manufacturers, and network operators around the world voluntarily implement and adopt the technical specifications and best practices described by RFCs.

The IETF states its purpose as follows:

> The Internet Engineering Task Force (IETF), founded in 1986, is the premier standards development organization (SDO) for the Internet. The IETF makes voluntary standards that are often adopted by Internet users, network operators, and equipment vendors, and it thus helps shape the trajectory of the development of the Internet. But in no way does the IETF control, or even patrol, the Internet.

IETF, *Introduction to the IETF* (2026).

The IETF along with the W3C implement the "WebRTC standard used by also helps bring WebRTC to the to the Microsoft Internet Explorer and Apple Safari desktop browsers."

10 Considerations for Running WebRTC Services on AWS, NETWORK WORLD (Nov. 22, 2016).

(B) W3C

The World Wide Web Consortium (W3C) is a voluntary standard organization that develops standards and guidelines predicated upon accessibility, internationalization, privacy and security. The W3C states its mission as "providing a productive environment for creating web standards that":

- Follow a consensus-based decision process.
- Cater for accessibility, privacy, security, and internationalization.

- Reflect the views of diverse industries and global stakeholders.
- Balance speed, fairness, public accountability, and quality.
- Benefit from Royalty-Free patent licensing commitments from participants.
- Are stable (and W3C ensures their persistence at the published URI).
- Benefit from wide review from groups inside and outside W3C.
- Are available at no cost.
- Are strengthened through interoperability testing.

W3C standards, technical specifications and guidelines are widely deployed on the web:

- Rendering of web pages
- Enabling access from any device
- Architecture of the web
- Linking data and services
- Authoring tools

World Wide Consortium (W3C), *Web Standards*, W3.ORG (March 5, 2026).

(C) IGF

The Internet Governance Forum (IGF) is a United Nations multistakeholder platform that facilitates the discussion of public policy issues pertaining to the Internet. The IGF "is the United Nations Secretary-General-convened platform for inclusive, multistakeholder dialogue on Internet governance and related digital technologies."

The IGF, established in 2006 "has convened 20 global annual meetings hosted by governments and developed a strong intersessional ecosystem in close cooperation with more than 180 national, regional, and youth IGF initiatives, supported by targeted capacity-development activities."

In December 2025, the United Nations confirmed that the IGF as a permanent forum of the United Nations. In February 2026, the Government of Norway in Lillestrøm "continues to advance inclusive, multistakeholder dialogue on Internet governance and digital policy issues."

United Nations, Internet Governance Forum, *About Us*, (2026).

(D) ICANN

The Internet Corporation for Assigned Names and Numbers (ICANN) is a private not-for-profit corporation that coordinates the Internet domain name system ("DNS") on behalf of the United States Department of Commerce. ICANN manages domain names, IP addresses, and the Domain Name System (DNS). ICANN describes its purpose is to:

> ensure the internet stays organized, accessible, and secure. By maintaining a structured system, ICANN allows users to easily find websites and

> services online. Without ICANN, websites could overlap, making it impossible to find the right one.

Danica Ubata, *What Is ICANN & What Do They Do?*, NETWORK SOLUTIONS (Aug. 23, 2025).

ICANN's lookup tool gives anyone the ability to look up publicly available contact and other information related to a domain name or an Internet number resource such as an Autonomous System number (ASN), or IP networks. ICANN describes its domain name registration lookup tool as:

> a JavaScript-based client application which makes use of the Registration Data Access Protocol (RDAP) to query, parse and display registration data in a human-friendly format. The results displayed come directly from registry operators and/or registrars in real-time. For domain name queries, if the queried information is not available in RDAP, the query will be redirected to the WHOIS service of the corresponding gTLD registry operator. This process is known as a WHOIS failover lookup which occurs when queried information is not available in RDAP and a WHOIS.

ICANN, *Registration Data Lookup Tool, Frequently Asked Questions (FAQs)*, (2026).

"As of Dec. 31, 2025, the 10 largest TLDs by number of reported domain names were .com, .cn, .de, .net, .org, .uk, .xyz, .ru, .nl and .top. For the top 10 TLDs with available data, recent quarterly renewal percentage estimates ranged from 78.9% for

.uk to 20.0% for .top." A December 2025 Domain Name Industry Brief concluded that:

> The top 10 ccTLDs, as of Dec. 31, 2025, were .cn, .de, .uk, .ru, .nl, .br, .fr, .au, .in and .eu. As of Dec. 31, 2025, there were 316 global ccTLD extensions delegated in the root zone, including internationalized domain names, with the top 10 ccTLDs comprising 57.4% of all ccTLD domain name registrations. For the top 10 ccTLDs with available data, recent quarterly renewal percentage estimates ranged from 80.0% for .eu to 71.4% for .ru.

DNIB Staff, *The DNIB Quarterly Report Q4 2025, Data and Analysis,* (Dec. 31, 2025).

(E) ISOC

The Internet Society (ISOC) is a "cause-driven voluntary organization that supports the IETF [Internet Engineering Task Force] and the IAB [Internet Architecture Board] to ensure that the Internet remains open and transparent." Internet Society (ISOC), *The Internet Is For Everyone* (2019).

> ISOC is the organizational home of the Internet Engineering Task Force (IETF), the Internet standards body responsible for developing the internet's technical foundations through its open global forum. The internet evolved rapidly in large part because of the role of nonhierarchical, open standards-setting organizations, such as ISOC.

ISOC's focus is connecting the world, collaborating with others, and advocating for equal access to the internet. ISOC works on issues such as access, privacy, Internet exchange points or hubs, children and the internet, net neutrality, spam, domain names, and open network standards. The organization provides insurance coverage for those involved in the IETF standards-setting groups.

The Internet Society Foundation describes its 2026 Action Plan as marking the second year of its 2030 Strategy:

> The Internet Society Foundation's goal remains clear: to be a strong and trusted supporting organization that amplifies the Internet Society's impact worldwide. We are dedicated to helping ensure that people everywhere have access to an affordable, reliable, and resilient Internet, one that is safe, secure, and protective of their rights online. Through our efforts, we continue to strengthen the global Internet community and advance the strategic goals that will define the Internet's future. The Internet Society Foundation contributes to the 2030 strategic goals by cultivating future Internet leaders, creating impact through funding mission-aligned initiatives, ensuring financial sustainability through revenue generation, and building a recognized global brand. Together, we focus on driving meaningful progress for universal and inclusive connectivity.

The Internet Society Foundation, ***2026** Action Plan.*

§ 1-4. The Future of the Global Internet

The Internet of the future creates opportunity and empowers people. The Internet Society (ISOC) made ten suggestions to ensure the future of the Internet for empowering its users:

- Human values must drive technical development and use.
- Apply human rights online as well as offline.
- Put users' interests first with respect to their own data.
- Act now to close digital divides.
- Make the internet economy work for everyone.
- Take a collaborative approach to security.
- Increase accountability for data handlers.
- Build strong, secure, resilient networks.
- Address the need for online social norms.
- Empower people to shape their own future.

Internet Society (ISOC), *Top Ten Recommendations for the Future of the Internet* (2019).

"Each of these recommendations calls for making the Internet user-centered. Of particular importance is the Internet of Things (IoT) with trillions of low-cost devices." *Investigators from Guangdong University of Technology Have Reported New Data on Telecommunication,* TELECOMMUNICATIONS DAILY (Mar. 5, 2021).

Consider what would happen if the Internet suddenly collapsed and shut down worldwide? Business operations have grown dependent upon the Internet. While businesses may suffer interruptions in supply chains and operations from malicious code and defective software design during daily operations, attacks on Internet hubs could result in a breakdown of critical information infrastructure.

Cell phones would shut down as well as desktop computers, laptops, and GPS devices. Electronic financial institutions around the world would go offline. Cloud computing would go offline, leaving countless businesses without access to key data; software applications, and critical infrastructure for businesses, nonprofits, and governments would suffer dislocations because of interruptions in key business, banking, military, fiscal, and governmental infrastructure; medical records, shipment and aircraft tracking systems, and much of the world's communications infrastructure would go down. Chapter 2 will examine Perspectives on Internet Law that shed light on how the Internet impacts every social, economic, and political institution.

CHAPTER 2
PERSPECTIVES ON GLOBAL INTERNET GOVERNANCE

§ 2-1. Overview of Cyberlaw

This chapter is divided into six sections. Section 2-1 is an overview of cyberlaw. This section presents arguments for and against whether there is a unique Internet law as opposed to just adapting existing law for cyberspace. Section 2-2 is an overview of Internet governance with an examination of five leading theories: (1) self-governance or libertarian, (2) global transnational, (3) code and Internet architecture, (4) national governments and law, and (5) market-based or economic-based regulation.

Next, Section 2-3 is a close examination of the libertarian approach to Internet governance, which is a leading approach followed in the United States.

Section 2-4 introduces Lawrence Lessig's influential argument that "code is law." Lessig's four modalities of Internet regulation are next covered: law, code, market and norms. Section 2-5 explains the role that national regulations of Internet activities plays in Internet law.

Section 2-6 critically examines Yochai Benkler's *The Wealth of Networks: How Social Production Transforms Markets and Freedom* (2006) that analyzes how the Internet's networked information economy enables new forms of collaborative, non-market production, like Wikipedia and open-source software, challenging traditional media and economic models.

The Internet is the world's largest marketplace, copy machine, and instrumentality for committing crimes, torts, and infringing intellectual property. Internet law is a relatively new field that began thirty years ago. The first web page was loaded in 1991. A year later, the first photograph of a female rock group, *Les Horribles Cernettes* became the first picture posted.

Gabriel H. Sanchez, *19 of The First Things To Ever Happen On The Internet* (May 28, 2016).

The early 1990s also resulted in numerous Internet law "firsts" such as the first online libel case decided in 1991.

> In *Cubby, Inc. v. CompuServe, Inc.*, a federal district court held an online service provider was not liable for defamatory postings made by a subscriber because it was classified as a distributor rather than a publisher.
>
> This case is a landmark because it represents the first time a court stretched defamation law developed for printed copies to internet publications. In 1993, a Florida federal district court became the first to find a computer bulletin board liable for copyright and trademark infringement. . . . That same year, a court ruled that a software program made infringing copies on the computer's random access memory (RAM) each time it was installed.

Michael L. Rustad & Diane D'Angelo, *The Path of Internet Law: An Annotated Guide to Legal Landmarks,* 2011 DUKE L. & TECH. REV. 1, 28 (2011).

The first spam email message was a message from a Digital Equipment Corporation (DEC) marketing representative sent to every address on the Advanced Research Projects Agency Network (ARPANET) in 1994. The 1990s was a decade of many other Internet firsts such as:

> *The First Web Browser:*
>
> That would be World Wide Web, and was developed by British computer scientist Tim Berners-Lee in 1990. Here in ChannelSight, we love a good TBL quote. For example: 'You affect the world by what you browse.' If you too fancy going down a wondrous rabbit hole of TBL quotes, pop over to Brainy Quote.
>
> *The First Website:*
>
> This was dedicated to information on the World Wide Web, went live on August 6th 1991, at http://info.cern.ch/hypertext/WWW/TheProject.html, and was made by Tim Berners-Lee.
>
> *The First Instant Message:*
>
> This was sent by Ted Leonsis, former AOL senior executive, to his wife Lynn on January 6th 1993.

Our 19 Favorite Internet Firsts, CHANNELSIGHT (Oct. 12, 2018).

The widespread use of the Internet has created new legal dilemmas and challenges in accommodating new information technologies since the mid-1990s. Global Internet law does not descend disembodied from the thin, rarefied air of the legal heavens but from legal opinions, statutes, industry standards, and social norms drawn from our lived experience. This chapter critically examines competing perspectives on the role of the Internet in society.

To paraphrase Grant Gilmore, Internet law is not "a brooding omnipresence in the sky." Justice Oliver Wendell Holmes Jr. famously stated that "the life of the law does not arise out of logic; it has been experience." Grant Gilmore, *Legal Realism: Its Cause and Cure*, 70 YALE L. J. 1037, 1038 (1961).

Courts and legislatures have significantly reworked the law to accommodate the Internet. New statutory provisions have evolved to address the liability of Internet service providers and search engines for postings of third parties.

The European Union's General Data Protection Regulation (GDPR), that took effect on May 25, 2018, provides comprehensive protection of personal data of individuals in the European Union/European Economic Area. The GDPR grants individuals rights to access, delete, and control their data, with penalties for non-compliance reaching up to 4% of annual global turnover. In contrast, the U.S. relies upon privacy torts and statutes that apply to limited sectors such as health, finance, and children's privacy.

Congress's express purpose in enacting Section 230 of the Communications Decency Act to protect the infant information industry from excessive defamation liability as publishers. Prior to 1996, courts disagreed as to whether online service providers would be liable for the defamatory postings of their subscribers. CDA Section 230's liability shield protecting Internet gatekeepers such as Facebook, Amazon, and Google will be explored in depth in Chapter 6.

The U.S. approach to the liability of websites and search engines for content provided by third parties also differs sharply from Europe. Section 230 of the Communications Decency Act of 1996 (47 U.S.C. § 230) protects interactive computer services (platforms, websites, ISPs) from liability for content posted by third-party users.

This liability shield enables platforms such as Amazon and eBay to moderate content without being treated as the publisher of that content.

CDA Section 230 stipulates that "no provider or user of an interactive computer service shall be treated as the publisher or speaker of any information provided by another information content provider." CDA Section 230 does not provide for a mechanism to takedown objectionable content.

In 2020, The U.S. Department of Justice released a report calling for reforming CDA Section 230 that made the following recommendations:

- The legislative proposal adds language to the definition of "information content provider" under current § 230(f)(3). Under the existing statute, an on line platform that is "responsible, in whole or in part, for the creation or development of information" is not entitled to Section 230 immunity. The proposal clarifies that being responsible "in whole or in part" "includes situations in which a platform solicits, comments upon, funds, or affirmatively and substantively contributes to, modifies, or alters the content of another person or entity." This amendment is consistent with the original purpose of Section 230. While online platforms do not have an obligation to monitor and screen all third-party content, they cannot avoid liability for harms arising from specific material if the platforms actively choose to modify or encourage it.

- The second category of amendments is aimed at incentivizing platforms to address the growing amount of illicit content online, while preserving the core of Section 230's immunity for defamation claims. Section 230 immunity is meant to incentivize and protect online Good Samaritans, as evidenced by the original title of § 230(c): "Protection for 'Good Samaritan' blocking and screening of offensive material." As the famous parable recounts, a Good Samaritan is someone who goes out of his or her way to help another in need. It therefore follows that platforms that purposely solicit and facilitate harmful criminal activity-in effect, on line Bad

Samaritans should not receive the benefit of this immunity. Accordingly, the proposed legislation adds a new Section, § 230(d). This section identifies three specific exclusions from immunity: platforms that (I) purposefully promote, facilitate, or solicit third-party content that would violate federal criminal law; (2) have actual knowledge that specific content it is hosting violates federal law; and (3) fail to remove unlawful content after receiving notice by way of a final court judgment.

- These new provisions are narrowly tailored in two important ways. First, they require a heightened *mens rea*-either acting "purposefully" or having actual knowledge. These requirements avoid sweeping in innocent or accidental acts or omissions by online platforms. Second, other than the court-order provision, the exclusions are limited to distribution or facilitation of third-party content that would violate federal criminal law. Providing platforms with civil immunity for facilitating such egregious illicit content is inconsistent with the purpose of Section 230 of the Communications Decency Act to encourage platforms to make the internet a safer place for children.

- In addition to new § 230(d), the proposal would add two sets of new carve-outs to those currently listed under § 230(e), which defines the statutory immunity's "effect on other laws." First, carved out from immunity are three specific categories of claims: (I) child exploitation and sexual abuse; (2) terrorism; and (3) cyber-stalking. These are targeted carveouts to address the over-expansion of Section 230 immunity that has limited the ability of victims of these specific offenses to seek civil redress in causes of action far afield from the statute's core objectives. The proposal also provides an explicit carve-out for claims brought under the federal antitrust laws, which promotes competition and clarifies that Section 230 immunity is unavailable to internet companies when they assert it against claims of anticompetitive conduct.

- Finally, the proposed legislation would amend current § 230(e) to expressly confirm that the immunity provided by this statute does not apply to civil enforcement actions brought by the federal government. In the decades since Congress passed Section 230, the widespread availability of internet access, the growth in the number of "interactive computer services," the ubiquity of smartphones, and the advent of social media have all contributed to an exponential increase in online crimes. Although federal criminal enforcement actions have always been outside the scope of Section 230 immunity, online crime is a serious and growing problem, and there is no justification for blocking the federal government from civil enforcement. The

> proposed provision is narrowly tailored to clarify that the government's civil enforcement capabilities are uninfringed by Section 230 without opening the floodgates to private damages lawsuits.

U.S. Department of Justice's Review of Section 230 of the Communications Decency Act of 1996 (2020).

Unlike CDA Section 230, the European Union (EU) adopted a notice and takedown regime for illegal content favored in the U.S. Department of Justice report.

The E-Commerce Directive is the foundational legal framework for online services in the EU. The Directive seeks to remove obstacles to cross-border online services. The E-Commerce Directive establishes harmonized rules on issues such as the transparency and information requirements for online service providers; commercial communications; and electronic contracts and limitations of liability of intermediary service providers.

The E-Commerce Directive (2000/31/EC) creates a "safe harbor" for online intermediaries, limiting their liability for hosting illegal content so long as they take down illegal content upon obtaining "actual knowledge" or awareness. This "notice and takedown" procedure requires the platform to remove content that constitutes copyright infringement, libel or other illegal content. Providers must disable access to avoid secondary liability.

The liability exemption only covers services which play a neutral, merely technical and passive role towards the hosted content. The Directive makes it clear that EU Member States cannot impose any monitoring obligation on intermediaries.

The European Union's Digital Services Act (DSA) was formally approved by the European Parliament on July 5, 2022, signed into law on October 19, 2022, and entered into force on November 16, 2022. It became fully applicable to all covered services across the EU by February 17, 2024. The DSA supplements and updates the law to address Amazon, Google or Facebook and other entities that evolved since the Directive.

The EU upgraded its rules governing digital services by introducing the Digital Markets Act (DMA) and the Digital Services Act (DSA), which created a single set of rules applicable across the EU. In December 2020, the European Commission published a proposal for a regulation on contestable and fair markets in the digital sector, otherwise referred to as the digital markets act (DMA). The European Parliament describes the DMA:

- The new DMA rules apply to those large companies.

- designated as gatekeepers—that provide an array of services, including social networks, video sharing, virtual assistants, web browsers, search engines and online advertising.

- The new legislation introduces a number of obligations for gatekeepers including an obligation to provide interoperable messaging services (interoperability of social media will be looked at in the next review) and an obligation to ensure that users have the right to unsubscribe from core platform services under similar conditions to subscription.
- Furthermore, the DMA prohibits various practices such as self-preferencing (i.e., ranking their own products or services higher than those of others) or reuse of private data collected during provision of one service for the purposes of another service.

European Parliament, *Digital Markets Act: Adoption in Plenary* (July 2022).

The DMA and the Digital Services Act (DSA) were both adopted in July 2025 to help advance a single Digital Single Market versus have the twenty-seven EU countries developed non-uniform national provisions. The DSA fortifies and updates rules for taking down objectionable content:

> The new rules also help protect users from harmful and illegal content. They significantly improve the removal of illegal content, making sure it is done as fast as possible. They also help tackle harmful content, which, like political or health-related disinformation, doesn't have to be illegal, and introduce better rules for the protection of freedom of speech.

European Parliament, *EU Digital Markets Act and Digital Services Act Explained* (updated June 26, 2025).

Chapter 7 will highlight the contrasting approaches to privacy in the U.S. and EU.

There is a deep divide between how the United States and the EU treat the liability of Internet Service Providers. The U.S. approach to privacy is market-based and online companies can freely collect, process, store and transfer personal data with few exceptions. Scott McNealy, founder of Sun Microsystems stated: "Consumer privacy is a red herring. You have zero privacy. Get over it."

In January of 2025, President Donald J. Trump contended that:

> Over the last 4 years, the previous administration trampled free speech rights by censoring Americans' speech on online platforms, often by exerting substantial coercive pressure on third parties, such as social media companies, to moderate, deplatform, or otherwise suppress speech that the Federal Government did not approve. Under the guise of combatting "misinformation," "disinformation," and "malinformation," the Federal Government infringed on the constitutionally protected speech rights of American citizens across the United States in a manner that advanced the Government's preferred narrative about significant matters of public debate.

Government censorship of speech is intolerable in a free society.

President Donald J. Trump, *Executive Order 14149—Restoring Freedom of Speech and Ending Federal Censorship* (Jan. 20, 2025).

The European Union approach is to create harmonized rules for online platforms enabling the "takedown" of illegal and harmful content.

In an increasingly cross-border legal environment, tortfeasors can defame, invade privacy, and misappropriate trade secrets at the click of a mouse in hundreds of jurisdictions simultaneously. Torts and crimes are increasingly carried out on Twitter, blogs, social media sites, e-mail transmissions, and website postings. Ideally, Internet law would develop sui generis rules and standards applicable in all of the countries connected to the Internet. At present, there is no single, codified body of global legal standards, statutes or norms that are enforceable universally. Internet law depends in large part where a user is located. U.S. Internet users, for example, do not have a 'right to be forgotten' or to erase objectionable content, whereas this is a fundamental right of European consumers.

(A) THE CASE AGAINST INTERNET LAW

In 1996, Judge Frank Easterbrook, a Seventh Circuit U.S. Court of Appeals judge, spoke at a University of Chicago academic conference on cyberspace law. Judge Easterbrook argued that the best way to approach any topic is through general rules, and supplementing one's education with an understanding of a specific subject's unique traits.

Judge Frank Easterbrook compared carving out Internet law as a special subject to creating a law governing horses, explaining:

> Lots of cases deal with sales of horses; others deal with people kicked by horses; still more deal with the licensing and racing of horses, or with the care veterinarians give to horses, or with prizes at horse shows. Any effort to collect these strands into a course on The Law of the Horse is doomed to be shallow and to miss unifying principles. Teaching 100 percent of the cases on people kicked by horses will not convey the law of torts very well. Far better for most students—better, even, for those who plan to go into the horse trade—to take courses in property, torts, commercial transactions, and the like, adding to the diet of horse cases a smattering of transactions in cucumbers, cats, coal, and cribs. Only by putting the law of the horse in the context of broader rules about commercial endeavors could one really understand the law about horses.

Frank H. Easterbook, *Cyberspace and the Law of the Horse,* 1996 U. CHI. LEGAL F. 207 (1996).

Judge Easterbrook's argument is that specialized Internet law is not required to apply the law to cyberspace. Instead, students interested in Internet law should study the overarching basic doctrinal fields, such as property, torts, contract law, and intellectual property, and stretch these principles to cases relevant to new information technologies.

Easterbrook was the first jurist to question Internet exceptionalism, which is the view that this novel technology required special laws. Internet exceptionalism is:

> whether the technological characteristics of the Internet (and, more generally, twenty-first century information technologies) justify treating regulation of information dissemination through the Internet differently from regulation of such dissemination through nineteenth-and twentieth-century media, such as print, radio, and television.

Mark Tushnet, *Internet Exceptionalism: An Overview from General Constitutional Law*, 56 WM. & MARY L. REV. 1637, 1648 (2015).

(B) IN DEFENSE OF INTERNET LAW

Lawrence Lessig, Harvard law professor and political activist, is a founding father of the Berkman-Klein Center at Harvard University. Lessig contends that Internet law has the potential to change every branch of the law, offering new perspectives on topics such as intellectual property, globalization, private regulation, and Internet governance.

Lawrence Lessig's theory of Internet law is that "Code is Law." He contends that that the Internet is regulated by four modalities: law, social norms, market forces, and architecture (code).

LAWRENCE LESSIG, CODE AND OTHER LAWS OF CYBERSPACE (1999).

Lawrence Lessig identified four modalities of Internet regulation: (1) Code/Architecture, (2) Market (economic forces), (3) the Law, and (4) Social Norms (enforced by the community). In CODE 2.0, Lessig explains that his book was written in opposition to those who argued that the Internet was beyond the reach of real-space regulation.

LAWRENCE LESSIG, CODE AND OTHER LAWS OF CYBERSPACE, VERSION 2.0 (2006) at ix.

Lessig describes the architecture of the Internet to include the TCP/IP protocols, as well as physical or technical constraints on activities enforced by many Internet-related protocols. The functions of architecture or real-space code are not a matter of technological necessity, but rather a human-created mechanism for controlling the Internet.

He also notes how privacy traditionally had physical limitations and high costs in monitoring behavior. For these reasons, the Internet requires a reconceptualization of data privacy rules in a world where online surveillance occurs on a 24/7 basis and disregards national borders.

Cyberlaw includes statutes and cases but also encompasses the architecture of the Internet, informal norms, as well as industry standards. The architecture of the Internet shapes the path of the law. The Internet is "layered architecture" which enables "specialized efficiency, organizational coherency, and future flexibility."

Tim Wu, *Application-Centered Internet Analysis*, 85 VA. L. REV. 1163, 1189 (1999).

The Internet of Things (IoT) calls for "an architecture for IoT applications where so-called 'accessors' provide an actor-oriented proxy for devices ('things') and services." Marten Lohstroh & Edward A. Lee, *An Interface Theory for the Internet of Things* in RADU CALINESCU & BERNHARD RUMPE, AN INTERFACE THEORY FOR THE INTERNET OF THINGS (2015).

The Children's Internet Protection Act (CIPA), for example, requires libraries that participate in the Library Services and Technology Act to implement software filters on their computers. These filters protect against visual depictions that are obscene, such as child pornography, as well as anything that may be considered harmful to minors. Software filters illustrate code as law.

Lawrence Lessig also acknowledges the role of the market, which is the second modality of Internet regulation:

> So too do markets regulate. Markets regulate through the device of price. The market constrains my ability to trade hours of teaching for potatoes, or my children's lemonade for tickets to the movies. This constraint functions differently from a sanction; so too is its meaning distinct from the meaning of a sanction. It is distinct from law and norms, even though parasitic on law (property and contract) and constrained by norms (again, one does not 'buy'

> a 'friend'). But given a set of norms, and scarcity, and law, the market presents a distinct set of constraints on individual and collective behavior. It establishes a third band of constraint on individual behavior.

Lawrence Lessig, *The New Chicago School*, 27 J. LEG. STUD. 661 (1998).

Law is the third modality of Internet regulation:

> Law (in its traditional, or Austinian, sense) directs behavior in certain ways; it threatens sanctions ex post if those orders are not obeyed. Law tells me not to deduct more than 50 percent of the cost of business meals from my income taxes; it threatens fines, or jail, if that order is not obeyed. Law tells me not to drive faster than 55 miles per hour on a highway; it threatens to revoke my license if that order is not obeyed. Laws tell me not to buy drugs, not to sell unlicensed cigarettes, and not to trade across international borders without first filing a customs form—all this with the threat that if these orders are not obeyed, I will be punished. In this way, we say, law regulates.

Additionally, Lessig recognizes that norms are the fourth modality of Internet regulation:

> Social norms regulate as well. They are a second sort of constraint. Norms say I can buy a newspaper, but cannot buy a 'friend.' They frown on the racist's jokes; they tell the stranger to tip a waiter at a highway diner; they are unsure about whether a man should hold a door for a

> woman. Norms constrain an individual's behavior, but not through the centralized enforcement of a state. If they constrain, they constrain because of the enforcement of a community. Through this community, they regulate.

Lessig, however, does not create a hierarchy, acknowledging that these modalities are not hierarchical but operate together in an interactive way:

> How obviously, these four modalities do not regulate to the same degree—in some contexts, the most significant constraint may be law (an appeals court); in others, it is plainly not. . . . Nor do they regulate in the same way—law and norms, for example, typically regulate after the fact, while the market or architecture regulates more directly. . . . But however they differ, we can view them from this common perspective—from a single view from which we might account for (1) the different constraints that regulate an individual and (2) the substitutions among these constraints that might be possible.

Lessig argued that government regulation not libertarianism is required to fix the Internet:

> Lessig believes that we should not sit idle and hope that the Internet will fix itself. He criticizes the belief that the Internet is a sovereign entity without ties to the traditional legal system and warns that this fallacy could lead to the demise

of core values such as free speech, privacy and anonymity, to name a few.

The Project—Stanford CS—Stanford University (Nov. 2010).

§ 2-2. Overview of Internet Governance

Classic Internet theories of governance are grand theories offering little guidance on practical problems. To date, five grand theories are most influential: (1) self-governance or libertarian, (2) global transnational, (3) code and Internet architecture, (4) national governments and law, and (5) market-based or economic-based regulation.

The chart below provides the basic attributes of each of the five major Internet governance theories. Lawrence Solum, Chapter 2 in MODELS OF INTERNET GOVERNANCE INFRASTRUCTURE AND INSTITUTIONS 48, 55 (Lee A. Bygrave ed. 2009).

Five Influential Theories of Internet Governance

Five Models of Internet Governance	*Domain Assumptions*
(1) Self-Governance or Internet Exceptionalism	The Internet should ideally be a government-free zone because it has decoupled the link between territory and regulation. The characteristics of the Internet require treating

	regulation differently than the real-world setting.
(2) Global Transnational	Transnational multi-stakeholder institutions must evolve to address Internet governance since this information technology transcends national borders.
(3) Code and Internet Architecture	Code is law, and therefore computer programmers make regulatory decisions when they construct protocols and create software parameters.
(4) National Governments and Law	National governments have regulated the Internet since its inception. Congress and the states have had little difficulty enacting statutes to address the Internet. Examples include CDA Section 230, which shields interactive service providers from liability for user-generated content, and Ohio extending its "harmful to juveniles" criminal statute to include Internet communications.
(5) Market-Based or	Since President William Clinton, Internet

Economic-Based Regulation	governance is based on "private ordering" or "do not fix what is not broken." Market forces, private ordering, and industry practices are emblematic of Internet governance. (No government invention except where there is market failure.)

§ 2-3. Libertarian Governance

(A) LIBERTARIAN MANIFESTO

Libertarianism asks questions such as how we can maximize human freedom but still have a stable social order. Internet libertarians contend that no national state has the authority to impose regulations in cyberspace. Libertarianism draws upon the nineteenth-century laissez faire capitalist ideology that asserts, "so long as we do not violate others' rights, we should be free to live as we choose."

JASON BRENNAN, LIBERTARIANISM: WHAT EVERYONE NEEDS TO KNOW (New York, New York: Oxford University Press, 2012) at 1–2.

Cyberlibertarians, like traditional libertarians, embrace maximizing freedom and have a distrust of government. In the late 1980s and early 1990s, cyber-libertarianism was the prevailing perspective on Internet governance. John Perry Barlow, in his 1996 Manifesto, entitled "A Declaration for Independence of the Internet," argued that no government could regulate the Internet:

> Governments of the Industrial World, you weary giants of flesh and steel, I come from Cyberspace, the new home of Mind. On behalf of the future, I ask you of the past to leave us alone. You are not welcome among us. You have no sovereignty where we gather.
>
> We have no elected government, nor are we likely to have one, so I address you with no greater authority than that with which liberty itself always speaks. I declare the global social space we are building to be naturally independent of the tyrannies you seek to impose on us. You have no moral right to rule us nor do you possess any methods of enforcement we have true reason to fear. In our world, all the sentiments and expressions of humanity, from the debasing to the angelic, are parts of a seamless whole, the global conversation of bits.

John Perry Barlow, *A Declaration of the Independence of Cyberspace* (1996).

> Barlow stated, 'On behalf of the future, I ask you of the past to leave us alone.' Barlow's brand of exceptionalism was the idea that the Internet is different, and no rules should apply. It inspired Internet activists and pirates alike. Internet exceptionalism was a perfect combination of an elitist message—'only we understand this new thing'—and the populist mantra—'no more paying for entertainment!'

Per Strömbäck, *The End of Internet Exceptionalism—Or Why the Pirates Bet on the Wrong Horse,* NETOPIA: FORUM FOR THE DIGITAL SOCIETY (Nov. 11, 2017).

Barlow's utopian view envisioned an Internet free from government censorship: "Governments of the Industrial World, you weary giants of flesh and steel, I come from Cyberspace, the new home of Mind." He famously thundered, "The First Amendment is a local ordinance, where is the consent from Netizens for any country imposing its laws on the Internet?" By what authority does the U.S. impose its First Amendment on the rest of the world?

This argument brings to mind a *Seinfeld* episode, "The Pothole" which featured Kramer complaining about a poorly maintained highway outside of New York City. After damaging his car running over an abandoned sewing machine, Kramer decides to adopt a one-mile piece of the "Arthur Burghardt Expressway" through the Adopt a Highway program. Kramer proceeded to repaint the four-lane highway, creating two extra-wide lanes with the intent to transform it into a "two lane comfort cruise."

By what authority did Cosmos Kramer have the right to repaint the lines on the highway, converting it to a two-lane comfort cruise zone? Similarly, by what authority can a national government impose its sovereignty on the borderless Internet?

The legitimacy of Internet governance ultimately come from the consent of Internet users in hundreds of countries. Barlow released his Manifesto shortly after the German government prosecuted a Bavarian Internet service provider for enabling German users to access objectionable content, such as Nazi memorabilia and hateful commentary posted by third parties.

By what authority can a Bavarian court order a U.S. service provider to block content to German citizens? Under this same argument, what gives the European Union the right to require U.S. companies, like Google, to comply with provisions in the EU's General Data Protection Regulation (GDPR), such as the right to be forgotten?

Barlow's concerns about widespread censorship on the Internet and national Internet regulations have since materialized around the world. China, Syria, Saudi Arabia and many other countries censor Internet content because their regimes do not allow free speech or expression. China's "great firewall" screens out information threatening to the regime. Libertarians are concerned that an alliance of authoritarian governments will use the United Nations as an instrumentality of control over Internet speech.

(B) DECENTRALIZED GOVERNANCE

David Johnson and David Post's article describe the sovereign Internet as a separate realm beyond the capacity of individual nation states to govern:

> Global computer-based communications cut across territorial borders, creating a new realm of human activity and undermining the

> feasibility—and legitimacy—of laws based on geographic boundaries. While these electronic communications play havoc with geographic boundaries, a new boundary, made up of the screens and passwords that separate the virtual world from the 'real world' of atoms, emerges. This new boundary defines a distinct Cyberspace that needs and can create its own law and legal institutions. Territorially based law-makers and law-enforcers find this new environment deeply threatening. . . . These new rules will play the role of law by defining legal personhood and property, resolving disputes, and crystallizing a collective conversation about online participants' core values.

David R. Johnson & David Post, *Law and Borders—The Rise of Law in Cyberspace*, 48 STAN. L. REV. 1367, 1367 (1996).

Johnson and Post argue that the Internet makes borders increasingly irrelevant:

> The rise of an electronic medium that disregards geographical boundaries throws the law into disarray by creating entirely new phenomena that need to become the subject of clear legal rules but that cannot be governed, satisfactorily, by any current territorially based sovereign.

It is naïve to assume that national governments could not regulate the Internet:

> For a long time, the Internet's enthusiasts have believed that it would be largely immune from state regulation. The theory was not so much

> that nation states would not want to regulate the Internet, it was that they would be unable to do so, forestalled by the technology of the medium, the geographical distribution of its users, and the nature of its content.

James Boyle, *Foucault in Cyberspace: Surveillance, Sovereignty and Hardwired Censors*, 66 U. CINC. L. REV. 177 (1997).

Cyberlibertarians exist across the political spectrum and heavily focus on the promotion of evading state regulation:

> Cyberlibertarianism, broadly speaking, refers to a discourse that claims that the Internet and related digital media technology can and should constitute spaces of individual liberty. Liberty here is understood as non-interference such that individuals are able to act and express themselves as they choose, and thus are self-governed.

Lincoln Dahlberg, *Cyberlibertarianism*, OXFORD RESEARCH ENCYCLOPEDIA (2021).

§ 2-4. Law, Code, Markets & Norms

Lawrence Lessig, was the first theorist to posit a model of the role of law in Internet governance. Lessig describes four methods of regulation that apply to both cyberspace and the natural world: (1) regulation through network architecture (code); (2) societal regulations (what is considered appropriate social behavior); (3) the market costs associated with maintaining parts of the Internet; and (4) the law.

"Combined, these modalities work together to regulate our internet behavior. Of these, however, Lessig believes the most effective form of regulation online is through architecture, '[online,] code is law.' "

LAWRENCE LESSIG, CODE AND OTHER LAWS OF CYBERSPACE, About the Project (2010).

Internet law, Lawrence Lessig argues, consists of interrelated conceptual layers with four interrelated modalities depicted in the chart below:

Four Modalities Comprising Internet Law: Code as Law

Law: "Norms constrain through the stigma that a community imposes; markets constrain through the price that they exact; architectures constrain through the physical burdens they impose; and law constrains through the punishment it threatens." LAWRENCE LESSIG, CODE AND OTHER LAWS OF CYBERSPACE, VERSION 2.0 (2006).	*Architecture* (computer software and hardware): "The code or software or architecture or protocols set these features, which are selected by code writers. They constrain some behavior by making other behavior possible or impossible. The code embeds certain values or makes certain values impossible. In this sense, it too is regulation, just as the architectures of real-

	space codes are regulations."
Market Forces: "Market forces encourage architectures of identity to facilitate online commerce. Government needs to do very little—indeed, nothing at all—to induce just this sort of development. The market forces are too powerful; the potential here is too great."	*Norms* (collectively determined social norms): "Talk about Democratic politics in the alt.knitting newsgroup, and you open yourself to flaming; 'spoof' someone's identity in a MUD, and you may find yourself . . . 'toaded' [take off and die] filter."

Lawrence Lessig's model of Internet governance is sophisticated in its interactivity and multi-dimensionality:

> Architecture, law, norms and markets together regulate behavior. Together, they set the terms on which one is free to act or not; together, they set the constraints that affect what is and is not possible. They are four modalities of regulation; they together determine how individuals and states within their scope are regulated.

Lawrence Lessig, *Architecting for Control: Version 1.0, Keynote given at the Internet,* CAMBRIDGE REVIEW OF INTERNATIONAL AFFAIRS, UK (May 11, 2000) at 4.

The National Security Agency's Homeland Security's surveillance activities illustrate Lessig's architecture of control. In December of 2011, the Electronic Privacy Information Center (EPIC) filed suit against the Department of Homeland Security to require it to disclose how it monitors and collects data on social networks such as Facebook.

(A) INTERNET-RELATED LAW & LEGAL SANCTIONS

The global Internet involves trans-border communications across hundreds of countries. These interactions raise inevitable jurisdictional issues for debate as cyberlaw lacks comprehensive international conventions or codes.

There are no inclusive global Internet directives or regulations covering topics such as computer security, electronic contracts, cybertorts, cybercrimes, online privacy, intellectual property, content regulation or cross-border jurisdictional rules.

Internet law is largely national law with notable exceptions such as the domain name system and the alternative dispute resolution system for conflicts over domain names often involving trademark owners. "What has changed significantly, however, is that under President Trump, the U.S. leadership in promoting a global Internet first faded, and now has become a force for active decoupling."

TikTok Case to Undermine U.S. Competitiveness, XINHUA NEWS BULLETIN (Sept. 27, 2020).

"On January 7, President Donald Trump issued a sweeping directive withdrawing from 66 international organizations, conventions, and treaties deemed 'contrary to the interests of the United States.'" Trump's directive withdrew the United States "from the Freedom Online Coalition (FOC)—the only alliance explicitly committed to defending human rights and openness on the Internet." Under the Trump Administration, the United States "has now formally stepped away from a core element of the normative architecture it helped build to shape the global Internet."

Konstantinos Komaitis, *Trump Ends Americas Leadership on Internet Freedom,* TECH POLICY PRESS (Jan 8, 2026).

Russia, too, has asserted national control over the Internet:

> The new amendments introduced in 2019 aim to give Russian authorities more centralized powers. Roskomnadzor—the Federal Service for Supervision of Communications, Information Technology, and Mass Media—and the central point for control over communication networks and facilities as well as personal data in Russia, wants to monitor traffic at its source, without having an ISP in between or internet services that do not comply with new regulations. . . .

Alena Epifanova, *Deciphering Russia's Sovereign Internet Law,* GERMAN COUNCIL ON FOREIGN RELATIONS (Jan. 16, 2020).

The Russian government targets users that spread fake news and disrespect the "authorities and the 'sovereign internet' law giving the Russian authorities greater control over the Internet." *Russian Lawmakers Seek to Control Email Communication,* BBC INTERNATIONAL (July 25, 2019). In early 2026, it is clear Russia is censoring Internet content on an unprecedented scale:

> The Kremlin has recently ramped up its internet censorship campaign by undertaking more decisive measures to restrict physical and cyber internet infrastructure and imposing stricter censorship regulations in 2025 and 2026. The Kremlin has been increasingly advancing this campaign by testing and legalizing mechanisms to shut down the mobile internet; throttling and blocking major messaging platforms such as Telegram and WhatsApp; trying to replace these platforms with a state-monitored messaging app; adopting restrictions on the use of virtual private networks (VPNs); systematically silencing and coopting social media creators and milbloggers; and strengthening general censorship laws and measures online.

Putin's Internet Crackdown Is Rooted in Weakness and a Need to Demand Greater War Sacrifices, ISW (Feb. 24, 2026).

There are many recent examples of Russia shutting down foreign platforms:

> Russian opposition outlets reported on February 11, 2026 that Russian federal censor

> Roskomnadzor blocked WhatsApp, YouTube, Facebook, Facebook Messenger, Instagram, the Tor browser, the BBC, Radio Free Europe/Radio Liberty (RFE/RL), RFE/RL's Systema investigative project, Deutsche Welle, the Moscow Times, virtual private network (VPN) service Windscribe, and a site for installing applications onto Android smartphones to bypass application stores.

Russian Offensive Campaign Assessment, ISW (Feb. 12, 2026).

(B) CODE AS INTERNET LAW

Lester Lawrence is the Roy L. Furman Professor of Law at Harvard Law School and the former director of the Edmond J. Safra Center for Ethics at Harvard University. He is the founder of Creative Commons and Equal Citizens. Lessig argued that Law, Norms, Market, and Architecture comprise Internet law.

Lawrence Lessig's theory of Internet law stems from his 1999 book, *Code and Other Laws of Cyberspace*. Lessig's thesis that Code including software architecture is law just as legal code regulates the physical world.

Lawrence Lessig's theory states "architecture, law, norms and markets together regulate behavior. Together, they set the terms on which one is free to act or not; together, they set the constraints affect what is and is not possible. They are four modalities of regulation."

Lawrence Lessig, *Architecting for Control: Version 1.0, Keynote given at the Internet,* CAMBRIDGE REVIEW OF INTERNATIONAL AFFAIRS, UK (May 11, 2000) at 4.

Lawrence Lessig argued that the world:

> is regulated by four sorts of constraints. Law is just one of those four constraints. Law regulates by sanctions imposed ex post—fail to pay your taxes, and you are likely to go to jail; steal my car, and you are also likely to go to jail. Law is the prominent of regulators. But it is just one of four.
>
> Social norms are a second. They also regulate. Social norms—understandings or expectations about how I ought to behave, enforced not through some centralized norm enforcer, but rather through the understandings and expectations of just about every-one within a particular community—direct and constrain my behavior in a far wider array of contexts than any law. Norms say what clothes I will wear—a suit, not a dress; they tell you to sit quietly, and politely, for at least 40 minutes while I speak; they organize how we will interact after this talk is over. Norms guide behavior; in this sense, they function as a second regulatory constraint.
>
> The market is a third constraint. It regulates by price. The market limits the amount that I can spend on clothes; or the amount I can make from public speeches; it says I can command less for my writing than Madonna, or less from my singing than Pavarotti. Through the device of

price, the market sets my opportunities, and through this range of opportunities, it regulates.

And finally, there is the constraint of what some might call nature, but which I want to call "architecture." This is the constraint of the world as I find it, even if this world as I find it is a world that others have made. That I cannot see through that wall is a constraint on my ability to know what is happening on the other side of the room. That there is no access-ramp to a library constrains the access of one bound to a wheelchair. These constraints, in the sense I mean here, regulate.

LAWRENCE LESSIG, THE LAWS OF CYBERSPACE (1998) at 3.

He describes regulation of code:

Ours is the age of cyberspace. It, too, has a regulator. This regulator, too, threatens liberty. But so obsessed are we with the idea that liberty means "freedom from government" that we don't even see the regulation in this new space. We therefore don't see the threat to liberty that this regulation presents.

This regulator is code—the software and hardware that make cyberspace as it is. This code, or architecture, sets the terms on which life in cyberspace is experienced. It determines how easy it is to protect privacy, or how easy it is to censor speech. It determines whether access to information is general or whether information is zoned. It affects who sees what, or what is

> monitored. In a host of ways that one cannot begin to see unless one begins to understand the nature of this code, the code of cyberspace regulates.

Lawrence Lessig, *Code Is Law: On Liberty in Cyberspace.*

He gave examples of Code as Law:

> Architectures for facilitating identification—or, more generally, for certifying facts about the user (that he is over 18; that he is a he; that he is an American; that he is a lawyer)—are emerging. Architectures for rating content (porn, hate speech, violent speech, political speech) have been described and are being implemented. Each is being developed without the mandate of government, and the two together could facilitate an extraordinary degree of control over behavior on the Net.

Under Lessig's theory of "Code as Law," digital rights management or access controls acts as a form of architecture useful for social control. Digital rights management are an example of how architecture is a form of social control. Software also functions as architecture of control.

Anti-circumvention software constrains fair use and has the potential of censoring content. Open source software that can be freely changed enables generativity because users improve the code and share it with the community. In contrast, proprietary software treats the source code as a trade secret.

Software code is a legal constraint on what Internet users can do, which threatens Internet freedom. In his book *CODE* AND OTHER LAWS OF CYBERSPACE, Lessig takes issue with libertarians and others who argue that the Internet should not be subject to national regulations. He maintains that the debate between regulation and no regulation is a false dichotomy:

> Our choice is not between 'regulation' and 'no regulation.' The code regulates. It implements values, or not. It enables freedoms, or disables them. It protects privacy, or promotes monitoring. People choose how the code does these things. People write the code.

Lawrence Lessig, *Code is Law: On Liberty in Cyberspace*, HARVARD MAGAZINE (Jan. 1, 2000).

> Lessig explains how the strategic location of the German Constitutional Court in Karlsruhe (a six-hour drive from the Bundestag in Berlin) is a geographic constraint against urban-based dissident groups. The six-hour drive from Berlin creates a barrier against demonstrations in Karlsruhe and thus functions as an architecture that controls social behavior. In the words of Winston Churchill: 'We shape our buildings, and afterwards our buildings shape us.' The Internet is a building of 'layered architecture' which enables specialized efficiency, organizational coherency, and future flexibility.

Tim Wu, *Application-Centered Internet Analysis*, 85 VA. L. REV. 1163 (1999).

Encryption or digital locks also illustrate how code functions as social control of Internet users. Digital locks prevent unauthorized users from accessing materials and act as a conduit to control use and treacherous conduct. An online company's failure to encrypt data may constitute a breach of the duty to protect the intangible assets of third parties.

The functions of architecture or real-space code are not a matter of technological necessity but rather human-created access controls for the global Internet. In Lessig's view, the software code infrastructure is, in effect, a form of law. Because of conscious decisions to encrypt or protect code, the Internet is creating new copyright wars that influence the future of the public domain of ideas. Encryption, for example, is a way to restrict access to data, information, or other knowledge.

(C) NORMS AS INTERNET LAW

Social norms constrain and shape Internet conduct. Sociologists define norms as social expectations, dividing them into mores (imperative) and folkways (customary). Folkways are informal expectations, while violating mores results in severe social sanctions.

"Open Internet standards are folkways that have contributed to many new products and services. Anonymity is a well-established folkway as is the norm of the free flow of information."

Daniel Levin, *Building Social Norms on the Internet*, 4 YALE J. L. & TECH. 99, 117–120 (2002).

Software engineers create social norms through architecture:

> First, architectural decisions affect what norms evolve and how they evolve. By allowing or facilitating certain types of behavior and preventing others, architecture can promote the growth of norms. On the flip side, architecture not tailored to promote certain positive norms of cooperation or compliance with the wishes of the designer (or in some cases the law) may allow the growth of antisocial norms. Second, because design decisions affect behavior directly as well as indirectly through norms, software engineers must recognize the regulatory function of the code they create. Although online architecture can promote productive social norms, design decisions can also create a backlash by fostering the development of norms that work against the sort of behavior the code is written to promote.

Informal norms had yet to develop in the early development of the Internet:

> The management problem is even more acute in the virtual context where, due to the newness of the medium, there are fewer existing traditions and folkways to rely on. Mailing lists are perhaps the most venerable Internet-based technology for self-organization of groups, but even here there are, as yet, few models of how a group can organize itself. I can testify from personal experience that mailing lists can engender a sense of community. But, it's a fragile community and can easily fall apart

> when there are disputes. For example, mailing lists sometimes fall prey to 'flame wars' or find that their community is being distracted by procedural wrangles, most often over what ground rules should govern posting rights to the list.

Michael Froomkin, *Building the Bottom Up From the Top Down*, 5 ISJLP 141, 155 (2009).

Communities, rather than the government, largely determine which norms constitute mores. Mores act as strict norms that control and punish conduct, regardless of the formal legal rules. Sending sexually charged text messages (a practice known as sexting) is part of today's high school rating, dating, and mating rituals. The Educational Development Center defines sexting as the act of:

> using the Internet, cell phones, or other electronic devices to send or forward nude, sexually suggestive, or explicit photos or videos of someone you know. It is a difficult behavior to study, though, because teens can be involved in many ways. They can create, receive, and/or share these messages. It can be tough to untangle individuals' roles and intentions.

Educational Development Center, *Sexting: A Cause for Concern* (Jan. 24, 2013).

Sexting is the act of sending sexually explicit messages, primarily between mobile phones. Fifty-three percent of sexters are girls. Seventeen percent of sexters share the messages they receive with others, and fifty-five percent of those share them with more than one person. *Sexting Statistics & Facts*, VISUAL.LY (Jan. 5, 2021).

A 2019 study of 5,593 American middle and high school students concluded that approximately 13% of students reported that they had sent a sext, while 18.5% had received a sext. Justin Patchin and Sameer Hinduja, *The Nature and Extent of Sexting Among a National Sample of Middle and High School Students in the U.S.*, 48(8) ARCHIVES OF SEXUAL BEHAVIOR (Nov. 2019) at abstract.

> Some states have downgraded it to a minor offense, while six states still regard the activity as a felony. . . . Statistics collected by the BBC indicate the authorities spoke to around 400 minors under the age of 12 that sexted someone between 2013 and 2017.

Sanela Puac, *15 Exciting Sexting Statistics & Facts to Know in 2021* (Jan. 12, 2021).

Overzealous prosecutors charged three Pennsylvania teenage girls with child pornography for sending photographs of their breasts to their boyfriends, who shared them with peer group members. The legislators who drafted the child pornography statute never anticipated applying it to sexting. As this case illustrates, a criminal statute first enacted to punish adult distributors of child pornography is too harsh for teenage sexters.

"Generally, however, the laws treat sexting between minors with more leniency than in child porn cases. For example, some states do not require sex offender registration, as is in Rhode Island,

Vermont, and Nevada." Haley Zapal, *State-by-State Differences in Sexting Laws* (Apr. 9, 2019).

Internet users enforced norms against a free loader who overused the free Wi-Fi available in a San Francisco Apple store preventing other users from accessing it. In response, social media users took to YouTube, posting a video to shame the moocher. The video achieved millions of views.

This "public shaming" video is an example of how user communities can deploy informal sanctions to establish norms and sanction those that break them. Folkways are informal norms for how to behave. Naming, blaming, and shaming celebrities is common on social networks like Facebook, which is often an organized response to controversial public figures' actions:

> Public actors include, for example, politicians who disregard political correctness norms, corporations that violate human rights, or academics who violate scientific norms by engaging in plagiarism. In this view, online firestorms enforce social norms by expressing public disapproval with the aim of securing public goods, for example, honesty of politicians, companies or academics. The stunning waves of aggression typical for online firestorms can be explained by the characteristic features of social media that ideally contribute to the solution of the second-order public good dilemma of norm enforcement. Digital norm enforcement in social media is cheap, and selective incentives and intrinsically motivated individuals are present.

Katja Rost et al., *Digital Social Norm Enforcement: Online Firestorms in Social Media,* PLOSONE (2016).

Conflict in online communities challenges norms and collective expectations. For example, member of a group complained about new posts, which were written in Italian:

> 'Why, oh, why do these RUDE BASTARDS *still* post here in a language only morons would speak?' Another member then replied that the complainer's post, besides being racist, had not included the obligatory ObHack. A spirited discussion and pursuit of the mysterious foreign messages ensued until an Italian hacker, Venom, bragged how a group of Italian hackers had decided to invade alt.hackers, 'They can read any message you post, the complaints too, they simply don't care, and taunt you.' Ultimately, the Italian hackers left, but at least one member of alt.hackers quit publicly in disgust because an alt.hacker member had violated the group's secret procedures.

University of Melbourne, *Norms in Online Communities: Introduction and Problem* 1 (2020).

A Cornell University study of social norms in Stack Overflow, a technical question and answer site concluded:

> Online communities are also expected to abide by the rules and regulations that are expressed in the code of conduct of a system. Even though community authorities continuously prompt their users to follow the regulations, it is

> observed that hate speech and abusive language usage are on the rise. . . . Even though the site has been dedicated to technical problem solving and debugging, hate speech as well as posting offensive comments make the community 'toxic.' By identifying and minimising various patterns of norm violations in different SO [Stack Overflow] communities, the community would become less toxic and thereby the community can engage more effectively in its goal of knowledge sharing.

Jithin Cheriyan et al., *Norm Violation in Online Communities—A Study of Stack Overflow Comments* (Cornell University Computer Science Department 2020).

Informal negative comments by individuals create a toxic online environment. A National Institute of Health study concluded that online attacks on public companies, officials, and celebrities is on the rise enabled by social media:

> In 2013, the company Amazon was accused of the ill treatment of temporary workers. The Amazon-affair led to floods of negative comments on Amazon's Facebook profile. Firestorms also shake academia: In 2011, the former minister of defense of Germany, Karl-Theodor zu Guttenberg, was accused of plagiarism. These accusations triggered widespread online debates and ultimately led to the denial of his PhD and to his resignation. Katja Rost et al., *Digital Social Norm*

Enforcement: Online Firestorms in Social Media, PLOSONE (2016).

(D) MARKETS AS INTERNET LAW

The Cato Institute contends that governments should not regulate the Internet. The Internet " 'came of age' in an ethos of rebellious libertarianism." 1 RIGHTS AND LIABILITIES IN MEDIA CONTENT § 4:1 (2d ed.).

Policymakers should resist intervention and allow the Internet to develop market-based solutions to problems. Regulators should not attempt to fix what is not broken and defer to the free market that has developed the World Wide Web.

> If the free market is working the way it should, then these networks might risk alienating some customers because of the filtering . . . At the moment, the free market is the best weapon we have for combating Internet piracy.

Net Neutrality and Free Speech on the Internet: Hearing, U.S. House of Representatives, *House Committee on the Judiciary. Task Force on Competition Policy and Antitrust Laws* (2008).

The Chicago School of Law and Economics argues that government intervention should only happen when there is acute market failure:

> The fundamental tenet of the Chicago approach is that competition within a perfect market will lead to efficiency, which is the desirable normative goal of the legal system. . . . Such a

> (market) failure exists when there are no multiple players on both sides of the market (the problem of monopolies), when these players do not have symmetric and full information relevant to their market activities, when any of the players bypass the market through involuntary actions. (the problem of externalities) or when the traded commodity is a public good.

NIVA ELKIN-KOREN & ELI M SALZBERGE, LAW AND ECONOMICS IN CYBERSPACE (2000) at 3.

The U.S. has a market-approach to content regulation. Opponents of this free-market perspective argue for government oversight in order to guarantee net neutrality. Consumer advocates point to the need for the government to enact mandatory minimum protection for Internet users due to the failure of the marketplace for privacy and consumer rights.

Problems of the free market approach include barriers making it difficult to enter and exit markets, the imperfect flow of information, and empirical evidence that consumers do not always make rational decisions:

> Capitalism has been a very successful system producing a host of innovations and generally increasing the standard of living around the world. . . . People make the markets, and people are not perfect. People do not exist in the abstract and are not controlled by assumptions we choose to place on them for market-based

> analytical purposes. The conditions necessary for the free market economy to function simply do not exist in today's world, if they ever did.

Presidio Economics, *The Fallacy of Free Markets*, TRIPLE PUNDIT (Dec. 27, 2011).

The call for universal Internet access troubles free-market activists:

> [I]f government requires cable firms to provide access to its cables to any ISP, the resulting increase in users would cut transmission speeds—a major reason why people prefer broadband in the first place! Congestion problems would undoubtedly then be blamed on the cable companies. In the long run, those companies would likely cut back on their investments in broadband technology, which would have the effect of limiting future access options for consumers.

Lawrence W. Reed, *Internet Access Should Be Left to the Free Market: Forced Access Legislation Will Not Achieve Its Intended Goals,* FEE FOUNDATION FOR ECONOMIC EDUCATION (Apr. 1, 2000).

Since the Internet was developed, the U.S. government has generally taken a market-based approach to Internet policy issues in contrast to the European Union countries that seek thick regulatory solutions to Internet policies issues such as access.

(E) THE GENERATIVE INTERNET

The strength of the Internet lies in its users' collective collaboration, which leads to improvements, a process he calls "generativity." Jonathan Zittrain's work illustrates Solum's third model because it emphasizes the myriad ways that software code and Internet architecture interact. See generally, JONATHAN ZITTRAIN, THE FUTURE OF THE INTERNET AND HOW TO STOP IT (2008).

The generative Internet is comprised of tens of millions of Internet users collaborating to produce code and content. Jonathan Zittrain writes about Apple's role in creating a generative Internet:

> The Apple II was quintessentially generative technology. It was a platform. It invited people to tinker with it. Hobbyists wrote programs. Businesses began to plan on selling software. Jobs (and Apple) had no clue how the machine would be used. They had their hunches, but, fortunately for them (and the rest of us), nothing constrained the PC to the hunches of the founders. The iPhone—for all its startling inventiveness—is precisely the opposite. Rather than a platform that invites innovation, the iPhone comes preprogrammed. You are not allowed to add programs to the all-in-one device that Steve Jobs sells you. Its functionality is locked in, though Apple can change it through remote updates.

Jonathan Zittrain, *Protecting the Internet Without Wrecking It: How to Meet the Security Threat,* BOSTON REVIEW (Mar. 1, 2008).

The Internet Engineering Task Force favors an open, generative Internet as opposed to a "walled garden" without significant user input. The public Internet is a generative technology because it allows individuals and voluntary organizations to improve it. Zittrain compared the open architecture of Apple II to the appliance-like platform incorporated in the tethered iPhone or iPad, which is under the total control of Apple.

In contrast, digital rights management (DRM) to prevent unauthorized use of copyrighted works is emblematic of the closed, walled Internet. Apple's products are in the closed paradigm. Apple protects its products through lockdown as illustrated by its 2018 message warning that it will deny service to any jailbreaker that installs unauthorized software:

> Unauthorized modifications to iOS (also known as 'jailbreaking') bypass security features and can cause numerous issues to the hacked iPhone, iPad, or iPod touch, including: (1) security vulnerabilities, (2) instability, (3) shortened battery life, (4) unreliable voice and data, (5) disruption of services, and (6) inability to apply future software updates.

Apple, *Unauthorized Modification of iOS Can Cause Security Vulnerabilities, Instability, Shortened Battery Life, and Other Issues* (2018).

Code architecture can either facilitate or constrain creative expression and innovation on the Internet. Zittrain's generative Internet requires interoperability enabled by reverse engineering and participation by the user community. He argues for developing policies enabling Internet generativity:

> That PCs are highly adaptable machines that are connected to a network with little centralized control, resulting in a grid that is nearly completely open to the creation and rapid distribution of the innovations of tech-savvy users to a mass audience that can enjoy these innovations.

BERIN SZOKA & ADAM MARCUS, THE NEXT DIGITAL DECADE: ESSAYS ON THE FUTURE OF THE INTERNET 117 (2011).

§ 2-5. Why National Regulation Still Matters

(A) LOCAL GOVERNANCE

Lawrence Solum's fourth model of Internet governance is local regulation by individual governments. The Communications Decency Act (CDA), 47 U.S.C. § 230, provides immunity from liability for providers and users of an "interactive computer service" who publish information provided by third-party users. The defendant must be a 'provider or user' of an "interactive computer service to qualify for the immunity." *Jefferson v. Zukerberg*, [sic] 2018 WL 3241343, at *5 (D. Md. July 3, 2018).

(B) NATIONAL REGULATION

"Internet governance has become a point of international conflict among states and a target of transnational policy advocates from business and civil society." MILTON MUELLER, NETWORKS AND STATES: THE GLOBAL POLITICS OF INTERNET GOVERNANCE (2010) at 2.

National governments frequently impose their extraterritorial will on cyberspace activities through directives and regulations.

Twitter obeyed a French court order to unveil anonymous speakers with Anti-Semitic hashtags on its service. The International Federation of Human Rights (FIDH) and the French League of Human Rights (LDH) filed suit on the U.S. National Security Agency for its PRISM data collection program.

Another example of national regulation is The Securities and Exchange Commission's settlement:

> with Elon Musk over his tweeting, because his tweeting, though it occurs online, is still material to his companies' fortunes. The Federal Trade Commission is expected to levy a 10-figure fine on Facebook, for which the company has already set aside $3 billion. The agency's previous record for a fine was $22.5 million. Alexis C. Madrigal, *The End of Cyberspace: Internet Theorists and Companies Once Declared Themselves Free of Nations and Governance, But That's All Over Now*, THE ATLANTIC (May 1, 2019).

§ 2-6. The Wealth of Networks

(A) ECONOMICS-BASED GOVERNANCE

Yochai Benkler of Harvard University's Berkman Center describes the shift from durable goods to an information-based economy as "the wealth of networks." He describes a networked information economy where Karl Marx's sharp division between workers and bourgeoisie is replaced with a more democratic division in a post-industrial information-based economy.

Marx predicted class conflict between the bourgeoisie, who controlled the means of production, and the proletariat, who were wage slaves. Benkler sees the rise of the Internet as democratizing the means of production, because it lowers the cost of the means of production. Law is also both a means of oppression and a means of resistance in Benkler's theory of networked society.

Benkler's principal point is that copyright law has the potential to either liberate or oppress information-based workers. Free and open source software, for example, is generative, controlled by those who produce it, whereas proprietary software distribution is an older model, where the software publishers own the code, and control the means of production.

With free and open source software, there is a complete freedom to tweak and change code, making those modifications available for other users.

> Benkler's concept of peer production in creating open software illustrates how a greater segment of the population has access and control to the means of production. Marxism is a theory that maintains that in every historical epoch, the means of production are owned by one class. Under a Marxist theory, the bourgeoisie, or member of the capitalist class, own factories and other means of production. For a farmer, the means of production will be the ownership of land. The means of production include tools and machinery to produce products critical to human survival and to satisfy human needs.

KEN MORRISON, MARX, DURKHEIM, WEBER: FORMATIONS OF MODERN SOCIAL THEORY 44 (2006).

In a durable goods-based economy, there is a constant push for investment in physical capital. By contrast, the information age economy allows larger proportions of the population to control the means of intellectual capital production. Individuals can communicate with millions around the world, which was not possible in an earlier stage of capitalism.

Benkler's concept of peer production argues that one class does not own today's means of production. He argues that a greater segment of the population currently accesses and controls the Internet, and other information-based means of production. Under industrial capitalism, the means of production is in the hands of the bourgeoisie or the wealthy class.

In a durable goods-based economy, there is a constant push for investment in physical capital. In contrast, the information age economy allows larger proportions of the population to control the means of intellectual capital production. Individuals can communicate with millions around the world, which was not possible in an earlier stages of capitalism.

YOCHAI BENKLER, THE WEALTH OF NETWORKS: HOW SOCIAL PRODUCTION TRANSFORMS MARKETS AND FREEDOM (2006).

The Internet blurs the boundary between workers and the owners of the means of production. The Internet is potentially democratizing because it enables workers to have access to the means of information production, granting greater access to digital information, which is the information age's equivalent of the means of production.

> Where there were once walls preventing ordinary persons from accessing mass media distribution, now, there is a free-flowing information superhighway, available to anyone with an internet connection. YouTube videos of cats being lazy or performing tricks go viral, getting millions of views. Another example of how social production of content has been extended to a larger population by the internet is the open source software movement. The production and improvement of open software by a decentralized community of users illustrates what Benkler calls 'commons-based peer production.'

Yochai Benkler & Helen Nissenbaum, *Common-Based Peer Production and Virtue*, 14 J. POLIT. PHIL. 394, 394 (2006).

Yochai Benkler and Helen Nissenbaum write:

> We suggest that the emergence of peer production offers an opportunity for more people to engage in practices that permit them to exhibit and experience virtuous behavior. We posit: (A) that a society that provides opportunities for virtuous behavior is one that is more conductive to virtuous individuals; and (B) that the practice of effective virtuous behavior may lead to more people adopting virtues as their own, or as attributes of what they see as their self-definition.

Free and open source software, for example, is generative—controlled by those who produce it—whereas proprietary software reflects an oppressive model, where the software publishers own the code. Open source represents the generative Internet as opposed to closed proprietary software where the source code is treated as a trade secret not accessed by users.

(B) COPYRIGHT COMMONS

Yochai Benkler contends that Hollywood and the recording industry are systematically undermining the innovations of the collaborative-networked economy by seeking control of the Internet. He concludes that we should not let "yesterday's winners dictate the terms of tomorrow's economic competition."

Urs Gasser, Benkler's Berkman Center colleague, describes the Internet as an information ecosystem that dramatically reduces the cost of production, and can potentially lead to a more participatory and egalitarian society with a broader governing class.

(C) THE SURVEILLANCE SOCIETY

The U.S. National Security Agency (NSA) mass surveillance program became the "focus of interest of experts and the global community after the speech made by Edward Snowden, former NSA contractor." *Civil Society Must Act Against Unlawful Surveillance of Internet Users*, EURASIA REVIEW (April 15, 2014).

A 2021 study of African speech control and suppression: concluded that "Internet shutdowns and online surveillance to social media taxes and arrests for anti-government posts" were threatening "basic freedoms and rights in many African countries." Nita Bhalla, *'Digital Authoritarianism' Threatening Basic Rights in Africa*, CNBC AFRICA (Mar. 2, 2011).

Surveillance capitalism is a term representing a new era where powerful interests "anticipate what you will do now, soon, and later."

> Companies operating in this mode seek not just to predict but also to 'shape our behavior at scale.' Companies like Google and Facebook possess, she declares, a new species of 'instrumentarian power,' the power to 'shape[ ]

> human behavior toward others' ends.' The result: an economic system that 'will thrive at the expense of human nature and will threaten to cost us our humanity.'

Shoshana Zuboff, *The Law of Informational Capitalism, The Age of Surveillance Capitalism: The Fight for a Human Future at the New Frontier of Power*, 129 YALE L. J. 1460 (2020).

The broader theories of Internet governance discussed in this chapter are the backdrop for understanding procedural and substantive topics in the following chapters.

CHAPTER 3
GLOBAL INTERNET JURISDICTION

This chapter examines the ways courts and legislatures have adapted jurisdiction to reflect of cyberspace transactions. This chapter is divided into eight sections. In the United States, Internet jurisdiction is established by a due process framework predicated upon minimum contacts.

§ 3-1. Introduction to Personal Jurisdiction

A federal court may not exercise personal jurisdiction over an out-of-state defendant unless "(1) an applicable statute authorizes service of process on that defendant and (2) the exercise of statutory jurisdiction comports with constitutional due process." U.S. states permit courts to "exercise jurisdiction on any basis consistent with the Constitution of this state and the Constitution of the United States,"

Exercising jurisdiction over a nonresident defendant "comports with constitutional due process" if there are "sufficient 'minimum contacts between the defendant and the forum state,'" such that "having to defend the lawsuit there would not offend traditional notions of fair play and substantial justice."

Section 3-1 of this chapter explains how minimum contacts for Internet jurisdiction require a non-resident defendant to have "purposeful availment" of the forum state, often determined by the interactivity of their website.

Section 3-2 presents the *Zippo* sliding scale test (from *Zippo Manufacturing Co. v. Zippo Dot Com, Inc.*, 952 F. Supp. 1119 (W.D. Pa. 1997) is a sliding scale test used by U.S. courts to determine personal jurisdiction over non-resident defendants based on their website activity. Under the *Zippo* test, the interactivity of the website determines whether a defendant purposefully availed themselves of the forum state,

Section 3-3 cover the *Calder* "effects test"—which is the test to establish personal jurisdiction over a defendant in Internet tort cases even if they have no physical contacts with the forum state. The "Calder effects test" originates from the U.S. Supreme Court case of *Calder v. Jones*, 465 U.S. 783 (1984).

This ruling established that a state may exercise personal jurisdiction over a defendant who engages in intentional, tortious acts aimed at the forum state, causing harm there.

In the context of Internet law, the test requires proof that a website or other entity engaged in an intentional, tortious act with knowledge that the effects will be felt in the forum state. Section 3-4 covers the "something more" test in establishing personal jurisdiction in cyberspace. The 'Something more' standard for Internet-based personal jurisdiction means something beyond mere website accessibility.

Next, Section 3-5 covers the topic of *in rem* jurisdiction applied to domain names. Under the Anticybersquatting Consumer Protection Act (ACPA) 15 U.S.C.A. § 1125(d)(2)(ii), trademark owners are permitted to sue a domain name itself, rather than the owner, when the registrant cannot be found or personal jurisdiction is impossible to obtain.

Section 3-6 introduces cross-border jurisdiction. Internet jurisdiction in international law is not governed by a single comprehensive treaty for all countries connected to the Internet.

Section 3-7 covers the Brussels Regulation Recast (2012). The European Union (EU) has enacted the Brussels Regulation governing jurisdiction in the twenty-seven EU Member States. Brussels I Regulation (Recast—1215/2012): applies to civil and commercial disputes (e.g., contracts, torts) initiated on or after January 10, 2015.

The principal default rule is that EU defendants are generally sued in their home Member State. The Brussels Regulation establishes a simple principle for the enforcement of judgments. Judgments from one Member State are generally enforceable in another without a special declaration. Section 3-8 calls for a global solution to Internet jurisdiction.

Since no international treaty or other agreement addresses Internet personal jurisdiction, U.S. courts have mechanically stretched the parochial minimum contacts approach to personal jurisdiction in cyberspace, creating jurisdictional dilemmas because no other country in the world has adopted a minimum contacts paradigm for personal jurisdiction.

§ 3-2. Adapting Personal Jurisdiction to the Internet

This section examines how courts have adapted principles of personal jurisdiction to the Internet. The exercise of personal jurisdiction is only permissible to the extent that it is "permitted by the forum state's long-arm statute and by the Due Process Clause of the Constitution." Due process requires that a defendant have certain 'minimum contacts' with the forum state for personal jurisdiction to be exercised.

State courts can only assert personal jurisdiction over an out-of-state corporation, consistent with the Due Process Clause of the Fourteenth Amendment, when the defendant corporation has such minimum contacts with the forum state such that the maintenance of the suit does not offend traditional notions of fair play and substantial justice, or in instances where the corporation's continuous operations in the state were so substantial and of such a nature as to justify suit against it on causes of action arising from dealings entirely distinct from those activities.

Under either form of personal jurisdiction, the defendant must have " 'certain minimum contacts with [the state] such that the maintenance of the suit does not offend traditional notions of fair play and substantial justice.' " (quoting *Int'l Shoe Co. v. Washington,* 326 U.S. 310 (1945)).

The *Washington Shoe* test focuses on the defendant's contacts with the state, and not the "random, fortuitous, or attenuated" contacts it has by interacting with other persons affiliated with the state. *Walden v. Fiore,* 571 U.S. 277, 284 (2014). To establish personal jurisdiction over a nonresident, a court employs a two-part inquiry: (1) a court must first examine whether jurisdiction is applicable under the state's long-arm statute and (2) whether a finding of jurisdiction satisfies the constitutional requirements of due process.

> Federal due-process requirements limit a state's power to assert personal jurisdiction over a nonresident defendant. Personal jurisdiction is proper when the nonresident defendant has established minimum contacts with the forum state, and the exercise of jurisdiction comports with traditional notions of fair play and substantial justice.

Schexnider v. E-Cig Cent., LLC, 2020 WL 6929872 at *4 (Tex. App. Nov. 25, 2020).

> Federal courts "ordinarily follow state law in determining the bounds of their jurisdiction over persons." *Daimler AG v. Bauman*, 571 U.S. 117, 125, 134 S.Ct. 746, 187 L.Ed. 2d 624 (2014) (citing Fed. R. Civ. P. 4(k)(1)(A)). But any state law governing personal jurisdiction must comport with the limitations of the Fourteenth Amendment, which require that a defendant have "such 'contacts' with the forum State that 'the maintenance of the suit' is 'reasonable, in the context of our federal system of government,'

and 'does not offend traditional notions of fair play and substantial justice.'" *Juselis v. Arlington Mgmt. Emps. LLC,* 2026 U.S. Dist. LEXIS 45669, *6 (D.C. Dist. Ct. Mar. 5, 2026).

Federal courts "ordinarily follow state law in determining the bounds of their jurisdiction over persons."

Daimler AG v. Bauman, 571 U.S. 117, 125 (2014).

A Texas federal court summarized the five factors that courts apply in determining whether the exercise of personal jurisdiction is reasonable or unfair:

Five factors determine if the exercise of personal jurisdiction would be unfair or unreasonable:

(1) the burden on the nonresident defendant,

(2) the forum state's interests,

(3) the plaintiff's interest in securing relief,

(4) the interest of the interstate judicial system in the efficient administration of justice, and

(5) the shared interest of the several states in furthering fundamental social policies.

Exxon Mobil Corp. v. Bonta, 2026 U.S. Dist. LEXIS 29952, *12–13 (E.D. Tex. Feb. 13, 2026).

The court observed that, "it is rare to say the assertion of jurisdiction is unfair after minimum contacts have been shown."

To determine whether a plaintiff in an Internet case has adequately alleged personal jurisdiction over a foreign defendant, a court must determine whether there is jurisdiction under a state's long-arm statute and next determine whether the exercise of jurisdiction comports with the Due Process Clause of the Fourteenth Amendment. A long-arm statute is a statutory means of serving process on a nonresident defendant.

There are "two types" of personal jurisdiction that satisfy this standard: "general" (sometimes called "all-purpose") jurisdiction and "specific" (sometimes called "case-linked") jurisdiction. General jurisdiction lies in the forum where the defendant is domiciled or "fairly regarded as at home."

Juselis v. Arlington Mgmt. Emps. LLC, 2026 U.S. Dist. LEXIS 45669 *7 (D.C. Dist. Ct. Mar. 5, 2026).

General personal jurisdiction applies only where a nonresident defendant's contacts are "so continuous and systematic as to render it essentially at home" in the forum state.

In *Ansys, Inc. v. SF Motors, Inc.,* 2021 WL 22453 at *1 (W.D. Pa., Jan. 4, 2021), the court explained the difference between general and specific jurisdiction:

> General jurisdiction applies if the defendant 'maintained systematic and continuous contacts with the forum state.' *Marten v. Godwin,* 499 F.3d 290, 296 (3d Cir. 2007). To establish specific jurisdiction, plaintiff must prove (1) defendant has purposefully directed his activities at the forum; (2) the plaintiff's claim arises out of or

> relates to at least one of those specific activities; and (3) the court's exercise of jurisdiction over the defendant comports with traditional notions of fair play and substantial justice. In addition, a party may consent to personal jurisdiction through a forum selection provision.

Burger King Corp. v. Rudzewicz, 471 U.S. 462, 472 n.14 (1985).

Specific jurisdiction, on the other hand, "covers defendants less intimately connected with a State, but only as to a narrower class of claims." A court may exercise specific jurisdiction over a defendant "only so long as there exist 'minimum contacts' between the defendant and the forum State."

To have the requisite "minimum contacts" with the forum State, a defendant must take 'some act by which [it] purposefully avails itself of the privilege of conducting activities within the forum State.'

These contacts must be of "the defendant's own choice and not random, isolated, or fortuitous," and they must show that the defendant "deliberately reached out beyond its home—by, for example, exploiting a market in the forum State or entering a contractual relationship centered there."

Juselis v. Arlington Mgmt. Emps. LLC, 2026 U.S. Dist. LEXIS 45669 *7 (D.C. Dist. Ct. Mar. 5, 2026).

Specific personal jurisdiction has three elements:

(1) the defendant "purposefully avail[s] itself of the privilege of conducting activities in the forum state,"

(2) the plaintiff's claim "arise[s] out of or relate[s] to" those purposeful contacts, and

(3) exercising jurisdiction is "fair and reasonable" to the nonresident defendant.

A defendant purposefully avails himself when he has "minimum contacts" with the forum state. Minimum contacts require an intentional act invoking the "benefits and protections of [the forum state's] laws." The defendant should "reasonably anticipate being haled into court" in the forum state based on that act.

Specific jurisdiction depends on "an 'affiliation between the forum and the underlying controversy,' principally, activity or an occurrence that takes place in the forum State and is therefore subject to the State's regulation."

Goodyear Dunlop Tires Operations, SA v. Brown, 564 U.S. 915, 919 (2011).

When specific jurisdiction is alleged, the focus of the minimum-contacts analysis is on the relationship between the defendant, the forum, and the litigation. *Brigade Elecs. (UK) Ltd. v. Dehaney,* 2020 Tex. App. 2020 WL 7391709, at *1 (Tex. App. Dec. 17, 2020). A court will typically focus on the interactivity of the website in determining whether there is personal jurisdiction as in *Poulin Ventures, LLC v. MoneyBunny Co.,* 2020 WL 6286440 (D.N.M. Oct. 27, 2020).

Poulin sold its LadyBoss-branded products on its website, www.ladyboss.com. Inc. magazine listed

LadyBoss as number four in its list of "2019 Inc. 5000: Poulin has about 222,000 Instagram followers, 816,000 Facebook followers, and 32,000 YouTube subscribers."

Poulin filed suit against MoneyBunny, which sold anti-blue light glasses using the same mark as registered by Poulin. The court held that Poulin made a prima facie showing that MoneyBunny's activities demonstrate purposeful direction at New Mexico, the forum state. "Plaintiff submits through its evidentiary proffers (Mr. Poulin's affidavit and screen shots of the LadyBoss website), that MoneyBunny does e-commerce as LadyBoss."

Purposeful availment may be shown where an out-of-state defendant causes its product to be distributed in the forum state. MoneyBunny has caused its products to be sold in New Mexico using a website that can be characterized as interactive. The interactive website for the sale of its products allows a user to select New Mexico as a ship-to destination from which the customer may choose.

MoneyBunny's website arranges for the sale of its products by particularizing shipping and tax costs associated with the sale of products to New Mexico. After arranging the sale, MoneyBunny then ships its products to New Mexico customers.

MoneyBunny admittedly sold about 100 glasses to New Mexico residents. These contacts are enough to find personal availment on MoneyBunny's part. *Id.* at *17–18. The essence of this test is that it is fair to subject the defect to jurisdiction as they have purposely directed activities toward the forum.

Internet-based conduct must have a connection to the forum state which goes beyond simply being directed at an individual who lives in the forum state in order for the minimum contacts test is satisfied. Every state has a long arm statute, which are state statutes that enable local courts to exercise personal jurisdiction over out-of-state or foreign defendants who have sufficient "minimum contacts" with that state, such as doing business, committing a tort, or owning property there. The purpose of the long arm statute is to ensure fairness in by allowing lawsuits against non-residents who have connections to the forum state.

Georgia's Long Arm Statute, O.C.G.A. § 9–10–90 et seq., defines the scope of personal jurisdiction that Georgia courts may exercise over nonresidents pursuant to O.C.G.A. § 9–10–91 and requires that an out-of-state defendant must do certain acts within the State of Georgia before he can be subjected to specific personal jurisdiction. O.C.G.A. § 9–10–90 defines nonresident for purposes of the Long Arm Statute.

Cooper Tire & Rubber Co. v. McCall, 312. Ga. 422, 422 (2021).

> Long arm statutes vary in their provisions. Florida's long arm statute, for example, provides two means for subjecting a foreign defendant to the jurisdiction of Florida courts: (1) a defendant is subject to specific personal jurisdiction—that

> is, jurisdiction over suits that arise out of or related to a defendant's contacts with Florida—for conduct specifically enumerated in the statute; and (2) a defendant is subject to general personal jurisdiction—that is, jurisdiction over any claims against a defendant, whether or not they involve the defendant's activities in Florida—if the defendant engages in substantial and not isolated activity in Florida.

Steelers Keys LLC v. High Tech Nat'l LLC, 2020 WL 7197822 (S.D. Fla. Dec. 7, 2020).

The landmark case of *Zippo Manufacturing Company v. Zippo Dot Com, Inc.*, 952 F. Supp. 1119 (W.D. Pa. 1997) led to many websites being subject to jurisdiction during the first decades of the World Wide Web. The *Zippo.com* case established the most influential test for determining jurisdiction on the Internet, often referred to as the "Zippo sliding scale test."

Zippo Manufacturing Company, a Pennsylvania corporation, created a popular brand of pocket lighters. Zippo.com was an unaffiliated California corporation that operated an Internet website offering access to USENET newsgroups.

Zippo Manufacturing Company filed suit against Zippo Dot Com, Inc., the operator of a California Internet news service corporation, alleging trademark infringement and other causes of action. This became a high profile case of a trademark owner filing suit against a domain name owner incorporating their famous trademarks.

An estimated 3,000 of Zippo.com's subscribers were Pennsylvania residents. Additionally, in Pennsylvania, Zippo.com entered into agreements with seven Internet service providers to enable their subscribers to access the defendant's news service. Zippo.com had obtained the exclusive right to use the Internet domain names "zippo.com," "zippo.net," and "zipponews.com." Zippo.com frequently used the word "zippo" in numerous locations on both its website and in newsgroup message headings posted by subscribers.

Zippo filed suit against Zippo.com in Pennsylvania for trademark dilution and violations of the Federal Trademark Act because Zippo.com owned a website that provided information about Zippo lighters, Zippo products, advertisements, and subscriptions to a news service about Zippo's products. Zippo.com moved to dismiss for lack of personal jurisdiction.

The *Zippo.com* court held that Zippo.com was subject to jurisdiction in Pennsylvania because it enabled website users to interact with the site. The following chart highlights the court's holding that the interactivity of a website is the strongest indicator of sufficient contacts to satisfy due process.

The court that it must apply a three prong test:

(1) the defendant must have minimum contacts with the forum state;

(2) the claim asserted must arise out of those contacts;

and (3) the exercise of jurisdiction must be reasonable. The court determines whether Zippo.com purposefully availed himself to the state.

(A) ZIPPO.COM'S INTERACTIVITY TEST

Three Levels of Interactivity

No Personal Jurisdiction	*Gray Area*	*Personal Jurisdiction Recognized*
Passive websites with little commercial activity.	A finding of jurisdiction turns upon the exchange of information but with little interactivity.	Interactive websites permit online orders.

Under *Zippo.com*'s sliding scale, websites are classified as "passive" if they merely post information and generally do not provide the contacts required to support jurisdiction. A 'passive' website, one that merely allows the owner to post information on the Internet, is at one end of the scale.

At the other end of the spectrum, interactive websites often give rise to a finding of personal jurisdiction because these cases exist in a "gray area," and the court assesses the level of interactivity in order to determine whether the exchanges are commercial or passive.

A Texas federal court compared passive to interactive websites, where there is personal jurisdiction:

> Passive websites cannot support personal jurisdiction. An interactive website "allows for bilateral information exchange with its visitors," which can create specific personal jurisdiction. A website is not passive (and therefore has some amount of interactivity) when it "receives purchases, allows customers to create accounts, and accepts product reviews."

Exxon Mobil Corp. v. Bonta, 2026 U.S. Dist. LEXIS 29952, *13–14 (E.D. Tex. Feb. 13, 2026).

The *Zippo.com* court described a "sliding scale" to guide the due process inquiry for Internet-based minimum contacts:

> The middle ground is occupied by interactive Web sites where a user can exchange information with the host computer. In these cases, the exercise of jurisdiction is determined by examining the level of interactivity and commercial nature of the exchange of information that occurs on the Web site.

Zippo Mfg. Co. v. Zippo Dot Com, Inc., 952 F. Supp. 1119 (W.D. Pa. 1997).

However, this bellwether decision is becoming less relevant as website design increasingly emphasizes interactivity. For example, Michigan rejected the *Zippo.com* approach observing:

> that the need for a special Internet-focused test for minimum contacts has yet to be established . . . [The] manner of establishing or maintaining those contacts, and the technological mechanisms used in so doing, are mere accessories to the central inquiry [of whether there are minimum contacts].

Winfield Collection, Ltd. v. McCauley, 105 F. Supp. 2d 746, 750 (E.D. Mich. 2000).

As of May 2, 2026 U.S. federal and state courts have cited *Zippo.com* more than 2,486 times. Post-*Zippo,* courts focus on "purposeful availment"—whether a defendant intentionally targeted a forum state—rather than mere website accessibility.

Courts evaluate the level of interactivity and commercial nature of the exchange of information on a website. Active websites (doing business in the forum) usually subject the operator to personal jurisdiction.

(B) PASSIVE JURISDICTION

If a website is passive meaning that it is not interactive, courts will find no personal jurisdiction because the website does not permit users to post comments. The leading case making interactivity the test for jurisdiction of websites is *Cybersell Inc. v. Cybersell, Inc.*, 130 F.3d 414 (9th Cir. 1997).

That case arose out of a dispute over two companies using the trade name Cybersell. Cybersell Incorporated (Cybersell AZ) registered its service mark with the U.S. Trademark Office in 1994. In

1995, a father and son running a family consulting business in Florida also created a website for their business under the trade name of Cybersell (Cybersell FL).

The Cybersell AZ plaintiffs, Laurence Canter and Martha Siegel, who were infamous spam e-mailers, filed a lawsuit for trademark infringement against Cybersell FL. The Arizona federal court dismissed the action, finding it had no personal jurisdiction over the Cybersell FL website since the site was not interactive and its owners were not conducting commercial transactions.

The Ninth Circuit found Cybersell FL's operation of a passive website did not purposefully avail itself of the privilege of doing business in Arizona, Thus, the court deemed Cybersell FL's contacts insufficient to establish personal jurisdiction. However, the court noted the operation of an interactive, commercial website often is insufficient to warrant personal jurisdiction. The defendant must do something akin to specifically targeting the forum, rather than merely posting a website accessible in the forum state.

In *Daly v. Francis*, 2026 U.S. Dist. LEXIS 15327 (N.D. N.Y. Jan. 28, 2026), Peter Daly, a New York resident filed suit against Distributed Ledger and BolsaDX, which are entities doing business in Alabama. Daly argued that Defendant Francis resides in Alabama and is the Chief Executive Officer of both Distributed Ledger and BolsaDX. He also alleges that Defendant Arnold was "the only human being listed on the BolsaDX website" and that she resides in Alabama.

Daly describes BolsaDX as a cryptocurrency exchange where customers could maintain a portfolio of digital currencies and engage in related cryptocurrency functions, including "deposits, withdrawals, transfers" and "trading activities." Daly stated that Defendants advertised BolsaDX "as a solution to the closing of Binance Exchange to all Americans." Daly alleged that Binance Exchange had "announced in November 2021 that it was banning all American accounts and leaving the United States."

Daly opened a BolsaDX account in 2019, but by December 2023, his cryptocurrency assets disappeared from his account. Daly filed suit against the defendants contending that they breached their duty and committed fraud. The court dismissed Daly's case ruling that there was no personal jurisdiction against the Alabama defendants.

The court found acknowledged that BolsaDX's website was interactive, but ruled that the defendants did not specifically target New York residents or purposefully avail themselves of New York law.

The court rejected Daly's argument that general accessibility to Americans via the Internet established jurisdiction in New York. The court also found Daly failed to show his injury occurred in New York or that Defendants should have expected consequences in New York. The court concluded that the defendant's solicitation through its website did not establish targeting of New York residents:

> Here, Plaintiff does not allege that BolsaDX, or any of the other Defendants, specifically targeted its advertising at or solicited use of its commercial services in New York through its website such that it "purposefully avail[ed] [it]self of the privilege of conducting activities within New York, thus invoking the benefits and protections of its laws." Even though Plaintiff alleges that he opened a BolsaDX account while present in New York, mere access does not amount to a transaction directed at New York for the purposes of the long-arm statute. . . .Thus, Plaintiff's allegation that he used BolsaDX's website in New York, without more, does not constitute a prima facie showing that BolsaDX or any other Defendant transacted business in New York.

Daly v. Francis, 2026 U.S. Dist. LEXIS 15327, *14–17 (N.D. N.Y. Jan. 28, 2026).

Similarly, in *ShopStyle, Inc. v. rewardStyle, Inc.*, 2020 WL 4187937 (Tex. App. July 21, 2020), the court concluded that the mere fact that a defendant had a website accessible everywhere, including in Texas, did not provide a sufficient notice for personal jurisdiction. The court noted:

> Texas courts have distanced themselves from a *Zippo*-style sliding scale analysis, with one court emphasizing that 'there needs to be more than the existence of a website (whether interactive

> or not) to support an inference that the forum was targeted by the website owner or that the latter directed its marketing efforts at the forum.'

The court found no purposeful availment reasoning:

> 'PopSugar uses its website to attract Texas residents by maintaining a Texas-specific web page with Texas-specific articles.' There is, however, no evidence of which we are aware regarding PopSugar's usage of the Texas web page—the existence of which the trial court judicially noticed—to attract Texas residents. PopSugar responds that its Texas web page is automatically generated based on the 'tag' a user selects in a search, and that users can generate any URLs (uniform resource locators) they like. PopSugar does not cite record evidence to support its assertion the Texas URLs are user generated. But in any event, the mere existence of a website at the Texas web address does not alone show PopSugar availed itself of the benefits and protections of Texas law.

In *Tufano v. Google LLC*, 2025 U.S. Dist. LEXIS 216885 (M.D. Pa. Nov. 4, 2025), the court characterized the plaintiff Frank Tufano, as a prodigious, but prodigiously unsuccessful, pro se litigant. Tufano filed suit against Google, an Internet search engine provider, Dr. Mehryar Ray Taban, and the doctor's medical practice, MTMD, seeking more than $484,000,000 in damages.

Tufano argued that he used Google to identify Dr. Taban as a health care provider. Tufano avers that the doctor "botched" a medical procedure in 2023, resulting in injuries to Tufano, and then asserts that the doctor and Google conspired to defeat his efforts to post negative reviews of the doctor online. Tufano's complaint then recites numerous claims against both Google and the doctor in support of his demand for more than $484,000,000 in damages.

The court dismissed this pro se case, concluding that Taban and MTMD's website was passive because it only provides information about their California-based medical practice, with no ability to purchase services directly, is insufficient to establish personal jurisdiction in Pennsylvania where they have no other contacts. The court found no personal jurisdiction as the California doctor had no minimum contacts in Pennsylvania.

The court concluded that Dr. Taban, a California doctor who never practiced in Pennsylvania, owns no property there, pays no taxes there, and has not advertised specifically to Pennsylvania residents cannot be subject to personal jurisdiction in Pennsylvania merely because a Pennsylvania resident found him through Google.

In *Freeman v. 3Commas Technologies, Ou*, the Ninth Circuit reversed a federal district court dismissal of a class action against an Estonian cryptocurrency software company finding no personal jurisdiction. The Ninth Circuit reversed finding that 3Commas, the defendant was subject to California personal jurisdiction.

The court applied the three-part jurisdiction test requiring that the (1) the defendant either purposefully directs its activities [at the forum] or purposefully avails itself of the benefits afforded by the forum's laws; (2) the claim arises out of or relates to the defendant's forum-related activities; and (3) the exercise of jurisdiction comports with fair play and substantial justice, i.e., it is reasonable. The court concluded that:

> 3Commas has exploited the California market by soliciting California investors, contracting with California businesses, and selling services to California residents. As a software provider for cryptocurrency trading, 3Commas contracts with Cloudflare, a California-based data server, to "optimize and maintain the availability of its website," and its contract with Cloudflare contains choice of law and forum selection clauses for California.

The court also found that 3Commas's website had a Privacy Policy page which included a section on California Privacy Rights. That 3Commas did not disclose or even mention any other jurisdiction's legal requirements indicates that 3Commas intentionally directed its activities toward California consumers.

Other evidence in the record indicates that 3Commas was aware that at least some of its users were California residents. 3Commas's Chief Legal Officer testified that "3Commas sees user IP addresses, which may allow for inferences regarding the user's general location." For users like Plaintiffs who purchased its service plans, 3Commas charges value added tax based on their location, which "is automatically determined by IP address of [the user's] device and/or manually provided by [the user] to 3commas when entering billing address." Finally, the court found that exercising jurisdiction over 3Commas satisfied fair play and substantial justice.

(C) GRAY ZONE

The *Zippo.com* court recognized a middle ground between the passive and interactive ends of the sliding scale "which permit the exchange of information between the website and the user." The court reasoned that in gray zone cases, jurisdiction is "determined by examining the level of interactivity and commercial nature of the exchange of information that occurs on the Web site." *Zippo Mfg. Co. v. Zippo Dot Com, Inc.*, 952 F. Supp. 1119, 1124 (W.D. Pa. 1997).

In *Parker v. Freiberger*, 2026 Cal. App. Unpub. LEXIS 168 (Calif. Ct. App. 2d App. Div. 3, Jan. 12, 2026), the court concluded that Freibergers' use of Zillow, an interactive 'middle ground' website, to list their Georgia property, without specifically targeting California residents or seeking benefits from California, was insufficient to establish personal jurisdiction in California.

The Freibergers were Georgia residents who own rental property in Georgia, and listed their property on Zillow.com. Parker, a California resident, applied to rent the property. The parties negotiated and signed a lease. Parker sent a security deposit but disputed when first month's rent was due.

Parker searched on Zillow for rental properties in Georgia "to eliminate the monthly travel of her military husband to Georgia for reserve duty." She applied to rent a property in Athens, Georgia owned by the Freibergers.

The parties negotiated a one-year lease and Parker sent a deposit. Parker alleged that the Freibergers had agreed to mail her the keys as soon as she paid the deposit, but they did not incorporate that agreement into the lease, and the Freibergers refused to send the keys until Parker sent the first month's rent. Parker sued the Freibergers for fraud, breach of the covenant of good faith and fair dealing, unfair business practices, and disgorgement.

The Freibergers did not specifically target California residents in their Zillow listing. The Freibergers who listed a rental property on Zillow and enter into a single lease agreement with a California resident, without specifically targeting California or conducting activities in California, have not purposefully availed themselves of California's benefits and protections and are not subject to personal jurisdiction in California.

The Freibergers timely removed this action and simultaneously moved to dismiss for lack of personal jurisdiction, improper venue, failure to effectuate proper service, and failure to state a claim. The court concluded that the website was classified as middle ground, because it allowed the Freibergers to "exchange information" with Parker and other potential tenants.

The court found no personal jurisdiction reasoning:

> Notably, Plaintiffs do not assert that this Court should find Defendants have minimum contacts with New Jersey based on Defendants' website. Rather, Plaintiffs allege that advertisements on Facebook and Groupon's websites give rise to jurisdiction over Defendants. The Court thus finds that this case falls into the third category where Defendant placed information about its hotels on the Internet as an advertisement, not as a means of conducting business.

In *Cambria Co. v. Pental Granite & Marble Co.*, 2013 WL 1249216 (D. Minn. March 27, 2013), a Washington company's website enabled the visitors of a Minnesota website to pay bills online, even though it had no agents, operations, or facilities in Minnesota. In addition, visitors could "like" the website on Facebook and follow it on Twitter.

The *Cambria* court found the website to be in the borderland between passive and active websites. A key factor in favor of jurisdiction was that the website advertised infringing products targeting Minnesota residents.

Courts adopting the *Zippo.com* test determine the exercise of jurisdiction by examining the level of interactivity and the commercial nature of the exchange of information which occurs on a given website. A growing number of courts, such as the *Cambria* court, recognize that the *Zippo.com* court's interactivity test is just one factor to be considered to determining Internet jurisdiction and "something more" is required.

§ 3-3. The Effects Test for Torts

Establishing jurisdiction when a tort takes place over the Internet depends on whether the defendant directed the harm to someone within the forum state. In *Calder v. Jones*, 465 U.S. 783 (1984), television star Shirley Jones (the Partridge Family matriarch) filed suit in California against the author and editor of a story published by National Enquirer that stated she was an alcoholic. Jones sued the National Enquirer and Calder who was the author of the article about Shirley Jones in California.

The magazine article was drawn from California sources, and the brunt of the harm, in terms of both the respondent's emotional distress and the injury to her professional reputation, was suffered in California. The court found California to be the focal point of the story and the harm suffered by Shirley Jones and found a sufficient basis for personal jurisdiction.

The *Calder* effects test asks whether the defendant: (1) committed an intentional act, (2) expressly aimed at the forum state, (3) causing harm that the defendant knows is likely to be suffered in the forum state. This test determines whether a tortfeasor purposefully directed his activity to the forum.

Vangheluwe v. Got News, 365 F. Supp. 3d 850 (2019) was the first case dealing with tort actions and social media, specifically Twitter. The court found Coulhart-Villanueva, a California defendant, was subject to jurisdiction in Michigan because she had doxed the plaintiffs, tweeting information about their physical home in Michigan.

Doxing is the malicious practice of publishing personal information about a particular individual on the Internet. The doxing here was misidentifying the driver of the vehicle that plowed into a crowd in Charlottesville, Virginia killing Heather Heyer, who was protesting against a white supremacist gathering.

The court concluded that Coulhart-Villanueva's malicious tweet was calculated to have an effect in Michigan unlike the retweeting of other defendants. The court did not hold "that all doxing amounts to constitutionally minimum contacts with the forum state." The court found that another defendant's tweet about the same incident did not satisfy minimum contacts.

> The mere existence of a website that is visible in a forum . . . is not enough, by itself, to subject a defendant to personal jurisdiction in that forum. . . . Given the 'omnipresence' of internet websites, such a rule would 'eviscerate' the limits on personal jurisdiction over out-of-state defendants.

Brown v. Dash, 2020 WL 6806433 at *11 (D. Mass. Nov. 18, 2020).

§ 3-4. "Something More" Test

The "express aiming" inquiry in Internet cases requires "something more" than "a foreign act with foreseeable effects in the forum state." For instance, the delivery or consumption of Internet services in the forum state that are "random," "fortuitous," or "attenuated" does not satisfy the express aiming analysis.

On the other hand, "where a defendant knows—as opposed to being able to foresee—that an intentional act will impact another state," then "the 'expressly aimed' requirement is satisfied." *Reflex Media, Inc. v. Chan*, 2020 WL 6694316 (C.D. Cal. Oct. 30, 2020).

"Internet advertisement alone" does not suffice; "rather, 'something more' is needed 'to indicate that the defendant purposefully . . . directed his activity in a substantial way to the forum state.' " *Hb Prods. v. Faizan*, 2020 WL 6784347 (D. Haw. Nov. 18, 2020).

§ 3-5. *In Rem* Jurisdiction

The application of *in rem* jurisdiction applies to real or personal property rather than jurisdiction over a natural person. Under U.S. law, *in rem* jurisdiction affects the right of all persons to property. The problem with the global Internet is that *in rem* jurisdiction may not be recognized or may have a different meaning; in the United Kingdom, where *in rem* jurisdiction applies only to admiralty cases.

However, applying *in rem* or *quasi in rem* jurisdiction to the Internet poses many problems.

First, *in rem* jurisdiction may not be recognized in all jurisdictions. Additionally, neither *in rem*, nor *quasi in rem* jurisdiction will extend to intangible Internet assets.

In *Briskin v. Shopify*, the Ninth Circuit crafted a more specific test for evaluating when Shopify ran an interactive website or platform with regular sales and exercises control over product distribution in the forum. Shopify is a Canadian company, while Briskin is a California resident.

The Ninth Circuit held that an interactive platform, as Shopify own here, "expressly aims its wrongful conduct toward" the forum "when its contacts are its own choice and not random, isolated, or fortuitous."

The *Shopify* court stated that " 'something more' than mere passive" access "was required to show express aiming at the forum . . ."

Commentators "are concerned that this decision could broadly expand the scope of personal jurisdiction and increase litigation risks for online platforms." *Proskauer on Privacy* (May 6, 2025).

In *Warehouse Goods, LLC v. GNLLN.COM*, 2019 WL 1375582 (E.D. Va. 2019), the federal court affirmed a federal magistrate's finding that the plaintiff was entitled to an *in rem* action to regain his domain name. The court entered a default judgment against defendant <GNLLN.COM> ("Defendant Domain Name") for violations of the Anti-Cybersquatting Consumer Protection Act, 15 U.S.C. § 1125(d).

In addition, the court granted permanent injunctive relief "stating that the registration, ownership, and control of Defendant Domain Name be maintained with Plaintiff." The court found the "Defendant Domain Name <gnlln.com> had a bad faith intent to profit from using the Defendant Domain Name, which is confusing similar to the distinctive mark owned by Plaintiff" in adopting the magistrate's report.

§ 3-6. Cross-Border Jurisdiction

To date, countries connected to the Internet have ceded their sovereignty in order to harmonize cyber-jurisdictional rules. Instead, courts adapt their own national rules to determine jurisdiction. *Google LLC v. Equustek Solutions Inc.*, 2017 WL 5000834 (N.D. Cal., Nov. 2, 2017) illustrates the conflicting jurisdictional rules in the U.S. and Canada.

"In 2011, Equustek filed suit in Canada against a group of individual and corporate defendants associated with Datalink, a rival computer hardware distributor and seller." "Equustek alleged that Datalink had colluded with a former Equustek engineer to incorporate Equustek's trade secrets into Datalink's products, and Datalink misled customers who believed they were buying Equustek's products." *Id.*

In 2012, Equustek obtained several Canadian court orders against Datalink. Datalink refused to comply and fled the country. The Canadian court issued an arrest warrant for the primary individual defendant, but he has not been apprehended.

In September 2012, Equustek requested that Google remove Datalink's websites from its search results, however Google refused. After the Canadian court granted Equustek's request for injunctive relief against Datalink, Google blocked more than 300 Datalink websites from appearing in its Canada-specific search results at www.google.ca.

However, Google did not remove Datalink websites from search results targeted to users outside of Canada. Equustek then sought a Canadian court order requiring Google to remove Datalink websites from its global search results. A Canadian trial court issued an order requiring Google to delist Datalink search results worldwide. This decision was affirmed by the Court of Appeals for British Columbia and the Canadian Supreme Court.

Canadian courts asserted jurisdiction over online activities by the mid-1990s:

> In part due to the *Equustek* doctrine, Canadian courts now more aggressively assert jurisdiction over online activities. Indeed, Canada could emerge as ground zero for internet litigation, with its courts and tribunals at ease with a principle that extends domestic law to an international arena.

Michael Geist, *The Equustek Effect: How One Case Has Sparked Canada's Aggressive Approach Over Internet Jurisdiction,* MICHAEL GEIST BLOG (Mar. 7, 2019).

The court entered an injunction against the enforcement of the Canadian court order stating:

The Canadian order would eliminate Section 230 immunity for service providers that link to third-party websites. By forcing intermediaries to remove links to third-party material, the Canadian order undermines the policy goals of Section 230 and threatens free speech on the global internet. Brussels Regulation Recast (2012)

The European Union (EU) updated its cross-border jurisdiction rules when The Brussels Regulation Recast (2012) replaced Regulation 44/2001 (the Brussels I Regulation) on January 10, 2015. The revised Brussels Regulation provides uniform rules for jurisdiction and enforcement of judgments throughout the European Union. The EU Commission states:

> The Regulation determines the courts of which Member State have jurisdiction to decide on a civil and commercial dispute where there is an international element.
>
> The Regulation further provides that a judgment given in a Member State shall be recognised in the other Member States without any special procedure being required. A judgment given in a Member State and enforceable in that State shall be enforced in another Member State without any declaration of enforceability being required.
>
> The Regulation provides for two forms, namely, the certificate concerning a judgment and the

certificate concerning an authentic court judgment or settlement.

Europa.eu, *National Information and Online Forms Concerning Regulation No. 1215/2012* (2019).

(A) SCOPE OF THE BRUSSELS REGULATION

The Brussels Regulation broadly applies to civil and commercial matters including Internet interactions. Article 1(1) of the Recast Brussels Regulation of 2012 states:

> This Regulation shall apply in civil and commercial matters whatever the nature of the court or tribunal. It shall not extend, in particular, to revenue, customs or administrative matters or to the liability of the State for acts and omissions in the exercise of State authority (*acta iure imperii*).

Article 1(2) notes that the Brussels Regulation (Recast) does not apply to: the status of natural persons, bankruptcy or insolvency, social security, arbitration, wills, trusts and family matters.

(B) JURISDICTION BASED ON DOMICILE

The basic principle is that jurisdiction is to be exercised based on domicile rather than nationality. Article 4 of the Brussels Regulation states:

> 1. Subject to this Regulation, persons domiciled in a Member State shall, whatever

their nationality, be sued in the courts of that Member State.

2. Persons who are not nationals of the Member State in which they are domiciled shall be governed by the rules of jurisdiction applicable to nationals of that Member State.

In the case of legal persons or corporations, domicile is determined by the country in which they have their statutory seat, central administration, or principal place of business.

(C) SPECIAL JURISDICTIONAL RULES

The Brussels Regulation devises special rules for determining jurisdiction where the offeror and offeree are located in different EU signatory countries. Article 7 provides the following cross-border jurisdictional rule for contracts:

> A person domiciled in a Member State may be sued in another Member State:
>
> (1)(a) in matters relating to a contract, in the courts for the place of performance of the obligation in question;
>
> (b) for the purpose of this provision and unless otherwise agreed, the place of performance of the obligation in question shall be:
>
> —in the case of the sale of goods, the place in a Member State where, under the contract, the goods were delivered or should have been delivered.

—in the case of the provision of services, the place in a Member State where, under the contract, the services were provided or should have been provided.

(c) if point (b) does not apply then point (a) applies.

The Brussels Regulation provides that a person domiciled in a Member State may be sued in another Member State for contract disputes "for the place of performance of the obligation" at issue unless the parties otherwise agree.

In tort actions, jurisdiction is the Member State where the place of the harm took place. Article 7(3) state other special rules for jurisdiction in civil claims for restitution:

(3) as regards a civil claim for damages or restitution which is based on an act giving rise to criminal proceedings, in the court seised of those proceedings, to the extent that that court has jurisdiction under its own law to entertain civil proceedings.

(D) MANDATORY CONSUMER RULES

The Brussels Regulation's mandatory consumer rules are at odds with U.S. law, where court enforce one-sided choice of law and forum clauses. However, U.S. companies are subject to the Regulation's mandatory rules if they target EU residents.

Under Articles 17–19 of the Recast Brussels Regulation, consumers in the EU Member States are entitled to have their disputes with providers settled in their home court or the country where they reside and this applies where the U.S. is a seller or provider.

Article 17 defines a consumer as being someone who is acting outside her trade or profession. Article 18 is a mandatory rule as to where a consumer may file actions:

> 1. A consumer may bring proceedings against the other party to a contract either in the courts of the Member State in which that party is domiciled or in the courts for the place where the consumer is domiciled.
>
> 2. Proceedings may be brought against a consumer by the other party to the contract only in the courts of the Member State in which the consumer is domiciled.
>
> 3. This Article shall not affect the right to bring a counter-claim in the court in which, in accordance with this Section, the original claim is pending.

Additionally, Article 19 of the Brussels Regulation prevents the parties of a consumer contract from agreeing to waive their right to jurisdiction in their home court. U.S.-based websites will therefore be unable to impose the stronger parties' choice of forum or choice of law clauses in any contract with EU consumers.

The parties may agree, however, to allow a consumer to have the option of bringing the case in another jurisdiction. Companies cannot compel

European consumers to waive the benefit of the Brussels Regulation's mandatory home court rule.

While the Brussels Regulation does not explicitly address electronic commerce related contracts, European courts should have little difficulty extending mandatory consumer rules for jurisdiction and the enforcement of judgments to cyberspace. U.S. companies need to do a complete audit of any mass-market contracts directed to the EU consumer marketplace or risk serious regulatory actions by EU authorities.

(E) ENFORCEMENT OF JUDGMENTS

The general rule of the Brussels Regulation on the enforcement of judgments is the default rule that judgments rendered in any one of the twenty-seven European Union Member States are enforceable in all of the other Member States. This means that a judgment rendered in one state is enforceable throughout the European Union without any special procedural requirements. If a party wants their judgment enforced in another EU Member State, they make an application in the courts of the Member State.

Plaintiffs seeking to enforce judgments apply to national courts or competent authorities as noted by Article 39 of the Regulation. "An appeal against the decision on the application for a declaration of enforceability is to be lodged with the court as notified by the Member State under Art 43(2) and 44 of the Regulation."

Judgments in Civil and Commercial Matters: Brussels I Regulation, EUROPEAN JUSTICE (2021).

Thus, "a judgment given in a Member State shall be recognized in the other Member States without any special procedure being required." Article 37 provides that a party who wishes to invoke a judgment needs only to produce a copy and certificate of the judgment. Brussels Regulation enables consumers in one country to enforce judgments and obtain jurisdiction over providers located in other EU countries. The Internet, to date, has no reciprocal jurisdiction and enforcement of judgment regime.

(F) EXTRATERRITORIAL IMPACT

The Brussels Regulation subjects the United States and other non-EU countries to its provisions if they direct or target commercial activities (i.e., offer goods or services) to EU consumers. If a consumer enters into a contract with a company:

> not domiciled in a Member State but has a branch, agency or other establishment in one of the Member States, that party shall, in disputes arising out of the operations of the branch, agency or establishment, be deemed to be domiciled in that Member State.

Regulation (EU) No 1215/2012 of the European Parliament and of the Council of 12 December 2012 on jurisdiction and the recognition and enforcement of judgments in civil and commercial matters (recast) at art. 17(2).

In *Air Canada v. United Kingdom*, (1995) 20 EHRR 150, the European Court of Human Rights held the seizure of an aircraft carrying illegal drugs belonging to the Canadian applicant had not infringed Article 1 of the First Protocol of the European Convention on Human Rights. The court did not find it persuasive that the applicant was a Canadian resident, and applied the European law of human rights.

As U.S.-based software publishers and platforms go global, one-sided terms of use will increasingly be under scrutiny within EU countries, and other nations with traditions of greater consumer protection. European courts will extend EU mandatory consumer rules to U.S. companies with subsidiaries in Europe. The Brussels Regulation is an important first step to a cross-border regime for Internet consumers giving them the right to file suit in their home country's forum rather than to submit to jurisdiction in a distant forum.

The United Kingdom (UK), which is not a member of the European Union, no longer follows the Brussels regulation:

> On jurisdiction, from 1 January 2021 the UK is no longer bound by the Brussels Recast Regulation and the Lugano Convention. This means that, save in legacy cases, English jurisdiction clauses and English judgments will no longer benefit from near automatic recognition under these longstanding regimes in EU Member States, Switzerland, Iceland and Norway.

Allen & Overy, *Brexit and Dispute Resolution Clauses: the Options for Finance Parties*, JD SUPRA (BLOG) (Mar. 1, 2021).

In addition to the Brussels Regulation, the EU has enacted the Rome I Regulation. Regulation (EC) No 593/2008 of the European Parliament and of the Council of 17 June 2008 on the law applicable to contractual obligations (Rome I). The Rome I Regulation adopts the fundamental principles that the parties generally have the freedom to choose the applicable law subject only to mandatory consumer rules.

The Rome I Regulation provides mandatory business-to-consumer rules for determining choice of law principles. Choice of law principles are employed by courts to determine which law applies when parties do not use a choice of law clause.

The parties to a contract may choose the law in business-to-business transactions. Rome I establishes default rules (unless the parties otherwise provide) for services, the sale of goods and franchise agreements. The general default rule where there is no parties' choice of law clause, courts will apply the law with the closest connection to the transaction.

This general rule of freedom of choice is subject to exceptions for consumer transactions. While parties generally have autonomy to select their own law, one notable exception is consumer transactions where mandatory rules apply.

EU consumers have the non-waivable right to consumer protection in the country where they reside. Council Regulation 593/2008, of the European Parliament and of the Council of 17 June 2008 on the Law Applicable to Contractual Obligations, 2008 O.J. (L 177/6) (EC). Article 6 defines a "consumer" as "being outside his trade or profession . . . with another person acting in the exercise of his trade or profession[.]"

The Rome I Regulation adopted the consumer's home court rule, meaning the governing law for consumers is where the consumer has their "habitual residence." Similar to the Brussels Regulation, the parties to a business-to-business transaction are free to choose what law applies with a parties' choice of law clause. The EU will enforce contracts specifying UK law, despite the UK's departure from Brexit:

> Prior to Brexit, Rome I Regulation provides that all EU member states give effect to the parties' choice of law. This includes the law of an EU member or non-EU member (e.g., New York law). Whilst the UK is now no longer a member of the EU and therefore not a member to Rome I Regulation, the . . . The EU courts will continue to apply Rome I and Rome II, and therefore give effect to the choice of any law (including English law as a law of a non-EU member state). Therefore, the choice of law and recognition of choice of law is largely unaffected by Brexit.

Brexit Update—Changes To Loan Documentation, MONDAQ (Mar. 1, 2021).

§ 3-7. Global Jurisdiction

An Internet presence automatically creates an international presence thereby triggering the potential for cross-border litigation. Clearly, Internet law requires harmonized jurisdictional rules, as evidenced by the lack of sovereign or any international treaty establishing rules for cyberspace.

It is theoretically possible for a U.S. business to be sued in hundreds of foreign countries for the same online conduct. However, this has not yet happened due to the jurisdictional barriers in filing cross-border lawsuits such as the Brussels Regulation for EU Member States.

To date, no international convention addresses how to resolve Internet jurisdiction, choice of law, or forum disputes. A growing number of U.S. courts are exercising jurisdiction over website activity occurring outside of the country's territorial boundaries. Conversely, U.S. companies are increasingly being sued in foreign venues for activities occurring on domestic Web servers. Presently, no case law covers international Internet jurisdiction. No statutory solutions exist to answer the question of cross-border enforcement of Internet judgments.

As companies use the border-defying Internet, they will increasingly become subject to foreign procedural and substantive law. Foreign websites, if they target U.S. users may be subject to personal jurisdiction in state and federal courts.

The next chapter examines how parties structure contracts in an online legal environment. In our information-based economy, the licensing of software and other digital information is rapidly displacing sales and leases.

CHAPTER 4

INTERNET-RELATED CONTRACT LAW

This chapter is divided into five sections. Section 4-1 begins with a discussion of licensing which is the principal form of contract formation on the Internet. Section 4-2 focuses on the concepts and methods of mass-market licensing, the chief means of transferring value in an information-based society. The discussion includes the evolution of wrap contracts from shrinkwraps in the 1980s to clickwraps, browsewraps, installwraps, and scrollwraps that evolved later.

The leading wrap contracts (shrinkwrap, browsewrap, clickwrap, installwrap and hybrid wraps) will be presented. Smart contracts that run on blockchain networks will be discussed next. Finally, U.S. consumer agreements where the stronger party dictates many terms will be contrasted to EU consumer contracts, where EU law enacts mandatory and non-waivable terms to protect the weaker party.

This section next assesses the enforceability of wrap contracts, rolling contracts, and mass-market agreements. Section 4-3 of this chapter presents cloud computing commonly known as software-as-a-service (SaaS). Finally, cloud computing or software-as-a-service is fundamentally an access agreement. Cloud computing, Cloud customers have access to applications in the "cloud" for the term of the agreement.

As cloud computing becomes more cost efficient, both startup companies and large corporations are investing in companies like Amazon Web Services for their capability to deliver extensive content.

Section 4-4 covers digital signatures and records at the state and federal level. Finally, Section 4-5 examines cross-border contracts.

Section 4-5 discusses cross-border contracts by considering the European Commission's mandatory consumer protection rules such as the Unfair Contract Terms Directive, which would invalidate many U.S. style mass-market terms widely used in one-sided Internet contracts.

§ 4-1. Types of Digital Contracts

With the sale of goods, title passes from seller to buyer and buyer takes possession of tangible goods or movable property, such as computer hardware (i.e., Dell sells laptop to customer) as well as title to the goods.

In a true Article 2A lease, the computer lessor gives possession and right to use a computer system to the lessee for a fixed term in return for renting the property. The title to the property and a meaningful residual interest remain with the lessor (i.e., Dell leases laptops to customers). A sale disguised as a lease is a financing transaction, not a true lease. If the transaction is a sale the express and implied warranties of Article 2 of the Uniform Commercial Code apply, not Article 2A. Article 9 of the UCC applies to "false leases." If a lease is for the entire life of the goods leased, UCC Article 9 applies not UCC Article 2. A true lease always has meaningful economic life in the goods when they are returned from the lessee to the lessor at the end of the term of the lease. This is referred to in case law as a "meaningful reversion. UCC § 1–203 states:

> [A] transaction in the form of a lease creates a security interest if the consideration . . . is an obligation for the term of the lease not subject to termination by the lessee, and . . . [the lease is for the remaining economic life of the goods.

UCC § 9–109(a)(1) states that secured transaction applies to disguised sales:

> [T]his article applies to a transaction, regardless of its form, that creates a security interest in personal property.

Suppose the Secured Party leases an auto to the Debtor for five years and gives the Debtor the right to purchase the auto for $1 at the end of the lease. This is a false lease subject to UCC Article 2 for the sale of goods and UCC Article 9 governing secured transactions not UCC Article 2A governing leases. When a licensee enters into a software license software with the licensor, they are, in reality, receiving only the right to use the software subject to terms and conditions. They are not purchasing the software, only the right to use it for the term of license agreement.

The term license includes an access contract, a lease of a computer program, and a consignment of a copy. The term does not include a reservation or creation of a security interest to the extent the interest is governed by Article 9 of the Uniform Commercial Code. UCITA § 102(41).

Calling an agreement a license agreement does not make it a license. "A licensing agreement is a type of contract in which an IP owner, also known as the licensor, grants another party permission to use their intellectual property under specific terms." *Contracting Basics: What Is a Licensing Agreement?*, ICERTIS, https://www.icertis.com/contracting-basics/licensing-agreement/.

To qualify as a license, a software publisher must place meaningful restrictions or conditions of use on its product or it will be deemed a "sale" subject to the first sale doctrine of copyright law.

To determine whether there is a legitimate license, we examine whether "the copyright owner (1) specifies that the user is granted a license; (2) significantly restricts the user's ability to transfer the software; and (3) imposes notable use restrictions." *Adobe v. Christenson,* 809 F.3d 1071, 1078 (9th Cir. 2011).

Software publishers like Adobe make copies of their product available to customers through Software license agreements. Users must accept the terms and conditions of the applicable licensing agreement before they can install the program on their computers.

Proprietary software licenses such as licensors such as Microsoft Word or Adobe typically restrict the licensee's right to copy, redistribute, or modify the software and normally do not grant access to the software's source code.

In contrast, open source licensors give the licensee access to the source code. The user has access, makes improvements; cannot restrict access to users downstream.

To determine whether an electronic contract is enforceable, courts focus on whether the plaintiffs had reasonable notice, and manifested assent to the terms of use or license. The key elements of Internet contract formation are notice and manifestation of assent and these "elements are generally required across the country." *Lewis v. Nat'l Bd. Of Osteopathic Medical Examiners*, 2020 WL 7260747 (E.D. Pa. Dec. 10, 2020).

"Four general types of online consumer contracts exist: (a) browsewrap; (b) clickwrap; (c) scrollwrap; and (d) sign-in-wrap." *Berkson v. Gogo LLC*, 97 F. Supp. 3d 359 (E.D.N.Y. 2015). The following four-part inquiry in analyzing sign-in-wraps, and electronic contracts of adhesion generally, is required:

> (1) Aside from clicking the equivalent of sign-in (e.g., log-in, buy-now, purchase, etc.), is there substantial evidence from the website that the user was aware that she was binding herself to more than an offer of services or goods in exchange for money? If not, the 'terms of use,' such as those dealing with venue and arbitration, should not be enforced against the purchaser.

(2) Did the design and content of the website, including the homepage, make the 'terms of use' (i.e., the contract details) readily and obviously available to the user? If not, the 'terms of use,' such as those dealing with venue and arbitration, should not be enforced against the purchaser.

(3) Was the importance of the details of the contract obscured or minimized by the physical manifestation of assent expected of a consumer seeking to purchase or subscribe to a service or product? If yes, then the 'terms of use,' such as those dealing with venue and arbitration, should not be enforced against the purchaser.

(4) Did the merchant clearly draw the consumer's attention to material terms that would alter what a reasonable consumer would understand to be her default rights when initiating an online consumer transaction from the consumer's state of residence: The right to (a) not have a payment source charged without notice (i.e., automatic payment renewal); (b) bring a civil consumer protection action under the law of her state of residence and in the courts in her state of residence; and (c) participate in a class or collective action? If not, then (a), (b), or (c) should not be enforced against the consumer.

In *Bell v. Royal Seas Cruises, Inc.*, 2020 WL 5639947 (S.D. Fla. Sep. 21, 2020), the plaintiff contended that she did not have actual knowledge of the Terms and Conditions of a website. The court found the website's design was such that the hyperlink to the terms and conditions was sufficiently conspicuous to put a reasonably prudent user on inquiry notice of the terms of the contract.

The court concluded that a reasonable user would see the statement understanding they were agreeing to the terms and conditions stating:

> Because it is nearly impossible that any user would not see that statement before hitting 'Continue,' this design is a far cry far from those wherein 'the hyperlink to the terms and conditions is buried at the bottom of the page, and the website never directs the user to review them[,]' which have been repeatedly deemed to provide insufficient notice.

Terms of service (also known as terms of use and terms and conditions, commonly abbreviated as ToS or TOS and TOU) are rules which one must agree to abide by in order to use a service. Terms of service can also be merely a disclaimer, especially regarding the use of websites.

The *Bell* court stated that the hyperlink to the terms and conditions was conspicuous enough to put a reasonably prudent person on inquiry notice of the Terms and Conditions, and clicking "Continue" directly below the relevant statement is sufficient to constitute assent to the Terms and Conditions. The court found no genuine dispute of material fact as to whether the person who clicked "Continue" on the Website assented to the Terms and Conditions, which included mandatory arbitration.

(A) DEFINITION OF LICENSING

Licensing is the chief contractual form used on the Internet, of which sales and leases hold the most significance. The licensor is the party that agrees to transfer software or to grant access to other computer information. The licensee's duty is to pay the licensing fee to the licensor in order to gain access to and/or for use of information under the terms and conditions specified in the agreement. Providers devised licensing to bypass the first sale doctrine of copyright law:

> Thus, if a software developer retains ownership of every copy of software, and merely licenses the use of those copies, the first sale doctrine (and Section 117) does not apply. A common sense example illustrates this logic—if you borrow a book from the library, you cannot sell it to someone else because it still belongs to the library. . . . The first sale doctrine rarely applies in the software world because software is rarely 'sold.' By licensing copies of their computer programs, instead of selling them, software developers avoid the effects of the first sale doctrine.

Christian H. Nadan, *Software Licensing in the 21st Century: Are Software "Licenses" Really Sales, and How Will the Software Industry Respond*, AIPLA Q. J. 555 (2004).

Software licensing protects the publisher's intellectual property rights, while simultaneously trying to avoid violating the rights of others. A software license is a contract as well as a transfer of intellectual property rights. Licensing is a contractual device to maximize the value of their intangible devices, while minimizing their liabilities.

By licensing copies of computer programs instead of selling computer programs, software publishers and developers have the ability to commodify their software, reallocate the risk of loss, and control multiple users of its software simultaneously. Essentially, a license is a contract that gives the licensee a right to use software for a specific term whereby the licensor agrees not to sue them for copyright (or patent infringement).

A license is an agreement granting the licensee the right to use computer software, data, or other information protected by copyright and patent law. The granting clause determines who and how licensed software may be used. A granting clause may specify whether the software may only be used or reproduced, sold, or sublicensed.

> Generally, most mass-market licenses give only access to the object code, not the source code. Object code licenses will have an anti-reverse engineering clause. Licensees must comply with the terms of the software license agreement as access is conditioned on their compliance. For example, a licensor filed a federal district court complaint alleging that its licensee accessed without authorization, its copyrighted software program at least 278 times over a five-year span.

Ansys Inc. v. Actox Corporation, No. 20–1694 (W.D. Pa. 2020) reported in 19–11 MEALEY'S LITIG. REP. COPYRIGHT 14 (2020).

In *Ansys Inc. v. Actox Corporation*, Ansys argued that its security software documented that:

> Actox Corp. used three different computers to access the ANSYS software, exceeding the terms of its software license agreement (SLA). Despite receiving warnings from ANSYS, 'defendants continue to infringe upon Plaintiff's Copyrights by using unlicensed' versions of the software.

This case filed against Actox and its CEO settled.

Licensing is rapidly replacing sales and leases as the chief contracting form in the information-age economy. For example, Uber, the popular ride-sharing app, uses Internet-based licenses to provide their services to customers. *Pintar v. State*, 432 P.3d 707 (Mont. Sup. Ct. 2018).

> The license grant provision or granting clause is the subject matter action of a software license agreement. The grant clause sets forth what rights are being conveyed. The [license] grant can be exclusive (i.e., only the licensee has the right to exploit the [license] rights) or non-exclusive (i.e., the licensor can grant similar rights to other parties). The grant can be limited by geography (such as U.S., worldwide), and field of use (such as for cellphones but not laptops).

The ABCs of Licensing Intellectual Property, NUTTER (Apr. 1, 2010).

(B) END USER LICENSE AGREEMENTS

Software publishers protect the intellectual property of their content by End-User License Agreements (EULAs). Typically, content downloaded from the Internet is subject to a license agreement, referred to as a EULA. EULAs are licenses between content providers and software licensors that govern the ultimate user's right to use software, data, or content. The EULA begins with the following disclaimer:

> NOTICE: BEFORE PROCEEDING, PLEASE READ THE FOLLOWING LEGAL AGREEMENT, WHICH CONTAINS RIGHTS AND RESTRICTIONS, ASSOCIATED WITH YOUR USE OF THE MCKESSON SOFTWARE AND ANY DOCUMENTATION PROVIDED TO YOU BY MCKESSON INFORMATION SOLUTIONS, LLC OR ITS AFFILIATES.

The EULA goes on to state:

> AS FURTHER DESCRIBED BELOW, USE OF THE SOFTWARE ALSO OPERATES AS YOUR CONSENT TO THE TRANSMISSION, FROM TIME TO TIME, OF CERTAIN COMPUTER AND SOFTWARE USAGE INFORMATION TO MCKESSON.
>
> Usage Information sent by the Software may include the following: Customer #/serial number; software name; software version; date

data was collected; total number of appointments in database; total number of visits in database; total number of transactions in database; for each item in doctor list: number of appointments in last n days, number of visits in last n days, number of charges in last n days; for each clearinghouse in the system: number of claims submitted in last n days, number of eligibility queries submitted in last n days.

True Health Chiropractic Inc. v. McKesson Corp., 332 F.R.D. 589 (N.D. Cal. 2019).

A typical EULA will specify: (1) geographic restrictions on use, (2) warranty disclaimers, (3) limitations on liability, (4) choice of law and form, and (5) restrictions on provisions including but not limited to assignment and transfer of the license.

In *MacIoce v. Hisense USA Corp.*, 2025 U.S. Dist. LEXIS 262350 (S.D. N.Y. Dec. 19, 2025), a consumer purchased a TV from Best Buy and agreed to Best Buy's terms containing arbitration provisions covering product advertising claims, the TV manufacturer (Hisense) could compel arbitration despite being a non-signatory because the manufacturer-retailer relationship was sufficiently close and the consumer's claims arose from advertising of products sold by Best Buy.

The court ruled that where a consumer's son set up a television and accepted the manufacturer's EULA containing an arbitration provision, the consumer was bound by the EULA because the son acted as the consumer's agent in setting up the TV. The court described contract formation:

> During the set-up process for a QD5 Hisense TV, a user is presented with "Terms and Conditions." The user is given the option to assent to any or all of (1) all terms and conditions; (2) the end user license agreement ("EULA"); and (3) a data protection policy. The user is presented with a box, alongside each option, and instructed to check or uncheck to signal his assent. . . .A button that reads "view details," situated to the right of each item, gives a user the ability to review a complete copy of the terms and conditions,

The EULA defines the "disputes" falling within arbitration to include a "claim or controversy, whether based on contract, statute, regulation, ordinance, tort—including, but not limited to, fraud, misrepresentation, fraudulent inducement, or negligence[ ] or any other legal or equitable theory."

The court noted that a user need not accept the EULA to use his Hisense TV:

> The EULA gives the user the opportunity to opt out of arbitration within 30 days of accepting the EULA by emailing "product.tv.info@gmail.com" and stating that he does not wish to be subject to the arbitration provision. Hisense does not have any record that Macioce opted out of the EULA arbitration agreement. And Macioce admits that he did not do so. Macioce states he did not personally accept the EULA during the

set up process, because his son set up the TV. Macioce's son does not recall either accepting or not accepting the EULA during the set up.

The court ordered that Macioce, the consumer, submit his claim to arbitration.

In *Avangrid Networks, Inc. v. Sec. Limits, Inc.*, 2026 U.S. Dist. LEXIS 37425 (S.D. N.Y. Feb. 23, 2026), Avangrid filed a lawsuit against Security Limits, Inc. (SLI), and Paulo Silva, alleging breach of contract and extortion. SLI created the 'Avangrid Secure Domain' using proprietary Ironclad technology as a subcontractor on Avangrid's cybersecurity project.

Avangrid, Inc., a sustainable energy company, with subsidiaries including Avangrid Networks, Inc., is owned by Iberdrola, A.S., a Spanish global energy company and non-party. SLI is a full-service technology, engineering, architecture, and consulting solutions firm.

In 2017, Avangrid sought to improve the reliability of its cybersecurity program and began hiring contractors and subcontractors to deliver on the cybersecurity improvement project.

In February 2019, Avangrid entered into a EULA licensing Ironclad:

Avangrid entered into an end-user license agreement ("EULA") with SLI for the licensing of Ironclad, The EULA licenses Ironclad to Avangrid and its subsidiaries "in perpetuity WITHOUT termination" and gives Avangrid unrestricted rights to utilize and modify the design for its own benefit or for the benefit of its operating companies, subsidiaries. The court enforced the EULA dismissing all claims:

> Even if the Court were to find that the parties entered an enforceable oral agreement, it was superseded by the subsequent EULA, which was a fully integrated agreement covering Avangrid's use of Ironclad.

The court concluded that the EULA granted Avangrid a license "in perpetuity," "WITHOUT termination," and with "unrestricted rights to utilize . . . the design . . .for its own benefit." The court ruled that SLI and Silva failed to allege a breach of contract claim.

(C) LICENSING DISPUTES

As of 2026, there is no comprehensive body of contracting law for software licensing. There is now a 60-year lag between the formation of the software industry and the development of specialized rules governing software licensing. See generally, Michael L. Rustad & Maria Vittoria Onufrio, *The Exportability of the Principles of Software: Lost in Translation*, 2 HASTINGS SCI. & TECH. L.J. 29, n.25 (2010).

In the 1970s and 1980s, there was uncertainty whether mass-market licenses were enforceable. By the mid-1990s, the industry was deploying rolling or layered contracts. With a layered contract, agreement to a contract may not occur at a single point in time.

Most, if not all, electronic standard forms used in social networking sites assert the right to modify their rolling terms of service "at any time, for any reason, or for no reason at all." YouTube, for example, reserves the right to unilaterally make changes to their service:

> YouTube is constantly changing and improving the Service. As part of this continual evolution, we may make modifications or changes (to all or part of the Service) such as adding or removing features and functionalities, offering new digital content or services or discontinuing old ones. We may also need to alter or discontinue the Service, or any part of it, in order to make performance or security improvements, make changes to comply with law, or prevent illegal activities on or abuse of our systems. These changes may affect all users, some users or even an individual user. When the Service requires or includes downloadable software (such as the YouTube Studio application), that software may update automatically on your device once a new version or feature is available, subject to your device settings. If we make material changes that negatively impact your use of the Service, we'll provide you with reasonable advance notice, except in urgent situations such as preventing abuse, responding to legal requirements, or addressing security and operability issues. We'll

also provide you with an opportunity to export your content from your Google Account using Google Takeout, subject to applicable law and policies.

YouTube, *Terms of Service* (Dec. 15, 2023) (accessed Mar. 7, 2026).

A NYU empirical study of terms of service was critical of their one-sided provisions. Contract scholars have established that very few consumers actually read or review standard-form boilerplate but have not determined whether these TOUs are, in fact, readable. Professor Florencia Marotta-Wurgler's research team found only one or two consumers out of 1,000 read consumer license agreements and that, of this miniscule number, the average reader spent only twenty-nine seconds with the form.

The NYU Law School researchers observed that, because the average length of the agreement was 2,277 words, it was implausible that users could review the complex terms in less than half a minute.

The NYU investigators concluded that the widespread practice of post-transaction marketing is deceptive because vendors exploit the empirical reality that consumers do not read online contracts.

The NYU researchers found that online vendors manipulatively positioned terms so that most consumers would overlook them. They

> recommended that marketers improve their disclosures and implement a means for consumers to cancel the contract and obtain a refund. The legal fiction of opportunity to review serves a useful purpose for the provider, but not for consumers who are stripped of all meaningful remedies and warranties and forced to litigate or arbitrate in a distant forum. Scholars have discussed the merits of requiring a general duty to make online contracts "user-friendly" or to "draft reasonably."
>
> Florencia Marotta-Wurgler & Robert B. Taylor, *Set in Stone? Change and Innovation in Consumer Standard-Form Contracts*, 88 N.Y.U. L. REV. 240, 243 (2013); See also, *Aggressive Sales Tactics on the Internet and Their Impact on American Consumers*: *Hearing Before the S. Comm. on Commerce, Sci. & Transp.*, 111TH CONG. 27 (2009).

An empirical study of the terms of use of the largest software companies concluded that mass-market license agreements are unreadable:

Software vendors generally draft clauses that take away rights and remedies at a reading level far beyond the reading comprehension of an average American consumer. The standard form agreements were drafted at a reading level only understood by users with two or more years of college education (Grade 14).

Software vendors draft clauses that foreclosure clauses that take away rights. The standard form agreements were drafted at a reading level only understood by users with two or more years of college education (Grade 14)

Michael L. Rustad, *Cancel Carte Blanche for the Information Industries: Federalizing UCC Article 2,* 89 MO. L. REV. 59, 106 (2024).

This empirical study of social media terms of use reveals how one-sided these mass market licenses are in favor of the social network providers:

> Imagine a profoundly unfair legal world in which businesses redirect consumer lawsuits away from state and federal courts into secret tribunals, in which a privately hired judge decides cases without precedents and with only limited grounds for an appeal. Under secretive forced arbitration, the social media service determines the arbitral provider and selects the rules that govern disputes with consumers.
>
> Visualize further that social media providers place legally binding terms of use (TOU) "agreements" that are seldom, if ever, read. Even if they are read, the TOU are composed of unnecessarily complex terminology, which is drafted at the comprehension level of a typical college graduate. In this dystopian legal world, users are required to waive their constitutional right to a jury trial, the right of liberal discovery, and the right of appeal by agreeing to "take-it-or-leave it" terms of use.
>
> This is not a law professor's far-fetched hypothetical. This legal dystopia is already here.

> The users of social networking websites (SNS) currently acquiesce to anti-class action waivers, damage caps, shortened statutes of limitations, "loser pays" rules, and choice-of forum clauses that are buried thousands of words deep in poorly indexed boilerplate. . . .A growing number of social media platforms contain predispute mandatory arbitration clauses specifying that hearings be conducted in the provider's home forum, which shifts the cost of air travel, hotels, and other expenses onto the consumer. These SNS are "rolling contracts" that reserve the right to unilaterally change or modify the rules of the game "at any time without further notice." Forced arbitration, under these imbalanced TOU, creates a liability-free zone for an increasing number of social media providers.

Thomas H. Koenig & Michael L. Rustad, *Fundamentally Unfair: An Empirical Analysis of Social Media Arbitration Clauses,* 65 CASE W. RES. L. REV. 341 (2014).

The principal finding of this large-scale study of the most important social media companies' terms of use study concluded:

> Our systematic examination of 329 of the world's largest social media providers reveals that 29 percent of these providers require users to submit to predispute mandatory arbitration as a condition of using their services. Forced consumer arbitration clauses are principally a U.S. phenomenon. Forty-two percent of the 188

U.S.-based social media providers contain forced arbitration clauses—in sharp contrast to only 13 percent of the 141 providers headquartered in foreign nations. Forty of the social networking websites (SNS) specify the American Arbitration Association (AAA) as the provider and nineteen specify JAMS, the two largest arbitration companies. We compare the fifty-nine social media terms of use (TOU) against the due process fairness tests that have been adopted by these two providers to mitigate the inevitable power imbalance in consumer arbitration proceedings. Our central finding is that the arbitration clauses of providers that specify the AAA and JAMS clearly fail the majority of the provisions of these two arbitral providers' consumer due process fairness tests. Arbitration clauses employed by social media have numerous "gotcha" provisions such as hard damage caps that place an absolute dollar limit on recovery that is significantly below the cost of filing an arbitral claim with either the AAA or JAMS. . . .In effect, social media providers, encouraged by the U.S. Supreme Court's endorsement of mandatory consumer arbitration, have constructed a liability-free zone where social media users have rights without remedies if social media providers breach their TOU, invade their privacy, or infringe their intellectual property rights.

Social media sites have created, what is in effect, a one-sided legal universe where users have no meaningful rights because they lack any practical way of obtaining a remedy.

Every social media site deployed webwrap agreement, which forecloses right and limits remedies of users. With webwrap contracts, for example, a party will manifest assent to different terms at different points in time. Terms of service agreements, for example, reserve the right to later modify or add to the terms of use or service. Many of these licenses were structured as "pay now, terms later."

On April 2, 2014, General Mills changed its terms of use to include the following clause:

> These terms are a binding legal agreement (Agreement) between you and General Mills. In exchange for the benefits, discounts, content, features, services, or other offerings that you receive or have access to by using our websites, joining our sites as a member, joining our online community, subscribing to our email newsletters, downloading or printing a digital coupon, entering a sweepstakes or contest, redeeming a promotional offer, or otherwise participating in any other General Mills offering, you are agreeing to these terms. These terms included, in bold, capital letters, a mandatory arbitration clause that extended to any consumer dispute with General Mills.
>
> General Mills revoked these new terms only a few weeks later in large part because of consumer protest to these one-sided provisions:

> Because of the copious negative attention, General Mills announced in a blog post this past Saturday that consumers' complaints have been heard and that as a result, the policy has been reversed and the original legal terms of use are back in place. The newest terms do not contain a "binding arbitration" clause.

Saya Weissman, *What Brands Should Learn From General Mills' Facebook Fiasco,* DIGIDAY (Apr. 22, 2014).

In the 1990s, the American Bar Association's Business Law Section began a project to update commercial law to create specialized legal infrastructure for software licensing. The Uniform Law Commission (ULC) (then called NCCUSL) and the American Law Institute (ALI) joined forces to develop a separate article of the Uniform Commercial Code called Article 2B, which was a proposed new article for software licensing.

The ABA and ALI withdrew from the UCC Article 2B project. "The National Conference of Commissioners of Uniform State Laws (NCCUSL) has been working on this issue for some time with what was originally called UCC Article 2B, later renamed the Uniform Computer Information Transaction Act after the American Law Institute withdrew from the project." *Conwell v. Gray Loon Outdoor Mktg. Group*, 906 N.E.2d 805, 811 (Ind. 2009).

NCCUSL drafted the Uniform Computer Information Transactions Act (UCITA), which was largely comprised of UCC Article 2B provisions. UCITA was a proposed model law designed to govern contracts for software licensing, multimedia products, and online database access.

UCITA adapted UCC Article 2 provisions and created new provisions applicable to the licensing of intangibles. UCITA is a stand-alone state contracting statute that customizes UCC Article 2 concepts for software licenses. In July of 1999, the ULC approved UCITA, for introduction into the states but it was adopted by only two states, Maryland and Virginia.

UCITA was the first uniform contract law designed to deal specifically with the new information economy. Transactions in computer information involve different expectations, different industry practices, and different policies from transactions in goods.

For example, in a sale of goods, the buyer acquires title for what she buys and thus has exclusive rights in that subject matter (e.g., a car, computer, or table). In contrast, someone that acquires a copy of computer information may or may not own that copy, but will be the owner of this information, as licensing give only a right to access.

UCITA developed contracting rules applicable to diverse license agreements including, terms of use, software license agreements, access contracts, clickwrap agreements, end-user agreements, online shopping, auction bidding agreements, terms of services agreements, and online licenses of all kinds.

UCITA validate "rolling contracts" if the person had reason to know that terms would come later, had a right to refund if he declined the terms, and manifested assent after an opportunity to review them. Online merchants typically offer consumers take it or leave it agreements. UCITA gave consumers a right to a refund if they have not had an opportunity to review the terms.

Critics claimed that UCITA was drafted by and for powerful software companies like Microsoft and Apple, legitimating one-sided terms such as the exclusion of warranties, remedies, and provider-centered choice of law and forum clauses.

Critics charged that UCITA would enable software publishers to shut down their customer's computer system without prior court approval. The Americans for Fair Electronic Commerce spearheaded an attack on self-help provisions in UCITA calling it "dangerous, anti-competitive, anti-business, anti-consumer measure."

UCITA opponents—large technology users and consumer rights groups who are strange bedfellows—contended that its provisions would give software companies a virtual stranglehold on technology contracts. The licensee community, too, joined the chorus against UCITA's self-help provisions. Consumers, the government and business objected to the following UCITA provisions:

- Unconditional validation of 'shrinkwrapped' or 'clickthrough' licenses combined with onerous default provisions.

- Restriction on number of permitted users as default provision.
- Limitation on duration of license as default provision.
- Limitation warranty of non-infringement.
- Permitted disclaimer of implied warranty regarding defects—even those known to the software publisher at time of license.
- Restriction on transferability—while prohibited under the recent proposed amendment to UCITA in the case of mergers or sales of business—are still allowed in other cases.
- Permitted use of automatic or passive restraint—for a reason as vague as the 'prevention of use inconsistent with the agreement.'
- Waiver of remedy for breach of contract.
- Deletion of the requirement to deliver a product conforming to the contract and the abandonment of perfect tender rule.
- Electronic repossession or self-help.

Letter of April 2001 to Oklahoma Attorney General Drew Edmundson (1999).

In 2002, the Uniform Law Commission withdrew UCITA from further introductions in the states. As of 2026, UCITA is the chief source of law for information transfers such as licensing in Maryland

and Virginia. Contracting parties in those states designate UCITA in the parties' choice of law clauses. Johns Hopkins University, for example, promulgates the following choice of law clause with UCITA as the designated law:

> This Agreement shall be governed by and construed in accordance with the laws of the State of Maryland (excepting the application of UCITA and any conflict of law's provisions which would serve to defeat application of Maryland substantive law). Each of the parties hereto agrees to attempt to resolve any dispute initially by mediation. However, if that is unsuccessful, each of the parties hereto agrees to venue in and submits to the exclusive jurisdiction of the state and/or federal courts located within the State of Maryland for any suit, hearing or other legal proceeding of every nature, kind and description whatsoever in the event of any dispute or controversy arising from or relating to this Agreement, or in the event any ruling, finding or other legal determination is required or desired hereunder. Both parties agree to waive their respective rights to a trial by jury.

Goodwin v. Johns Hopkins Univ., 2025 U.S. Dist. LEXIS 59616, *3 (D. Md. Mar. 31, 2025).

The American Law Institute (ALI) proposed the Principles of the Law of Software Contracts (Principles) to fill a gap left in the law of software contracts by UCITA's demise.

The ALI's Principles of the Law of Software Contracts is a contracting law for all transactions involving software, Key principles focus on addressing issues with standard-form agreements, clarifying intellectual property rights, establishing clear warranties, and defining remedies, with a strong emphasis on disclosure and good faith.

The ALI approved the Principles in 2009 as "soft law" as opposed to UCITA, which was a stand-alone statute for information transfers. The Reporters for the Principles explain its limited scope;

> The first question the Principles faced was how to define the transactions to which they applied. The Principles intentionally define their scope narrowly to software as traditionally understood.
>
> As drafters, we understood the danger of over-inclusiveness: In particular, we wished to avoid the trap of including all types of digital information within our project's scope. As a result, digital media and digital databases are not part of the project.

Robert A. Hillman & Maureen A. O'Rourke, *Law and Technology: Principles of the Law of Software Contracts, Viewpoint*, 53(9) COMMUNICATIONS OF THE ACM (Sept. 2010).

The ALI describes the Principles of the Law of Software Contracts as a "comprehensive set of legal principles intended to guide the drafting of software contracts and assist in judicial resolution of disputes involving software transactions." The Principles' Reporters divide the Principles into four chapters:

- Chapter 1: Definitions, Scope, and General Terms.
- Chapter 2: Formation and Enforcement.
- Chapter 3: Performance.
- Chapter 4: Remedies.

Chapter 1 covers three topics: definitions, scope, and general terms. Section 1.06 states the Principles Sphere of Application:

> (a) These Principles apply to agreements for the transfer of software for a consideration. Software agreements include agreements to sell, lease, license, access, or otherwise transfer or share software.
>
> (b) These Principles do not apply to
>
> > (1) the transfer of any disk, CD-ROM, or other tangible medium that stores the software, or
> >
> > (2) the transfer of a security interest in software.

The ALI Principles apply to any transfer of any software, including sales, leases, and licenses, as long as the transfer of software is supported by consideration, which encompasses sales, leases, and licenses, thus avoiding the problem of determining whether a given software transaction was a sale, lease, or license.

Open source licenses where the licensor does not charge a licensing fee (or other consideration) are outside the sphere of application of the Principles of the Law of Software Contracts. The Principles guide courts to refuse to enforce license agreements if enforcement would violate important public policies. The Principles also presume that pro-provider choice of forum clauses are broadly enforceable. Official Comment (a) to Section 1.06 states:

> Software, as defined in § 1.01(j), consists of information used by a computer to produce a particular result. It does not include digital art or a digital database (digital content), as defined in § 1.01(f). However, courts can look to these Principles by analogy to resolve issues involving digital content if appropriate Principles of the Law of Software Contracts § 1.06.

Section 114 of the Principles allow the parties to submit to jurisdiction and agree to an exclusive forum so long as it is not unfair or unreasonable. The Principles adopted the "opportunity to review" test in UCITA, which gives the licensee reasonable accessibility to terms prior to the transfer.

The Principles of the Law of Software Contracts validated mass market license agreements such as clickwrap and shrinkwrap, but do not validate browsewrap because it does not give the licensee reasonable accessibility to terms prior to the transfer.

The ALI Reporters for the Principles argued that software contracting law should reflect well-established principles from sales such resale, market price, specific performance, and liquidated damages to software contracts. The ALI Reporters contended that software licensors should provide their customers with a minimally adequate remedy. In the absence of agreement, they adopted the expectation theory of damages.

See generally, American Law Institute, *ALI Reporters Memorandum to the Principles of the Law of Software Contracts* (2009).

As of May 2, 2026, 386 U.S. courts have cited the Principles of the Law of Software Contracts in a judicial opinion but no court has adopted any of its substantive provisions. Despite the low impact in judicial opinions, the Principles provides useful licensing legal infrastructure adaptable to many software contracts. The Principles nevertheless suffered the same fate as UCITA because of a perception that the proposed restatement-like rules were skewed in favor of the software industry.

The growth of the Internet has also prompted Congress to bring up-to-date statutory licenses for webcasting. The D.C. Circuit explained that Congress updated copyright law to develop statutory copyright licenses for non-interactive webcasters in the Copyright Act:

> The statutory license permits non-interactive webcasters to transmit recordings by paying a standard royalty rate rather than negotiating individual licensing agreements with countless copyright holders. Every five years, the Copyright Royalty Board sets the standard rates

non-interactive webcasters must pay to play recordings over the Internet under the statutory license.

SoundExchange Inc. v. Copyright Royalty Board, 904 F.3d 41 (D.C. Cir. 2018).

Increasingly, Internet contractual disputes involve the breach of licensing agreements. In *Malibu Media LLC v. Bayko*, 2019 WL 414917 (M.D. Pa. Feb. 1, 2019), the court enjoined the defendant from directly, contributorily, or indirectly infringing plaintiff's rights under federal or state law in its copyrighted works. The court also enjoined the defendant from making plaintiff's copyrighted works available for distribution to the public, except pursuant to a lawful license or with the express authority of plaintiff.

In *Recursion Software v. Interactive Intelligence*, 425 F. Supp. 2d 756 (N.D. Tex. 2006), the dispute raised the issue of whether Interactive agreed to the terms of the license agreement to Voyager 2.0.1 when they clicked "Yes" on the clickwrap license. Interactive maintained there was no evidence that it ever agreed to the terms of the agreement. The court disagreed, finding that Interactive was bound to a clickwrap agreement:

> It is undisputed that Interactive used Voyager 2.0.1 and embedded it in Interaction Recorder. There is unchallenged testimony in the record that, to install Voyager 2.0.1, a user must accept the license terms under the website protocol discussed above. In addition, even if the software were not obtained from the website, the

user would still have to accept the license terms before the software could be installed.

> Without accepting the terms of the license, installation is impossible. Therefore, the Court finds that the record evidence is sufficient to support the conclusion that Interactive could not have incorporated Voyager 2.0.1 in the software without clicking 'Yes' to the terms of the license agreement.

Software licenses impose duties surviving termination (e.g., duty to keep the other party's trade secrets confidential), regardless of whether they take the form of terms of use, wrap contracts, or software.

The Software Publishers Association (SPA) describes the diversity of licenses evolving in recent years:

> (1) *Use License*: permits a discrete set of ways in which the software may be used (2) *Single-Use Licenses*: permits by only one user; *Machine License*: Permits use on a particular computer or device; *Per-Seat License*: permits use by a group of individually-specified us *Concurrent Use License*: Use by a specified number of simultaneous users; *Server License*: permits use by all users connected to a particular server; and *Site Licenses*: permits use by users in a specified geographic area(s), building(s), organization(s), or other entities.

Amicus Brief of BSA Foundation, Software.org, in *Kornkrumpf v. Adobe Systems* (9th Cir. 2013).

§ 4-2. Mass-Market Licenses

(A) SHRINKWRAP LICENSES

In the 1970s, the software industry developed the "shrinkwrap" agreement, which was the earliest form of a quickwrap license. The shrinkwrap agreement received its name from the practice of vendors physically printing shrinkwrap licenses beneath the shrinkwrap or directly on the box holding the CD-ROM or disk. By the early 1980s, vendors were widely using the term to describe a specific form of contracting. Shrinkwrap licenses have three common features:

> (1) notice of a license agreement on product packaging (i.e., the shrinkwrap), (2) presentation of the full license on documents inside the package, and (3) prohibited access to the product without an express indication of acceptance. These licenses could not be reviewed until the consumer purchased the software and opened the box by removing the shrinkwrap.

Savetsky v. Prepaid Legal Services, Inc., 2015 WL 604767 at *3 (N.D. Cal. Feb. 12, 2005).

In a caricature of mass-market licenses, Dilbert states: "I didn't read all of the shrinkwrap license agreement on my new software until after I opened it,"—and concludes with Dilbert lamenting: "Apparently, I agreed to spend the rest of my life as a towel boy in Bill Gates' new mansion."

Samsung employs shrinkwrap agreements for all its Galaxy Book 3 devices.

> Samsung represents, all Galaxy Book 3 devices were packaged in this way, Faridian—who purchased his Galaxy Book 3 from Samsung—must have also received his Galaxy Book 3 with the above labeling. This kind of notice, "where notice of contractual terms is provided on the exterior physical packaging containing the product," is commonly referred to as a "shrinkwrap agreement."

Williams v. Samsung Elecs. Am., Inc., 2026 U.S. Dist. LEXIS 38012, *24 (D.N.J. Feb. 24, 2026).

In Samsung's shrinkwrap agreement, the limited warranty conspicuously modified implied warranties by limiting duration to one year and required contact with Samsung for exclusive repair/replace remedy, defeating breach of implied warranty claims by plaintiffs. In the Samsung case, the court compelled arbitration enforcing the shrinkwrap agreement.

(B) CLICKWRAP AGREEMENTS

"Today, virtually every Internet user is familiar with what have become known as clickwrap agreements—agreements formed by requiring a computer user to consent to any terms or conditions by clicking on a dialog box on the screen in order to proceed with a transaction."

Bazemore v. Jefferson Capital Sys., LLC, 827 F.3d 1325, 1327 (11th Cir. 2016).

Clickwraps evolved out of shrinkwrap and premises consumer assent by a consumer clicking the "I Agree" button. The typical "clickwrap" or "clickstream" agreement calls for express agreement from the consumer licensee by clicking the "I Agree" button. Note, *The Electronic "Sign-in-Wrap" Contract: Issues of Notice and Assent, the Average Internet User Standard, and Unconscionability*, 50 U.C. DAVIS L. REV. 535, 539 (2016).

"Clickwraps are mechanisms that require a user to click on a dialog box, which contains terms and conditions, on a screen in order to proceed." *Ansys, Inc. v. SF Motors, Inc.*, 2021 WL 22453 at *1 (W.D. Pa. Jan. 4, 2021).

The Ninth Circuit explains clickwrap agreements as follows:

> If the consumer does not click 'I agree,' the licensee is asked to leave the site. The clickwrap standard form displays terms electronically and the user demonstrates assent to the terms by clicking the acceptance button. 'Under a clickwrap arrangement, prospective licensees are presented with the proposed license terms and forced to expressly and unambiguously manifest either assent or rejection prior to being given access to the product.'

Nguyen v. Barnes & Noble, 763 F.3d 1171 (9th Cir. 2014).

The court in *Savetsky v. Prepaid Legal Services, Inc.*, 2015 WL 604767 (N.D. Cal. Feb. 12, 2005), describes how clickwraps demonstrate the manifestation of assent:

> The first, a clickwrap agreement is familiar to most internet users and requires a user or prospective customer to check a box or click an 'I agree' button after being presented with terms and conditions (or more realistically after declining the opportunity to review the often voluminous terms and conditions).

Clickwrap licensors typically disclaim warranties, however licensors typically offer only to repair or replace the software disk or other media as the sole and exclusive remedy. Many clickwraps impose arbitration and anti-class action waivers such as in the clause below:

> YOU AND [PROVIDER] AGREE THAT EACH MAY BRING CLAIMS AGAINST THE OTHER ONLY IN YOUR OR ITS INDIVIDUAL CAPACITY, AND NOT AS A PLAINTIFF OR CLASS MEMBER IN ANY PURPORTED CLASS OR REPRESENTATIVE PROCEEDING.

The characteristic "click through" website agreement requires end users to click an "I agree" icon, thus creating a contract where the user agrees to submit to all of the licensor's terms and conditions. For example, Dell's software agreement binds the consumer to all the terms of its license agreement once the preloaded software is used.

The court upheld an arbitration clause in a clickwrap agreement in *Doe v. Massage Envy*

Franchising (MEF), LLC, 2020 WL 7624622 (Del. Super. Ct. Dec. 21, 2020), which was a case that arose out of the plaintiff's sexual assault by a franchise employee. The plaintiff argued that the franchise failed to provide basic safety to clients and systematically and intentionally conspired and concealed the problem of massage therapists sexually assaulting customers.

The court dismissed the action ruling that the plaintiff had agreed to arbitration when she created a profile on the Massage Envy website, agreed and assented to arbitrate all claims against the franchise. The court ruled that the arbitrator had "the power to determine whether Plaintiff's claims fall within the scope of the purported arbitration agreement."

In *Campbell v. Princess Cruise Lines Ltd.*, 2021 WL 75663 (N.D. Cal. Jan. 8, 2021), Brenda Campbell filed an admiralty action on behalf of the Estate of Carl E. Weidner based on the death of her husband from COVID-19 following his time on the Grand Princess cruise ship. She contended that, despite knowledge of the risks of COVID-19, Defendants issued an "Emergency Notification" to their passengers in advance of Mr. Weidner's voyage, indicating that the Grand Princess would be safe to board.

She also contended that the Princess cruise ship learned of outbreaks of COVID-19 aboard several of their other cruise ships and of at least one passenger with COVID-19 symptoms aboard the Grand Princess, but failed to take proper precautions. "Plaintiff asserts that Mr. Weidner relied on

Defendants' representations about the safety of the trip and boarded the Grand Princess, where he contracted COVID-19."

Shortly after disembarking, Mr. Weidner tested positive for COVID-19, and on March 26, 2020, he died "because of infection related to the COVID-19 virus."

The cruise line argued that the action be transferred to the Central District of California because he agreed to that forum:

> Defendants cite to their booking records, which indicate that Mr. Weidner booked the cruise on the Grand Princess on December 23, 2019. Defendants then sent Mr. Weidner an email, which contained a 'Booking Confirmation PDF'. . . . The email and PDF prompted Mr. Weidner to complete mandatory additional booking information, including reading and accepting the terms of the Passage Contract. The bottom of the PDF reads:
>
> > IMPORTANT NOTICE: Upon booking the Cruise, each passenger explicitly agrees to the terms of the Passage Contract. Please read all sections carefully as they affect the passenger's legal rights.

The cruise company stated that Weidner agreed to the "Forum and Jurisdiction for Legal Action," the Passage Contract that states:

> *Claims for Injury, Illness or Death*: All claims or disputes involving Emotional Harm, bodily

> injury, illness to or death of any Guest whatsoever, including without limitation those arising out of or relating to this Passage Contract or Your Cruise, shall be litigated in and before the United States District Courts for the Central District of California in Los Angeles, or as to those lawsuits over which the Federal Courts of the United States lack subject matter jurisdiction, before a court located in Los Angeles County, California, U.S.A., to the exclusion of the courts of any other country, state, city, municipality, county or locale. You consent to jurisdiction and waive any objection that may be available to any such action being brought in such courts.

The court concluded that the clickwrap agreement was valid and enforceable like any other contracts:

> And 'clickwrap' agreements made through websites, where a user is presented with the terms and conditions and must click on a button or box to indicate that he agrees before he may continue, are considered valid and enforceable. . . . Here, Mr. Weidner not only agreed to the Passenger Contract, but he had ample opportunity to review it. He accepted the terms of the Passage Contract on January 3, 2020, over a month before boarding the Grand Princess.
>
> The Court does not in any way minimize the tragedy of Mr. Weidner's death. But on the record before it in this case, the Court cannot find any hardships that would make

enforcement of the forum selection clause unreasonable or unfair. The Court finds that Plaintiff has not met her burden of establishing that this is one of the few 'exceptional cases' where the forum selection clause should not be enforced.

Massachusetts' highest court was unwilling to enforce a clickwrap agreement in *Kauders v. Uber Technologies, Inc.*, 486 Mass. 557 (2021). The Kauders commenced a lawsuit against Uber "claiming, among other things, that three Uber drivers refused to provide Christopher Kauders with rides because he was blind and accompanied by a guide dog." "Each of the plaintiffs registered with Uber through its cellular telephone application (app)."

Uber sought to compel arbitration, which was opposed by the plaintiffs. Uber sought to compel arbitration. The plaintiffs opposed arbitration on various grounds, including that there was no enforceable arbitration agreement. The judge granted Uber's motion, and the parties arbitrated their dispute. The arbitrator ruled in favor of Uber on all of the plaintiffs' claims.

(C) BROWSEWRAP

'Browsewrap' refers to terms of use that are mentioned on a website but posted in full on a separate web page accessible via hyperlink. Like a shrinkwrap agreement, a browsewrap agreement does not require affirmative assent, and considers continued use of a website, like

> continued use of a shrink wrapped product, as assent to the terms of use.

Disney Enterprises, Inc. v. Redbox Automated Retail, Inc., 336 F. Supp. 3d 1146, 1153 n.4 (C.D. Cal. 2018).

> In a pure-form browsewrap agreement, the website will contain a notice that—by merely using the services of, obtaining information from, or initiating applications within the website—the user is agreeing to and is bound by the site's terms of service.

Fteja v. Facebook, Inc., 841 F. Supp. 2d 829, 837 (S.D.N.Y. 2012).

Courts are unwilling to enforce browsewrap agreements if there is no actual proof the consumer had reasonable notice of the terms. In *Linders v. Festival Fun Parks, LLC*, 2026 U.S. Dist. LEXIS 46407 (D. Conn. Mar. 6, 2026), a Connecticut federal district court concluded that theme park did not establish that Alexandria Linders unambiguously manifested assent to the Terms, including their requirement to arbitrate any disputes or their prohibition on bringing a class action. The court dismissed the action compelling arbitration.

The court concluded that while the content of the Website is not cluttered, the lack of additional instruction or clarifying language concerning the Terms; and the layout of the Website, having the Terms visually separated from the purchase process, support a finding that Defendant has not carried its burden and demonstrated that Plaintiff was on inquiry notice as to the Terms. The court stated:

> To determine whether an offeree knew or should have known of the terms of a web-based contract such that they unambiguously manifested assent, courts consider the following three factors: (1) "whether the interface clearly warned the user that taking a specific action would constitute assent to certain terms"; (2) "whether notice of the contractual terms was presented to the consumer in a location on the interface and at time when the consumer would expect to receive such terms"; and (3) the "course of dealing between the parties, including whether the contract terms were conspicuously presented to the consumer at each use of the offeror's service and the consumer's conduct in response to the repeated presentation of conspicuous terms."

The court applied these criteria to the theme park's browsewrap concluding that Linder did not unambiguously manifest her intent to be bound by the agreement to arbitrate disputes:

> First, the interface here did not clearly warn customers that clicking the "Continue" button and proceeding through the purchase process would constitute acceptance of the Terms. Unlike with the "Park Rules," which had to be checked before the purchase could be completed, the Terms hyperlink does not contain any indication that clicking continue or completing the purchase would bind Plaintiff to the Terms

> as part of her purchase. . . [T]here is no message indicating that "selecting 'Confirm and continue' . . . constitutes [a customer's] confirmation that they 'agree to the payment terms'" that were hyperlinked. Here, the Court cannot find any such indication in the screenshots of the Website. Thus, the first factor weighs against an unambiguous manifestation of assent. Defendant fares no better under the second factor. While the Terms appear "at time when the consumer would expect to receive such terms" throughout the purchase process, they are not in a location a customer would expect. . . .The Terms are located on their own box at the bottom of the screen, separate from the continue button and separate from any price information for the items a customer is looking to purchase. This location—a distinct box that is above and to the left of the continue button and the price information, rather than "directly above" the continue button—weighs against finding that the Terms were incorporated into the purchase. Finally, the parties' course of dealing is short, and Defendant has not alleged a prior repeat relationship with Plaintiff.

"Browsewraps" seeks to bind users to an agreement without an affirmative click. Courts acknowledge that browsewraps are problematic and there is uncertainty whether they are enforceable.

(D) SCROLLWRAP & SIGN-IN WRAP

Scrollwrap requires users to physically scroll through an Internet agreement and click on a separate "I agree" button to manifest assent to terms and conditions. A federal district court outlined the four general types of online consumer contracts, identified as: (a) browsewrap; (b) clickwrap; (c) scrollwrap; and (d) sign-in-wrap. Browsewrap exists:

> where the online host dictates that assent is given merely by using the site. Clickwrap refers to the assent process by which a user must click 'I agree,' but not necessarily view the contract to which she is assenting. Scrollwrap requires users to physically scroll through an internet agreement and click on a separate 'I agree' button in order to assent to the terms and conditions of the host website. Sign-in-wrap couples assent to the terms of a website with signing up for use of the site's services[.]

Berkson v. Gogo LLC, 97 F. Supp. 3d 359, 394–395 (E.D.N.Y. 2015).

Sign-in agreements and scrollwraps were described by one court in the following way:

> In a scrollwrap, which provides "the strongest notice" and are usually enforced, the user must scroll through all the terms before the website allows her to click a box to agree. Finally, a sign-in wrap lives somewhere in the middle: the website provides a link to terms of use and indicates that some action may bind the user but does not require that the user actually review those terms.

Hernandez v. Event Ticket Ctr., Inc., 2026 U.S. Dist. LEXIS 45687, *7 (E.D. Calif. Mar. 4, 2026).

The California federal court found that the plaintiff was not on inquiry notice to a sign-in agreement:

> The parties disagree whether the agreement here should be labeled as a sign-in wrap agreement or a hybrid click wrap agreement. The parties do agree, however, that the agreement notice read, "By clicking 'Place Order,' you are agreeing to EventTicketsCenter.com's terms & policies. All sales are final," and that the phrase, "terms & policies," was a hyperlink to the Terms and Policies. The court concludes that this agreement is akin to a sign-in wrap agreement because the website provides a link to the Terms and Policies but does not require the user to review the terms.

Hernandez v. Event Ticket Ctr., Inc., 2026 U.S. Dist. LEXIS 45687, *7 (E.D. Calif. Mar. 4, 2026).

> The court found that the Event Ticket sign-in was inconspicuous and unenforceable observing: Courts are more likely to enforce agreements with weak visual notices when the context of the transaction puts users on notice to look for a link to the terms of the relationship. . . .Here, the weak visual notice of defendants' Terms and Policies is not saved by the context of the transaction. Rather, a reasonably prudent internet user would not necessarily see the notice, especially when, as here, the context of

> the transaction does not suggest an ongoing relationship in which a user may expect to be governed by terms and policies. . .Based on the foregoing, and when considering the context of the transaction in conjunction with the weak visibility of the notice provision, the notice provision here did not sufficiently notify users of the Terms and Policies they purportedly agreed to. The "lack of notice is dispositive" because it is a necessary element to enforce the contract based on inquiry notice.

Hernandez v. Event Ticket Ctr., Inc., 2026 U.S. Dist. LEXIS 45687, *18–20 (E.D. Calif. Mar. 4, 2026).

Courts will not enforce wrap contracts unless the website design and placement of terms of use is calculated to give users reasonable notice of terms and an opportunity to decline the terms.

A California federal district court described the features of sign-in-wrap agreements as:

> those in which a user signs up to use an internet product or service, and the sign-up screen states that acceptance of a separate agreement is required before the user can access the service. . . . Sign-in wrap agreements do include a textual notice indicating the user will be bound by the terms, but they do not require the consumer to review those terms or to expressly manifest their assent to those terms by checking a box or clicking an 'I agree' button. Instead, the consumer is purportedly bound by clicking some other button that they would otherwise need to

click to continue with their transaction or their use of the website—most frequently, a button that allows the consumer to 'sign in' or 'sign up' for an account. *Smith v. Inflection Risk Sols., LLC*, 2026 U.S. Dist. LEXIS 46036, *24 (N.D. Calif. Mar. 6, 2026).

Courts will not enforce sign-in agreements where notices were not "sufficiently conspicuous" to provide inquiry notice to users. The California federal district court concluded that Infection provided constructive notice of its terms:

> Inflection's evidence shows that (1) prior to accessing his report on Inflection's website, Smith was required to check a box next to the following statement: "Yes, I agree to Inflection's Terms of Use and Privacy Policy"; (2) the words "Terms of Use" were a hyperlink to Inflection's Terms; and (3) Smith affirmatively This sufficiently establishes constructive notice of Inflection's Terms because the Terms were presented to Smith in a manner that made clear he was assenting to the Terms by checking the box next to the terms. . .Therefore, Smith's act of affirmative assent (checking the box) is sufficient to impute knowledge of Inflection's Terms.

(E) HYBRID AGREEMENTS

Hybrid contracts combine features of clickwraps and browsewraps. In *Church v. Hotels.com*, 2018 WL 3130615 (D.S.C. June 26, 2018), Joseph Church used the hotel booking website Reservations.com to purchase two nights in a guest room at the Hyatt Regency Orlando Hotel.

> To make a transaction, the Reservations.com website prompts a customer to select the desired hotel room and enter payment information into a form, at the bottom of which is a button labeled Confirm Reservation.
>
> Next to the 'Confirm Reservation' button is a paragraph of text stating, 'Your information is protected and SSL encrypted secure. By clicking the 'Complete Reservation' button you agree to our Terms of Service and hotel room cancellation policy.'
>
> The phrase 'Terms of Service' is hyperlinked to a web page containing the Reservations.com 'Terms of Service and Dispute Resolution ('Agreement'),' which contains a provision titled 'Mandatory Arbitration' requiring both parties to submit 'Any and all claims' to 'binding arbitration, rather than in court' unless the claim may be brought in small claims court.

He "incurred credit card charges for the 'Room Subtotal,' Reservations.com's 'Service Fee,' and 'Tax & Fees.' " Church alleges:

> that Reservations.com knowingly charged him $108.68 in 'Tax & Fees,' that the correct cost was $69.97, and that Reservations.com knowingly kept the excess $38.71. Plaintiff alleges Reservations.com has done the same for 'nearly every reservation booked on the website, and [is]

> illegally retaining millions of dollars in overcharges annually.'

The court found that Church was subject to an arbitration clause:

> By clicking the "Complete Reservation" button you agree to our Terms of Service. In any event, to the extent Plaintiff argues that he was not given sufficient notice of the Terms of Service, the type of agreement implemented by Reservations.com has been found enforceable. Reservations.com implements a hybrid between a clickwrap and browsewrap agreement: by expressly agreeing to click and 'Complete Reservation,' the consumer is impliedly agreeing to the Terms of Service, of which he is put on sufficient notice by the clear hyperlinked disclaimer directly adjacent to the 'Complete Reservation' button.

In *Regan v. Pinger, Inc.*, 2021 WL 706465 (N.D. Cal. Feb. 23, 2021), the defendant Pinger developed Sideline that is a paid service that allows users to create a "virtual," alternative telephone line for their mobile phone. The issue was whether the consumer had notice of Sideline's terms of us.

The *Regan* court found that the (TOS) was "neither a 'true browsewrap agreement' nor a 'pure-form clickwrap agreement.' " See *Nevarez v. Forty Niners Football Company, Inc.*, 2017 WL 3492110, at *7 (N.D. Cal. Aug. 15, 2017) (explaining a middle-ground between these approaches). The court found that the hybrid agreement gave the user reasonable notice upholding Pinger's arbitration agreement reasoning:

> Regardless of the precise label, based on the design and function of the Sideline App, the Court finds that Plaintiff assented to the Sideline TOS by creating an account. As the Court has already explained, the Sideline App sufficiently informed Plaintiff either (1) that by creating an account the user agreed to Sideline's TOS, or (2) that by clicking the 'Create Account,' 'For Professional Use,' 'For Personal Use,' or 'Login' button, Plaintiff was agreeing to the Sideline TOS. Plaintiff was also repeatedly reminded that he agreed to the TOS by creating an account when Plaintiff clicked the 'Login' button upon returning to use the Sideline App. As such, when Plaintiff created each account, Plaintiff assented to the Sideline TOS by creating that account.

§ 4-3. Cloud Computing Service Agreements

"Cloud computing is the delivery of computing services—including servers, storage, databases, networking, software, analytics, and intelligence—over the internet." Sebastian Straub, *49 Cloud Computing Statistics You Must Know in 2025* (June 25, 2025). "The public cloud market alone is expected to exceed $1 trillion by 2026." *Id.* The following cloud computing statistics demonstrate the growth of the market:

- By 2026, the cloud computing market is forecast to be worth $947.3 billion.

- Amazon Web Services remains the biggest public cloud provider, with 32% of the market.
- 96% of companies use the public cloud.
- 84% of companies use the private cloud.

Mariusz Michalowski, *55 Cloud Computing Statistics for 2026*, SPACELIFT (Jan. 1, 2026). Cloud computing is often referred to as "Software as a Service (SaaS)":

> Software as a service is one of three cloud computing service models, the others being platform as a service and infrastructure as a service. In the platform as a service, or PaaS, model, end users can deploy their software applications on the PaaS provider's cloud infrastructure. Meanwhile, the servers, storage and networking are managed by the PaaS provider.

The Evolution Of Software As A Service Taxes Post-Wayfair, LAW360 (May 17, 2019).

> In the infrastructure as a service, or IaaS, model, end users can access the service provider's processing, storage, networks, servers, operating systems or other computing resources, which can be more convenient for many users than having to purchase their own hardware (or reduce their hardware ownership when they no longer need it). IaaS is similar to traditional information technology resources used by organizations' IT departments and developers.

> Where the second wave leveraged the internet, the third wave began with advances in cloud computing. Beginning in November 2004, when Amazon Web Services first launched, cloud computing became increasingly affordable to the masses, enabling small teams of researchers and innovators, in schools, at startups, and in big companies, to run experiments on large data sets, quickly and often.

The Third Wave of Legal Technology Transformation: Changing What Lawyers Do, With Structured Data, LEGALTECH NEWS (Jan. 11, 2021).

> Under cloud computing, data is stored on the Internet on remote servers, rather than on a computer or server in the office. Personal cloud computing, allowing one to store and access personal data from any personal device, is steadily growing. Similarly, applications for business cloud computing, suitable for law firms, continue to expand. Cloud-based practice management applications, such as Clio, facilitate access to data from wherever needed.

OHIO ELDER LAW (2020 ed.) at § 4:11, Cloud Computing.

The term, "cloud," is an unsatisfactory metaphor used to describe remote storage of software applications, tools and data accessed via the Internet. A University of California Berkeley Distributed

Systems Laboratory research report describes the paradigm of cloud computing as follows:

> Cloud Computing refers to both the applications delivered as services over the Internet and the hardware and systems software in the datacenters that provide those services. The services themselves have long been referred to as Software as a Service (SaaS). The datacenter hardware and software is what we will call a Cloud. When a Cloud is made available in a pay-as-you-go manner to the public, we call it a Public Cloud; the service being sold is Utility Computing.

MICHAEL ARMBRUST ET AL., ABOVE THE CLOUDS: A BERKELEY VIEW OF CLOUD COMPUTING (Feb. 10, 2009).

> Worldwide IT spending is projected to total $3.4 trillion in 2020, a decline of 8% from 2019, according to the latest forecast by Gartner, Inc. The pandemic and effects of the global economic recession are causing CIOs to prioritize spending on technology and services that are deemed 'mission-critical' over initiatives aimed at growth or transformation. However, as the COVID-19 pandemic continues to spur remote working, sub segments such as public cloud services (which falls into multiple categories) will be a bright spot in the forecast, growing 19% in 2020. Cloud-based telephony and messaging and cloud-based conferencing will also see high levels of spending growing 8.9% and 24.3%, respectively.

Gartner Says Global IT Spending to Decline 8% in 2020 Due to Impact of COVID-19, GARTNER (May 13, 2020).

> The National Institute of Standards and Technology (NIST) explains cloud computing as a model for enabling convenient, on-demand network access to a shared pool of configurable computing resources (e.g., networks, applications and services) that can be rapidly provisioned and released with minimal management effort or service provider interaction.

Peter Mell & Timothy Grance, *The NIST Definition of Cloud Computing*, National Institute of Standards, U.S. Dept. of Commerce (Sept. 2011).

> The NIST definition of cloud computing consists of five essential characteristics: (1) On-demand self-service, (2) broad network access, (3) resource pooling, (4) rapid elasticity, and (5) measured service. Cloud providers deploy three basic service models (1) Cloud Software as a Service (SaaS), (2) Cloud Platform as a Service (PaaS), and (3) Cloud Infrastructure as a Service (IaaS). The four most common deployment models are: (1) Private cloud, (2) Community cloud, (3) Public cloud, and (4) Hybrid cloud.

National Institute of Standards, *NIST Cloud Computing Program* (2013).

Cloud computing is a flexible paradigm, enabling applications and data to be accessed and shared seamlessly from any location, on any device. Cloud computing has five qualities:

- Cloud computing is an on-demand self-service allowing the customers to unilaterally access the desired service whenever required.
- Cloud service capabilities are available through broad and ubiquitous network access (virtual web platform) by way of different devices (laptops, smartphones etc.).
- Cloud computing enables resource pooling (also called multi-tenancy), i.e., services are offered to multiple parties at the same time in a flexible way.
- Resource pooling forms the bases for the rapid elasticity of the service provision and the mass customization of computing power on the demand and the supply side.
- Cloud computing enables measured service provision leading to transparency on the provider and the customer side.

Rolf H. Weber & Dominic Nicolaj Staiger, "*Cloud Computing: A Cluster of Complex Liability Issues,*" 20(1) EUROPEAN JOURNAL OF CURRENT LEGAL ISSUES (2014).

(A) CLOUD COMPUTING SERVICE MODELS

The service provider makes it clear it keeps all proprietary rights and the customer does not own the software or the media on which it is inscribed. Subscription based licenses frequently incorporate services (24/7 telephone support, installation, or maintenance) in addition to the licensing of software. The foremost cloud-based storage products are DropBox, Google Drive, and Apple iCloud. In cloud computing agreements, the following terms are often significant:

- Technical Specifications.
- Warranties and Service Levels.
- Ownership and Protection of Data.
- Data Conversion and Transition.
- Indemnity and Limitation on Liability.

Don't SaaS Me: Key Areas of Negotiation in Software as a Service Agreements, FLORIDA BUSINESS REVIEW (Mar. 4, 2019).

Companies increasingly outsource their IT operations to cloud computing providers as opposed to installing software on their computer systems. Cloud-based providers give companies access to a network of remote servers that are hosted on the Internet. The businesses can use these to store, manage and process data, rather than doing this on their local server. Najiyya Budaly, *Financial Firms Warned To Watch Risks of Cloud Services*, LAW360 (Dec. 18, 2020).

(B) EDGE COMPUTING

"Edge computing refers to datasets, applications and servers that exist beyond the standard, centralized access points of an enterprise network."

CCSI, *What Is Edge Computing?* (2019). "By 2029, generative AI is projected to be part of 60% of all edge computing deployments, a sharp increase from just 5% in 2023." Vitaly Kurduban, Principal Product Manager, Digi International. *Edge Computing Trends in Industrial and Enterprise Applications* (Mar. 30, 2026).

The platform comprises a mesh framework that facilitates local—typically disk-based—storage of mission-critical data while keeping recently received data within a central storage repository for quick access. Unlike Cloud Computing, which depends on data centers and communication bandwidth to process and analyze data, Edge Computing keeps processing and analysis near the edge of a network, where the data was initially collected. Charles McLellan, *Edge Computing: The State of the Next IT Transformation*, ZDNET.COM (Oct. 1, 2018).

Edge Computing truncates the distance between devices and cloud resources:

> In practical terms, this means distributing new resources and software stacks along the path between today's centralized data centers and the increasingly large number of devices in the field, concentrated, in particular, but not exclusively, in close proximity to the last mile network, on both the infrastructure and device sides.
>
> The benefits of Edge Computing are:
>
> By solving the proximity problem, you solve the latency problem. The on-device processing approach ensures that only non-critical data is

> sent over the network and that critical data can be acted upon immediately. That is important for latency-sensitive applications, such as autonomous vehicles, where having to wait milliseconds may be untenable. . .
>
> Outage reduction and intermittent connectivity are also improved with edge computing because it doesn't solely rely on the cloud for processing. This can aid in avoiding server downtime, ensuring reliable operations in remote locations and avoiding unplanned downtime.

Eric Hamilton, *What is Edge Computing? The Network Edge Explained*, CLOUDWARDS (Dec. 27, 2018).

§ 4-4. Electronic Signatures & Records

(A) STATE DIGITAL SIGNATURES & RECORDS

A digital signature is an electronic identifier created by computer with the same legal validity as a handwritten signature. The Uniform Electronic Transactions Act (UETA) is a model state law act proposed by the National Conference of Commissioners on Uniform State Laws (NCCUSL) to create more uniformity in state law for electronic transactions.

Forty-seven U.S. states have enacted the Uniform Electronic Transactions Act (UETA), which has functionally equivalent provisions. New York, Illinois, and Washington, the only states not to have adopted UETA have functionally similar laws recognizing the validity of electronic signatures.

To constitute a valid electronic signature under the Uniform Electronic Transactions Act, there must be a showing that the signer intended to do a legally significant act. To constitute an electronic signature, however, the "electronic sound, symbol, or process . . . associated with a record" must be executed or adopted by a person with the intent to sign the record.

The UETA accepts a non-regulatory approach to electronic signatures and writings and validates electronic signatures and records in order to remove barriers to electronic commerce. E-SIGN's central provision is:

> With respect to any contract, agreement, or record entered into or provided in, or affecting, interstate or foreign commerce, notwithstanding any statute, regulation, or other rule of law, the legal effect, validity, or enforceability of such contract, agreement, or record shall not be denied—(1) on the ground that the contract, agreement, or record is not in writing if the contract, agreement, or record is an electronic record; or (2) on the ground that the contract, agreement, or record is not signed or is not affirmed by a signature if the contract, agreement, or record is signed or affirmed by an electronic signature.

15 U.S.C. § 7001(a)(1).

The UETA has been enacted in forty-seven of the fifty states and the District of Columbia, as well as by the territories of Puerto Rico and the Virgin Islands. What this means is that an e-signature or e-record has the same validity as a paper and pen signature or writing. A document bearing an electronic signature may be contested on the ground that an alleged signatory did not execute, adopt, or authorize the electronic signature.

UETA applies to electronic records and electronic signatures relating to a transaction. UETA § 3. The scope of UETA is "inherently limited by the fact that it only applies to transactions related to business, commercial (including consumer) and governmental matters." UETA § 3, cmt. 1.

> For example, when a person orders goods or services through a vendor's website, the person will be required to provide information as part of a process, which will result in receipt of the goods or services. When the customer ultimately gets to the last step and clicks 'I agree,' the person has adopted the process and has done so with the intent to associate the person with the record of that process.
>
> The actual effect of the electronic signature will be determined from all the surrounding circumstances; however, the person adopted a process which the circumstances indicate s/he intended to have the effect of getting the goods/services and being bound to pay for them. The adoption of the process carried the intent to do a

legally significant act, the hallmark of a signature.

UETA § 2, cmt. 7.

Section 8(a) of UETA provides the rules for what constitutes an electronic record. UETA § 8(a). Electronic records must minimally be "capable of retention." UETA § 8(a). An online communication that prevents the recipient from either printing or storing the record does not qualify as a retained record.

An "attribution procedure" is a method used to identify the person who sent an electronic message or to verify the integrity of its content. In general, an attribution procedure has a substantive effect only if it was agreed to or adopted by the parties or established by applicable law.

The parties must agree to contract electronically in order for digital signatures to be binding. Section 5 of UETA notes that the model act "does not require a record or signature to be created, generated, sent, communicated, received, stored, or otherwise processed or used by electronic means or in electronic form." UETA § 5(a).

UETA applies where the parties decide to enter into contracts electronically. UETA "does not require a record or signature to be created, generated, sent, communicated, received, stored, or otherwise processed or used by electronic means or in electronic form."

UETA states, "A record or signature may not be denied legal effect or enforceability solely because it is in electronic form." Section 8 of UETA requires that electronic record be capable of retention or enforcement will be denied.

"If a sender inhibits the ability of a recipient to store or print an electronic record," it is not enforceable against the recipient. Section 9 sets forth the rules of attribution and the effect of electronic records and signature.

For electronic contracts to be feasible, there must be some mechanism of attribution enabling the parties to learn each other's identity and whether they have authority to contract. For example, passwords are a well-established attribution method. A Westlaw or TWEN user supplies a password authenticating the user's identity for each login.

The attribution of messages between sender and receiver is a fundamental feature of the infrastructure of online contracting. Attribution procedures also verify whether a message contains errors or alterations using algorithms or other codes, identifying words or numbers. UETA Section 9 states;

> (a) an electronic record or electronic signature is attributable to a person if it was the act of the person. The act of the person may be shown in any manner, including a showing of the efficacy of any security procedure applied to determine the person to which the electronic record or electronic signature was attributable.

> (b) The effect of an electronic record or electronic signature attributed to a person under subsection (a) is determined from the context and surrounding circumstances at the time of its creation, execution, or adoption, including the parties' agreement, if any, and otherwise as provided by law.

UETA § 9.

UETA's method for apportioning the risk of errors in electronic records places the risk of loss of a transmission error on the party failing to employ an agreed upon security procedure. Thus, if both parties fail to use an agreed upon security procedure, the rule does not apply.

The party following reasonable security procedures will avoid the effect of the changed or erroneous electronic record only if the other party deviates upon the agreed upon procedure. Persons entering into electronic contracts must be able to avoid and correct errors. UETA § 10 states the rules for change or error. UETA Section 11 allows notaries to perform their acts through electronic signatures:

> If a law requires a signature or record to be notarized, acknowledged, verified, or made under oath, the requirement is satisfied if the electronic signature of the person authorized to perform those acts, together with all other information required to be included by other applicable law, is attached to or logically associated with the signature or record.

UETA § 11.

Section 12 deals with the serviceability of electronic records as retained records and originals. UETA Section 12 provides:

> So long as there exists reliable assurance that the electronic record accurately reproduces the information, this section continues the theme of establishing the functional equivalence of electronic and paper-based records. This section assures that information stored electronically will remain effective for all audit, evidentiary, archival and similar purposes.

UETA § 12.

UETA Section 13 treats electronic evidence the same as evidence in other forms making it broadly admissible. UETA § 13. Section 14 of UETA validates the enforceability of machine-to-machine transactions where there are no human agents. Section 14 provides default rules:

> regarding when and from where an electronic record is sent and when and where an electronic record is received. This section does not address the efficacy of the record that is sent or received.

UETA § 14.

That is, whether a record is unintelligible or unusable by a recipient is a separate issue from whether that record was sent or received. "The effectiveness of an illegible record, whether it binds any party, are questions left to other law." UETA § 15.

Section 16 of UETA recognizes the concept of the "acquisition of 'control' over an electronic record serves as a substitute for 'possession' in the paper analog." Section 16(c) then sets forth a safe harbor list of stringent requirements for such a system. See UETA § 16.

UETA Section 17 gives government agencies the discretion to set rules on electronic records, whereas Section 18 provides that government agencies determine rules for accepting and controlling electronic records. See UETA §§ 17, 18.

Section 19 calls for agencies to approve rules facilitating interoperability. Comment 1 to UETA § 19 states that Sections 17 to 19 are broad optional provisions. UETA § 19, cmt. 1. Section 20 is a standard severability clause while Section 21 is the effective date for UETA. See UETA §§ 20, 21.

As of April 6, 2021, UETA was mentioned in one hundred and forty-two court decisions. UETA is most influential and widely cited state law for electronic signatures and records.

(B) FEDERAL DIGITAL SIGNATURE LAW

The Electronic Signature in Global and National Commerce Act of 2000 (E-SIGN), 15 U.S.C. § 7001 et seq. is a federal statute that made electronic contracts and electronic signatures (E-Signatures) legally binding.

E-SIGN carves out nine statutory exceptions outside its sphere: (1) wills, codicils, and testamentary trusts; (2) laws governing domestic law matters; (3) state Uniform Commercial Code, except Sections 1–107 and 1–206, Articles 2 and 2A; (4) court orders or notices; (5) utility cancellation notices; (6) default, foreclosure, or eviction notices; (7) health or life insurance benefit cancellation notices; (8) product recall notices; and (9) hazardous, toxic, or dangerous materials notices. E-SIGN § 103.

Together, UETA and E-SIGN recognize technologies for e-signatures that presently take the following forms:

> *Password or personal identification number (PIN)*—a set of characters, numbers, or combination thereof, created by the system user and encrypted when transmitted over an open network;
>
> *Smart Card*—a plastic card (like an ATM or credit card) containing a microprocessor or 'chip' that can generate, store, and process data and that has programming capacity for activation when the user enters another identifier such as a PIN;
>
> *Biometrics*—technological method that measures and analyzes unique human characteristics, such as fingerprints, eye retinas and irises, voice and facial patterns, and hand measurements. The devices consist of a reader or sensor, and software that convert the received information into a digital form, and a database that stores the individual's known biometric data;

> *Digitized Signature*—a type of biometric, consisting of a graphical image of a handwritten signature, entered using a special digitized pen and pad input device that is automatically compared with a stored copy of the digitized signature of the user and authenticated if the two signatures meet specifications for similarity; and
>
> *Digital Signature*—a unique signature produced on a message that uses a key (a large, binary number) known only by the signer, and a signature algorithm (mathematical formula) that is publicly known.

Kathy D. Smith, Chief Counsel & Milton Brown, Deputy General Counsel, *ELECTRONIC SIGNATURES: A Review of the Exceptions to the Electronic Signatures in Global and National Commerce Act* (June 2003) at 6.

§ 4-5. Cross-Border Contracts

The Internet is increasingly a cross-border legal environment because more and more online contracts are being created online:

> The Internet is becoming a key platform for commerce that is increasingly happening between buyers and sellers located in different countries, thereby driving international trade. Additionally, as the Internet enables cross-border data flows this is also underpinning global economic integration and international trade.

> For instance, cross-border data flows are now intrinsic to commerce, from Internet-based communications like email and platforms such as eBay and Facebook that bring buyers and sellers together, from the financial transaction to purchase the product in other countries to the downloading of the goods and services.

Joshua Meltzer, *The Internet, Cross-Border Data Flows and International Trade* (Brookings Institution 2013) at 1 (Executive Summary).

Contract law in cyberspace must consider radically different social, economic, and legal systems. Over the past century, movements to devise uniform rules for private international law have evolved rapidly. U.S. companies need to tailor their contracts for the cross-border Internet:

> 'Cross-border e-business' refers to international business activity, in which trading parties within different customs territories reach an agreement on a transaction, use an e-business platform to conduct payment and settlement procedures, then deliver goods through cross-border logistics to conclude the transaction.
>
> The cross-border e-business platform integrates various transaction links such as overseas promotion, transaction support, cross-border logistics, customs inspection taxes, remittance and payment, after-sales services, credit systems and dispute resolution. Because it features paperless, anonymous, borderless, cross-border and transnational legal-systems,

the main legal issues are characterized by their aggregation and multi-dimensional complexity.

Watson & Band Law Office, *Internet+ Legal Issues in Cross-Border Import E-Businesses* (Sept. 10, 2015).

This chapter has examined Internet-related contract issues. Chapter 5 will focus on consumer protection issues in contracts executed on the Internet.

CHAPTER 5
CONSUMER LAW IN CYBERSPACE

Consumers are defined as a natural person who seeks or acquires goods or services for personal, family, or household use. In the European Union, consumers are defined as any natural person acting for purposes outside their trade, business, craft, or profession.

Consumer Protection by federal agencies will often turn on which party in in control of the U.S. Presidency. In 2026, the Trump-Vought Consumer Financial Protection Bureau (CFPB) has moved to make it harder for people to seek help with financial problems when filing a complaint with the consumer agency.

Consumers who file a complaint with the Consumer Financial Protection Bureau (CFPB) are given a warning alerting them not to submit a credit reporting complaint to the consumer agency unless a dispute has already been formally filed with the credit reporting agency (CRA).

The Trump-CFPB makes it more difficult for people to file complaints, CONSUMERACTION (Feb. 9, 2026). This chapter focuses on protecting consumers from unfair, deceptive, and fraudulent business practices on the Internet.

Consumer protection on the Internet focuses on safeguarding users from fraud, identity theft, invasion of privacy, and unfair business practices.

Chapter 7 is an in depth examination of Internet privacy. The tort of fraud is covered in greater depth in Chapter 6.

This chapter is divided into eight parts. Section 5-1 examines Federal Trade Commission Enforcement, while Section 5-2 is a study of deceptive advertising on the Internet. Section 5-3 covers website disclosures, while Section 5-4 examines Internet antitrust.

Section 5-5 covers FTC actions against spammers and the CAN-SPAM act. Section 5-6 is a study of consumer rights lawsuits. Section 5-7 describes European Union consumer law and how it compares to U.S. law. Finally, Section 5-8 is a case study of COVID-19 frauds.

§ 5-1. Overview of FTC Enforcement

The primary federal agency enforcing Internet-related consumer issues is the Federal Trade Commission (FTC). The FTC, created by statute, is an independent agency of the United States Government, charged with enforcing Section 5(a) of the FTC Act.

Section 5 of the FTC Act prohibits "unfair or deceptive acts or practices in or affecting commerce." The prohibition applies to all persons engaged in commerce. In 1994, Congress amended the FTC Act to specify that an unfair act or practice is one that causes or is likely to cause substantial injury to consumers that is not reasonably avoidable and is not outweighed by countervailing benefits to consumers or competition.

In late 2025, the Federal Trade Commission sued Uber Technologies, Inc. and Uber USA LLC (collectively, "Uber") for alleged violations of Section 5 of the FTC Act and the Restore Online Shoppers' Confidence Act (ROSCA). The FTC complaint alleges that:

> Uber charges consumers for its subscription service, Uber One, through a negative option feature but has failed to provide a simple mechanism to stop recurring charges. The complaint also alleges Uber has charged consumers without their consent in violation of the FTC Act and ROSCA. Further, the complaint alleges Uber falsely claims that consumers can cancel Uber One at "any time" with no additional fees.

The FTC filed a lawsuit against Uber, alleging the rideshare and delivery company charged consumers for its Uber One subscription service without their consent, failed to deliver promised savings, and made it difficult for users to cancel the service despite its "cancel anytime" promises.

In 2025, the FTC filed an action against the operator of the Sendit anonymous messaging app. The FTC states that its complaint was for Sendit:

> unlawfully collecting personal data from children, misleading users by sending messages from fake "people," and tricking consumers into purchasing paid subscriptions by falsely

promising to reveal the senders of anonymous messages.

The Federal Trade Commission argues that it has ample authority to police unfair and deceptive trade practices on the Internet:

> The FTC has plenty of existing authority to bring enforcement actions against companies that are acting in a deceptive or unfair manner on the Internet. Since our first Internet case in 1994, the FTC has brought over 100 Internet-related cases involving over 300 defendants. The Commission has obtained injunctions stopping illegal schemes, collected over $20 million in redress for victims, and obtained orders freezing another $65 million in cases that are still in litigation. Most of these cases have involved the migration of traditional kinds of fraud to the Internet, such as business opportunity schemes, credit repair scams, pyramid schemes, and false claims for health-related products, to name a few.

Federal Trade Commission, *Internet Issues Facing Consumers/Citizens* (Mar. 14, 2000).

In early 2026, the FTC issued a policy statement announcing that the Commission will not bring an enforcement action under the Children's Online Privacy Protection Rule (COPPA Rule) against certain website and online service operators that collect, use, and disclose personal information for the sole purpose of determining a user's age via age verification technologies. The FTC describes its new policy rule as follows:

> The COPPA Rule requires operators of commercial websites or online services directed to children under 13, and operators with actual knowledge they are collecting personal information from a child, to provide notice of their information practices to parents and to obtain verifiable parental consent before collecting, using, or disclosing personal information collected from a child under 13. Since COPPA was enacted in 1998, there's been an explosion in the use of internet-connected technologies by children. To help parents navigate the challenges associated with their children's online activities, some states have started requiring some websites and online services to use age verification mechanisms to help determine the age of users. But as noted at the FTC's recent workshop on age verification technologies, some age verification technologies may require the collection of personal information from children, prompting questions about whether such activities could violate the COPPA Rule.

In December 2025, the FTC settled its case against Disney for $10 million. The FTC contended that Disney allowed personal data to be collected from children who viewed kid-directed videos on YouTube without notifying parents or obtaining their consent as required by the Children's Online Privacy Protection Rule (COPPA Rule).

On December 22, 2025, the FTC issued an order to reopen and set aside a 2024 final consent order involving Rytr LLC.

In January 2026, the FTC filed suit Facebook, alleging that the company is illegally maintaining its personal social networking monopoly through a years-long course of anticompetitive conduct. The FTC charged Facebook with acquiring Instagram, WhatsApp calculated to protect its monopoly.

In 2025, the FTC issued orders against seven companies that provide consumer-facing AI-powered chatbots seeking information on how these firms measure, test, and monitor potentially negative impacts of this technology on children and teens.

The FTC inquiry seeks to understand what steps, if any, companies have taken to evaluate the safety of their chatbots when acting as companions, to limit the products' use by and potential negative effects on children and teens, and to apprise users and parents of the risks associated with the products:

> Chatbots may use generative artificial intelligence technology to simulate human-like communication and interpersonal relationships with users. AI chatbots can effectively mimic human characteristics, emotions, and intentions, and generally are designed to communicate like a friend or confidant, which may prompt some users, especially children and teens, to trust and form relationships with chatbots.

> The FTC inquiry seeks to understand what steps, if any, companies have taken to evaluate the safety of their chatbots when acting as companions, to limit the products' use by and potential negative effects on children and teens, and to apprise users and parents of the risks associated with the products.

Federal Trade Commission, *FTC Launches Inquiry into AI Chatbots Acting as Companions Agency issues 6(b) Orders to Seven Companies That Operate Consumer-Facing AI Chatbots* (Sept. 11, 2025).

The FTC is issuing the orders using its 6(b) authority, which authorizes the Commission to conduct wide-ranging studies that do not have a specific law enforcement purpose. The recipients include:

- Alphabet, Inc.;
- Character Technologies, Inc.;
- Instagram, LLC;
- Meta Platforms, Inc.;
- OpenAI OpCo, LLC;
- Snap, Inc.; and
- X.AI Corp.

The FTC is interested in particular on the impact of these chatbots on children and what actions companies are taking to mitigate potential negative impacts, limit or restrict children's or teens' use of these platforms, or comply with the Children's Online Privacy Protection Act Rule.

As part of its inquiry, the FTC is seeking information about how the companies:

- Monetize user engagement;
- Process user inputs and generate outputs in response to user inquiries;
- Develop and approve characters;
- Measure, test, and monitor for negative impacts before and after deployment;
- Mitigate negative impacts, particularly to children;
- Employ disclosures, advertising, and other representations to inform users and parents about features, capabilities, the intended audience, potential negative impacts, and data collection and handling practices;
- Monitor and enforce compliance with Company rules and terms of services (e.g., community guidelines and age restrictions); and
- Use or share personal information obtained through users' conversations with the chatbots.

The FTC received 200 complaints mentioning ChatGPT between November 2022 and August 2025.

Several attributed delusions, paranoia, and spiritual crises to the chatbot:

> In recent months, there has been a growing number of documented incidents of so-called AI psychosis in which interactions with generative AI chatbots, like ChatGPT or Google Gemini, appear to induce or worsen a user's delusions or other mental health issues. Chatbots can sometimes be overly sycophantic, which often keeps users happy and engaged. In extreme cases, this can end up dangerously inflating a user's sense of grandeur or validating fantastical falsehoods. People who perceive ChatGPT as intelligent, or capable of perceiving reality and forming relationships with humans, may not understand that it is essentially a machine that predicts the next word in a sentence. So if ChatGPT tells a vulnerable person about a grand conspiracy or paints them as a hero, they may believe it.

Caroline Haskins, *People Who Say They're Experiencing AI Psychosis Beg the FTC for Help*, WIRED (Mar. 13, 2026).

The Federal Trade Commission (FTC) administers diverse laws applicable to cyberspace activities including *The Undertaking Spam, Spyware, and Fraud Enforcement With Enforcers Beyond Borders Act of 2006* (Safe Web). Safe Web amended Section 5's "unfair or deceptive acts or practices" to include "such acts or practices involving foreign commerce" causing reasonably foreseeable injury within the United States. Section 5 of the FTC Act prohibits, in part, "unfair . . . acts or practices in or affecting commerce." 15 U.S.C. § 45(a).

In late 2025, the FTC filed a Section 5 action against Amazon for its years-long effort to enroll consumers into its Prime program without their consent while knowingly making it difficult for consumers to cancel their subscriptions to Prime. The FTC stated that it was charging that:

> Amazon has knowingly duped millions of consumers into unknowingly enrolling in Amazon Prime. Specifically, Amazon used manipulative, coercive, or deceptive user-interface designs known as "dark patterns" to trick consumers into enrolling in automatically-renewing Prime subscriptions. Amazon also knowingly complicated the cancellation process for Prime subscribers who sought to end their membership. The primary purpose of its Prime cancellation process was not to enable subscribers to cancel, but to stop them. Amazon leadership slowed or rejected changes that would've made it easier for users to cancel Prime because those changes adversely affected Amazon's bottom line.

Chegg Inc., an American educational technology company that functions primarily as an online platform, provides digital services like homework help, textbook rentals, and AI-powered learning tools to students. The FTC described its settlement with Chegg as follows:

> In September 2025, the Federal Trade Commission announced that Chegg Inc. will be required to pay $7.5 million to settle FTC allegations that the education technology provider made it extremely difficult for consumers to cancel recurring subscriptions while also failing to honor consumers' cancellation requests.
>
> The FTC's Office of Technology is policing "model-as-a-service" companies in this post, develop and host models to make available to third parties via an end-user interface or an application programming interface (API):
>
> - For example, a company can train a large language model (LLM) and sell access to this model to businesses (online stores, hotels, banks, etc.) who apply it to customer service chatbots. . . .There's also a risk that a model-as-a-service company may, through its APIs, infer a range of business data from the companies using its models, such as their scale and precise growth trajectories.
>
> - Model-as-a-service companies that fail to abide by their privacy commitments to their users and customers, may be liable under the laws enforced by the FTC. This includes promises made by companies that they won't use customer data for secret purposes, such as to train or update their models—be it directly

or through workarounds. In its prior enforcement actions, the FTC has required businesses that unlawfully obtain consumer data to delete any products—including models and algorithms developed in whole or in part using that unlawfully obtained data. . . .

- Model-as-a-service companies must also abide by their commitments to customers regardless of how or where the commitment was made. This includes, for instance, commitments made through promotional materials, terms of service on the company's website, or online marketplaces. Failure to do so can expose a firm to enforcement action by the FTC. For example, the FTC has brought actions against companies that disclosed people's data for ad targeting despite assuring them in privacy policies or during the registration process that it would keep their data private. The FTC brought an action against a company that, among other things, claimed not to use its facial recognition technology on consumers' images unless consumers affirmatively chose to activate the feature—but omitted the fact that this was only true for consumers in some jurisdictions. . . .Misrepresentations, material omissions, and misuse of data associated with the training and deployment of AI models also pose potential risks to competition. . . .Model-as-a-service companies that appropriate the competitively significant information of business customers may also run afoul of the prohibition against unfair

> methods of competition. In short, the data practices of model-as-a-service companies can violate antitrust laws as well as consumer protection laws.

Artificial Intelligence (AI) companies are subject to FTC enforcement actions if they "deceive customers or users about how their data is collected—whether explicitly or implicitly, by inclusion or by omission—may be violating the law." Federal Trade Commission, *AI Companies: Uphold Your Privacy and Confidentiality Commitments* (Jan. 9, 2024).

§ 5-2. Deceptive Online Advertising

The FTC brings hundreds of cases every year involving fraud, scams, identity theft, false advertising, privacy violations, anti-competitive behavior and more. The Commission typically brings these cases in federal court or through their internal administrative process, called an adjudicative proceedings.

The Federal Trade Commission has conducted a large number of investigations and enforcement actions for Internet-related advertising.

In late 2025, the Commission sued Zillow and Redfin over an unlawful agreement:

> that eliminates Redfin as a competitor in the market for placing advertising of rental housing on internet listing services (ILSs)—the websites that millions of Americans use to find their next rental home. The complaint alleges that in February 2025, Zillow and Redfin entered into

> an illegal agreement to dismantle Redfin as a competitor in the ILS advertising market for multifamily rental properties.

In 2012, the Federal Trade Commission investigated www.seewinter.com, which was operated by the Clearwater Aquarium for violating the Children's Online Privacy Protection Act. In March of 2026, the Commission the FTC filed a complaint:

> alleging that Mercury Marketing, LLC, and other defendants impersonated substance use disorder treatment clinics in Google search ads to deceptively route consumers trying to call those clinics to defendant clinics.
>
> Federal Trade Commission, *Stipulated Order for Permanent Injunction, Civil Penalty Judgment, and Other Relief Against Behavioral Healthcare Group of America, LLC, JHEL Holdings, LLC, Malibu Detox, LLC, and Robby Stempler* (Mar. 2, 2026).

Advertisers must determine which claims might need qualification and what information should be provided in a disclosure. "If a disclosure provides information that contradicts a claim, the disclosure will not be sufficient to prevent the ad from being deceptive. In that situation, the claim itself must be modified."

Beginning in the mid-1990s, the FTC has investigated websites to ensure that they do not contain unfair or deceptive advertisements. For example, the Federal Trade Commission agreed to scrutinize whether Google's YouTube Kids application was unfair and deceptive. Consumer groups studied YouTube Kids video finding videos disturbing for young children and potentially harmful, including examples such as:

- Explicit sexual language presented amidst cartoon animation.
- A profanity-laced parody of the film Casino featuring Bert and Ernie from Sesame Street.
- Graphic adult discussions about family violence, pornography and child suicide.
- Jokes about pedophilia and drug use.
- Modeling of unsafe behaviors such as playing with lit matches.

In 1997, the Commission released a statement

In early 2026, the FTC shut down a deceptive charity fund raising schemes and its operators who made false or deceptive online claims to U.S. donors.

> Kars-R-Us.com, Inc. (Kars) and its operators, Michael Irwin and Lisa Frank, solicited charitable donations nationwide on behalf of United Breast Cancer Foundation, Inc. (UBCF), a charity that claims to assist individuals affected by breast cancer, according to a complaint filed by the FTC.

The FTC applies three basic principles to determining if advertisements are deceptive: (1) whether they are truthful and not misleading; (2) whether advertisers have evidence to back up their claims (substantiation); and (3) whether the advertisements are unfair. To comply with the FTC.com disclosures, online advertisers, must identify:

> all express and implied claims that the ad conveys to consumers. When identifying claims, advertisers should not focus only on individual phrases or statements, but should consider the ad as a whole, including the text, product name, and depictions. If an ad makes express or implied claims that are likely to be misleading without certain qualifying information, the information must be disclosed.

Federal Trade Commission, *.com Disclosures: How to Make Effective Disclosures in Digital Advertising* (March 2013).

In late 2025, the FTC entered into a consent order with Rytr over deceptive AI-generated reviews:

> According to the FTC's complaint, Rytr's service generated detailed reviews that contained specific, often material details that had no relation to the user's input, and these reviews almost certainly would be false for the users who copied them and published them online. In many cases, subscribers' AI-generated reviews featured information that would deceive potential consumers who were using the reviews to make purchasing decisions. The complaint further alleges that at least some of Rytr's subscribers used the service to produce hundreds, and in some cases tens of thousands,

of reviews potentially containing false information.

The proposed order settling the Commission's complaint is designed to prevent Rytr from engaging in similar illegal conduct in the future. It would bar the company from advertising, promoting, marketing, or selling any service dedicated to—or promoted as—generating consumer reviews or testimonials.

In March of 2026, the FTC filed a complaint alleging that Mercury Marketing, LLC, and other defendants impersonated substance use disorder treatment clinics in Google search ads to deceptively route consumers trying to call those clinics to defendant clinics.

§ 5-3. Website Disclosures

The Federal Trade Commission requires online advertisers "to ensure that consumers receive material information about the terms of a transaction . . . [and they] must be clear and conspicuous."

Federal Trade Commission, *.com Disclosures: How to Make Effective Disclosures in Digital Advertising* (March 2013) at 1.

The FTC's emphasis on the location of the disclosure as well as its proximity to the underlying claim also applies to online advertisements. The FTC gives the following guidelines when websites use hyperlinks for disclosures:

- Make the link obvious.
- Label the hyperlink appropriately to convey the importance, nature, and relevance of the information it leads to.
- Use hyperlink styles consistently, so consumers know when a link is available.
- Place the hyperlink as close as possible to the relevant information it qualifies and make it noticeable.
- Take consumers directly to the disclosure on the click-through page.
- Assess the effectiveness of the hyperlink by monitoring click-through rates and other information about consumer use and make changes accordingly.

The FTC guideposts include illustrations where paid bloggers failed to disclose material connections for endorsed products or services. Both Internet advertisers and bloggers are subject to liability for misleading or unsubstantiated statements made in social media or website endorsements. The FTC used the example of a blogger promoting a skin care product:

> If an advertiser requests that a blogger try a new body lotion and writes a review of the product on her blog, she has an affirmative duty to disclose

> any financial remuneration or connection that may have influenced her endorsement.

> In late 2018, the FTC entered into a settlement with four companies that allegedly withheld money from consumers trying to start online businesses from home, and banned [the companies] from selling purported business coaching or development services under court-approved settlements with the Federal Trade Commission.

Federal Trade Commission, *Owners of Business Coaching and Development Service Scam Are Banned* (Oct. 29, 2018).

The FTC complaint against the Business Coaching defendants stated:

> The scheme took $8.4 million from consumers interested in starting an online business. The defendants bought the contact information of these consumers and then tried to sell them a series of business coaching and related services, each of which cost thousands of dollars. . . In one call, a salesman touting a program that cost $10,000 claimed it was 'almost impossible' to make less than $3,000 to $5,000 a month using defendants' foolproof methods: '[W]e don't have any students we've built the business for that have ever failed. There's just—there's literally no way to fail.'

The other FTC settlement imposes a $6.75 million judgment on the owners of the Internet coaching business.

§ 5-4. Antitrust Actions

Google is the world's largest search engine, with an index somewhere between 500 billion and 600 billion web pages. "Now, as regulators around the world examine ways to curb Google's power." *Google Dominates Thanks to an Unrivaled View of the Web*, N.Y. TIMES (Dec. 16, 2020). In December 2020, the State of Utah joined 10 states in a multistate lawsuit against Google, which asserted violations of Federal and State Antitrust Laws, including:

> Anticompetitive conduct, exclusionary practices, and deceptive misrepresentations in connection with its role in the multibillion-dollar online display advertising industry.
>
> Google's monopolization of online display advertising includes an anticompetitive agreement with Facebook, misrepresenting customers, suppressing competition and harming consumers in violation of antitrust and consumer protection laws.

AG Schmitt Joins Multistate Lawsuit Against Google for Anticompetitive Practices and Deceptive Misrepresentations in Online Display Advertising, STATES NEWS SERVICE (Dec. 16, 2020).

A number of large Internet companies face antitrust actions and regulatory actions by the European Union:

> The EU wants to be able to force the separation of companies' businesses, separating—for example—the WhatsApp and Instagram

> services from Facebook (NASDAQ:FB)—if they are fined under the new laws three times within five years, according to the Financial Times. The fines foreseen are up to 10% of global revenue, in line with broader EU antitrust policy.

Geoffrey Smith, *EU Aims at Big Tech,* SYNDIGATE (Dec. 15, 2020).

The FTC filed suit against Facebook, contending that the social media giant:

> is illegally maintaining its personal social networking monopoly through a years-long course of anticompetitive conduct. The complaint alleges that Facebook has engaged in a systematic strategy—including its 2012 acquisition of up-and-coming rival Instagram, its 2014 acquisition of the mobile messaging app WhatsApp, and the imposition of anticompetitive conditions on software developers—to eliminate threats to its monopoly.

Federal Trade Commission v. Facebook, Inc., No. 191 0134 (D.D.C. Dec. 9, 2020).

The FTC's action against Facebook was in cooperation with a coalition of attorneys general of forty-six states and the District of Columbia as well as Guam:

> the complaint alleges that Facebook has engaged in a systematic strategy—including its 2012 acquisition of up-and-coming rival Instagram, its 2014 acquisition of the mobile

> messaging app WhatsApp, and the imposition of anticompetitive conditions on software developers—to eliminate threats to its monopoly. This course of conduct harms competition leaves consumers with few choices for personal social networking, and deprives advertisers of the benefits of competition.

The FTC sought a permanent injunction in federal court that could, among other things: require divestitures of assets, including Instagram and WhatsApp; prohibit Facebook from imposing anticompetitive conditions on software developers; and require Facebook to seek prior notice and approval for future mergers and acquisitions.

The FTC recognized that a remedy could include breaking up Facebook:

> If we prevail in showing that Facebook has broken the law, we will ask the court to provide full and adequate relief to restore competition. We currently expect that that will include divestiture of Instagram and WhatsApp. (For context, divestiture is the standard remedy in our merger cases.) But it's too early to say definitively what would be necessary and appropriate to restore competition here.

Federal Trade Commission, *The FTC's Facebook Suit: Questions and Answers* (Dec. 9, 2020).

§ 5-5. FTC Actions Against Spammers

Congress enacted the Controlling the Assault of Non-Solicited Pornography and Marketing Act of

2003 (CAN-SPAM), 15 U.S.C. §§ 7701–7713. CAN-SPAM, which prohibits fraudulent, abusive and deceptive commercial e-mail. The CAN-SPAM Act requires the Commission to issue regulations "defining the relevant criteria to facilitate the determination of the primary purpose of an electronic mail message."

The CAN-SPAM Act applies almost exclusively to "commercial electronic mail messages." The federal anti-spam statute provides for enforcement of the Act by the FTC as well as by Internet service providers (ISPs). CAN-SPAM requires the commercial e-mailer to include a functioning return e-mail address and a method for opting out of future messages.

To state a claim under the CAN-SPAM Act, the government or a service provider must allege that the spammer sent an e-mail containing "materially false or materially misleading" header information. CAN-SPAM defines false or materially misleading headers to include a false and fraudulent electronic mail address, domain name, or Internet Protocol address.

For text messages, CAN-SPAM needs consumers to give "prior express authorization" prior to transmittal. Commercial messages must identify the company and include an opt-out mechanism functioning for at least 30 days.

If the consumer elects to unsubscribe from receiving more messages, the company must stop sending any other promotional messages within 10 days. CAN-SPAM does not authorize private lawsuits by aggrieved consumers.

CAN-SPAM provides standing for governmental entities such as the FTC or providers of "internet access services" if they are adversely affected by a violation of the Act. CAN-SPAM has defined Internet access services as:

> a service that enables users to access content, information, electronic mail, or other services offered over the Internet, and may also include access to proprietary content, information, and other services as part of a package of services offered to consumers.

15 U.S.C. § 7701(a)(11).

The Federal Trade Commission's CAN-SPAM rule specify further obligations. For example, commercial emails with sexual content must be conspicuously labeled:

> (a) Any person who initiates, to a protected computer, the transmission of a commercial electronic mail message that includes sexually oriented material must:
>
> (1) Exclude sexually oriented materials from the subject heading for the electronic mail message and include in the subject heading the phrase 'SEXUALLY-EXPLICIT:' in capital letters as the first nineteen (19) characters at the beginning of the subject line.
>
> The phrase 'SEXUALLY-EXPLICIT' comprises 17 characters, including the dash between the two words. The colon (:) and the space following the phrase are the 18th and 19th characters.

Federal Trade Commission, CAN-SPAM Rule, 16 CFR § 316.4 (current as of Feb. 26, 2021).

The FTC's CAN-SPAM Rule also prohibits commercial emailers from charging an opt-out fee:

> Neither a sender nor any person acting on behalf of a sender may require that any recipient pay any fee, provide any information other than the recipient's electronic mail address and opt-out preferences, or take any other steps except sending a reply electronic mail message or visiting a single Internet Web page, in order to: (a) Use a return electronic mail address or other Internet-based mechanism, required by 15 U.S.C. 7704(a)(3), to submit a request not to receive future commercial electronic mail messages from a sender; or (b) Have such a request honored as required by 15 U.S.C. 7704(a)(3)(B) and (a)(4).

(A) EMBLEMATIC CAN-SPAM AWARDS

In *ZooBuh, Inc. v. Savicom, Inc.*, 2019 WL 1099024 (D. Utah Mar. 8, 2019), ZooBuh sought statutory damages and treble damages against DG International for violating CAN-SPAM. DG International (DGI), a St. Kitts company, contracted with a Delaware company to send emails to persons on DGI's customer lists.

The customer list contained email addresses for persons who had supposedly registered for the dating website xdating.com.

> DGI used Mindshare to send email advertisements to the email addresses associated with the xdating.com customer list.
>
> ZooBuh alleges that it and its customers have received thousands of email advertisements for xdating.com. All of these emails arrived on ZooBuh's email servers, which are located in Utah. The emails contain links to a registration page for xdating.com.
>
> Many of the emails contain misleading information: they purport to identify people registered on xdating.com, but in reality the people identified in the emails do not exist and are not users of xdating.com.
>
> Rather, the emails are sent from 'virtual cupids' that are fake users created by DGI LLC and/or DG International who communicate with users in the same way actual users would.

The court characterized ZooBuh's CAN-SPAM complaint in the following passage:

> ZooBuh alleges that all of the emails at issue violate at least one or more provisions of CAN-SPAM. ZooBuh alleges that it has suffered harms to its business, including financial harm, lost time, and server crashes. ZooBuh regularly receives customer complaints concerning spam email, and some customers have stopped using ZooBuh because of the spam emails.

ZooBuh pointed to the following violations by DGI:

ZooBuh alleges that DG International initiated at least 24,024 emails promoting DGI LLC and/or DG International all of which contained false sender names purporting to be actual women. For example, ZooBuh provides an email that in the sender line contains the name 'Cassidy Fox,' and the email address 'XDmembers@reply.m100.net.' ECF No. 33–1 at 94. But Cassidy Fox is not a real person. Because the email identifies a false sender, the header information is materially false or misleading in accordance with 15 U.S.C. § 7704(a)(1)(B). ZooBuh is entitled to judgment on the 24,024 emails identifying a false sender. ZooBuh also claims that 60,000 emails contained false sender domains purporting to be online users such as 'Addict2Bang,' 'BANGmeHARD,' and 'iBendover4U.'

But usernames are not domain names. The domain name is part of the email address. For example, 'xdating.com' and 'dgmailservice.com' are domain names. 'Addict2Bang' and 'BANGmeHARD' and other such usernames are not domain names. . . . Thus, ZooBuh is not entitled to judgment under the act on these 60,000 emails. ZooBuh is only entitled to judgment for 24,024 violations of 15 U.S.C. § 7704(a)(1).

§ 5-6. Consumer Rights Lawsuits

In recent years, consumers have prevailed in a number of class action lawsuits arising out of unfair and deceptive Internet practices. In 2016 alone, "the U.S. Judicial Panel on Multidistrict Litigation (JPML) centralized 20 class action lawsuits accusing Vizio Inc. of secretly installing tracking software in its Smart TVs to find out what users were watching."

Anne Bucher, *Vizio Smart TV Data Privacy Class Actions Grouped in California,* TOP CLASS ACTIONS (April 14, 2016).

> Vizio, the largest manufacturer of 'smart' televisions, agreed to pay $2.2 million to settle charges by the Federal Trade Commission and the Office of the New Jersey Attorney General that it installed software on its TVs to collect viewing data on 11 million consumer TVs without consumers' knowledge or consent.

Federal Trade Commission, *Vizio to Pay $2.2 Million to FTC, State of New Jersey* (Feb. 6, 2017).

In December 2018, the New York Attorney General announced that Charter agreed to a $72 Million Consumer Payout by an Internet Service Provider in U.S. History. New York consumers will receive $62.5 Million in direct refunds as well as over $100 million in premium channels and streaming services.

In *In re Apple Inc. Device Performance Litigation,* 2018 WL 4772311 (N.D. Cal. Oct 1, 2018), plaintiffs filed a class action against Apple claiming that, in an effort to fix battery life issues, "it included code in updates to its mobile operating system (iOS) that significantly reduced the performance of certain models of the iPhone."

The complaint arose out of Apple's misleading "response to software capability and battery capacity issues in certain older-model iPhones and iPads." "Plaintiffs alleged that Apple's conduct violated federal and state computer-intrusion laws, as well as state consumer-protection laws and common law."

In early 2018, the Judicial Panel combined all cases in multidistrict litigation (MDL). The plaintiff's consumer law causes of action were based upon the claim that Apple made misrepresentations or concealed information about the characteristics of Plaintiffs' iPhones and the nature of the iOS updates.

The court stated that the plaintiff's consumer protection claims "centrally focus on allegations that Apple made misrepresentations or concealed information about the characteristics of Plaintiffs' iPhones and the nature of the iOS updates."

However, the court found the consumers did not sufficiently state a claim for violation of California Computer Data Access and Fraud Act (CDAFA). The consumers' first theory of liability under the CLRA, "the 'fraudulent' prong of the UCL, and the FAL is that Apple affirmatively misrepresented the characteristics of Plaintiffs' devices."

The court ultimately characterized the consumers' claim as being "relatively skimpy and unfocused." The court found "Apple's broad statements about improving features and product superiority" as insufficient to constitute affirmative misrepresentation. The court dismissed all of the claims against Apple arising out of its iPhones and its updates.

§ 5-7. Global Consumer Law

(A) UNFAIR CONTRACT TERMS DIRECTIVE

The Unfair Contract Terms Directive of 1993 (UCTD) is a European Union directive applicable to all consumer transactions. The UCTD applies only to non-negotiated, consumer software licenses. It does not apply to business-to-business license agreements. The European legislature defines a consumer as a natural person who "is acting for purposes which are outside his trade, business or profession." Council Directive 93/13/EEC at art. 2.

The language of the UCTD mandates courts apply a two-part test to determine whether a given contractual provision is unfair under the general test. First, there must be a significant imbalance to the detriment of the consumer, and the imbalance should be "contrary to good faith."

This language in UCTD Article 3 addresses newly emergent electronic contracting terms not found in the annex. In effect, the UCTD gives all European consumers a fundamental right to read, review, and understand standard terms before committing to a contract.

In addition to the UCTD's general requirement of "good faith" and "balance," the UCTD's Annex lists specific terms that may be judged unfair. These suspect terms include:

- Terms which exclude/limit a trader's liability if a consumer dies or is injured because of an act/omission by that trader.
- Terms which inappropriately exclude/limit consumers' rights to compensation if the trader doesn't keep to his side of the contract.
- Terms which bind the consumer but allow traders to get out of providing a service just because it doesn't suit them.
- Terms which allow a trader to keep pre-payments if the consumer cancels the contract without allowing for equivalent compensation to the consumer where the trader cancels.
- Terms which allow the trader to alter a contract unilaterally, unless the contract states a valid reason for doing so.
- Terms which restrict how and where consumers can take legal action and obliging them to provide proof which is the responsibility of the other party to the contract.

European Union, *Unfair Contract Terms: What the Directive Does* (2019).

Article 7 of the UCTD requires:

Member States . . . [to take] the necessary measures to ensure that the consumer does not lose the protection granted by the Directive by virtue of the choice of the law of a non-Member country.

The UCTD invalidates choice of forum clauses where EU consumers are required to litigate disputes in Washington. The UCTD would also invalidate Amazon's choice of forum clauses to litigate disputes arising out of their service in Seattle, Washington.

The EU Commission views the UCTD as the chief tool to achieving a fair result and preventing unfair surprise and oppression. The UCTD's purpose is to free EU consumers from distortions of competition that impede cross-border contracts making browsewrap and many clickwrap agreements unenforceable, as their provisions include clauses that are in favor of the stronger party.

(B) EU ENFORCEMENT OF U.S. CONTRACTS

The United Kingdom's National Consumer Council (NCC) surveyed twenty-five U.S. software license agreements, concluding that typical end user license agreements (EULAs) "mislead consumers and remove legal rights." The NCC charges 17 firms, including Microsoft, Adobe and Symantec, of using unfair "end user license agreements."

Computer Software Terms 'Unfair', BBC NEWS (Feb. 19, 2008).

The consumer group recommends an investigation by the Office of Fair Trading due to the failure of software companies to provide up-front information on key provisions and "pay now, terms later" licenses.

European courts may reject insufficiently precise contract terms in consumer contracts even if they are not substantively unfair.

In 2019, the European Commission began the process of modernizing the UCTD so it will be harmonized with other directives that had recently been updated. The proposed changes in EU consumer protection law provide for:

- Enhanced harmonisation and streamlining of some of the criteria to be used to determine the level of penalties for infringements of EU consumer law.
- A right to individual remedies for consumers when they are harmed by unfair commercial practices, such as aggressive marketing, and provided that these remedies are proportionate, effective and do not affect the application of other remedies available to consumers under EU or national law.
- Enhanced transparency in online transactions, in particular regarding the use of online reviews, personalised pricing based on algorithms or higher ranking of products due to 'paid placements.'
- The obligation of online marketplaces to inform consumers on whether the responsible trader in a transaction is the seller and/or the online marketplace itself.
- The protection of consumers in respect of 'free' digital services, namely digital services for

which consumers do not pay money but provide personal data, such as: cloud storage, social media and email accounts.

- Clear information for consumers in case of price reduction.
- The removal of disproportionate burdens, such as the obligation to use outdated means of communication, imposed on businesses by existing legislation.
- Clarifications regarding member states' freedom to adopt rules to protect the legitimate interests of consumers with regard to some particularly aggressive or misleading marketing or selling practices in the context of off-premises sales.
- Clarifications regarding the way misleading marketing of 'dual quality' products should be dealt with by member states.

European Commission, *EU to Modernise Law on Consumer Protection* (Mar. 29, 2019).

U.S. companies are subject to EU enforcement actions if targeting EU consumers with sales or services. The EU's Unfair Contract Terms Directive would overturn many contractual clauses routinely upheld by U.S. courts. Standard U.S. contract terms including warranty disclaimers, liability limitations, anti-class action, and employer's choice of law and forum clauses. Are not enforceable in EU consumer contracts. Unlike the U.S., Europe has mandatory consumer rules that cannot be modified by contract.

(C) THE DSA AND THE DMA

The European Union protects online consumers through comprehensive legislation like the Digital Services Act (DSA) and the Digital Markets Act (DMA), ensuring a safer, transparent, and fair digital environment. The DSA is part of the Digital Services Act package which aims, together with the Digital Markets Act, to:

- Ensure digital users have access to safe products and protect users' fundamental rights.
- Allow free and fair competition in the digital sectors to boost innovation and growth. Key protections include strict rules against scams, clear advertising disclosures, 14-day withdrawal rights for purchases, robust data privacy (GDPR), enhanced safety for minors, and the banning of manipulative "dark patterns."

(1) DSA Rules for Online Services

The DSA applies to all online intermediary companies that connect users with content, products and services in the EU single market, whether they are established inside or outside the Union. The Digital Services Act (DSA) introduces rules for online services used by European citizens in their everyday life.

These services include marketplaces, social media networks, app stores, and online travel and accommodation platforms. The DSA requires digital platforms to institute measures to better protect users and enhance transparency:

- Counter and quickly react to illegal content (fake news, propaganda, hate speech, harassment and child abuse), and allow users to flag such content.
- Combat the sale of illegal products and services.
- Use content moderation tools that include the option to contest decisions when users' content is removed or restricted.
- Increase transparency for users regarding terms and conditions and how algorithms recommend content.
- Ban advertising for children and the use of sensitive personal data to target ads (gender, sexual orientation, race, religion, or political beliefs).
- Ban 'dark patterns', i.e., misleading interfaces intentionally designed to trick users into, for instance, subscribing to services without noticing.

DSA rules vary dependent upon companies' size and impact on society. Very small platforms are exempt from most obligations. Stricter rules apply to very large online platforms (VLOPs) and search engines (VLOSEs) with more than 45 million active users, considering the key role they play in e-commerce, in disseminating information and in facilitating the exchange of opinions and ideas. The

European Commission identified 23 VLOPs and 2 VLOSEs:

> AliExpress, Amazon Store, AppStore, Bing Booking.com, Facebook, Google Play, Google Maps, Google Search, Google Shopping, Instagram, LinkedIn, Pinterest, Pornhub, Shein, Snapchat, Stripchat, Temu, TikTok, Wikipedia, X (previously known as Twitter), XNXX, XVideos, YouTube and Zalando.

The DSA imposes additional requirement on these companies:

- Establish mitigation plans, subject to audits, for the systemic risks they pose, such as disinformation, manipulation during electoral processes, cyber violence against women, or abuse of minors.
- Share data with researchers and authorities.
- Let users decide if they wish to receive personalised recommendations and, if so, how (e.g., not based on their online searches).

Companies that do not comply with the DSA do so at their peril:

- Companies that do not follow the DSA face penalties and fines proportionate to their size.
- Companies with less than 45 million active users may get penalties, including fines, as laid down in Member States' national laws.

- Companies with more than 45 million active users may get fines of up to 6% of their global turnover.

European Council, Council of the European Union, *Digital Services Act* (2026).

The European Union describes the Digital Services Act (DSA) and the Digital Markets Act (DMA) as follows:

> The main goal of the DSA is to create a digital space that respects citizens and consumers' fundamental rights. By establishing a clear set of rules across the EU, the DSA also enables smaller platforms, SMEs and start-ups to scale up in Europe, fostering innovation, growth and competitiveness. The DSA and the Digital Markets Act (DMA) complement each other. The DMA includes rules for gatekeeper online platforms. Gatekeepers function as bottlenecks between businesses and consumers for digital services, affecting competition and the functioning of the EU internal market. Some of these services are also covered in the DSA, but for different reasons and with different types of provisions. Find out more about how the DMA benefits you.

European Commission, *The Digital Services Act* (2026).

The EU Commission states the following benefits of the DSA for businesses:

- One single set of rules across the EU—The DSA replaces 27 different regulations with one unified framework, giving you legal certainty and the ability to scale up across the EU.
- A proportionate approach—The DSA's obligations are tailored to each online services' role, size and impact in the online ecosystem. Micro and small companies have lighter requirements based on their size, to keep them accountable while helping them scale up, while bigger platforms have more responsibilities and therefore, obligations.
- Simplified reporting of illegal content—You can use a user-friendly mechanism to flag illegal content and goods that infringe your rights, including intellectual property rights. Your company may also become 'trusted flaggers', whose notices of illegal content or goods gain priority in platforms' assessment.
- Better protection against unfair content moderation decisions—New appealing mechanisms through the platform or through out-of-court dispute settlement bodies allow you to protect your online presence in case you disagree with a content moderation decision by a platform.
- More transparency on marketplaces—New obligations for marketplaces, such as the

> requirement to list a seller's contact information, enhance transparency and trustworthiness in E-Commerce. For the same reason, the DSA requires marketplaces to make reasonable efforts to perform random checks on products sold on their service or adopt new technologies for product traceability.

All online business are subject to the DSA, but obligations depend upon the size of the company:

> The DSA follows a proportionate approach, which means that the obligations assigned to the different online players match their role, size and impact in the online ecosystem. Micro and small companies have lighter requirements based on their size, to keep them accountable while helping them scale up, while bigger platforms have more responsibilities and therefore, obligations.
>
> The DSA recognises that the biggest online platforms—those with over 45 million monthly users in the EU—play a significant role in our societies and democracies. They must therefore follow specific rules to ensure they do not pose unintentional risks to us, such as amplifying illegal content and shaping opinion at scale, and to minimise the possibility of malicious actors using them to inflict harm on Europe.

(2) Digital Markets Act Governing Gatekeepers

The Digital Markets Act (DMA) is an EU regulation, in force since November 2022 and largely active since May 2023, that forces major tech "gatekeepers" (e.g., Alphabet, Amazon, Apple, Meta, Microsoft, ByteDance) to ensure fairer, more contestable digital markets.

The DMA mandates interoperability, prohibits self-preferencing, and allows third-party app stores to prevent market abuse. Non-compliance can result in fines up to 20% of global turnover.

In particular, these large platforms must identify and analyze wide-spread risks. These risks include:

- The spreading of illegal content, as defined in national or EU laws.
- Threats to fundamental rights, such as freedom of expression.
- Threats to media freedom and pluralism, public security and electoral processes.
- Gender-based violence, public health, protection of minors and physical and mental well-being.
- Once these risks are identified, these larger platforms must put measures in place to reduce them. Similarly, these platforms must meet other requirements to enhance transparency and accountability. A full list of

these platforms is published on the Commission's website.

The DMA sets clear rules for big platforms, 'gatekeepers', providing so-called 'core platform services', to make sure that they do not abuse their position, for instance, by favoring their own products or preventing users from installing external applications.

To be considered a gatekeeper, a digital platform must:

- either have had an annual turnover within the European Union of at least €7.5 billion in the past three years or have a market valuation of at least €75 billion
- have at least 45 million monthly end users
- have at least 10 000 business users established in the EU
- control one or more core platform services in at least three member states

Due to their size, gatekeepers enjoy significant advantages over smaller competitors and have a dominant position in the digital market. Of the 10 000 digital platforms that exist in the EU, just a handful qualify as gatekeepers under the DMA, and most of those are based in the United States.

The European Commission has so far designated seven of them, providing 23 core platform services:

- Alphabet

- Amazon
- Apple
- Booking
- ByteDance
- Meta
- Microsoft

The DMA establishes the following rules for gatekeepers:

What gatekeepers are not allowed to do:

- They cannot rank their own products or services higher than those of other companies.
- They cannot prevent developers from using third-party payment platforms for app sales.
- They cannot process users' personal data for targeted advertising, unless consent has been granted.
- They cannot establish unfair conditions for business users.
- They cannot pre-install certain software applications or prevent users from easily un-installing them.
- They cannot restrict business users of platforms.

What gatekeepers will have to do:

- They must offer greater choice, such as the choice of certain software on a user's operating system.
- They need to ensure that unsubscribing from core platform services is as easy as subscribing.
- They have to provide information on the number of users that visit their platforms to determine whether the platform can be identified as a gatekeeper.
- They need to give business users access to their marketing or advertising performance data on the platform.
- They must inform the European Commission of any acquisitions and mergers.
- They have to ensure that the basic functionalities of instant messaging services are interoperable, i.e., users must be able to send messages, voice messages or files.

What happens if gatekeepers do not comply with the rules?

- When a large online company has been identified as a gatekeeper, it has to comply with the rules of the DMA within six months.
- If a gatekeeper violates the rules laid down in the DMA, it risks a fine of up to 10% of its total worldwide turnover. For a repeat offence, a

fine of up to 20% of its worldwide turnover may be imposed.

- If a gatekeeper systematically fails to comply with the DMA, i.e., it violates the rules at least three times in eight years, the European Commission can open a market investigation and, if necessary, impose behavioural or structural remedies.

The European Commission states the following Benefits of the Digital Markets Act (DMA):

- Fair competition of digital services is key to ensuring that companies and consumers can all benefit in the same way from digital opportunities.
- By establishing a set of rules for large online platforms, the DMA makes it easier for smaller companies and start-ups to enter the digital market, innovate and compete.
- By increasing choice, consumers also benefit from lower prices and higher-quality services.

The Council adopted the DMA on 18 July 2022, and it entered into force on 2 May 2023. The DMA is part of the EU's digital services package, which also includes the Digital Services Act (DSA).Both the DMA and the DSA seek to protect users from unfair practices, while supporting innovation in the digital economy.

CHAPTER 6
GLOBAL INTERNET TORTS

§ 6-1. Overview of Cybertorts

(A) DEFINING CYBERTORTS

Cybertorts address injurious social conduct not prosecuted under the criminal law. In virtual space, all torts are information-based versus accident law in the physical world. Cybertorts may be broadly defined as civil wrongs arising from Internet communications such as harassment, the invasion of privacy, defective software, and other vulnerabilities rapidly evolving in the connected world. Examples of cybertorts include:

(1) Cyber Defamation

(2) Invasion of Privacy

(3) Cyber Harassment/Stalking

(4) .Intellectual Property Infringement

(5) Trespass to Chattels/Conversion.

(6) Data Breaches/Negligence

Cybertorts often occur in a cross-border legal environment, where tortfeasors can defame, invade privacy and misappropriate trade secrets at the click of a mouse in hundreds of jurisdictions simultaneously:

> Internet-related publication torts arise out of heated Twitter (now X) exchange, blogs, social

> media sites, email transmissions, website posting, and the distribution of defective software.

THOMAS H. KOENIG & MICHAEL L. RUSTAD, GLOBAL INFORMATION TECHNOLOGIES: ETHICS AND THE LAW, (2d ed. 2023) at 122–123.

This chapter is divided into seven sections. Section 6-1 is an overview and definition of cybertorts as well as an introduction to CDA Section 230, which shields Internet service providers for torts committed on their services. Cybertorts are stymied by how large providers use one-sided contracts to eliminate tort rights and remedies.

Section 6-2 demonstrates that cybertorts are largely intentional torts. This section covers how courts apply ancient torts such as trespass to chattels to address e-mail spam, bots, and trespass to i-Phones. This section also show how courts have adapted the tort of conversion to the theft of domain names.

Section 6-3 covers information-based torts, which is the largest category of cybertorts: cyberfraud, trade libel in cyberspace, Internet defamation and privacy-based torts. Section 6-4 is a study of negligence-based cybertorts including negligent enablement, negligence per se, computer professional negligence, and negligent data-brokering.

Section 6-5 is a study of Internet products liability, while Section 6-6 is a prediction of cybertorts of the future. Finally, international cybertorts and transborder security breaches are covered.

(B) BARRIERS TO CYBERTORTS

(1) CDA Section 230

Congress enacted the Communications Decency Act (CDA) in 1996 "to promote the continued development of the Internet and other interactive computer services and other interactive media." CDA Section 230 shields Internet service providers, search engines, websites and countless other interactive computer services from liability arising out of third party postings on their services.

Representatives Chris Cox and Ron Wyden proposed Section 230 as an amendment to the CDA "to encourage the unfettered and unregulated development of free speech on the Internet, and to promote the development of e-commerce." Chris Cox explained CDA Section 230's purpose:

> Without Section 230, social media platforms would be exposed to lawsuits for users' reviews of products, restaurants, books, and movies. Airbnb would be exposed to lawsuits for users' negative comments about a rented home. Any service that connects buyers and sellers, workers and employers, content creators and website visitors, or victims and victims' rights groups—or provides any other interactive engagement opportunity one can imagine—could not continue to function on the Internet absent fear of liability for user-generated content.

In 1996, CDA Section 230 shielded America Online, CompuServe, and Prodigy from having to defend against a predicted flood of defamation lawsuits launched by those claiming harm from third party postings on their services.

Section 230(c)(1) of the CDA, entitled "Protection for private blocking and screening of offensive material" states: "No provider or user of an interactive computer service shall be treated as the publisher or speaker of any information provided by another information content provider." 47 U.S.C. § 230(c)(1).

CDA Section 230 defines "information content provider" to mean a third party "that is responsible, in whole or in part, for the creation or development of information provided through the Internet or any other interactive computer service." 47 U.S.C. § 230(f)(3).

To be successful with a CDA Section 230 defense, a defendant must establish (1) it is a provider or user of an "interactive computer service," (2) the claim is based on information provided by another information content provider, and (3) the claim treats the defendant as the publisher or speaker of that information.

"The CDA provides that no state law claim may be brought that is inconsistent with its provision." 47 U.S.C. § 230(e)(3). However, state claims consistent with the CDA still may be pursued, and the statute does not "limit or expand any law pertaining to intellectual property." 47 U.S.C. § 230(e)(2).

Because of CDA Section 230, Internet providers have no legal liability for postings by their users even if the post constitutes an ongoing tort:

> For example, that Amazon is not liable for unsafe or counterfeit products sold on its site by third parties, and that internet service providers are not responsible for the plight of people 'who found themselves targeted or terrorized by mostly anonymous users.'

Carl Watner, *Computers and Privacy: National Identification Revisited from a Voluntarist Perspective,* 190 VOLUNTARIST 1 (July 1, 2021).

As of March 8, 2026, courts have cited CDA Section 230 in more than 8,000 cases. In hundreds of cases each year, websites are shielded from liability by this federal statute. CDA Section 230 has been described as the "twenty-six words that created the internet." This provision allowed platforms like Facebook, Amazon, YouTube, and the largest digital platforms to host user-generated content without liability for third parties posting on their services.

In *McNeal v. Calvin*, 2026 U.S. Dist. LEXIS 71224 (E.D. Mo. Mar. 31, 2026), a Missouri federal district court concluded that YouTube, Google, and TikTok were immune from McNeal's claims seeking to hold them liable for Content Creator Defendants' allegedly defamatory posts about McNeal, even where McNeal complained about selective enforcement of content standards and platforms' failure to remove requested content.

McNeal's 116-page Amended Complaint asserted 14 causes of action against 21 defendants, alleging that she was harassed, defamed, and otherwise harmed by various online commentators and members of the show Love & Marriage: Huntsville (LAMH). *Id.* at *3. McNeal named ten individuals who were online commentators of LAMH. *Id.* at *4.

McNeal, who was an attorney, participated in public chats using only her first initial and last name to attempt keep her identity secret, asking YouTube content creators to refer to her only as "Anonymous." *Id.* at *5.

The court described the gist of McNeal's complaint as follows:

Plaintiff alleges that Defendant Carlos King "plotted with other LAMH cast members," particularly Defendant Maurice J. Scott, "to attack YouTube content creators and subscribers, like the Plaintiff" for the opinions they shared online in support of Rodgers. She alleges that Defendant King worked with a gang to engage in a coordinated effort to "dox, harass, cyber-stalk, threaten, and strike" commentators who spoke in support of Rodgers, including Plaintiff. *Id.* at *6. The court dismissed several defendants for "failure to state a claim." The court concluded that CDA Section 230 shielded the media defendants:

> Broad federal statutory immunity protects internet platforms like YouTube and Tik Tok from liability for content created by third parties. Plaintiff's claims against YouTube LLC,

> its parent company Google LLC, and Tik Tok Inc. are categorically barred by Section 230 of the Communications Decency Act, 47 U.S.C. § 230(c)(1) ("Section 230" or the "CDA"). Section 230 immunizes "interactive computer services" like YouTube and Tik Tok against any claim that seeks to treat them as the "publisher or speaker" of information posted online by third parties. Courts routinely apply Section 230 to dismiss claims against online service providers like YouTube and Tik Tok for hosting disputed content created by third parties. *Id.* at *18–19.

In *Doe v. Snap, Inc.*, 2025 WL 2926161 (Del. Super. Ct. Oct. 15, 2025) (unreported decision), Joan Doe purchased an iPhone for her 10-year-old daughter Jane with Verizon's Smart Family App. The 10-year-old girl downloaded Snapchat with her mother's permission.

Snapchat's contact synchronization function linked Joan's contact information with Jane's iPhone, enabling Omeire to add Jane as a contact. Anthony Omeire used Snapchat to contact Jane, impersonated a teenage girl and later a friend of her mother, and eventually sexually assaulted her. "Omeire has been convicted of two counts of first-degree rape and imprisoned for a term of sixty years. Omererire was convicted of rape and sentenced to sixty years in prison."

The young girl's mother filed a tort lawsuit against Snapchat, Verizon, and Apple. The Delaware Superior Court determined that all three high tech defendants qualified as interactive computer service providers shielded from liability by CDA Section 230:

> Defendants Snap, Verizon, and Apple did not "develop" the challenged communications in whole, or even part. Under the Complaint's allegations, the content at issue was created entirely by Mr. Omeire. Ms. Doe's claims rest on the theory that Snap, Verizon, or Apple allowed such material to circulate and make its way to Jane. That theory falls squarely within the editorial and structural functions Congress chose to immunize. The Defendants are not "information content providers" under the CDA.

CDA Section 230 has been under attack by critics that are concerned that harmful and illegal content is posted on websites without recourse. In 2020, President Donald J. Trump called for repealing CDA Section 230 and "signed an executive order attempting to curb some of its protections, though the order has been challenged in court." *Trump and Section 230: What to Know*, COUNCIL ON FOREIGN RELATIONS (Dec. 2, 2020).

"More recently, those critics have become more vocal in blaming Section 230 for enabling the worst of the internet (e.g., hate speech, revenge porn, disinformation and other objectionable content) and for giving large tech platforms too much leeway in moderating or presenting content." Proskauer, *A Final Bow for Section 230? Latest Plea for Reform Calls for Sunset of Immunity Law*, (June 12, 2024).

In December 2025, a bipartisan Senate proposal "introduced the Sunset Section 230 Act, which would repeal Section 230 two years after the date of enactment so that those harmed online can bring legal action against companies and finally hold them accountable for the harms that occur on their platforms."

Durbin, Graham Introduce Bill To Sunset Section 230 Immunity For Tech Companies, Protect Americans Online, (Dec. 18, 2025).

In recent years, courts have rejected CDA Section 230 immunity claims where websites or other Internet service providers went beyond being mere conduits contributing to creating content An influential decision concluding that a website was not shielded from third party tort liability was *Fair Housing Council of San Fernando Valley v. Roommates.com, LLC,* 521 F.3d 1157 (9th Cir. 2008), In the *Roommates.com* case:

> Roommates.com operated a housing website that required all users to disclose protected characteristics such as sex, sexual orientation, and family status before posting or searching for listings. It then used this information to create profile pages and to filter search results and email notifications so that users were channeled toward or away from listings based on those protected traits. The federal appeals court held that Roommates.com was not merely hosting third-party content but was itself "responsible, in whole or in part, for the creation or development" of the discriminatory material. By

> designing and mandating a system that solicited unlawful preferences and enforced them through search and notification tools, the company "contribute[d] materially to the alleged illegality of the conduct," forfeiting CDA immunity.

Doe v. Snap, Inc., 2025 Del. Super. LEXIS 495, *15–16 (Del. Super. Ct. Oct. 15, 2025) (discussing *Roommates.com exception to CDA Section 230*).

The court in *Fleites v. MindGeek S.A.R.L.*, 801 F. Supp. 3d 1045 (C.D. Cal. 2025) concluded that MindGeek is not entitled to Section 230 immunity because it materially contributed to the alleged illegality of child sexual abuse material (CSAM) content.

In 2014, thirteen-year-old Serena Fleites was induced to make a sexually explicit video by her then high school boyfriend. Her boyfriend uploaded the video to Pornhub.com, a pornography website owned and operated by the MindGeek Defendants, without Fleites knowledge or consent.

MindGeek delayed removing videos when Fleites reported them and videos were repeatedly reuploaded, generating millions of views. It earned advertising revenue from videos depicting Fleitas and optimized them to attract more viewers. MindGeek maintained an "unrestricted content" business model that embraced and monetized CSAM despite knowledge of its prevalence.

The court described how Serena Fleites' life spiraled out of control. She was harassed and bullied in school to such a degree that she started skipping school and finally unenrolled to attend courses online. The court observed that:

> From 2013 to 2023, MindGeek was the dominant online pornography company in the world. MindGeek operates several pornographic websites which fall into two broad categories: (1) free "tubesites" that contain free, user populated content and (2) premium "paysites" where it sells content, services, and merchandises.

Serena Fleites filed fourteen causes of action including torts against Mindgeek, which contended that they were immune under CDA Section 230. The plaintiff responded that CDA Section did not shield Mindgeek because they materially contributed to the CSAM content and went thus classified as a content creator. The court agreed with the plaintiff reasoning that:

> The Court finds that the Complaint sufficiently alleges that MindGeek itself, not its users, engaged in acts which was specifically designed to drive traffic to Plaintiff's videos, thereby "materially contributing" to the value of the CSAM. . . . While the Court agrees that Plaintiff's pleadings as to MindGeek's involvement in the videos as specific to her leave more to be desired, the Court finds that these allegations paired with the general allegations found in the rest of the SAC detailing MindGeek's tools that are not neutral in nature but rather encourage criminality are sufficient

at this stage of the litigation when all reasonable inferences are drawn in favor of Plaintiff.

The court allowed Plaintiff's TVPRA beneficiary liability claim, CSAM distribution claims, and most privacy tort claims to proceed.

High Tech companies defend CDA Section 230 because its liability shield enabled the Internet to grow:

> Google's head of global intellectual property policy, Katherine Oyama, told Congress [PDF] in October 2019 that without the law, companies could be subject to a host of lawsuits. Review sites such as Yelp or TripAdvisor could be sued for defamation by a restaurant with bad ratings, for example. The Internet Association, an industry group that represents major tech companies including Google, Facebook, Amazon, and Microsoft, has said the 'best of the internet would disappear without Section 230.'
>
> In 2026, there are frequent bipartisan calls for reforming or even eliminating CDA Section 230. Internet service providers in the European Union are not shielded from liability and have a duty to takedown illegal or objectionable content. Defenders of CDA Section 230 argue that this provision protects free expression on the Internet.

(2) Contracts Cannibalizing Cybertorts

Social media providers use one-sided terms of use to eliminate rights and all significant remedies of their users through one-sided clauses such as fixed caps on damages (i.e., no recovery beyond $100 or what the consumer paid in fees), mandatory predispute arbitration, anti-class action waivers, and choice of law and forum clauses that require the consumer to arbitrate in distant forums losing rights they had in their home forum.

Online businesses routinely employ terms of use (TOU) to redirect consumer lawsuits away from state and federal courts into non-public tribunals, in which privately hired judges decide cases without precedents and with almost no grounds for appeal. Users of social media sites such as Facebook, Instagram, and Match.com are:

> often—and often unknowingly—agreeing to give up their basic legal rights in disputes involving loss of privacy, disclosure of credit card information, rights of publicity, intellectual property rights and breaches of contract, disclosure of credit card information, rights of publicity, intellectual property rights and breaches of contract.

Michael L. Rustad & Thomas H. Koenig, *Rebooting Cybertorts for the Internet of Things*, HARVARD LAW RECORD (Nov. 16, 2017).

Chapter 4 examines numerous cases where providers use contract law to eliminate all warranties, cap damages, impose arbitration, and other one-sided provisions.

§ 6-2. Intentional Cybertorts Against the Person

(A) CYBER-ASSAULT

An assault is the intentional creation of a reasonable apprehension of an imminent battery, where the unprivileged touching of a person, including harmful or offensive contacts with the body, constitute the tort of battery. The tort of assault requires the plaintiff prove the defendant threatened the plaintiff who understood that a physical attack was imminent. The defendant must have the present ability to carry out either a harmful or an offensive touching of the plaintiff's body.

President Donald Trump's retweeting a GIF of him striking Hillary Clinton in the back with a golf ball is not actionable as a battery because there was no physical touching, nor is there an action for assault because there was no imminence of a harmful or offensive touching.

Threatening words transmitted in an email or website posting do not constitute the tort of assault. The target of these online threats will have no way of determining whether the threat is imminent or the sender nearby.

An assault requires an overt act evidencing an attempt to do bodily harm, which actually falls short of a battery. In *Marczeski v. Law*, 122 F. Supp. 2d 315, 325 (D.Conn. 2000), the court held that a threat by telephone or an Internet communication does not qualify as a civil assault.

While plaintiffs have found it difficult to recover for tort liability for cyberstalking, there have been successful criminal prosecutions as evidenced by a 2025 Massachusetts case:

> A Plymouth, Mass. man has been sentenced in federal court in Boston for cyberstalking more than a dozen Massachusetts women over a 16-year period. Beginning as early as 2008 and continuing into 2024, the defendant engaged in elaborate online harassment campaigns that targeted and tormented women he knew personally—including two who were minors when the conduct began. Among other things, the defendant hacked into victims' personal accounts and used over sixty accounts across thirty platforms to relentlessly impersonate, intimidate and abuse them—sharing thousands of fake sexually explicit images of the victims along with their personal information and urging others to contact, shame and sextort them.

U.S. Department of Justice, United States Attorney's Office for the District of Massachusetts, *Serial Cyberstalker Who Terrorized Women for 16 Years Sentenced to Nine Years in Prison* (July 25, 2025).

Vermont recognizes a civil action for stalking, but its state statute does not recognize a private cause of action.

(B) INTERNET-RELATED BATTERY

Battery is the tort of intentionally creating an unconsented harmful or offensive contact with a person. An actor is liable for battery if "(a) he acts intending to cause a harmful or offensive contact with the person of the other . . . or an imminent apprehension of such a contact, and (b) a harmful contact with the person of the other directly or indirectly results." Restatement (Second) of Torts § 13 (1965). Courts have yet to accept the argument a woman "virtually groped" in an online game has an action for the tort of battery.

Jordan Belamire, *My First Virtual Reality Groping*, MEDIUM.COM (October 20, 2016).

A battery requires proof of harmful or offensive touching, which will seldom occur in Internet cases. Hackers attacked the nonprofit Epilepsy Foundation website through the injection of JavaScript into some posts redirecting the users' browsers to a page whose pulsating pattern of squares flashing in different colors was calculated to trigger seizures in epileptics.

Kevin Poulsen, *Hackers Assault Epilepsy Patients via Computer*, WIRED.COM (March 28, 2006).

Photo and pattern-sensitive sufferers would need to convince courts to stretch the law to prove it was substantially certain that epileptics would suffer harmful or offensive contact, even though there was no physical touching. The victims of this attack did not file a tort lawsuit because the perpetrators could not be identified.

(C) INTENTIONAL INFLICTION OF EMOTIONAL DISTRESS

Plaintiffs in cyberstalking cases have been successful in pursing the intentional infliction of emotional distress (IIED). A plaintiff must satisfy three requirements to state a claim for IIED: (1) the conduct involved must be truly extreme and outrageous, i.e., it must go beyond all bounds of decency and be considered intolerable in a civilized community; (2) the actor must either intend his conduct will inflict severe emotional distress or know there is at least a high probability his conduct will cause severe emotional distress; and (3) the conduct must in fact cause severe emotional distress.

In *FitzGerald v. Brady*, 2025 Vt. Super. LEXIS 792 (Vt. Super. Ct., Dec, 23, 2025), Liam FitzGerald filed suit against Daniel Brady, alleging that he stalked him over a 12-month period. FitzGerald claims that Brady violated a Relief from Abuse (RFA) Order, engaged in civil stalking, committed intentional infliction of emotional distress, and invaded his privacy, and also seeks punitive damage.

The court found that FitzGerald's claim for IIED was sufficiently pleaded and the issue was for a jury to decide:

FitzGerald claims that Brady's conduct was "extreme and outrageous," that Brady intended to cause him severe emotional distress or acted with reckless disregard, and that he has suffered "psychological damage requiring medical and therapeutic care."

More specifically, he points to his allegations that Brady repeatedly violated a court order by contacting him directly or through third parties, contacted him via burner phone numbers, surveilled him online, and disseminated private transgender-related information.

FitzGerald further argues that, because he lives in the "Deep South," the disclosure of transgender status "exposes individuals to heightened risk of harassment, discrimination, and violence." The Court observes that several of the messages that FitzGerald alleges were sent by Brady were sexually explicit. FitzGerald here has pled a pattern of repeated harassment under the backdrop of a restraining order whereby Brady knew such contact was unwelcome.

Repeated harassment may compound the outrageousness of incidents which, taken individually, might not be sufficiently extreme to warrant liability for infliction of emotional distress. Accordingly, FitzGerald has sufficiently pled a claim for IIED, and the ultimate determination must be left for summary judgment or a jury trial after further factual development.

In *Butler v. Continental Express,* 2002 NLP IP Company—American Lawyer Media, J: 98: 05227, No. 96-1204096 (Montgomery, Texas June 8, 1998), Rainer Krebs, a pilot for Continental Express, took a photograph of a female pilot and used a software application to superimpose the plaintiff's face onto nude pictures of women in sexually suggestive poses.

Krebs posted these pornographic images on the Internet and the airline's intranet.

The female pilot victimized by this sexual harassment by her male co-workers was awarded damages for defamation per se, intentional infliction of emotional distress, invasion of privacy, and punitive damages for acting with malice.

(D) TRESPASS TO VIRTUAL CHATTELS

Trespass to chattels is a personal property tort committed by intentionally: (1) dispossessing another of a chattel, or (2) using or intermeddling with a chattel in the possession of another. The tort of trespass to chattels allows recovery for interferences with possession of personal property not sufficiently important to be classed as conversion, and so to compel the defendant to pay the full value of the thing with which he has interfered. A California Appeals Court concluded that owners did not have possessory or property interest in copies of their websites sufficient to give rise to trespass to chattels claim.

As an equitable remedy for trespass to chattel, the trial court ordered the transfer of a website. The appeals court affirmed the trial court's denial of relief as to other causes of action, which included a claim of an unlawful business practice as well.

Best Carpet Values, Inc. v. Google, LLC, 90 F.4th 962 (9th Cur, 2024).

In *Doe v. E. Me. Healthcare Sys.*, 2025 Me. Bus. & Consumer LEXIS 1 (Jan. 9, 2025), EMHS installed tracking "pixels" on its website that collected and transmitted patients' private information to Facebook and other third parties without patients' knowledge or consent.

Doe's browsing activity and IP address on EMHS's website were shared with Facebook, which then linked that information to Plaintiff's Facebook profile. Facebook used this information to show Doe targeted health-related advertisements. The court concluded that when EMHS collected IP address and browsing activity, it lacked the tangible component to constitute "chattel."

(1) E-Mail Spam as Trespass to Chattels

The first U.S. court to stretch trespass to chattels to email spamming was *CompuServe v. Cyberpromotions, Inc.*, 962 F. Supp. 1015 (S.D. Ohio 1997). CompuServe filed for a preliminary injunction against Cyberpromotions, a bulk e-mailer.

The court held CompuServe had a viable trespass to chattels claim against Cyberpromotions because the emailer sent a substantial volume of spam and continued to sidestep the service provider's blocking software to protect its computer system from the unsolicited e-mail. The *CompuServe* court ruled that the provider did not violate the spammer's First Amendment rights in seeking to enjoin the spam.

The *CompuServe* court explained that a service provider could sustain an action for trespass to chattels however could not sustain an action for conversion without a showing of substantial interference with its right to possession of its computer system. Under the logic of this modern case, physical contact is satisfied by the mere reception of electrons.

In *EBay, Inc. v. Bidder's Edge, Inc.*, 100 F. Supp. 2d 1058 (N.D. Cal. 2000), the court entered a preliminary injunction preventing Bidder's Edge from accessing eBay's web site with spiders, or automated querying software programs. The eBay court concluded that Bidder's Edge "trespassed" on eBay's web site because it breached the terms of service agreement.

In *Intel Corp. v. Hamidi,* 94 Cal. App. 4th 325 (2001), a disgruntled ex-employee flooded Intel's company-wide computer system by transmitting six separate e-mails to 29,000 current employees. When Intel was unable to block or otherwise filter out the unwanted messages, it sent a letter demanding that the defendant cease sending the e-mails criticizing the company.

The court enjoined the commercial e-mail campaign rejecting the defendant's argument that he had a First Amendment right to transmit mass e-mailings. The California Supreme Court reversed the intermediate court, ruling that Intel had not met its evidentiary burden of proving that Hamidi's e-mails had caused actual damages, an essential element of the tort of trespass to chattels.

The court concluded that Hamidi's e-mails to current employees had not caused any physical damage, disrupted Intel's computers, nor prevented the company from accessing its computers' e-mail messages.

(2) Bots as Trespassers

In *Microsoft v. Does*, 2014 WL 1338677 (E.D. Va. 2014), the federal court ruled Microsoft alleged sufficient facts to demonstrate the defendant, whose botnet infected a large number of computers, committed the common law tort of trespass to chattels. The defendant allegedly used various techniques to lure victims to websites where malicious botnet code was secretly installed on their computers.

(3) Trespass to iPhones

In *In re Apple Inc. Device Performance Litigation*, 347 F. Supp. 3d 434 (N.D. Cal. 2018), plaintiffs filed a class action against Apple, claiming the updated code for its mobile operating system (iOS) significantly reduced the performance of certain models of the iPhone.

The class action complaint alleged Apple failed to adequately disclose the iOS updates would affect the performance of their iPhones and, more broadly, Apple made representations and omissions regarding the capacity of iPhone and iPad devices.

The court summarized the case as primarily concerning Apple's misleading response to battery capacity issues in certain older-model iPhones and iPads. The court stated that:

> Beginning in late 2015, consumers began reporting that their iPhone and iPad devices were experiencing unexpected shutdowns despite showing more than 30% remaining charge on the battery. When the device shut down, it would remain dead until the user reconnected the device to power.

In 2017, Apple reduced occurrences of unexpected shutdowns a small number of users were experiencing with their iPhone. After a user installed Apple updates, independent research identified a performance deficit. Then, on December 28, 2017, Apple released another statement that confirmed some consumers' suspicions that the iOS updates had intentionally slowed down the processing speeds of iPhone 6 and iPhone 7 models.

The plaintiffs contended that Apple knew a phone may shut down as a battery ages because the battery could not deliver the peak power demanded by the phone's processor. Faster and more powerful processing units, which required more power, they claimed, caused batteries to degrade over time by discharge/recharge cycles, elevated temperatures, and aging.

Plaintiffs filed a number of consumer class action lawsuits against Apple. The complaint alleged that Apple's conduct violated federal and state computer-intrusion laws, as well as state consumer-protection laws and common law. The court found that the plaintiffs stated evidence for each element of the trespass to chattels.

The court concluded that the plaintiffs asserted facts establishing each of the elements of the tort of trespass to chattels. First, the court found that the complaint contained sufficient allegations that Apple intentionally and without authorization interfered with Plaintiffs' possession of their iPhones.

The court found Apple trespassed by exceeding the consent of iPhone users. Plaintiffs alleged the iOS updates were designed to slow their iPhones' processing speed. They also contended Apple did not inform consumers the updates would do so. Apple's disclosures were inadequate because they did not advise users processing speed would be reduced.

In two similar cases again Apple, the plaintiffs argued that Facetime was intentionally nonfunctional in older operating systems. Apple argued that:

> Per that agreement, Apple did not sell or otherwise transfer its ownership of IOS to [Plaintiff]. For this reason, the plaintiff lacks a sufficient possessory interest to bring a trespass claim. One court rejected such argument finding that software license did not give Apple the right to disable a key function of the phone.

Nathan Hale, *Fla. Judge Cuts Cord on Class Claims Over iPhone Updates,* LAW360 (Apr. 14, 2020).

(E) CONVERSION IN CYBERSPACE

Cyberconversion, like its bricks and mortar counterpart, is the wrongful exercise of dominion over personal property on the Internet. Plaintiffs file a large number of Cyberconversion claim with little success. Plaintiffs were mostly unable to win conversion cases arising out of photographs, design, and coding used on a website.

See e.g., *Liegey v. Gadeh*, 198 A.D.3d 460 (N.Y. Sup. Jud. Ct., Oct. 12, 2021).

A Virginia court ruled that Verizon, as a matter of law, was not liable for conversion for transferring the domain name <radaris.com>, registered to plaintiff Accuracy Consulting Ltd. ("Accuracy"), and the website located at that domain name, operated by plaintiff Bitseller Expert Limited as directed by a third-party.

Bitseller Expert Ltd. v. Verisign, Inc., 2019 U.S. Dist. LEXIS 248005 (E.D. Va. Dec. 20, 2019).

The *Bitseller* court ruled that Verizon had a lawful justification for interfering with the alleged converted property. Courts have regarded a defendant's compliance with a valid court order as lawful justification.

In *K3b, Inc. v. Collectors Universe*, 2016 Cal. Super. LEXIS 22534 (Calif. Super. Ct. Nov. 17, 2016), the plaintiff claimed that the tort of conversion applied to an entire website, i.e., the Forums, by change of the underlying website software that controls what is seen by a visitor to the website. The court dismissed this claim because the plaintiff failed to plead facts demonstrating its exclusive control of the Forums reasoning:

> Because the Defendant could exercise control over the software upon which the Forums were run, Plaintiff has not establishes that it had exclusive possession and control over the Forums. Thus this element is not adequately alleged.

(1) Conversion of Domain Names

Few plaintiffs have been successful in pleading claims for the conversion of domain names. In *Kremen v. Cohen*, 337 F.3d 1024, 1029–30 (9th Cir. 2003), the Ninth Circuit ruled that the district court erred in concluding that domain names, although a form of property, were intangibles not subject to conversion. The Ninth Circuit became the first to rule that an intangible such as a domain name was protected by the tort of conversion.

Michael L. Rustad & Thomas H. Koenig, *Cybertorts and Legal Lag: An Empirical Analysis*, 13 S. CAL. INTERDISC. L.J. 77, 122 (2003).

In *Gizmo Beverages, Inc. v. Park,* 2019 WL 141461 (C.D. Cal. Jan. 9, 2019). Gizmo's complaint alleged Park committed trademark infringement, cybersquatting, and conversion, by: (a) continuing to use the domain www.gizmoclosure.com (i.e., "www. gizmoclosures.com" without the "s") (the gizmoclosure domain); and (b) refusing to turn over the log-in information for the "teaofakind" domain.

The court found the domain names at issue in the conversion claim, "gizmoclosure.com" and "teaofakind.com," were created and registered prior to Gizmo's creation as a legal entity. Since the domain names were registered in the name of Daniel Park, there could be no evidence of the essential element Gizmo owned the domain names at issue. There was no evidence that the domain names were ever transferred to Gizmo.

(2) Conversion of Bitcoins

"Bitcoin is a decentralized digital currency uses a ledger to track the ownership and transfer of every bitcoin in existence." *Kleiman v. Craig*, 2018 WL 6812914 (S.D. Fla. Dec. 28, 2018).

A federal district court explained how the Bitcoin Blockchain worked:

> In order to complete a transaction with bitcoins, you must have a bitcoin wallet. 'Wallets' are computer files dedicated to storing bitcoin information. Each bitcoin wallet has a 'public key' used as the 'address' to receive bitcoin from others. Each wallet is also assigned a 'private key.' To send bitcoin out of a wallet, an individual must have the private key associated with that bitcoin wallet.

The *Kleinman* court noted it was unsettled whether bitcoins were currency for the purpose of the tort of conversion. The court surveyed other jurisdictions where courts held bitcoin qualified as money for the purposes of indicting and prosecuting a defendant on federal money laundering statutes. The court agreed with the plaintiffs that they sufficiently identified their ownership of the bitcoins and that conversion applied to bitcoins.

(F) MALICIOUS PROSECUTION

To prevail on a malicious prosecution tort claim, the plaintiff must prove three elements: (1) that the prior action was commenced by or at the direction of the defendant and was pursued to a legal termination in the plaintiff's favor; (2) was brought without probable cause; and (3) the lawsuit was initiated with malice.

This difficult burden was not satisfied in *Hartnett v. Hardenbergh,* 2026 U.S. Dist. LEXIS 38122 (E.D. Va. Feb. 24, 2026) where defendants' Facebook posts compared plaintiff to a convicted murderer, promised 'more details' about 'past victims,' and displayed a sign with plaintiff's photo labeled 'LIAR' alongside 'REGISTERED SEX OFFENDERS.' The jury found defendants liable for defamation but rejected assault, battery, and malicious prosecution claims.

The court reasoned that Defendants' statements were not protected opinion because they implied undisclosed defamatory facts, unlike true opinion based on fully disclosed facts.

The Facebook posts' comparison to a convicted murderer and promises of 'more details' suggested hidden defamatory information. The jury's rejection of other tort claims did not necessarily establish

Plaintiff lied, as different elements and burdens apply to different torts.

(G) ABUSE OF PROCESS

Abuse of process is misusing legal process for an unlawful purpose. To establish an abuse of process claim, a plaintiff must show the defendant (1) used a legal process against the plaintiff, (2) primarily to accomplish a purpose for which the process was not designed, and (3) harm has been caused to the plaintiff Abuse of process is a post-litigation claim in response to a frivolous lawsuit or case brought for an improper purpose.

In *Ghrist v. CBS Broadcasting, Inc.*, 40 F. Supp. 3d 623 (W.D. Pa. 2014), Christopher William Ghrist had a similar name to Christopher Wayne Ghrist, a convicted drug dealer. The plaintiff filed suit against the television-broadcasting network alleging false light, invasion of privacy, defamation, intentional infliction of emotional distress (IIED), and abuse of process, for wrongly identifying him and using his likeness in an Internet news story regarding the convicted criminal.

The plaintiff's abuse of process claim was based upon the television company's motion to dismiss his case. The *Ghrist* court found this allegation "wholly insufficient to plead a cause of action for abuse of process."

The court found no evidence that the motion to dismiss was being used for an unlawful purpose that caused the plaintiff harm. "Simply put, the Plaintiff cannot base its abuse of process claim on the Defendant's efforts under Rule 12 to defend itself against the Plaintiff's lawsuit."

§ 6-3. Intentional Information-Based Torts

(A) CYBERFRAUD

The elements of a cyberfraud claim include: (1) a knowingly false representation by the defendant, (2) an intent to deceive or induce reliance, (3) justifiable reliance by the plaintiff, and (4) resulting damages. Fraud or misrepresentation includes willfully deceiving another with the intent to induce a person to alter their position to their detriment.

In *Bhotiwihok v. Fairlife, LLC*, 2026 U.S. Dist. LEXIS 30859 (C.D. Cal. Feb. 13, 2026), Fairlife launched in 2014 as Select Milk-Coca-Cola partnership, with Coca-Cola acquiring full ownership in 2020 while Select Milk retained operational control.

Multiple Animal Recovery Mission investigations documented systematic animal abuse at Fairlife supplier farms including beatings, neglect, and abandonment. Fairlife bottles display 'Recycle Me' labels and chasing arrow symbols despite being 0% recyclable.

The court concluded that Fairlife's brand name combining 'fair' and 'life' above a cartoon cow image misleads reasonable consumers into believing dairy cows live abuse-free lives, making it actionable misrepresentation rather than puffery given documented animal abuse at supplier farms. In granting Fairlife's motion to dismiss the fraud claims the court reasoned that:

> Plaintiffs' First Amended Complaint is sprawling. For example, Plaintiffs group several misrepresentations together as "Animal Care Claims," including those relating to the Fairlife Logo and multiple statements on Fairlife's website. Plaintiffs also group several other unspecified claims as "Sustainability Claims." However, Plaintiffs explicitly plead reliance on only two specific misrepresentations: the Fairlife Logo and the recyclability claims on Fairlife's bottle label.
>
> However, Plaintiffs do not plead any other misrepresentations with sufficient particularity under Rule 9(b)'s exacting pleading standard because they fail to identify any other statements on which they relied. . .Plaintiffs allege that Fairlife "intentionally fail[ed] to disclose material information about the products," including that Fairlife's products are derived from abused cows and that the products' packaging is not recyclable. However, Plaintiffs do not plead where this information should or could have been revealed. Nor do they identify on which specific "advertisements, offers, or other representations" they relied that omitted critical information about Fairlife's animal care and sustainability practices.

In *Bloomsybox.com, LLC v. Userway, Inc.*, 2026 U.S. Dist. LEXIS 30698 (D. Del. Feb. 13, 2026),

Bloomsybox operated e-commerce website selling flowers and gifts. UserWay sold accessibility widget software claiming to ensure ADA/WCAG compliance. Bloomsybox purchased UserWay subscription in July 2023 after viewing website representations.

UserWay's website claimed 'full WCAG & ADA compliance from day one' and litigation protection. Bloomsybox was served with ADA class action lawsuit in December 2023. UserWay required annual subscription upgrade for legal support, then provided only generic guide and closed case within days.

The plaintiff identified a list of alleged misrepresentations, and the complaint alleges facts connecting those misrepresentations to Plaintiff's purchase of the Widget and documented losses suffered as a result. For examples, the plaintiff stated that the defendant offered litigation support, but that was not the case. Another example was that the defendant inaccurately represented full Americans with Disabilities Act compliance. The court denied dismissal of the plaintiffs' negligent misrepresentation claim, dismissing all other causes of action.

(B) TRADE LIBEL IN CYBERSPACE

To prevail in a claim for trade libel, a plaintiff must demonstrate the defendant: (1) made a statement that disparages the quality of the plaintiff's product; (2) that the offending statement was couched as fact, not opinion; (3) that the statement was false; (4) that the statement was made with malice; and (5) that the statement resulted in monetary loss.

A company must present evidence of special damages arising out of an online defamatory falsehood such as a Facebook posting. A court may presume, as a matter of law, the defendant intended to make false statements (susceptible of only one meaning) creating public hatred, contempt, or ridicule.

Online "publication" requires proof the libelous statement reached even a single third person who understood both the defamatory meaning and its connection to the plaintiff. Trade libel requires proof of special damages, while libel *per se* does not have this requirement. "Special damages" are limited to actual pecuniary losses must be specially pleaded and proved.

(C) INDIVIDUAL & MEDIA *PRIMA FACIE* DEFAMATION CASE

The potential for Internet-related defamation in is staggering. Virtual torts-such as the invasion of privacy or defamation-are frequently difficult to expunge once they go viral:

> Plaintiffs in virtual injury cases will find that an injurious comment is difficult to expunge from the Internet, unlike a newspaper where a retraction and the passage of a few days may reduce the radius of the injury significantly. Even with the help of companies such as Reputation Defender that will attempt to expunge tortious postings, you cannot really "unring the bell" once information is posted, copied, and forwarded around the globe.

Michael L. Rustad, *The Internalist/Externalist Debate*, 88 IND. L. J. 419, 439 (2013).

Like a traditional defamation case, a private figure in an Internet libel case must establish: (1) publication; (2) of a defamatory statement; (3) concerning the plaintiff; (4) in a negligent breach of the professional standard of care; and (5) that resulted in demonstrable injury. Internet libel cases frequently arise out of anonymous postings.

Before compelling disclosure of an anonymous speaker's identity, a defamation plaintiff must (1) undertake reasonable efforts to notify the anonymous poster that disclosure is sought and (2) support his defamation claim to defeat a summary judgment motion. Plaintiffs will typically serve subpoenas on X (formerly known as Twitter), Google, and other digital platforms to identify anonymous users.

In defamation actions against anonymous speakers on the Internet, a Plaintiff seeking to compel disclosure of a defendant's identity must make a prima facie evidentiary showing of the elements of defamation, including falsity, before X, Google or other platforms must disclose the defendant's identity.

In a 2025 California state case, the plaintiff filed an action for defamation against anonymous actors he contends are responsible for posting defamatory statements on social media accounts, leading his employer to fire him. He was unable to learn the identities of the anonymous parties or to convince the trial court that they had made general appearances, and the court dismissed his libel claim.

(1) Libel *Per Quod*

"Libel per quod" is a publication not obviously defamatory but when considered with innuendo, colloquium, and explanatory circumstances becomes libelous. For publications which are libelous per quod, the innuendo and special damages must be alleged and proved. Special damage means pecuniary loss, and emotional distress and humiliation alone are not enough to support a claim actionable per quod.

In *Nguyen v. Taylor*, 684 S.E.2d 470 (N.C. Ct. App. 2009), the court dismissed a libel per quod action filed by the Greensboro N.C. police against Taylor a/k/a the rap artist "The Game." a DVD publisher, website, and others arising out of claims that the rapper was wrongfully arrested and brutalized by the police. To state a claim for libel per quod, a party must specifically allege and prove special damages as to each plaintiff, which was not done in the *Taylor* case.

(2) Libel *Per Se*

As with the common law, cyberlibel per se cases requires proof the plaintiff maliciously: (1) accused a person of commission of crime, (2) imputed unchastity to a woman, (3) stated a person had a loathsome disease—e.g., AIDS, mental illness etc., or (4) made any statement damages a person in his business or standing in the community—e.g., crooked lawyer, drunken doctor. A plaintiff need not prove actual damages with defamation *per se;* damages are presumed.

In *Araya v. Deep Dive Media*, 966 F. Supp. 2d 582 (W.D. N.C. 2013), Frances Araya filed a lawsuit against Deep Dive Media, LLC and Gawker that published separate news stories on their Internet news websites showing a cropped, altered, and partially censored picture of the Plaintiff allegedly exposing her genitals in her high school yearbook. The headline to Gawker's story read "Female High School Student Accused of Flashing Vagina in Yearbook Photo." Gawker's story stated:

> On page 14 of the Lake Norman High School yearbook there is a photo of a girl lifting her graduation gown and exposing her hooha.
>
> Or so it would seem: A spokeswoman for the Iredell-Statesville School District in North Carolina left open the possibility that what appeared to be the student's "genitalia" was merely her thighs bunched together.

Prominently displayed above the article was a still photograph in which the Plaintiff appeared in her cap and gown—her face and pelvic area, however, had been obscured by black bars. The Plaintiff's complaint alleged:

> that the photograph, as altered, deliberately misconstrued the context of the original scene; that she was sitting, not standing as the pictorial evidence might suggest; that she was with a crowd of over one hundred students and did not pose for the picture, nor was she aware

it was being taken at that very moment; that she was holding a ceremony program and not lifting her gown; and that, finally, she was wearing a dress and undergarments beneath her graduation gown.

The court concluded that the Internet news website article was capable only of a libelous reading per se, under North Carolina law, where operator falsely accused that graduate intentionally lifted her graduation gown when the photograph was taken, tending to disgrace and degrade graduate.

(3) Publishers & Conduits or Distributors

Internet distributors are third party platforms such as Facebook, search engines such as Google, or web posts. Distributors do not have liability for third party content because of CDA Section 230.

CDA Section 230 shield ISPs and digital platforms for defamation and other torts arising out of content posted by third-parties. Distributors in the brick and mortar world include conduits such as "telegraph and telephone companies, libraries and news vendors." DAN B. DOBBS, THE LAW OF TORTS § 402, at 1123 (2000).

A bookstore owner, for example, would not be liable for defamatory statements made in books the store sold absent actual knowledge. Nevertheless, if a bookstore had notice of defamatory content, it could be liable as a distributor. In contrast, a publisher is liable for defamatory statements in their works and the plaintiff need not prove the publisher had knowledge of the defamatory content.

Distributors are subject to an intermediate standard between publishers and conduits. Conduits are common carrier type defendants, who are not liable for defamatory content because they have no ability to screen or control defamatory material.

(4) Single Publication Rule

The "single publication rule" treats the communication to the entire group as one publication giving rise to only one cause of action for defamation. This "one and done" rule means that for mass publications on the Internet, there is a single cause of action, which arises at the first posting of an allegedly defamatory statement. See Restatement (Second) of Torts § 577A.

The single publication rule protects Internet publishers from infinite liability and multiple, repetitive lawsuits for the same content. The date of publication is deemed the date the allegedly defamatory content was posted. Many states have adopted the single publication rule by statute. A single publication case arose when:

> On Sept. 7, 2000, The Atlanta Journal-Constitution published an article about a controversy surrounding a local social club for the overweight. According to the group's Web site, "Hipsters" was created to "provide social gatherings that included size-positive spectacles for persons of size, and those who support them,

> in the form of an atmosphere conducive to interaction and camaraderie—usually including a bar, music and dancing."

Kristen Murphy, *Single-Publication Rule Receives Double Protection,* REPORTERS COMMITTEE FOR FREEDOM OF THE PRESS (2004).

The *Atlanta Journal-Constitution* wrote an article about a lawsuit filed against the author the article and stated:

> The Hipster party in metro Atlanta was noted on the cover of 'Plumper and Big Women': 'Five thousand pounds of Sex-Starved Fatties.' A similar sentence appeared in a follow-up article on Nov. 7, 2000. Both stories were archived on the newspaper's Web site.

Two years later, the author of the article filed suit against the Atlanta newspaper. A trial court dismissed the case under the state's statute of limitations, and on Jan. 8, 2004, the Georgia Court of Appeals affirmed that decision, holding that the "single-publication rule" applies to Internet postings.

(5) John Doe Subpoenas

John Doe subpoenas, also called *subpoena duces tecum*, are requested by prosecutors or private litigants to unveil anonymous bloggers, posters, and others potentially liable for trade libel or the infringement of intellectual property rights.

The leading test for granting these subpoenas was articulated in *Dendrite Int'l, Inc. v. Doe*, 775 A.2d 756

(N.J. Super. Ct., App. Div. 2001). The *Dendrite* court held a plaintiff seeking to unveil an anonymous speaker must: (1) give notice, (2) identify the exact statements that constitute allegedly actionable speech, (3) establish a *prima facie* cause of action against the defendant based on the complaint and all information provided to the court, and (4) produce sufficient evidence supporting each element of its cause of action, on a *prima facie* basis, prior to a court ordering the disclosure of the identity of the unnamed defendant.

Assuming the plaintiff establishes a *prima facie* cause of action; the court must balance the defendant's First Amendment rights against the strength of the case presented, considering the importance of disclosing the anonymous defendant's identity to allow the plaintiff to prove her case.

Courts do not issue John Doe subpoenas unless the ISP gives notice to the anonymous speaker and an opportunity to be heard. A New Hampshire Jane Doe plaintiff filed suit against Friendfinder.com, an adult networking site, for defamatory third party postings under the screen name "petra03755."

The anonymous poster created a false defamatory profile of the Jane Doe plaintiff, which depicted her as a "swinger." The court granted Friendfinder.com's motion to dismiss the plaintiff's claims for invasion of privacy and defamation on grounds of the federal immunity under Section 230 of the Communications Decency Act.

The federal court ruled Friendfinder.com was not transformed into a content provider merely because it changed the wording of the age of Jane Doe's profile from age 40 or 41 into "early forties." However, a website operator making extensive editorial modifications risks losing its Section 230 immunity. *Doe v. Friendfinder Network*, 2008 WL 2001745 (D. N.H. May 8, 2008).

(D) DEFAMATION DEFENSES

(1) Public Official

A plaintiff classified as a public official must demonstrate that a defamatory statement was made with actual malice by clear and convincing evidence. The statement must be false or made with reckless disregard toward the truth or falsity of the avowal.

The rule requiring public officials to prove actual malice is based on First Amendment principles, reflecting the U.S. Supreme Court's commitment to encouraging robust and wide-open debate of public issues. Examples of public officials would include Donald J. Trump, Pete Buttigieg, Bernie Sanders, Gavin Newsom, Zohran Mondami, Lindsey Graham, Stacey Abrams, and Elizabeth Warren.

(2) General Purpose Public Figure

In 1967, the Court expanded *New York Times v. Sullivan's*, 376 U.S. 254 (1964), constitutional limitations on suits against public officials to public figures in *Curtis Publ'g Co. v. Butts*, 388 U.S. 130 (1967). The Court in *Gertz v. Robert Welch, Inc.*, 418

U.S. 323 (1974), extended the malice standard to public figures.

General-purpose public figures are individuals who achieve pervasive fame or notoriety so they qualify as public figures for all purposes and in all contexts. Examples of public figures would be Madonna, Taylor Swift, Bad Bunny, Bill Gates, Michael Jordan, Oprah Winfrey, Scarlett Johansson, Leonardo DiCaprio, Adam Sandler, Johnny Depp, Britney Spears, and Tiger Woods.

The general public figure possesses general fame or notoriety in the community and pervasive involvement in the affairs of society. *Gertz v. Robert Welch, Inc.*, 418 U.S. 323, 324 (1974). To qualify as a general public figure, the person's fame must be very great; the individual must be a household name on a national scale. The actual malice standard applies to both public figures and public officials.

To be liable for the defamation of a public figure, a distributor of allegedly defamatory material must act with actual malice—that is, with knowledge the material was false or with reckless disregard of whether it was false or not. Public figures may be celebrities, other well-known individuals, or public officials.

As with elected or appointed public officials, a celebrity must prove a defamatory statement was made with malice by clear and convincing evidence.

(3) Limited Purpose Public Figure

A limited-purpose public figure is an individual who voluntarily injects themselves or is drawn into a specific, public controversy to influence its outcome. When I testified before both Houses of Congress on whether punitive damages should be limited, I was a limited public figure. In contrast to the general public figure, persons who thrust themselves to the forefront to influence resolution of a public issue are limited public figures only with respect to that issue.

A "limited public figure," also called a limited-purpose public figure, for purposes of defamation actions is an individual who voluntarily injects himself or is drawn into a particular public controversy and thereby becomes a public figure for a limited range of issues. Thus, I was only a limited public figure for the issue of tort reform of punitive damages and a private person for all other purposes.

A court determined that an evangelical minister was a limited public figure in *Carter v. Jones*, 581 P.3d 1050, 202 (Wash. Ct. of App. 2025), In that case, Pastor Micahn Carter filed a defamation suit against former parishioner and assistant Mary Jones who claimed that he raped her during his previous tenure at Together Church in Yakima, Washington.

Carter filed suit because Ms. Jones she sent two letters (Hodge letters) and authored a blog post entitled "Moving Forward." Mary Jones characterized the sexual intercourse as rape while Micahn Carter referred to the intercourse as consensual sex.

Micahn Carter filed a defamation action against Mary Jones. The complaint alleged that Jones published a false accusation of rape in the Hodges letter and blog post. According to the complaint, Jones' false claims cost Carter his job, damaged his community reputation, caused mental anguish, humiliation, and embarrassment, and led to lost paid publishing contracts and other paid speaking engagements.

Mary Jones filed a motion to dismiss, a summary judgment motion, and a special motion for expedited relief Declarations from Jones, her mother Laurie and Pastor Kevin Gerald accompanied the motion. The trial court granted Jones' motion to seal the requests. Mary Jones contended that Micahn Carter failed to present facts to comply with four elements of defamation: unprivileged communication, factual statement, falsity, and fault of the speaker.

Mary Jones argued that Micahn Carter had the status of a limited public figure or to label the nature of her communications as imbued with public interest with regard to both communications: the Hodges letter and the blog post. The trial court labeled Carter a private figure. The appeals court reversed finding Carter to be a limited public figure:

> Scandals involving the Catholic clergy are matters of public concern. Evangelists such as Micahn Carter, who reach hundreds through media, embrace similar characteristics to office holders and Catholic clergy. The public possesses an interest in the pastor's fitness to serve the Lord and a congregation. Thus, sexual

scandals of an evangelist should be a subject of public concern. Carter was a limited public figure.

(4) Liability Standard for Private Persons

Private individuals in U.S. defamation cases need only to prove negligence to win a defamation lawsuit, which is a lower standard than the "actual malice" required for public officials and public figures. The plaintiff only needs to prove that the defendant failed to exercise reasonable care in determining the truth of a statement before publishing it.

Thus, in Internet defamation cases against private individuals (not general or limited public figures or public officials), the plaintiff must prove: (1) a false and defamatory statement concerning another, (2) unprivileged publication to third party, (3) fault amounting to at least negligence on the publisher's part, and (4) either actionability of statement irrespective of special harm, or existence of special harm caused by publication.

(5) Truth as a Complete Defense

Under the law of defamation, truth is a complete defense. In U.S. defamation actions, the defense of truth is constitutionally required where the subject of the publication is a public official or public figure. The courts require only the defendant establish the Internet-related posting is substantially true.

(6) Qualified Privileges

To establish defamation, a plaintiff must prove the defendant made an unprivileged publication of a defamatory statement to a third party causing damages. There are two classes of privileged statements: those subject to an absolute privilege, and those subject to a conditional or qualified privilege.

An absolute privilege provides a complete bar to a claim for defamation. In contrast, a qualified privilege can be exceeded, and the privilege lost such as when an ex-employer makes false statements with an intent to injure his former employee.

(7) Anti-SLAPP Suit Statutes

Several states have enacted Strategic Lawsuits Against Public Participation Statutes (Anti-SLAPP) giving a cause of action to a person who is sued while exercising free speech discussing public issue. Anti-SLAPP actions apply to either the First Amendment or an expression right recognized by a state constitution.

For example, California's Anti-SLAPP Statute was enacted in response to a "disturbing increase in lawsuits brought primarily to chill the valid exercise of the constitutional rights of freedom of speech." *Manufactured Home Communities Inc. v. County of San Diego*, 544 F.3d 959 (9th Cir. 2008).

To dismiss a cause of action under California's Anti-SLAPP Statute, the court must determine whether: (1) the defendant has made a sufficient threshold showing the challenged cause of action is subject to a special motion to strike and (2) the threshold showing has been made. The court must find the plaintiff has demonstrated sufficient minimal merit to be allowed to proceed.

A California appellate court ruled websites were accessible to the public—thus being public forums for the purposes of California's Anti-SLAPP statute. *Kroneymer v. Internet Movie Database Inc.*, 150 Cal. App. 4th 941 (Cal. Ct. App. 2007).

To date, many defendants who post derogatory statements on so-called "gripe websites" have successfully deployed anti-SLAPP suits. In *Macdonald v. Paton*, the Massachusetts Appeals Court ruled that the operator of web site was entitled to grant of her special motion to dismiss town selectman's complaint for defamation under Massachusetts' statute governing strategic lawsuits against public participation (anti-SLAPP statute). *MacDonald v. Paton*, 57 Mass. App. Ct. 290 (2003).

(8) Retraction Statutes

Thirty-three U.S. states have retraction statutes that require plaintiffs to request a retraction from media defendants as a condition to filing a lawsuit or to limit the amount of damages (especially punitive damages) if a timely, appropriate retraction is published. Oregon's retraction statute provides:

(1) In an action for damages on account of a defamatory statement published or broadcast in a newspaper, magazine, other

> printed periodical, or by radio, television or motion pictures, the plaintiff shall not recover general damages unless:
>
> (a) A correction or retraction is demanded but not published as provided in ORS 30.165; or
>
> (b) The plaintiff proves by a preponderance of the evidence that the defendant actually intended to defame the plaintiff.

Oregon's retraction statute, like many other states requires demands for retraction or correction to be in writing signed by the defamed person or her attorney the attorney and delivered to the publisher of the defamatory statement.

The demand must specify which statements are false and defamatory and request that they be corrected or retracted. The demand may also refer to the sources from which the true facts may be ascertained with accuracy.

Under Oregon's retraction statute, the publisher of the defamatory statement shall have not more than two weeks after receiving receipt of the demand for correction or retraction in which to investigate the demand.

(E) PRIVACY BASED CYBERTORTS

The right of privacy includes four causes of action: (1) the right to be free from invasion into one's solitude or intrusion upon seclusion, (2) the right to be free from public disclosure of private facts, (3) the right to be free from placement in a false light, and (4) the right not to have one's identity appropriated for commercial purposes.

(1) Intrusion upon Seclusion

The elements required to state a claim for the intrusion upon seclusion invasion of privacy tort are: "(1) an unauthorized intrusion or prying into a plaintiff's seclusion; (2) the intrusion would be 'highly offensive or objectionable to a reasonable person;' (3) the matters upon which the intrusion occurred were private; and (4) the intrusion caused anguish and suffering." *Huon v. Breaking Media LLC*, 75 F. Supp. 3d 747 (N.D. Ill. 2014).

The Vermont Superior for Chittenden County found a sufficient basis for an intrusion upon seclusion claim arising out of a cyberstalking case:

> To establish an invasion of privacy, FitzGerald must show that Brady "intentionally interfered with [his] interest in solitude or seclusion in a way that would be highly offensive to a reasonable person" and the intrusion must be "substantial."
>
> Here, the alleged sixteen instances of intrusion over a year include sexually explicit messages where FitzGerald already had a restraining order against Brady. These actions, if proven, could constitute persistent conduct that would be highly offensive to a reasonable person. cannot conclude at this early stage of the

proceedings that sixteen alleged instances of intrusion over a one-year period is insufficient as a matter of law.

(2) Appropriation & Right of Publicity

"The right of publicity is an intellectual property right that protects against the misappropriation of a person's name, likeness, or other indicia of personal identity—such as nickname, pseudonym, voice, signature, likeness, or photograph—for commercial benefit." International Trademark Association, *Right of Publicity: What Is Right of Publicity?* (2026).

The elements of the tort of the right of publicity are: (1) the defendant's use of the plaintiff's identity, (2) the appropriation of plaintiff's name or likeness to defendant's advantage, commercially or otherwise, and (3) the plaintiff has not given the defendant consent.

The right of publicity applies to anyone "who appropriates the commercial value of a person's identity by using without consent the person's name, likeness, or other indicia of identity for purposes of trade is subject to liability." Restatement (Third) of Unfair Competition § 46 (2005).

The right of publicity is exercised by public figures such as movie stars and famous athletes, but ordinary persons also has remedies for the nonconsensual use of their name, likeness, or identity.

Famous celebrities can prevail in a right of publicity case, where there is no First Amendment interest in the content such as a private sex tape. The federal district court enjoined an adult entertainment website from distributing the video sex tape of celebrity couple, Pamela Anderson Lee, and musician Brett Michaels.

The court found the site liable for copyright infringement as well as the celebrities' right of privacy and publicity. *Michaels v. Internet Ent. Group Inc.*, 5 F. Supp. 2d 823 (C.D. Cal. 1998).

Deep-fakes makers use the likeness of a celebrity to sell porn and are the latest frontier in right of publicity cases. Celebrities would have a right of publicity action against deep fakes used to make it appear that it is a famous movie star, singer, or other public figure in a porn video.

In 2018, four prominent rappers filed a right of publicity and copyright infringement case against Epic Games arguing the popular game copied their dance moves. Nicholas Camillo, *Fortnite Sparks a Battle Royale Over the Right to Use Dance Moves*, FINNEGAN (Feb. 11, 2019).

> The specific Fortnite emotes at issue in the lawsuits are 'Swipe It,' 'Floss,' 'Hype,' and 'Fresh.' The 'Swipe It,' 'Floss,' and 'Hype' emotes are reminiscent of the viral 'Milly Rock,' 'Floss,' and 'Shoot' dances created and performed by Terrance Ferguson, Russell Horning, and James Baker, respectively. Currently, dance moves cannot be copyrighted.

In *Upper Deck Co. v. Pixels.Com, LLC*, 2026 U.S. Dist. LEXIS 46911 (S.D. Calif. Mar. 6, 2026), Pixels operates print-on-demand websites allowing users to upload images and sell physical prints. Products on Pixels' site featured Hall of Fame basketball player Michael Jordan, who played fifteen seasons for the Chicago Bulls. Jordan's likeness and Upper Deck's hologram trademark was used without authorization. Upper Deck sent cease-and-desist letters in 2022; Pixels continued operations.

Upper Deck asserted a right of publicity claim under California tort law as it had standing to sue as the licensee of Jordan's right to publicity. The court refused Pixel's request for summary judgment of the right of publicity claims:

However, the record is replete with evidence that at the very least, triable issues remain as to both Jump 23's and Upper Deck's publicity rights to Jordan's likeness. First, the definition of Jordan's Attributes in the Jump 23 Agreement, § 1(A), originated in 1991 from an agreement between Jordan and Jump 23.

Upper Deck and Jump 23 have been operating under that same definition of Jordan's Attributes for decades, as Upper Deck has conducted national and international sales of products containing Jordan's likeness pursuant to its licensing rights under the Jump 23 Agreement.

Jump 23 granted Upper Deck merchandising rights to use Jordan's likeness (including Jordan's Marks) in its memorabilia via the Jump 23 Agreement. Additionally, in an addendum to the Jump 23 Agreement, Jump 23 explicitly granted

Upper Deck rights to pursue legal claims against Pixels for Pixels' misuse of Jordan's name and likeness.

(3) Public Disclosure of Private Fact

To pursue a public disclosure of private facts action, the plaintiff must plead that: (1) publicity was given to the disclosure of private facts, (2) the facts were private, not public, (3) the matter made public was such as to be highly offensive to a reasonable person, and (4) the matter publicized was not one of legitimate public concern.

In *Davidson v. Hewlett-Packard*, 2018 WL 3659053 (N.D. Cal. Aug. 2, 2018), Jonathan Davidson's claim for public disclosure of private facts arose out of the defendants' unauthorized access of Davidsons' online communication and their use of the United HealthCare website and portal to intrude in the laptop, computing or communication devices of Jonathan and his family.

The court held that Davidson adequately pleaded a claim for public disclosure of private facts stating:

> Construed liberally and viewed in the light most favorable to Plaintiffs, these allegations plausibly state a claim for public disclosure of private facts. The TAC alleges that Defendants 'communicated, disseminated and publicly distributed private information and records of Corinna and Jonathan Davidson' including 'details of the physical, emotional and mental health and condition of Jonathan and Corinna

Davidson.' . . . Taken as true, these allegations are sufficient to plausibly allege a claim for public disclosure of private facts.

In *F.B.C. v. MdWise, Inc.*, 122 N.E.3d 834 (Ind. Ct. of App. 2019), the wife of a policyholder filed an action against the health insurer after the insurer indicated that she had been tested for various sexually transmitted diseases on an online portal. The husband viewed this information, ceased the reconciliation of their marriage, and divorced her. The court dismissed the wife's public disclosure of private facts, because Indiana does not recognize this cause of action.

(4) False Light

One who gives publicity to a matter concerning an individual in a way that places the said individual before the public in a false light is subject to liability to the other for invasion of his privacy, if (1) the false light in which the other was placed would be highly offensive to a reasonable person; and (2) the actor had knowledge of or acted in reckless disregard as to the falsity of the publicized matter and the false light in which the other would be placed.

In *Lograsso v. Frey,* 10 N.E.3d 1176 (Ohio Ct. of App. 2014), a city law director brought action against website operators and city resident for defamation and false-light invasion of privacy, and sought punitive damages. The appeals court affirmed a dismissal of the false light claim. Holding that the resident's statements about director were non-actionable opinion; and the director's conclusory allegations about inferences from city resident's statements were insufficient to state a claim.

The court found was no evidence that political website operator, who filed grievance with disciplinary counsel of the Ohio Supreme Court to obtain review of whether city law director should continue to practice law, publicized the grievance, as required for the law director to prevail on defamation or false-light invasion of privacy claims against the website operator, though city resident who spoke against law director at city council meeting allegedly referred to information contained in operator's "packet" to disciplinary counsel. The court concluded:

> Because we have found that the alleged comments made at the city council meetings could not sustain a cause of action for either defamation or false-light invasion of privacy, we also necessarily find that such causes of action cannot be sustained by DiFranco and Furry's posting a video of the meetings on the internet.

§ 6-4. Negligence Based Actions

(A) INTERNET RELATED NEGLIGENCE

The elements of Internet negligence are duty, breach, causation (cause-in-fact and legal causation), and damages. Duty is a legal obligation to conform to a reasonable person standard of care in order to protect others against unreasonable risks of harm. A breach of the duty of care is the failure of a defendant to conform to the standard of reasonable care.

(B) NEGLIGENT ENABLEMENT

The failure to implement reasonable cybersecurity poses great risks to our networked society. Increasingly, the world's infrastructure is software-driven and networked, creating new vulnerabilities. For example, LinkedIn.com used outdated methods to secure information of subscribers that enabled 6.5 million passwords to be purloined by some unknown cybercriminal.

Assuming they are able to prove duty and breach, the biggest barrier to a negligent enablement claim for stolen passwords is for plaintiffs to demonstrate a nexus between substandard security and a concrete injury they suffered.

The proposed tort of the "negligent enablement of cybercrime," would hold software vendors, ISPs, or other entities liable for damages when their insecure products or services allow third-party criminals to commit cyberattacks or fraud.

Michael L. Rustad & Thomas H. Koenig, *The Tort of Negligent Enablement of Cybercrime*, 20 BERKELEY TECH. L.J. 1553, 1598 (2005).

Courts have been slow to recognize a company's duty to secure their website or computers system to prevent hackers from compromising their computer system. Plaintiffs in inadequate computer security cases are often customers harmed when their personal data or valuable trade secrets are misappropriated. New York has not yet recognized a cause of action for the negligent enablement of imposter fraud. In most cases, customers have lost these claims as they are unable to establish standing or proven damages.

Plaintiffs had a rare victory in *Lone Star Nat. Bank, N.A. v. Heartland Payment Sys.*, 729 F.3d 421 (5th Cir. 2013), where the Fifth Circuit applying New Jersey law held the economic loss doctrine did not bar credit card issuer banks' negligence claim against the processer of credit card transactions.

This case arose out of hackers' breach of Heartland Payment Systems, Inc.'s (Heartland's) data systems, compromising confidential information belonging to customers of the plaintiff banks. The federal district court dismissed the Issuer Banks' claims. The lower court dismissed the negligence claim reasoning that the economic loss doctrine precludes a party from recovering purely financial damages in tort lawsuits.

The Fifth Circuit reversed and remanded allowing the banks' negligence claims to go forward. The court held that the economic loss doctrine did not bar the Issuer Banks' negligence claim at this preliminary stage. The court stated that the Issuer Banks would be left with no remedy for Heartland's alleged negligence, which defies "notions of fairness, common sense and morality." Heartland's negligence caused the issuer banks documented financial losses because they had to (1) compensate consumers for fraudulent charges and (2) issue a large number of replacement cards.

Lone Star National Bank v. Heartland Payment Systems, 729 F.3d 421 (5th Cir. 2013).

"Injury in fact is 'an invasion of a legally protected interest' that is 'concrete and particularized' and 'actual or imminent, not conjectural or hypothetical.'" *Kenny v. Wilson*, 885 F.3d 280, 287 (4th Cir. 2018) (quoting *Spokeo, Inc. v. Robins*, 136 S.Ct. 1540, 1548 (2016)). For a dispute to be within the power (the subject-matter jurisdiction) of a federal court, the plaintiff must have standing—that is, the plaintiff must have alleged a sufficient interest in the dispute.

This "irreducible constitutional minimum" of standing has three elements: (1) the plaintiff has suffered a concrete injury; (2) that injury is fairly traceable to actions of the defendant; and (3) it must be likely—not merely speculative—that the injury will be "redressed by a favorable decision." *Lujan v. Defenders of Wildlife*, 504 U.S. 555, 560–61 (1992).

(C) NEGLIGENCE *PER SE*

The plaintiff must prove three things to establish negligence *per se*: (1) the violation must have caused the injury, (2) the injury must be the type intended to be prevented by the statute, and (3) the injured party must be one of the class intended to be protected by the statute.

In *Stassi v. Immediata Health Group Corp.*, patients whose personal and medical information was compromised as a result of medical billing provider's data breach filed a class action against billing provider, alleging tort claims including negligence per se. Defendant moved to dismiss for lack of subject matter jurisdiction and for failure to state a claim.

The federal district court concluded that negligence per se doctrine supported the plausibility of patients' negligence claim, California law makes medical billing provider liable if a data breach results in posting Internet patients' confidential medical information, which was protected by California Confidentiality of Medical Information Act (CMIA).

In deciding the providers' motion to dismiss for failure to state a claim, it was reasonable to infer that alleged injuries resulting from posting of medical information on the Internet were the injuries the statute was intended to prevent, and that patients, as persons who initially provided confidential medical information that provider possessed, were within class of persons for whose protection the statute was adopted, The court imposed a duty on Immediata to protect patient information even though they were not the defendant's customers:

> Immediata owed a duty to protect Plaintiffs' information despite the fact that Plaintiffs were not Inmediata's customers or otherwise in privity with Immediata. As noted above, Plaintiffs allege they lost time responding to Inedita's breach notification, and that they noticed an increase in spam/phishing e-mails and/or calls, . . .It is foreseeable that these alleged harms would result from posting Plaintiffs' personal and medical information on the Internet. It can also reasonably be said that Immediata bears some "moral" blame for failing

to protect medical information concerning persons who were likely unaware that Immediata possessed their medical information in the first place.

The duty of care was also the issue in *Daniel v. Armslist*, 926 N.W.2d 710 (Wisc. 2019). In *Daniel,* the daughter of a shooting victim filed a lawsuit against interactive computer service operator of firearms advertising website, asserting numerous tort claims arising from mass casualty shooting at salon. The trial court dismissed on the grounds that the federal Communications Decency Act barred the claims. Daughter appealed, and the Court of Appeal reversed and remanded.

In 2019, the Wisconsin Supreme Court reversed the Court of Appeals holding that a website hosting advertisements for firearm-related sales which enabled the illegal purchase of firearms used in a mass shooting: Daniels asserted a negligence per se cause of action and other tort claims. Arms list argued that the CDA immunizes it from liability for the information posted by third parties on armslist.com, and moved to dismiss Daniel's complaint for failure to state a claim. The appeals court agreed with Armslist that CDA Section 230 barred Daniel's negligence per se claim (as well as other tort causes of action):

In this case, Armslist did not develop the content of Linn's firearm advertisement, so Armslist is not an information content provider with respect to the advertisement. Daniel's argument is based primarily on the assertion that Armslist's design features make it easier for prohibited purchasers to illegally obtain firearms. She asserts that Armslist should have known, actually knew, or even intended that its website would facilitate illegal firearm sales to dangerous persons.

The text and purpose of the CDA require us to reject Daniel's intent argument. Again, Section 230(c)(1) contains no good faith requirement; we analyze only whether Armslist materially contributed to the unlawfulness of third-party content such that it "developed" the content as provided in § 230(f)(3).

Because it did not, it is not an information content provider with respect to the content; therefore, Daniel's claims depend on content provided only by third parties.

(D) COMPUTER PROFESSIONAL NEGLIGENCE

U.S. courts have concluded "that computer professionals are not subject to a higher duty of care based on their profession." *Superior Edge, Inc. v. Monsanto Co.*, 44 F. Supp. 3d 890, 911 (D. Minn. 2014). "Of the courts to consider the question, the overwhelming majority have determined that a malpractice or professional negligence claim does not lie against computer consultants or programmers."

As of 2026, no U.S. court has recognized an action for computer malpractice for inadequate security.

For example, New York does not recognize a cause of action for malpractice by computer professionals. *Nielsen Media Research Inc. v. Microsystems Software Inc.*, 2002 WL 31175223 (S.D.N.Y. Sept. 30 2002). A New York federal court noted that computer consultants are not held to a professional standard of care:

> New York law is clear in limiting imposition of a duty, the breach of which can support a claim in tort, to a limited class of professionals and circumstances. Falconstor is a provider of computer software, hardware, and related installation services. While such goods and services require specialized knowledge, New York State law does not 'recognize a cause of action for professional malpractice by computer consultants.' *Avazpour Networking Services, Inc. v. Falconstor Software, Inc.*, 937 F. Supp. 2d 355, 364 (E.D.N.Y. 2013).

(E) NEGLIGENT DATA BROKERING

Negligent data brokering occurs when an information broker sells information to a client pertaining to a third party, when they have a cognizable legal duty to that third party with respect to the sale of the information.

In *Remsburg v. Docusearch, Inc.*, 816 A.2d 1001 (N.H. 2003), the New Hampshire Supreme Court held an online data broker owed a duty to Amy Boyer, a murder victim, because the data broker breached a duty of care in providing the killer with her Social Security number and other personal contact information without taking steps to determine how the data would be used.

On July 29, 1999, New Hampshire resident Liam Youens contacted Docusearch through its Internet website and requested the date of birth for Amy Lynn Boyer, a former high school classmate. Youens provided Docusearch his name, New Hampshire address, and a contact telephone number along with a $20 fee. He e-mailed Docusearch inquiring whether it would be possible to get better results using Boyer's home address, which he provided, giving Docusearch a different contact phone number.

Later that same day, Youens again contacted Docusearch and placed an order for Boyer's social security number (SSN), paying the $45 fee by credit card. On August 2, 1999, Docusearch obtained Boyer's social security number from a credit-reporting agency and provided it to Youens.

The next day, Youens placed an order with Docusearch for Boyer's employment information, paying the $109 fee by credit card, and giving Docusearch the same phone number he had provided originally.

Shortly after obtaining information from Docusearch, Youens drove to Boyer's workplace and fatally shot her as she left work. Youens then shot and killed himself. The New Hampshire Supreme Court ruled that the data broker owed a duty to third persons whose information was disclosed if the company was subjecting them an unreasonable risk of harm. The N.H. Supreme Court concluded that the harm of selling information was foreseeable based upon Docusearch's own knowledge as well as the danger inherent in selling personal information.

To date, the New Hampshire Supreme Court case is the only negligent data broker legal opinion case where the intermediary was held liable for contributing to the harm by supplying personal information or data to a criminal or stalker.

§ 6-5. Internet-Related Products Liability

(A) OVERVIEW OF PRODUCTS LIABILITY

Products liability is predicated upon three types of defects: manufacturing defects, design defects, and "warning defects," meaning inadequate warnings or failures to warn. Section 1 of the Restatement (Third) makes each seller in the chain of distribution liable if there is proof that the product was sold with a defect.

Plaintiffs have had little success in classifying video games, movies, and websites as 'products' for purposes of products liability. The landmark case was *James v. Meow Media, Inc.*, 300 F.3d 683 (6th Cir, 2002),

On December 1, 1997, Michael Carneal walked into the lobby of Heath High School in Paducah, Kentucky, and shot several of his fellow students, killing three and wounding many others. The parents and estate administrators of Carneal's victims filed a products liability action against the creators of the violent video games, movies, and Internet sites. The parents' complaint noted that:

> Carneal regularly played video games, watched movies, and viewed internet sites produced by the defendant firms. These activities, James argues, "desensitized" Carneal to violence and "caused" him to kill the students of Heath High School. James claims that the distribution of this material to impressionable youth like Carneal constitutes actionable negligence under Kentucky law, entitling James to recover wrongful death damages from the distributing firms.

The Sixth Circuit acknowledged that Carneal viewed violent content created by the defendants:

> . . .Carneal regularly played "Doom," "Quake," "Castle Wolfenstein," "Redneck Rampage," "Nightmare Creatures," "Mech Warrior," "Resident Evil," and "Final Fantasy," which are interactive computer games that, in various ways, all involve the player shooting virtual opponents. Carneal also possessed a video tape containing the movie, "The Basketball Diaries," in a few minutes of which the high-school-student protagonist dreams of killing his teacher and several of his fellow classmates. Investigators examined Carneal's computer and discovered that he had visited "www. persiankitty.com," which appears to catalogue and link to sites with sexually-suggestive material. It also appeared that through "www. adultkey.com," www.adultkey.com, a site operated by Network Authentication Systems and designed to restrict access to certain

websites to viewers over certain ages, Carneal was granted age verification sufficient to visit many other pornographic sites.

In response to the plaintiffs' argument that violent video games and Internet content made these companies liable for products liability, the Sixth Circuit stated: James's theory of product liability in this case is deeply flawed. First, and something none of the parties have mentioned, the "consumers or ultimate users" of the alleged products are not the ones claiming physical harm in this case. Restatement (Second) of Torts § 402A. Carneal was the person who "consumed" or "used" the video games, movie, and internet sites. Allegedly because of Carneal's consumption of the products, he killed the victims in this case. . . .Kentucky courts, but certainly not all courts, have extended the protection of products liability to "bystanders" who are injured by the product, but are not "using" or "consuming" the product. . . .Imposing strict liability for the injuries suffered in this case would be an extension of Kentucky's bystander jurisprudence, as the decedents were not directly injured by the products themselves, but by Carneal's reaction to the products.

The appeals court concluded that the plaintiffs failed to demonstrate a prior requirement, that the video games, movies, and Internet sites are "products" for purposes of strict liability. When dealing with ideas and images, courts have been willing to separate the sense in which the tangible containers of those ideas are products from their communicative element for purposes of strict liability.

In *Amazon v. McMillan*, 625 S.W.3d 101 (Tex. 2021), the Texas Supreme Court held that third-party e-commerce platforms—such as Amazon, eBay, Etsy, and Alibaba—were not strictly liable for defective products manufactured and owned by third parties.

The court concluded that Amazon.com was not a "seller" under Texas law as it does not hold title to third-party products sold on its website. Amazon describes itself as a marketplace where other sellers exhibit their wares but allows the marketplace to handle the payment mechanism of any subsequent sales.

In *Wallace v. Tri-State Assembly, LLC*, 201 A.D.3rd 65 (N.Y. Sup. Ct., App. Divis. First Dept. 2021), the plaintiff sustained injuries when the handlebars of an electric bike his father purchase for him through Amazon loosened while he was riding causing him to fall.

Nonparty Eshion, a China based company, listed the bicycle for sale on Amazon.com. At the time of purchase, plaintiff's father also elected to buy a service option to have the bicycle assembled.

Former codefendant Tri-State Assembly (Tri-State), which offers its services for sale on Amazon.com and is an Amazon approved service provider, assembled it. Tri-State was uninsured at the time it provided assembly services to plaintiff.

After Tri-State was dismissed from the case, the trial court granted summary judgment in Amazon's favor. In so doing, the trial court found that Amazon had impliedly warranted neither the bike nor Tri-State's assembly services. Wallace appealed to the New York Appellate Division. There, Wallace argued that Amazon was liable for breach of the implied warranties under New York law. Alternatively, Wallace argued that the court should create an equitable remedy extending the implied warranties to Amazon because he had no other means of recovery.

The Appellate Court concluded that Amazon could not be held liable for negligence and breach of implied warranties related to a product sold by a third-party seller and assembled by an independent service provider. The Appellate Division of the Supreme Court of New York affirmed the lower court's decision to grant Amazon summary judgment, dismissing the claims against it.

The court found that Amazon's role was simply providing the Internet platform for the sale. They also observed that Amazon disclaimed warranties for third-party products in their conditions of use. The plaintiff's breach of warranty claim failed as Amazon submitted sufficient evidence to prove it was not a seller.

The court noted that expanding liability to Amazon would conflict with settled New York law, which limits liability to sellers and those within the manufacturing, selling, or distribution chain.

This court takes a narrow and formalistic approach that Amazon never owned the electric bicycle and could therefore not be the seller nor make anno implied warranty of merchantability. Plaintiffs in future cases will argue that Amazon is functionally equivalent to a seller and should therefore be accountable as a seller.

In *Oberdorf v. Amazon.com Inc.*, 930 F.3d 136 (3rd Cir. 2019), Heather Oberdorf purchased a dog collar on Amazon.com from a third-party vendor identified as "The Furry Gang." Amazon did not design, manufacture, have title to, or ever possess the dog collar. While Oberdorf was walking her dog on a retractable leash, the D-Ring on the collar broke, causing the leash to recoil, hitting her in the eye, and resulting in permanent blindness.

Neither Amazon nor Oberdorf could locate The Furry Gang, so Oberdorf sued Amazon, asserting strict liability under § 402A because it "facilitated and participated in the sale and distribution of the subject dog collar." The district court granted summary judgment in favor of Amazon.

In a 2–1 decision, a panel of the Third Circuit vacated the summary judgment and ruled that Amazon was strictly liable for the injuries caused by the defective dog collar. A series of California decisions have followed the Third Circuit's lead by holding that a marketplace can be liable in products cases, even where it never took custody of the products at issue.

On July 14, 2021, the Consumer Product Safety Commission (CPSC) filed an administrative complaint against Amazon, directing the online retailer to recall hazardous products sold on its site. Future cases will determine whether digital platforms like Amazon should be classified as part of the product distribution chain.

(B) TYPES OF PRODUCTS DEFECTS

Section 2 of the Restatement (Third) of Torts: Products Liability requires a product defect to be determined "at the time of sale or distribution." Section 19 of the Third Restatement defines a product for purposes of strict liability as tangible personal property distributed commercially. (Restatement (Third) Torts: Products Liability, § 19, subds. (a), (c).) A court concluded that a virtual reality game was not a product for purposes of strict liability. *Wilson v. Midway Games, Inc.*, 198 F. Supp. 2d 167, 173 (D. Conn. 2002).

(1) Manufacturing Defects

A product has a manufacturing defect when the product departs from its intended design even though all care was exercised in the preparation and marketing of the product. Manufacturing defects tend to occur on the assembly line, during construction or in packaging an item. Unlike design flaws, these are usually isolated to a specific batch or unit. Examples would include a loose bolt, foreign object in food, or improper wiring or assembly of a single unit.

(2) Design Defects

A design defect in product liability occurs when a product causes injury because of it fundamental design, rendering it unreasonably dangerous even if manufactured perfectly. If a product has a design defect, all products of the same type have the same defect. The foremost test for determining design defects is the consumer expectations test.

A product has a design defect if it "fails to meet ordinary consumer expectations as to safety" or "the design is not as safe as it should be." Restatement (Second) § 402A. The consumer must use the product for its intended use. Product misuse in product liability cases occurs when a consumer uses a product in a way that is not foreseen by the manufacturer, causing injury. For example, a consumer cannot use a lawn mower to trim the hedges. Consuming laundry detergent packets would constitute product misuse. If misuse is foreseeable, the manufacturer has a duty to warn the consumer.

The Restatement (Third) considers a defective design to occur:

> when the foreseeable risks of harm posed by the product could have been reduced or avoided by the adoption of a reasonable alternative design by the seller or other distributor, or a predecessor in the commercial chain of distribution, and the omission of the alternative design renders the product not reasonably safe.

Restatement (Third) Torts: Products Liability § 2(b) (American Law Institute, 1997).

In a 2019 case, a plaintiff sued Apple Inc. and one hundred unknown defendants, alleging "that Apple's iOS 12.1 software was defective in allowing unknown third parties to eavesdrop on users, without their permission, during a group Facetime." *Williams v. Apple Inc.*, 2019 WL 2057960 (S.D. Tex. May 9, 2019). Williams argued that Apple is strictly liable:

> to him because the iOS 12.1 software had a design defect and failed to give him and other users warning or instruction about the defect. To state a Texas design-defect claim, a plaintiff must allege facts showing that '(1) the product was defectively designed so as to render it unreasonably dangerous; (2) a safer alternative design existed; (3) the defect was a producing cause of the injury for which plaintiff seeks recovery.'

The court dismissed William's case because he did not allege facts about any available alternative design:

> He fails to allege facts about the iOS 12.1 software as to whether the defect that allegedly allowed a third party to 'eavesdrop' on his group Facetime call was 'unreasonable' for the product's ordinary use. Williams's generalized allegation that the iOS 12.1 software was 'unreasonably dangerous' and caused him injury falls short of the Rule 8 threshold.

(3) Failure or Inadequate Warning

When a manufacturer fails to properly warn of a product's dangerous propensities, that failure may make an otherwise non-defective product unreasonably dangerous. The Restatement (Third) states that a product may be "defective because of inadequate instructions or warnings when the foreseeable risks of harm posed by the product could have been reduced or avoided by the provision of reasonable instructions or warnings by the seller or other distributor." Restatement (Third) § 2(c).

In a failure to warn case, the plaintiff must prove that:

> (1) a risk of harm exists that is inherent in the product or that may arise from the intended or reasonably anticipated use of the product; (2) the product supplier must actually know, or could reasonably foresee, the risk of harm at the time the product is marketed; (3) the product must have a marketing defect; (4) the absence of the warning or instructions must render the product unreasonably dangerous to the ultimate user or consumer of the product; and (5) the failure to warn or instruct must constitute a causative nexus in the product user's injury.

(C) STRICT PRODUCTS LIABILITY

Strict product liability is the leading theory of product liability having been adopted in 1965 by the Restatement (Second) § 402A. Section 402A was adopted by all but a few jurisdictions by the 1980s

Strict liability eliminated the need for plaintiffs to demonstrate manufacturer's fault or to prove privity of contract.

A manufacturer, distributor, component parts supplier or other defendant in a supply chain may be liable for negligent products liability. The only significant difference between a strict products liability cause of action and negligence is the additional requirement that the plaintiff prove that the seller breached a standard of care.

(D) WARRANTY-BASED PRODUCTS LIABILITY

(1) Breach of Warranty as a Theory of Product Liability

Breach of warranty actions in products cases may be divided into actions based upon UCC § 2–313 express warranties; the implied warranty of merchantability under UCC § 2–314; and the implied warranty of fitness for a particular purpose, UCC § 2–315.

In strict liability and negligence-based products liability, the plaintiff must prove that a defect had a causal relationship with the plaintiff's injuries. The liability for breach of express warranty may be thought of as a form of strict liability but one difference from Section 402A is that the claimant need not demonstrate a manufacturing defect, design defect or failure to warn.

(2) Express Warranty

The product has no burden of proof to show that a product is defective only that the seller breached the warranty which was the cause of her injury. An express warranty is created by any affirmation of fact or promise made by the seller to the buyer which relates to the goods and becomes part of the basis of the bargain. UCC § 2–313(1)(a).

(3) Implied Warranty of Merchantability

To be "merchantable" the goods must pass without objection in the trade under the contract description and be fit for the ordinary purposes for which they were intended. A products liability plaintiff must prove five elements to establish a UCC § 2–314 claim: (1) that a merchant sold goods, (2) which were not merchantable at the time of sale, (3) proximately causing by the defective nature of the goods, (4) injury and damages to the claimant or his property, and (5) notice to the seller of the injury.

The issue is not the degree of care exercised in the design and manufacture manufacturing of the product, but rather whether the goods meet the various quality standards of UCC § 2–314 which states:

> [A] warranty that the goods shall be merchantable is implied in a contract for their sale if the seller is a merchant with respect to goods of that kind. . . . Goods to be merchantable must be . . . fit for the ordinary purposes for which such goods are used. UCC § 2–314.

(4) Fitness for a Particular Purpose

Section 2–315 of the UCC creates a cause of action for breach of implied warranty of fitness for a particular purpose where the seller at the time of contracting has reason to know any particular purpose for which the goods are required and that the buyer is relying on the seller's skill or judgment to select or furnish suitable goods.

(E) INTERNET-RELATED PRODUCTS LIABILITY

Tort law has "progressively expanded the obligation owed by manufacturers to those foreseeable harmed by their products." *Hamilton v. ACTU-TEK*, 1999 U.S. Dist. LEXIS 8264 (E.D.N.Y. June 3, 1999). Only one products liability lawsuit was filed against a website for selling defective goods on a website in the past three decades.

The court ruled in favor of the defendant in the sole successful products liability action, a 2003 case, arose out of the website sale of a field-monitoring device for tracking criminals under house arrest.

The manufacturer's website advertised that its field-monitoring unit in the offender's home would detect any tampering. However, when a murderer cut off the ankle device, he was out of range of the monitoring unit, so the home unit did not detect the tampering. The court refused to impose a legal duty on the manufacturer to make a tamper-proof field-monitoring device.

Similarly, the court found that the monitoring device did not breach any express or implied warranty, nor was it defectively manufactured. The victim's estate successfully brought an action only for misrepresentation based on false statements about the field-monitoring unit on the company's website.

Kirby v. B.I. Inc., 2003 U.S. Dist. LEXIS 16964 at *49–50 (N.D. Tex. Sept. 26, 2003).

Products Liability will evolve to address connected devices:

> If an IoT device is hacked and/or malfunctions, there will be new challenges with regard to product liability law. Traditional notions of product liability law provide that a product manufacturer, component part supplier, or seller (and others who make products available to the public) are to be held liable if they put a defective product into a consumer's hands and the defect causes personal injury or property damage. . . . With an IoT device, however, these traditional notions will be challenged. What product liability law will look like in 2020 is an unknown. Today, unfortunately, there are more questions than answers.

Letta E. Gorman, *The Era of the Internet of Things: Can Product Liability Laws Keep Up?*, DEFENSE COUNSEL JOURNAL (Feb. 7, 2020).

Tort law must recognize a new duty of care for IoT providers:

> Like other fiduciaries, IoT companies would have a duty of care; specifically, a duty not to foreseeably cause harm to their consumers by discontinuing service, remotely altering a device, or otherwise engaging in digital repossession. IoT companies would also have a duty of loyalty, which would require them to act in the interests of the IoT device user. . . . This duty could also forbid terminating service, digitally repossessing, or otherwise altering how an IoT device operates absent adequate warning or notice.

Rebecca Crootof, *Accountability for the Internet of Torts*, BALKINIZATION (BLOG) (July 25, 2018).

§ 6-6. International Cybertorts

Torts play a far more significant role in the U.S. and other common law countries, whereas civil law countries rely mostly upon administrative fines or penalties as opposed to private causes of action. If the Chinese influencer case occurred in the U.S., the victim would have actions for the torts of assault, battery, and conversion in addition to the criminal law offenses.

Outside the U.S. and common countries, social media and Internet-related torts are seldom treated as such. Rather, it would be a matter for regulators or prosecutors. Cybertorts are undeveloped in civil law countries. Rebecca Crootof conceptualizes international cybertorts as:

> an act that employs, infects, or undermines the internet, a computer system, or a network and thereby causes significant transboundary harm. Like the definition of transnational cybercrime, the international cybertort definition is means-based and encompasses a broad range of harmful activities.

Rebecca Crootof, *International Cybertorts: Expanding State Accountability in Cyberspace*, 103 CORNELL L. REV. 565, 592 (2018).

(A) INTERMEDIARY LIABILITY

U.S. courts have overextended Congress's express language in § 230 of the Communications Decency Act from the narrow purpose of immunizing ISPs as publishers to the expanded purpose of shielding them from all tort liability. In contrast, Internet intermediaries in European countries do not enjoy immunity for third party postings because there is no equivalent to CDA Section 230.

In *Tamiz v. Google, Inc.*, No. 2013 EWCA Civ. 68 (EWWA 2013), an English and Welsh court ruled that Google Inc. could be held liable as the publisher of an allegedly defamatory blog posting because of its failure to remove the post after receiving a complaint.

The strong administrative state in many civil code countries is an alternative to a strong cybertort regime. For example, in Sweden claimants look to insurance first and to torts second for accident compensation. In Sweden, the tort system serves as a backup for those few individuals, such as foreigners, not covered by the nation's social security compensation agency, the *Forsakringskassan*.

In Europe, cybertorts are patrolled by consumer regulatory agencies, not private litigants. The United States is the only country connected to the Internet depending upon the tort system to fulfill public law functions. For example, the countries of the European Union arm consumer regulatory agencies with roving powers to protect privacy and other rights of persons.

Unlike CDA Section 230, the European Union's E-Commerce Directive imposes a takedown duty on websites for ongoing torts or crimes. As is in the United States, EU intermediaries have no duty to monitor websites for illegal third-party generated content.

(B) TRANSBORDER SECURITY BREACHES

Data security breaches are cross-border cybertorts affecting victims in scores of countries. "From Adidas (two million records compromised) to Facebook (up to two billion accounts scraped), 2018 has seen more than its fair share of massive global data breaches." Ed Targett, *6 Months, 945 Data Breaches, 4.5 Billion Records,* CBR (Oct. 9, 2018).

"Gemalto reveals that 945 data breaches led to a staggering 4.5 billion data records being compromised worldwide in the first half of 2018." "Hotel chain Marriott suffered the year's biggest breach, after uncovering one of its systems containing up to 500 million guests' details had been jeopardised."

Jamie Harris, *The Biggest Global Data Breaches of 2018,* SKYWIRE (Dec. 31, 2018).

In 2016, 3 billion Yahoo accounts were hacked in one of the biggest breaches of all time. In 2017, the WannaCry virus infected 100,000 groups in at least 150 countries and more than 400,000 machines costing $4 billion.

Note on Wanna Crypt Infection Count Accuracy, MALWARE TECH (May 19, 2017).

The vast majority of high-profile cybersecurity breaches create cross-border harm where there is no remedy or even notification to the victims:

> The Sony hack, DNC hack, and other recent malicious cyberoperations have highlighted a significant gap in the international law of cyberspace: states are not being held accountable for these kinds of harmful cyberoperations, in part because classifications created in physical space do not map well onto the cyber domain and in part because states appear unwilling to extend existing definitions of wrongful state acts to these activities.

Rebecca Crootof, *International Cybertorts: Expanding State Accountability in Cyberspace*, 103 CORNELL L. REV. 565 (2018).

CHAPTER 7
INTERNET-RELATED PRIVACY

§ 7-1. Overview of Online Privacy Issues

Privacy is evolving as one of the hot practice areas in U.S. law firms. Boston's Foley, Hoag, where I was an associate before becoming a law professor formed a Privacy and Data Security Practice that advices major corporations on compliance with global privacy laws:

- Privacy and information security policies
- Third-party data security agreements
- Security incidents including competitive espionage and proprietary data leaks
- Corporate governance
- Company records, financial information, and other information assets
- Data privacy-specific due diligence in mergers and acquisitions

Dan Solove gives many examples of privacy and the law positions with the federal government:

> There are privacy offices in nearly every government agency. Numerous government agencies regulate privacy, including the Federal Trade Commission, the Consumer Financial Protection Bureau, the Federal Communications Commission, the Department for Health and Human Services, the National

Labor Relations Board, and the Department of Education, among others. Within various agencies are privacy oversight departments, such as the Department of Homeland Security.

This chapter examines a large number of Internet-related privacy questions such as:

- How long do digital footprints last? What control do Internet user have over who uses our information? How does that right differ between the United and the European Union (EU)?
- What degree of control do EU vs. U.S. data subjects have over digitized personal information? How much control do U.S. data subject have over who, when, where, and how information about you is shared?
- Do Internet users have a right to rectify inaccurate information or a right to forget?
- Do consumers have a right to notification upon a data breach? This chapter examines the most significant online privacy issues including topics such as facial, iris, or fingerprint recognition technologies that collect and process biometric information to identify individuals. This chapter is divided into six sections. Section 7-1 is an overview of online privacy issues. Section 7-2 addresses privacy issues raised by biometric technologies.

Section 7-3 covers the role of The Federal Trade Commission (FTC) as the chief federal agency concerned with privacy issues. The FTC privacy disclosures and enforcement will be critically evaluated. Recently, the FTC is studying what limits should be placed upon biometric tracking to protect consumer privacy and data security concerns and limit the potential for bias and discrimination.

Section 7-4 covers privacy, data security and security risks in in the Internet of Things (IoT) will be covered. There are now an estimated twenty billion Internet-connected devices, including smart light bulbs, wearable fitness trackers, and even smart homes. The IoT poses new threats where inadequate security enables cybercriminals to intercept confidential information transmitted by the device.

Data and security breach notification will next be required in Section 7-5. All U.S. jurisdictions have enacted data breach notification to those affected. The FTC also requires that providers notify them of security breaches involving unencrypted information of five hundred or more consumers within 30 days of discovery.

Finally, Section 7-6 covers global privacy regulations focusing on the European Union's General Data Protection Regulation. The EU has comprehensive privacy covering every sector. The U.S., in contrast protects privacy in selected industries supplemented by privacy torts.

§ 7-2. Biometric Technologies

Biometrics is the automated recognition of individuals based on their biological and behavioral characteristics from which distinguishing, repeatable biometric features can be extracted for the purpose of biometric recognition. Biometric data includes any data that depict or describe physical, biological, or behavioral traits, characteristics, or measurements of or relating to an identified or identifiable person's body. The U.S. Department of Homeland Security uses biometric recognition technologies:

> These characteristics, often called modalities, include—but are not limited to—fingerprints, iris patterns, or facial features that can be used for automated recognition. At the Department of Homeland Security (HS), biometrics are used for detecting and preventing illegal entry into the United States, granting and administering proper immigration benefits, vetting and credentialing, facilitating legitimate travel and trade, enforcing federal laws, and enabling verification for visa applications to the United States. HS provides biometric and identity capabilities to protect the Nation through its Office of Biometric Identity Management (OBIM), which supplies the technology for storing, comparing, and sharing biometric data. his system, called the Automated Biometric Identification System or IDENT, is owned and operated by OBIM. IDENT currently holds more than 320 million unique identities and processes

> more than 400,000 biometric transactions per day.

Biometrics, *Homeland Security* (2026).

Homeland Security also shares this vast data base with the U.S. Department of Defense and the U.S. Department of Justice "to support the homeland security, defense, and justice missions."

Companies use biometric technology for identification and authentication of an individual; therefore it is becoming increasingly popular for social media websites to use this technology in their services.

Apple and Samsung use biometric technology in their mobile phones, while retail websites use this technology to pinpoint measurements on a person's face allowing the user to virtually try on makeup or a hairstyle. Companies are increasingly using biometrics to validate identity:

> In 2026, that reality is closer than ever. These everyday credentials—and the frustrations they create—are fading away. The world is moving toward a time where you are the only element needed to validate your identity. Cards, keys and passwords are being replaced by biometric identity frameworks that let you prove who you are instantly across systems and environments.

Daniel Asraf, *The Future Is You: 8 Biometric Trends Redefining Identity in 2026,* HIDGLOBAL.COM (Jan. 27, 2026).

As of 2026, no comprehensive federal statute governs the collection and use of biometric data in the United States. The federal statutes addressing biometric data do not address misuses or abuses of data. The Department of Homeland Security's statutory provision notes that DHS may collect this information:

> An individual may be required to submit biometric information by law, regulation, Federal Register notice or the form instructions applicable to the request type or if required in accordance with 8 CFR 103.2(b)(9). DHS may collect and store for present or future use, by electronic or other means, the biometric information submitted by an individual. DHS may use this biometric information to conduct background and security checks, adjudicate immigration and naturalization benefits, and perform other functions related to administering and enforcing the immigration and naturalization laws.

76 FR 53782, Aug. 29, 2011, as amended at 81 FR 73331, Oct. 24, 2016.

In 2023, the Federal Trade Commission issued a policy statement on biometric data:

> The Commission said the agency is committed to combatting unfair or deceptive acts and practices related to the collection and use of consumers' biometric information and the marketing and use of biometric information technologies.

The FTC policy statement on biometric information states that it will consider several factors in determining whether a business's use of biometric information or biometric information technology could be unfair in violation of the FTC Act including:

- Failing to assess foreseeable harms to consumers before collecting biometric information;
- Failing to promptly address known or foreseeable risks and identify and implement tools for reducing or eliminating those risks;
- Engaging in surreptitious and unexpected collection or use of biometric information;
- Failing to evaluate the practices and capabilities of third parties, including affiliates, vendors, and end users, who will be given access to consumers' biometric information or will be charged with operating biometric information technologies;
- Failing to provide appropriate training for employees and contractors whose job duties involve interacting with biometric information or technologies that use such information; and
- Failing to conduct ongoing monitoring of technologies that the business develops, offers for sale, or uses, in connection with biometric information to ensure that the technologies are functioning as anticipated and that the

technologies are not likely to harm consumers. Illinois, Texas, and Washington enacted biometric privacy regulations, but only Illinois recognizes a private cause of action for consumers:

> The Illinois Biometric Information Privacy Act is the only statute of the three that enshrines a private right of action for those who fail to properly handle biometric data. Both the Texas Capture or Use Biometric Identifier Act Information Act and the Washington Biometric Privacy Act allow for state Attorneys General to bring suit on behalf of aggrieved consumers.
>
> Maya E. Rivera, *Face Off: An Examination of State Biometric Privacy Statutes & Data Harm Remedies,* 24 FORDHAM INTELL. PROP. MEDIA & ENT. L.J. 571 (2019).

The Illinois Biometric Information Privacy Act (BIPA) codified an individual's right to privacy in and control over their biometric identifiers and biometric information. 740 Ill. Comp. Stat. Ann. 14/10, 14/15(a), 14/15(b), 14/20. BIPA was the country's first biometric data protection statute and is the only state statute-recognizing individuals as having a private right of action. The Seventh Circuit stated:

> A key part of the right to control biometric information is 'the power to say no by withholding consent.' When an entity fails to adhere to the statutory procedures and thereby denies someone the ability to make an informed decision about whether to provide her biometric

> identifier, 'the right of the individual to maintain his or her biometric privacy vanishes into thin air.'

Bryant v. Compass Group, Inc., 958 F.3d 617, 621–622 (7th Cir. 2020) (quoting Illinois Supreme Court).

BIPA prohibits the unauthorized collection and storing of some types of biometric data. 740 ILCS 14/1 et seq. BIPA defines "biometric identifier" to mean "a retina or iris scan, fingerprint, voiceprint, or scan of hand or face geometry." 740 ILCS 14/10.

BIPA defines "Biometric information" to mean:

> means any information, regardless of how it is captured, converted, stored, or shared, based on an individual's biometric identifier used to identify an individual. Biometric information does not include information derived from items or procedures excluded under the definition of biometric identifiers.

BIPA requires private companies retaining biometric information to develop retention and destruction guidelines. 740 ILCS 14/15.

BIPA recognizes a cause of action for the non-consensual collection and storage of biometric information:

> Right of Action. Any person aggrieved by a violation of this Act shall have a right of action in a State circuit court or as a supplemental claim in federal district court against an

offending party. A prevailing party may recover for each violation:

(1) against a private entity that negligently violates a provision of this Act, liquidated damages of $1,000 or actual damages, whichever is greater;

(2) against a private entity that intentionally or recklessly violates a provision of this Act, liquidated damages of $5,000 or actual damages, whichever is greater;

(3) reasonable attorneys' fees and costs, including expert witness fees and other litigation expenses; and

(4) other relief, including an injunction, as the State or federal court may deem appropriate.

740 ILCS 14/20.

A 2025 law firm survey identified a large number of Illinois BIPA lawsuits resulting in settlements:

> Many of these cases have resulted in massive settlements. In a landmark 2020 settlement, Facebook paid $650 million to resolve a BIPA class action alleging its facial-recognition photo tagging feature scanned Illinois users' faces without consent. In 2021, the parent company of TikTok agreed to a $92 million settlement to end litigation over alleged unlawful collection of face and voice data through the TikTok app. In 2022, Google settled an Illinois class action for $100 million over its Google Photos tool, which had

used face-recognition to group similar faces without the explicit consent required by BIPA.

Epstein, Becker, Green, *Biometric Backlash: The Rising Wave of Litigation Under BIPA and Beyond* (Aug. 21, 2025).

In 2026, YouTube and Google agreed to settle a class action lawsuit for $6 million arising out the Face Blur feature that "collected biometric data without proper consent, violating Illinois' Biometric Information Privacy Act (BIPA)."

$6M BIPA Settlement Approved in YouTube and Google Face Recognition Lawsuit, TOP CLASS ACTIONS (Feb. 2, 2026).

§ 7-3. FTC's Role as Chief Privacy Regulator

(A) FTC PRIVACY DISCLOSURES

The Federal Trade Commission (FTC) is the chief U.S. federal agency protecting individual privacy. The FTC polices privacy primarily through Section 5 of the Federal Trade Commission Act (FTC Act), which bars unfair and deceptive acts and practices in or affecting commerce.

In addition to Section 5 of the FTC Act, the agency also enforces other federal laws relating to consumers' privacy and security. The FTC has primary jurisdiction to enforce the Privacy Act of 1974, The Children's Online Privacy Protection Act, the Fair Credit Reporting Act, Telemarketing Sales Rule, and many other privacy-related statutes.

The FTC primarily uses injunctive relief to enjoin unlawful behavior. When appropriate, the FTC orders that companies implement comprehensive privacy and security programs. In addition, the FTC can impose civil penalties and order restitution to consumers.

The U.S. has not adopted the EU's General Data Protection Regulation (GDPR), but that comprehensive data protection has aggressive extraterritorial impacts for U.S. companies. A U.S. business collecting, storing, using or transferring EU consumer data must comply with the GDPR. The FTC is committed to enforcing the Data Privacy Framework agreed to by the United States and the European Union:

> On July 17, 2023, the European Commission issued an adequacy decision on the EU-U.S. Data Privacy Framework (DPF). This new voluntary Framework, which replaces the Privacy Shield program, provides a mechanism for companies to transfer personal data from the EU to the United States in a privacy-protective way consistent with EU law. To join the Data Privacy Framework, a company must self-certify to the Department of Commerce that it complies with the Data Privacy Framework Principles. A participating company's failure to comply with the Principles may violate Section 5 of the FTC Act's prohibition on unfair and deceptive acts.

Federal Trade Commission, *Data Privacy Framework* (2026).

The EU/U.S. Data Privacy Framework was developed because the EU does not regard the U.S. privacy rule to adequately protect EU consumer's personal data. There is no comprehensive federal privacy law. U.S. privacy law is a complex patchwork of state and federal law and the common law torts of privacy. Federal privacy statutes enforced by the FTC include:

- The Privacy Act of 1974, 5 U.S.C. 552a, provides privacy protections for records containing information about individuals (i.e., citizen and legal permanent resident) that are collected and maintained by the federal government and are retrieved by a personal identifier. The Act requires agencies to safeguard information contained in a system of records (SOR). It is currently being revised. It is currently being revised.

- The Federal Information Security Modernization Act of 2014 (amends the Federal Information Security Management Act of 2002, 44 U.S.C. 3541), requires agencies to develop, document, and implement an agency-wide program to provide information security for the information and information systems that support the operations and assets of an agency.

- The E-Government Act of 2002 (44 U.S.C. 3601 et seq.) establishes procedures to ensure the privacy of personal information in electronic records.

- Freedom of Information Act (FOIA) generally provides that any person has a right, enforceable in court, to obtain access to federal agency records, except to the extent that such records (or portions of them) are protected from public disclosure by one of nine exemptions or by one of three special law enforcement record exclusions.
- Children's Online Privacy Protection Act of 1998 (15 U.S.C. 6501–06) (COPPA) regulates the online collection and use of personal information provided by and relating to children under the age of 13 (COPPA's Online Privacy Protection Rule).

Industry-specific federal statutes have also been enacted such as The Gramm-Leach-Bliley Act requires financial institutions—companies that offer consumers financial products or services like loans, financial or investment advice, or insurance—to explain their information-sharing practices to their customers and to safeguard sensitive data.

California is one of the only U.S. states to enact more comprehensive data protection with statutes that include:

- Data breach notification laws.
- Obligation to display privacy policies. A California Online Eraser law applies to teens, no right to be forgotten.

"Currently, there are 20 states—including California, Virginia, and Colorado, among others—

that have comprehensive data privacy laws in place." *Which States Have Consumer Data Privacy Laws?*, BLOOMBERG LAW (Apr. 7, 2025).

(B) FTC PRIVACY ENFORCEMENT

The FTC launches investigations and enforcement actions when businesses are suspected of violating Section 5 of the FTC Act, barring unfair and deceptive acts and practices in or affecting commerce.

In 2026, the FTC entered into a settlement with General Motors for privacy abuses arising out of their offering a connected car feature in their GM-branded vehicles called OnStar. Initially, the OnStar module within a vehicle could connect the driver to an OnStar representative who could relay information to first responders in an emergency. The FTC contended that that the privacy policy of OnStar connected services was unfair and deceptive:

> The May 2018 Privacy Statement does not present the collection, use, and sharing disclosures in a form that would allow a consumer to understand the invasiveness of the data collection and sharing. . . In addition, a consumer would reasonably understand this policy to mean that additional user consent or authorization would be collected for sharing a consumer's driving information for marketing activities or uses related to third-party services. Subsequent revisions to the Privacy Statement presented the information in similar fashion until September 2024. Consequently, from May 2018 to September 2024, consumers were asked

to give their consent to the collection, use, and disclosure of their data with incomplete information.

In the Matter of General Motors, Inc., Docket No. C-1428 complaint at 3–4.

The FTC's complaint against General Motors' OnStar connected system also contended that:

> Since at least 2018, Respondents have collected precise geolocation data from millions of Gen10+ OnStar vehicles through a particular task that collected and transmitted precise geolocation data every three seconds, starting from ignition on, to Respondents' (GMC) storage systems. . . .This precise geolocation data consisted of latitude and longitude (intended to be precise up to six decimal places by contractual requirements with third parties, which could pinpoint geolocation accuracy to approximately 111 millimeters, or 4.5 inches), along with elevation, heading, current speed, a date and time stamp, and a trip identifier that could be used to tie multiple transmissions together to identify the entire route of a specific trip taken by a second vehicle.

Section 5(a) of the FTC Act, 15 U.S.C. § 45(a), prohibits "unfair or deceptive acts or practices in or affecting commerce."

The FTC contended that GMC's misrepresentations or deceptive failures to disclose a material fact constitute deceptive or unfair practices. Count I of the complaint charged that GMC sold personal data of drivers without their consent:

> Respondents sell consumers' precise geolocation data and Driver Behavior Data (a) to third parties to license to other entities for transportation planning, infrastructure construction and management, outdoor advertising analytics, and retail and real estate location planning, and (b) to consumer reporting agencies to compile consumer reports that could be used to deny consumers auto insurance coverage or raise their car insurance.
>
> In January 2026, the FTC finalized an order with General Motors and OnStar settling claims that they collected, used, and sold consumers' precise geolocation data and driving behavior data from millions of vehicles without adequately notifying consumers and obtaining their affirmative consent.

Under the agreement, GM is prohibited from sharing certain consumer data with consumer reporting agencies. The auto giant must take steps to provide greater transparency and choice to consumers over the collection, use, and disclosure of their connected vehicle data, The final order also:

> imposes a five-year ban on GM disclosing consumers' geolocation and driver behavior data to consumer reporting agencies. This

> fencing-in relief is appropriate given GM's egregious betrayal of consumers' trust. And for the entire 20-year life of the order, GM will be required to:
>
> - Obtain affirmative express consent from consumers prior to collecting, using, or sharing connected vehicle data (including sharing data with consumer reporting agencies), with some exceptions such as for providing location data to emergency first responders;
> - Create a way for all U.S. consumers to request a copy of their data and seek its deletion;
> - Give consumers the ability to disable the collection of precise geolocation data from their vehicles if their vehicle has the necessary technology; and
> - Provide a way for consumers to opt out of the collection of geolocation and driver behavior data, with some limited exceptions.

The FTC entered into a settlement agreement with Disney on December 31, 2025. Disney agree to a $10 million settlement arising out a complaint that the company allowed personal data to be collected from children who viewed kid-directed videos on YouTube without notifying parents or obtaining their consent as required by the Children's Online Privacy

Protection Rule (COPPA Rule). The FTC describes the final order as follows:

- Pay a $10 million civil penalty for violating the COPPA Rule;
- Comply with the COPPA Rule, including by notifying parents before collecting personal information from children under age 13 and obtaining verifiable parental consent for collection and use of that data; and
- Establish and implement a program to review whether videos posted to YouTube should be designated as MFK—unless YouTube implements age assurance technologies that can determine the age, age range, or age category of all YouTube users or no longer allows content creators to label videos as MFK. This forward-looking provision reflects and anticipates the growing use of age assurance technologies to protect kids online.

A 2025 enforcement action against the Sendit anonymous messaging app for unlawfully collecting personal data from children, misleading users by sending messages from fake "people," and tricking consumers into purchasing paid subscriptions by falsely promising to reveal the senders of anonymous messages.

The Federal Trade Commission describes its complaint as follows:

> The complaint alleged that Iconic Hearts knew that numerous Sendit users were under the age

of 13 but failed to comply with the COPPA Rule. For example, in 2022, more than 116,000 users reported their age as under 13 while using Sendit, according to the complaint. Iconic Hearts also received complaints from parents who indicated that their children were under 13. Even though it was aware that many users were under 13, Iconic Hearts failed to notify parents that it collected personal information from children, including their phone numbers, birthdates, photos and usernames for Snapchat, Instagram, TikTok and other accounts, and did not obtain parents' verifiable consent to such data collection.

The complaint also alleged that Iconic Hearts and Rice deceived Sendit's users, many of whom were children and teens, into purchasing its premium "Diamond Membership" using methods such as:

- Misrepresenting that when users received anonymized Sendit messages, those messages came from users' friends and social media contacts—when, in fact, many messages were fake and generated by Iconic Hearts;
- Sending fake messages that were often provocative and sexual in nature—such as "have you done drugs" or "would you ever get with me?"—and then encouraging users to buy its Diamond Membership to reveal who sent the message;

- Misrepresenting that users would find out the identity of message senders if they purchased a Diamond Membership—when, in reality, users received either false information (if the message was fake) or generic information like location or phone type (if the message was from a real person); and
- Failing to clearly disclose to Diamond Membership purchasers that they would automatically be billed as much as $9.99 every week, rather than paying a one-time fee to see who sent a particular message.

The FTC has taken other enforcement measures in 2025 as follows:

- FTC Will Require Illusory Systems to Return Money Stolen by Hackers and Implement an Information Security Program (December 16, 2025)
- FTC Announces Workshop on Age Verification Technologies (December 8, 2025)
- FTC Denies Petition from SpyFone App CEO to Vacate 2021 Order (December 8, 2025)
- FTC Sends Payments to Consumers Impacted by Avast's Deceptive Privacy Claims (December 2, 2025)
- FTC Acts Against Education Technology Provider for Failing to Secure Students' Personal Data (December 1, 2025)

- Dun & Bradstreet Agrees to Pay $5.7 Million to Resolve Alleged Violations of FTC Order (September 29, 2025)
- FTC Alleges Sendit App and its CEO Unlawfully Collected Personal Data from Children, Deceived Users About Messages, Subscription Memberships (September 29, 2025)

Federal Trade Commission, *Privacy and Security Enforcement* (2026).

(C) CHILDREN'S ONLINE PRIVACY PROTECTION ACT (COPPA)

In 1998, Congress enacted The Children's Online Privacy Protection Act (COPPA), making it illegal for companies to harvest personally identifiable information from children without the consent of a parent. The COPPA Rule:

> applies to operators of commercial websites and online services (including mobile apps and IoT devices) directed to children under 13 that collect, use, or disclose personal information from children. It also applies to operators of general audience websites or online services with actual knowledge that they are collecting, using, or disclosing personal information from children under 13.

Federal Trade Commission, *Complying With COPPA: Frequently Asked Questions* (July 20, 2020).

The amended COPPA Rule, which took effect on July 1, 2013, also protects the privacy of children by making it illegal for companies to harvest personally identifiable information without their parents' consent. COPPA applies only to websites or online services that target children thirteen or younger.

The Children's Online Privacy Protection Act (COPPA) (15 U.S.C. § 6501) makes it illegal for companies to harvest personally identifiable information from children aged 13 and under without their parents' consent. COPPA requires companies collecting personal information from children under thirteen online follow steps to ensure children's information is protected.

These steps include clearly disclosing to parents the information it collects, how the information will be used, and seeking verifiable parental consent. Companies must take reasonable measures to protect the confidentiality, security, and integrity of the personal information they collect about children.

The FTC's COPPA Rule mandates that the site operator obtain verifiable parental consent and give conspicuous notice of their information practices. A website may not condition a child's use of the website in its terms of service on disclosing personal information. The FTC requires that a website give a child's parents the opportunity to restrain further use or collection of information. A website must have reasonable security to protect the confidentiality, security, and integrity of personal information collected from children.

The FTC's COPPA Rule provides websites with safe harbor protections only if they comply with the approved self-regulatory guidelines formulated by marketing or online industries. Self-regulatory guidelines must subject operators to the same or greater protections for children as contained in Sections 312.2 through 312.9 of the FTC's COPPA Rule.

All websites are required to conduct periodic reviews of subject operators' information practices. The FTC states the website must comply with COPPA if the operator has a "general audience web site and actual knowledge that they are collecting personal information" from children aged 13 or under. 16 C.F.R. § 312.

In February 2026, The Federal Trade Commission issued a policy statement in today announcing that the Commission will not bring an enforcement action under the Children's Online Privacy Protection Rule (COPPA Rule) against certain website and online service operators that collect, use, and disclose personal information for the sole purpose of determining a user's age via age verification technologies.

The FTC policy statement states that the Commission will not bring an enforcement action under the COPPA Rule against operators of general audience sites and services and mixed audience sites and services that collect, use, or disclose personal information for the sole purpose of determining a user's age without first obtaining verifiable parental consent—if they comply with certain conditions, specifically that they:

- Do not use or disclose information collected for age verification purposes for any purpose except to determine a user's age;
- Do not retain this information longer than necessary to fulfill the age verification purposes, and delete such information promptly thereafter;
- Disclose information collected for age verification purposes only to those third parties the operator has taken reasonable steps to determine are capable of maintaining the confidentiality, security, and integrity of the information, including by obtaining certain written assurances from those third parties;
- Provide clear notice to parents and children of the information collected for age verification purposes;
- Employ reasonable security safeguards for information collected for age verification purposes; and
- Take reasonable steps to determine that any product, service, method, or third party utilized for age verification purposes is likely to provide reasonably accurate results as to the user's age.

§ 7-4. Privacy & the Internet of Things

(A) IOT & DATA SECURITY

The Internet of Things (IoT) requires manufacturers, service providers, distributors purchasers, and policymakers to understand, assess, and embrace effective security and privacy measures. The IoT enables consumers to easily share a photo with family or watch from the office what's going on at home. However, the IoT creates new privacy risks like enabling hackers to "gaze at the live feed from your family room, or have your personal conversations remotely recorded? (Shudder.)"

Leslie Fair, *D-Link Case Alleges Inadequate Internet of Things Security Practices* (Jan. 5, 2017).

Privacy regulations will continuously be updated for a rapidly evolving IoT landscape as revealed by the following:

- The Global IoT Device Management Market is valued at approximately USD 6.4 billion in 2026.
- Based on application, the Connected & Smart Home segment led the market with a 31.35% revenue share in 2025.
- The IoT industry is expanding at an annual growth rate of 4.88%, supported by 257.3K patents and a global workforce of 7.6 million employees, with 2.4K new hires added last year.
- Around 400 active IoT (Internet of Things)

- The global number of IoT devices is projected to increase from 22 billion in 2026 to over 40.6 billion by 2034.
- Approximately 75% of IoT attacks are routed through routers, with an average of 5,200 attacks per router per month.

IoT Device Statistics By Market Share And Trends (2026), BAYELSA WATCH (Mar. 5, 2026).

The Internet of Things (IoT) is shifting from simple data-gathering to AI-driven devices in countless consumer products:

> Devices for consumer use include connected vehicles, wearable technology, connected health, appliances, and home automation or "smart home" devices, including lighting, heating and air conditioning, media and security systems, and camera systems. Other, more tailored, IoT devices are used in many industries to facilitate operations, including medical and healthcare (IoMT), transportation, manufacturing, agriculture, and energy. With the adoption of the Matter protocol, an open, smart-home connectivity protocol developed by the Connectivity Standards Alliance (CSA) that enables communication between devices, mobile apps, and cloud services, has standardized device communication, making smart homes more interoperable, but also creating a more uniform landscape for potential attackers.

New Jersey Cybersecurity and Communications Integration Cell (NJCCIC) (2026).

This New Jersey Report contends that:

IoT devices have remained a primary target for threat actors over the years as user adoption continues to grow. Threat actors can exploit vulnerable devices, impact other connected devices and networks, and result in unauthorized access, alteration, disclosure, destruction, or unavailability of data. Vulnerable home routers, combined with compromised IoT devices, such as home security cameras, increase the risk of criminal activity and cyberattacks. Compromised IoT devices and connected home networks could have further implications when devices connected to the home network also connect to a corporate network.

The following 2026 statistics on IoT data breaches reveals the radius of the risk:

- *820,000+ IoT Attacks Per Day (2025)*: In 2025, there were on average 820,000 malicious IoT hacking attempts every day, a 46% increase from the previous year. Early 2026 data suggests this automated onslaught is not slowing down.

- *124% Surge in IoT Malware*: Global IoT malware attacks spiked by 124% year-over-year in 2025, indicating that the pool of IoT devices recruited into botnets and other malware campaigns more than doubled. 2026 is on track to see continued expansion of these threats.

- *75% of IoT Attacks Target Routers:* Routers remain the single most attacked IoT device, accounting for over 75% of observed IoT-related cyberattacks. Attackers exploit home and office routers (often via command injection flaws) to hijack traffic and spread malware, with popular brands like Netgear frequently targeted.

IoT Hacking Statistics 2026, Global Trends and Key Insights, MALWARE NEWS (Mar. 10, 2026).

In February 2026, a cybercriminal exploited a memory corruption vulnerability in Apple's Dynamic Link Editor:

> Apple states that an attacker with memory write capability may be able to achieve arbitrary code execution, and notes the issue may have been used in an "extremely sophisticated attack" against specific targeted individuals.

Daryna Olyniychuk, *CVE-2026-20700: Apple Patches Zero-Day Exploited in Sophisticated Cyber Attacks*, SOCPRIME.COM (Feb. 12, 2026).

In July of 2025, Google experienced an IoT data breach of smart TVs:

> Google, in partnership with Human Security and Trend Micro, disclosed BadBox 2.0, the largest known botnet of internet-connected TVs. More than 10 million smart TVs, digital projectors, in-car infotainment systems, and even digital picture frames were compromised. . . . Once infected, devices were

> enrolled into a global botnet used for click-fraud campaigns, account hijacking, residential proxy services, and distributed denial-of-service (DDoS) attacks. The operation relied on BadBox's ability to evade threat detection by blending in with legitimate network traffic and leveraging the vast reach of consumer IoT to scale its activity worldwide.

The Top Internet of Things (IoT) Cybersecurity Breaches in 2025, SIMILY (2025).

(B) CROSS-DEVICE SECURITY ISSUES

Smartphones, personal fitness trackers, smart televisions, and smart appliances produce substantial amounts of sensitive information, including but not limited to browsing habits, purchasing patterns, real-time location, and personal health information. *Data Privacy in the Age of IoT,* TRENDMICRO (Feb. 1, 2018). Cross-device privacy and security involves protecting consumer data across interconnected devices against data breaches, unauthorized access, and tracking.

The Internet Engineering Task Force (IETF) explain how cross-device communications occur:

> Cross-device flows enable a user to initiate an interaction on one device (e.g., a smart TV) and complete or continue it on a second device (e.g., a mobile phone). This specification addresses two distinct cross-device use cases:
>
> - Cross-Device Authorization:* In the cross-device authorization use case, the second

device is used to authenticate the user or grant authorization before passing control back to the first device.

- Cross-Device Session Transfer* In the cross-device session transfer use case, the user is already authenticated on the first device, before the session is transferred to the second device without requiring the user to re-authenticate. . .

These flows typically involve using a mobile phone to scan a QR code or enter a user code displayed on the first device (e.g., Smart TV, Kiosk, Personal Computer, or other electronic devices).

IETF, *Cross-Device Flows: Security Best Current Practice: draft-ietf-oauth-cross-device-security-16* (latest update Mar. 4, 2026).

Through cross-device tracking, companies can associate multiple devices with the same person. "Companies can gather information about consumers across their connected devices, including smartphones, tablets, personal computers, smart televisions, and even smartwatches and other wearables."

Federal Trade Commission, *Cross-Device Tracking: An FTC Staff Report* (Jan. 2017).

The practice of cross-device tracking raises difficult challenges in obtaining consent or giving consumers a right to opt-out of such data sharing.

The most pressing privacy issues arising out of this practice are:

- Transparency and control gaps: probabilistic methods often operate behind the scenes, making it hard for users to understand how they're linked or to meaningfully opt out. Effective privacy programs pair transparency with technical accuracy, ensuring that notices and opt-outs reflect the real mechanics of cross-device tracking.
- Sensitive-data creep: cross-device contexts can accumulate location, health-adjacent, and financial-adjacent signals quickly, heightening risk if processes don't filter or silo sensitive categories. Regulators emphasize the importance of limiting sensitive data and enforcing truthful disclosures.
- Accountability blind spots: complex vendor webs, including ad tech, analytics, and consent tools, create ambiguity in accountability. Evolving interpretations under California law, including "share" (cross-context behavioral advertising) and "sell," can turn a single tag into a compliance trigger.

A 2017 *FTC Report on Cross-Device Tracking* recommends that companies engaged in cross-device tracking:

(1) Be transparent about their data collection and use practices;

(2) Provide choice mechanisms that give consumers control over their data;

(3) Provide heightened protections for sensitive information, including health, financial, and children's information; and

(4) Maintain reasonable security of collected data.

FTC, *Cross-Device Tracking*, An FTC Staff Report (Jan. 2017).

§ 7-5. Data Breach Notification Law

All fifty states, the District of Columbia, Guam, Puerto Rico, and the Virgin Islands have enacted legislation requiring private or government entities to notify individuals of security breaches involving their personally identified information. Data breach notification statutes require entities maintaining personally identifiable information to give notice if there is a breach in the security of the information. These data security laws:

> typically have provisions regarding who must comply with the law (e.g., businesses, data/information brokers, government entities, etc.); definitions of 'personal information' (e.g., name combined with SSN, driver's license or state ID, account numbers, etc.); what constitutes a breach (e.g., unauthorized acquisition of data); requirements for notice (e.g., timing or method of notice, who must be notified); and exemptions (e.g., for encrypted information).

Michael L. Rustad & Thomas H. Koenig, *Towards a Global Data Privacy Standard*, 71 FLA. L. REV. 365, 422 (2019).

In October 2025, California enacted a new data breach provision that has the following sphere of application:

> Existing law requires an individual or a business that conducts business in California, and that owns or licenses computerized data that includes personal information, to disclose a breach of the security of the system following discovery or notification of the breach in the security of the data to a resident of California whose unencrypted personal information was compromised, as specified, and requires that disclosure to be made in the most expedient time possible and without unreasonable delay, consistent with the legitimate needs of law enforcement, as specified, or any measures necessary to determine the scope of the breach and restore the reasonable integrity of the data system. This bill would require that data breach disclosure to be made within 30 calendar days of discovery or notification of the data breach but would authorize an individual or business to delay the disclosure to accommodate the legitimate needs of law enforcement, as specified, or as necessary to determine the scope of the breach and restore the reasonable integrity of the data system.
>
> Existing law also requires an individual or business that is required to issue the security

breach notification described above to more than 500 California residents as a result of a single breach of the security system to electronically submit a single sample copy of that security breach notification, excluding any personally identifiable information, to the Attorney General.

California's Senate Bill 446 (SB 446), which went into effect on January 1, 2026 mandates:

> that businesses and state agencies notify affected residents of a data breach within 30 calendar days of discovery, replacing the previous "without unreasonable delay" standard. For breaches affecting over 500 residents, the Attorney General must be notified within 15 days of the consumer notification.
>
> *California SB-446 Data Breaches: Customer Notification* (2025–2026).

California's data breach notification requires the following information be included in a notice:

> The security breach notification shall be written in plain language, shall be titled "Notice of Data Breach," and shall present the information described in paragraph (2) under the following headings: "What Happened?" "What Information Was Involved?" "What We Are Doing," "What You Can Do," and "For More Information." Additional information may be provided as a supplement to the notice.

Many states limit the data breach notification requirement to unencrypted data. Similar to other jurisdictions, Massachusetts imposes civil penalties for failing to give consumers notice of security breaches. Data breaches for e-commerce companies, will rarely affect citizens in a single state. Counsel must ensure their client complies with the data breach statutes for all states.

In 2018, California took a momentous step to protect its citizens, their data, and the authority they possess over the usages of their personal information when it passed the California Consumer Privacy Act of 2018 (CCPA), which adapts many provisions of the EU's General Data Protection Regulation.

§ 7-6. Global Privacy Issues

(A) DATA PROTECTION DIRECTIVE

In 1995, The European Commission adopted the Data Protection Directive, Directive 95/46/EC with two objectives in mind: (1) to protect the fundamental right to data protection and (2) to guarantee the free flow of personal data between Member States.

In particular, the Directive achieves this by giving data subjects control over the collection, transmission, and use of personal information. The Directive gave data subjects the right to be notified of all uses and disclosures concerning the collection and processing of their personal data. Directive 95/46/EC.

Each EU Member State enacted legislation fulfilling the legal grounds defined in the Directive: consent, contract, legal obligation, vital interest of the data subject, and the balance between the legitimate interests of the people controlling the data versus the people on whom data is held (i.e., data subjects).

(B) SAFE HARBOR 2.0

On February 2, 2016, the European Commission and the United States agreed to a new framework for transatlantic data transfers: "the EU-U.S. Privacy Shield" or Safe Harbor 2.0 that replaced Safe Harbor 1.0, which was a new adequacy decision by the European Commission, officially adopted on July 12, 2016, for transfers to U.S. organisations subscribing to the Privacy Shield.

Under Safe Harbor 2.0, the U.S. Department of Commerce administers self-certification program where U.S. companies will register their promise to comply with EU data protection principles. The Safe Harbor 1.0 agreement, in place during the Data Protection Directive, lacked a meaningful enforcement mechanism, whereas the GDPR assesses significant fines against non-compliant U.S. companies.

Article 83(5) of the GDPR provides that fines can be up to twenty million euros, or in the case of an undertaking, up to 4% of their total global turnover of the preceding fiscal year, whichever is higher.

The European Commission issued a press release announcing the European Court of Justice's invalidating of the EU-U.S. Privacy Shield:

> On July 16, 2020, the Court of Justice of the European Union (ECJ) issued a judgment declaring as 'invalid' the European Commission's Decision (EU) 2016/1250 of 12 July 2016 on the adequacy of the protection provided by the EU-U.S. Privacy Shield. As a result of that decision, the EU-U.S. Privacy Shield Framework is no longer a valid mechanism to comply with EU data protection requirements when transferring personal data from the European Union to the United States. This decision does not relieve participants in the EU-U.S. Privacy Shield of their obligations under the EU-U.S. Privacy Shield Framework.

European Commission, *FAQs—EU-U.S. Privacy Shield Program Update* (Aug. 20, 2020).

On July 10, 2023, the European Commission adopted an adequacy decision for the EU-U.S. Data Privacy Framework (DPF), replacing the invalidated Privacy Shield. The DPF replaces the Privacy Shield program, provides a mechanism for companies to transfer personal data from the EU to the United States. To join the Data Privacy Framework, a company must self-certify to the U.S. Department of Commerce that it complies with the Data Privacy Framework Principles.

A participating company's failure to comply with the Principles may violate Section 5 of the FTC Act's prohibition on unfair and deceptive acts. The Data Privacy Framework site also features a searchable list of participating businesses.

(C) GENERAL DATA PROTECTION REGULATION

The General Data Protection Regulation (GDPR) is the European Union's comprehensive data privacy law, effective since May 25, 2018, governing how personal data is collected, used, and stored. It grants individuals significant rights over their data, mandates transparency, and imposes heavy fines on organizations, including those outside the EU targeting EU residents.

The General Data Protection Regulation (GDPR) naturally applies to multi-national companies that have a base in the European Union (EU) or do business in the EU, although simply closing an EU operation is not sufficient to avoid compliance with GDPR. The GDPR is about data not where an organization the company or organization is located,

The European Commission takes the position that the GDPR applies to any U.S. (or other country), where an organization collects, processes, or stores personal data. U.S. companies doing business in Europe or even interacting with EU consumers in any of the twenty-seven EU Member States must comply with the GDPR.

The European Commission described the statutory intent of the General Data Protection Regulation as follows:

> The General Data Protection Regulation (GDPR) is the toughest privacy and security law in the world. Though it was drafted and passed by the European Union (EU), it imposes obligations onto organizations anywhere, so long as they target or collect data related to people in the EU. The regulation was put into effect on May 25, 2018. The GDPR will levy harsh fines against those who violate its privacy and security standards, with penalties reaching into the tens of millions of euros.
>
> With the GDPR, Europe is signaling its firm stance on data privacy and security at a time when more people are entrusting their personal data with cloud services and breaches are a daily occurrence. The regulation itself is large, far-reaching, and fairly light on specifics, making GDPR compliance a daunting prospect, particularly for small and medium-sized enterprises (SMEs).

GDPR.eu, *What is GDPR, the EU's New Data Protection Law?* https://gdpr.eu/what-is-gdpr/.

A U.S. company's only option is not to do business with any EU consumer if they wish to avoid compliance. This means that any company with a website accessible by any EU consumer is subject to the GDPR. The GDPR applies to all organizations as well as companies of all sizes, from SME to multinationals such as Amazon, Facebook, or Google. The EU Commission describes the GDPR as follows

> First, if you process the personal data of EU citizens or residents, or you offer goods or services to such people, then the GDPR applies to you even if you're not in the EU. . . .
>
> Second, the fines for violating the GDPR are extremely high. There are two tiers of penalties, which max out at €20 million or 4% of global revenue (whichever is higher), plus data subjects have the right to seek compensation for damages.
>
> The GDPR defines an array of legal terms at length:
>
> - *Personal data*—Personal data is any information that relates to an individual who can be directly or indirectly identified. Names and email addresses are obviously personal data. Location information, ethnicity, gender, bio-metric data, religious beliefs, web cookies, and political opinions can also be personal data. Pseudonymous data can also fall under the definition if it is easy to ID someone from it.
>
> - *Data processing*—Any action performed on data, whether automated or manual. The examples cited in the text include collecting, recording, organizing, structuring, storing, using, erasing. . . so basically anything.

- *Data subject*—The person whose data is processed. These are your customers or site visitors.
- *Data controller*—The person who decides why and how personal data will be processed. If you are an owner or employee in your organization who handles data, this is you.
- *Data processor*—A third party that processes personal data on behalf of a data controller. The GDPR has special rules for these individuals and organizations. These could include cloud servers, like Google Drive, Proton Drive, or Microsoft OneDrive, or email service providers, like Proton Mail.

GDPR.eu, *What is GDPR, the EU's New Data Protection Law?* https://gdpr.eu/what-is-gdpr/.

The GDPR is divided into five chapters: (1) Chapter 1 (Art. 1–4) General provisions; (2) Chapter 2 (Art. 5–11) Principles; (3) Chapter 3 (Art. 12–23) Rights of the data subject; (4) Chapter 4 (Art. 24–43) Controller and processor, and (5) Chapter 5 (Art. 44–50) Transfers of personal data to third countries or organizations. *Safeguarding Privacy in a Connected World—A European Data Protection Framework for the 21st Century*, COM (2012).

(1) Key Data Protection Rights

The GDPR requires data controllers to document verifiable consent. Data processors must present written requests for data subject consent "in a manner which is clearly distinguishable from the other matters." Article 7 of the GDPR requires data processors to obtain data-subject consent prior to the processing of personal data. Article 7(3) allows data subjects to withdraw their consent at any time.

(1) The definition of and conditions for consent provided for under Articles 4(11) and 7 of Regulation (EU) 2016/679/EU shall apply.

(2) Without prejudice to paragraph 1, where technically possible and feasible, for the purposes of point (b) of Article 8(1), consent may be expressed by using the appropriate technical settings of a software application enabling access to the internet.

(3) End-users who have consented to the processing of electronic communications data as set out in point (c) of Article 6(2) and points (a) and (b) of Article 6(3) shall be given the possibility to withdraw their consent at any time as set forth under Article 7(3) of Regulation (EU) 2016/679 and be reminded of this possibility at periodic intervals of 6 months, as long as the processing continues.

The principle of user consent is the cornerstone of European Union data protection. The GDPR restricts personal data processing to data "collected for specified, explicit and legitimate purposes and not further processed in a manner that is incompatible with those purposes."

Under the GDPR, "businesses will be able to collect and process data only for a well-defined purpose.

They will have to inform the user about new purposes for processing." The GDPR adopts the concept of data protection by design.

The GDPR requires companies "to take into account the protection of the rights of individuals, both before and during their processing activities, by implementing the appropriate technical and organization measures to ensure that they fulfil their data protection obligations."

Article 25 requires that data controllers "shall implement appropriate technical and organizational measures for ensuring that, by default, only personal data which are necessary for each specific purpose of the processing are processed." The GDPR grants EU consumers the following rights:

- The right to be informed
- The right of access
- The right to rectification
- The right to erasure
- The right to restrict processing
- The right to data portability
- The right to object
- Rights in relation to automated decision making and profiling.

U.S. consumers, in contrast have none of these rights under either the common law or statutory law at the state or federal level.

(2) Article 17: Right to Be Forgotten

The GDPR's Article 17 provides the data subject with a right to be forgotten and to erasure. Article 17 further elaborates the right of erasure while providing the conditions of the right to be forgotten, including but not limited to the obligation of the controller allowing personal data to be public to inform third parties on the data subject's request to erase any links to, or copy or replication of that personal data. The "right to be forgotten" is set forth in GDPR that states:

The EU Commission's *Explanatory Memorandum* makes a policy-based decision the data controller, not the data subject, must notify third-party websites a data subject has requested it "erase any links to, or copy or replication of . . . personal data." Article 17(1) sets forth the ground rules for when data subjects have a right to be forgotten:

> The data subject shall have the right to obtain from the controller the erasure of personal data relating to them and the abstention from further dissemination of such data, especially in relation to personal data, which are made available by the data subject while he or she was a child, where one of the following grounds applies:
>
> (a) the data are no longer necessary in relation to the purposes for which they were collected or otherwise processed;
>
> (b) the data subject withdraws consent on which the processing is based according to point (a) of Article 6(1), or when the storage

period consented to has expired, and where there is no other legal ground for the processing of the data;

(c) the data subject objects to the processing of personal data pursuant to Article 19;

(d) the processing of the data does not comply with this Regulation for other reasons.

Article 17(2) of the GDPR states:

> Where the controller has made the personal data public and is obliged pursuant to paragraph 1 to erase the personal data, the controller, taking account of available technology and the cost of implementation, shall take reasonable steps, including technical measures, to inform controllers which are processing the personal data that the data subject has requested the erasure by such controllers of any links to, or copy or replication of, those personal data.

GDPR at Art. 17(2).

The GDPR creates many affirmative duties on data controllers backed by serious penalties and administrative actions. Companies and organizations need to establish procedures for receiving and addressing requests to delete personal data. Consumers need to provide companies and organizations with sufficient information for them to make the decision to delete. Companies and organizations need to determine how long they should keep personal data.

Controllers making decisions as to delete need to critically evaluate all individual requests. The right to erasure is not an absolute right. Controllers need to balance the right to be forgotten with the EU fundamental right of expression.

(3) Exceptions to the Right to Be Forgotten

The data controller is not required to initiate erasure if the subject of the data request falls into one of four exceptions in Article 17(3). Article 17(3) makes clear the right to be forgotten is subject to other fundamental rights as noted below:

(a) for exercising the right of freedom of expression in accordance with Article 80;

(b) for reasons of public interest in the area of public health in accordance with Article 81;

(c) for historical, statistical, and scientific research purposes in accordance with Article 83;

(d) for compliance with a legal obligation to retain the personal data by Union or Member State law to which the controller is subject; Member State laws shall meet an objective of public interest, respect the essence of the right to the protection of personal data and be proportionate to the legitimate aim pursued.

The European Commission provides little guidance on how to respond to data requests to accommodate the policy interest in public health.

Similarly, it is unclear how data controllers should determine what data requests are important for historical, statistical, or scientific purposes.

Finally, Article 17(3) sets forth a general standard data controller can retain personal data if retention accords with EU or member state law, requiring balancing a data subject's request against the public interest, "respect[ing] the essence" of the right to data protection, and remaining "proportionate to the legitimate aim pursued." GDPR at art. 17(3).

(4) GDPR's Class-Action Like Remedy

Article 80 of the GDPR provides for representation through lawsuits filed by not-for-profit associations to protect data subjects' privacy rights. The GDPR gives European data subjects the right to lodge a complaint with a supervisory authority for misuses of their data.

In addition, Article 77 indicates that data subjects can choose to apply personally rather than be represented by a non-profit organization under Article 80. By permitting private lawsuits, the GDPR supplements public enforcement, with private enforcement.

(5) GDPR's Wealth-Based Punishment

The GDPR levies fines up to €20 million, or 4% of the worldwide annual revenue of the prior fiscal year, whichever is higher. These fines shall be issued for infringements of:

- The basic principles for processing, including conditions for consent, under Articles 5, 6, 7, and 9.
- The data subjects' rights under Articles 12–22.
- The transfer of personal data to a recipient in a third country or an international organisation under Articles 44–49.
- Any obligations pursuant to Member State law adopted under Chapter IX.
- Any non-compliance with an order by a supervisory authority.

The CMS.Law GDPR Enforcement Tracker is an overview of fines and penalties which data protection authorities within the EU have imposed under the EU General Data Protection Regulation The European Commission reported hundreds of fines to companies, including Google and Facebook, more than €114 million in the first 20 months of GDPR. The largest GDPR fine ever was imposed in 2023:

> Meta Platforms Ireland Limited (Meta IE) was issued a 1.2 billion euro fine following an inquiry into its Facebook service, by the Irish Data Protection Authority (IE DPA). This fine, which is the largest GDPR fine ever, was imposed for Meta's transfers of personal data to the U.S. on the basis of standard contractual clauses (SCCs) since 16 July 2020. Furthermore, Meta has been

ordered to bring its data transfers into compliance with the GDPR.

1.2 Billion Euro Fine for Facebook as a Result of EDPB Binding Decision, EUROPEAN DATA PROTECTION BOARD: EDPB (May 22, 2023).

(6) Towards a Global Privacy Standard?

U.S. companies doing business in Europe need to comply with the EU's General Data Protection Regulation because of its extraterritorial scope. U.S. companies collecting any personal data of Europeans need to comply with the GDPR. Even if a U.S. company collected or transferred email addresses in a marketing list or the IP addresses of Europeans who visit your website, they are subject to the GDPR. The European Commission creates the following checklist for U.S. companies:

- Conduct an information audit for EU personal data.
- Inform your customers why you are processing their data.
- Assess your data processing activities and improve protection.
- Make sure you have a data processing agreement with your vendors.
- Appoint a data protection officer (if necessary).
- Designate a representative in the European Union.

- Know what to do if there is a data breach.
- Comply with cross-border transfer laws (if applicable).

GDPR.eu, *GDPR Compliance Checklist for U.S. Companies* (2020).

U.S. companies that do not comply with the GDPR face fines of hundreds of millions or even billions of euros as evidenced by the largest fines against organizations:

- €1.2 Billion—Meta (Ireland, 2023): For transferring personal data of EU users to the U.S. in violation of the 2020 Schrems II ruling.
- €746 Million—Amazon Europe Core (Luxembourg, 2021): For non-compliant processing of personal data for targeted advertising.
- €530 Million—TikTok (Ireland, 2025): For breaches related to user, particularly children's, data protection.
- €479 Million—Meta (2025): Added to their series of large fines regarding compliance.
- €405 Million—Meta/Instagram (Ireland, 2022): For failings in processing children's data.
- €390 Million—Meta/Facebook (Ireland, 2023): For illegal data processing practices.

- €345 Million—TikTok (Ireland, 2023): Regarding children's account settings and data processing.
- €310 Million—LinkedIn (Ireland, 2024): For violations related to targeted advertising.
- €290 Million—Uber (Netherlands, 2024): For, among other things, transferring driver data to the US.
- €265 Million—Meta/Facebook (Ireland, 2022): Following a data scraping incident.

10 Biggest GDPR Fines (Until 2025), DATA PRIVACY MANAGER, https://dataprivacymanager.net/5-biggest-gdpr-fines-so-far-2020/.

The "Brussels Effect" hypothesis projects a "race to the top" as multinational entities find it easier to adopt the most stringent data protection standards worldwide, rather than satisfying divergent data privacy rules. The GDPR is said to be a prime example of the Brussels Effect because of its aggressive extraterritorial scope that unilaterally imposes EU law on U.S. entities.

Michael L. Rustad & Thomas H. Koenig, *Towards a Global Data Privacy Standard*, 71 FLA. L. REV. 365 (2019).

The GDPR adopts long-established U.S. tort law remedies, including deterrence-based fines, bringing EU data protection law closer to American practices. Under the GDPR, collective redress, wealth-based punishment, and arming data subjects with the right to initiate public enforcement are recognized for the first time in European legislative history. Innovations first instituted in the U.S., such as Privacy by Design, wealth-based punishment, and security breach notification obligations are essential to the GDPR.

The European Commission notes how countries outside of Europe have enacted GDPR-style privacy protection:

> The GDPR has inspired many imitators, from Brazil's LGPD to the CCPA in California. While many of these laws agree on the broad terms of data protection, each implements these protections in its own way. And these two new regulations are just the start: Canada and Australia are both considering new data protection regulations, and India's legislature will vote on its Personal Data Protection Bill. In the US, several states, including Nevada, New York, Texas, and Washington, are considering following California's lead and passing their own data protection law.

GDPR.eu, *How the GDPR Could Change in 2020* (Dec. 9, 2019).

(D) THE DATA PROTECTION LAW ENFORCEMENT DIRECTIVE

The European Union enacted Directive (EU) 2016/680 on the protection of natural persons regarding processing of personal data connected with criminal offences or the execution of criminal penalties, and on the free movement of such data.

The Commission notes the purpose of this directive in balancing privacy rights against law enforcement interests:

> The directive protects citizens' fundamental right to data protection whenever personal data is used by criminal law enforcement authorities for law enforcement purposes. It will in particular ensure that the personal data of victims, witnesses, and suspects of crime are duly protected and will facilitate cross-border cooperation in the fight against crime and terrorism. The directive entered into force on 5 May 2016 and EU countries had to transpose it into their national law by 6 May 2018.

Europa, European Commission, *The Data Protection Law Enforcement Directive* (2021).

The European Commission describes the Directive as modernizing privacy law for the digital age:

> The reform was made to make the EU's data protection standards fit for the digital age, and future-proof for technological developments. The Directive protects individuals when their personal data are processed by authorities for the purposes of prevention, investigation, detection, or prosecution of criminal offences or for the execution of criminal penalties. The rules deliver on the EU's Agenda on Security, the EU's strategy in the fight against terrorism, organised crime, and cybercrime. The exchange of such data is essential in the fight against terrorism and cross border crime. Thanks to the

> new rules, sharing such data will be more efficient both at EU-level and international level. They will build trust and ensure legal certainty crossborder.

Věra Jourová, Directorate-General for Justice and Consumers, *How Will the Data Protection Reform Help Fight International Crime?*, EUROPEAN COMMISSION (Fact Sheet 2016).

(E) ELECTRONIC PRIVACY & COMMUNICATIONS DIRECTIVE (EPRIVACY)

> The ePrivacy Directive ensures the protection of fundamental rights and freedoms, in particular the respect for private life, confidentiality of communications and the protection of personal data in the electronic communications sector. The Directive also guarantees the free movement of electronic communications data, equipment, and services in the Union. It implements in the Union's secondary law the fundamental right to the respect for private life, with regard to communications, as enshrined in Article 7 of the Charter of Fundamental Rights of the European Union ('Charter').

European Commission, *Explanatory Memorandum* (2020).

The following provisions will be incorporated in the ePrivacy Regulation that will replace the ePrivacy Directive:

- Use of technologically neutral definitions to apprehend new services and technologies to ensure that the Regulation is future-proof.
- Repeal of the security rules to eliminate regulatory duplication.
- Clarification of scope to help eliminate/reduce the risk of divergent implementation by Member States (point 3 of the Opinion).
- Clarification and simplification of the consent rule for the use of cookies and other identifiers, as explained in Sections 3.1 and 3.4 (point 2 of the Opinion).
- Alignment of the supervisory authorities with the authorities competent to enforce the GDPR and reliance on the consistency mechanism of the GDPR.

§ 7-7. Conclusion

Safeguards for the collecting, processing, and transfer of big data must keep pace with the harvesting of ever-larger quantities of personal data. Most multinational private and public entities stand to benefit from the efficiencies created by a globalized Internet privacy regime.

Major U.S. information companies such as eBay, Facebook, and Google have already agreed to comply with the GDPR and, in some cases, extend the EU-style data protections to citizens around the world. The GDPR is rapidly evolving into the transnational gold standard of data protection, applicable to all domestic and cross-border transfers of personally identifiable data.

CHAPTER 8
INTERNET-RELATED CRIMES

§ 8-1. Overview of Cybercrimes

(A) OVERVIEW OF INTERNET CRIMES

Historically, Internet crimes, or cybercrimes were local attacks individual computers. The Federal Bureau of Investigation stated that the three leading cybercrimes, by number of complaints reported by victims in 2024, were (1) phishing/spoofing, (2) extortion, and (3) personal data breaches.

Victims of investment fraud, specifically those involving cryptocurrency, reported the most losses—totaling over $6.5 billion. Examples of computer crime include computer intrusions, denial of service attacks, viruses, and worms. Spending on cybersecurity products and services to $1 trillion (USD) annually by 2031. *Official 2026 Cybersecurity Market Report: Predictions And Statistics*, CYBERCRIME MAGAZINE (Nov. 17, 2025).

This chapter is divided into five sections. Section 8-1 overviews Internet crimes with examples of emerging cybercrime categories such as election Darknet, Dark Market, Disinformation on Social Media, Cyberbullying, and revenge porn. Section 8-2 covers the Computer Fraud and Abuse Act and Section 8-3 covers the Electronic Privacy Communications Act, the two most important computer crime statutes. Internet-Related Specific

Purpose Acts such as identity theft, anti-staking, and access fraud are covered in Section 8-4.

Finally, Section 8-5 covers global cybercrime enforcement with a close study of the Cybercrime Convention and the United Nations Convention on Cybercrime as well as global cybercrime enforcement.

Cybercrimes can be broadly divided into three categories:

(1) *Organized Crime Groups* that are primarily threatening the financial services sector, and they are expanding the scope of their attacks.

(2) *State Sponsors*—foreign governments that are interested in pilfering data, including intellectual property and research and development data from major manufacturers, government agencies, and defense contractors.

(3) *Terrorist Groups* who want to impact this country the same way they did on 9/11 by flying planes into buildings.

Federal Bureau of Investigation, *The Cyber Threat: Part I: On the Front Lines with Shawn Henry* (Mar. 27, 2012).

The FBI counters the cyberthreat with the following actions:

- The FBI has specially trained cyber squads in each of our 56 field offices, working hand-in-hand with interagency task force partners.

- The FBI leads the National Cyber Investigative Joint Task Force (NCIJTF), a task force of more than 30 co-located agencies from the intelligence community and law enforcement.
- The rapid response Cyber Action Team can deploy across the country within hours to respond to major incidents.
- With cyber assistant law enforcement attachés in embassies across the globe, the FBI works closely with our international counterparts to seek justice for victims of malicious cyber activity.
- The Internet Crime Complaint Center (IC3) collects reports of internet crime from the public. Using such complaints, the IC3's Recovery Asset Team has assisted in freezing hundreds of thousands of dollars for victims of cybercrime.
- CyWatch is the FBI's 24/7 operations center and watch floor, providing around-the-clock support to track incidents and communicate with field offices across the country.

Federal Bureau of Investigation, *The Cyber Threat* (2026).

Cybercrimes are increasingly attacking computer systems and the perpetrator may be located in a distant foreign forum. Cybercrime respects no national borders and is often difficult to detect because although online criminals sometimes leave digital footprints, there is no traditional crime scene. Internet crimes, unlike conventional crimes, do not involve face-to-face criminality.

Most cybercriminals are not physically present at the crime scene. The Internet allows anonymous communications impossible to trace through Internet telecommunications. Internet criminals frequently use false e-mail headers and anonymous remailers. Cybercrimes are frequently committed one-time. Relational crimes, in contrast, are easier to prosecute because we can often do an investigation focusing on multiple clues.

Cybercrimes or Internet crimes are a product of a connected world where malicious individuals target computer systems. The Internet enables anonymous communications impossible to trace because computer records are so easy to alter. Anonymity is emblematic of cybercrime enabled by anonymous remailers and false e-mail headers.

Internet crimes are difficult to investigate because they are often perpetrated in distant offshore forums. Victims of unauthorized computer entry or other Internet crimes are often reluctant to report that they had been victimized by a swindle.

During the COVID-19 pandemic, cybercriminals masqueraded as the Center for Disease Control and Prevention (CDC) or World Health organization (WHO) representatives in sophisticated e-mail phishing schemes. Malware, or malicious software, is any piece of software that was written with the intent of doing harm to data, devices or to people:

- Types of malware include computer viruses, Trojans, spyware, ransomware, adware, worms, file-less malware, or hybrid attacks.
- Recent malware attacks have become more sophisticated with the advent of machine learning and targeted spear phishing emails.
- More than 250,000 unique users were attacked by Trojan-Banker, a malware application.
- Ninety-eight percent of mobile malware target Android devices.
- Over the last year, MacOS malware has increased by 165%.
- Malware development rates for Windows decreased by 11.6% since reaching an all-time high in 2015.

Cybercrime Up 600% Due To COVID-19 Pandemic, PURPLESEC (2020).

INTERPOL reported that:

In one four-month period (January to April) some 907,000 spam messages, 737 incidents related to malware and 48,000 malicious URLs—all related to COVID-19—were detected by one of INTERPOL's private sector partners.

INTERPOL, *INTERPOL Report Shows Alarming Rate of Cyberattacks During COVID-19* (Aug. 4, 2020).

(B) THE INTERNET OF THINGS & CRIMES

"IoT devices—also known as "smart objects"—can range from simple "smart home" devices like smart thermostats, to wearables like smartwatches and RFID-enabled clothing, to complex industrial machinery and transportation systems."

IBM, *What is the Internet of Things (IoT)?* (2026).

"The global Internet of Things (IoT) market is forecast to be worth around 419.8 billion U.S. dollars in 2025, and rise to more than 908 billion U.S. dollars in 2034, more than doubling its revenue in ten years."

Internet of Things (IoT) Total Annual Revenue Worldwide From 2020 to 2034 (in billion U.S. dollars) STATISTICA (2026).

With the IoT, "your smartphone will be able to lock your house, turn on the air conditioning, check whether the milk is out of date, or even heat up your iron." Nevertheless, IOT also creates the possibility of hackers taking over one's "home life, gathering valuable personal data, or even use stolen information to extort money from victims."

U.S. Department of Justice, U.S. Attorney's Office, District of New Hampshire (Dec. 9, 2020).

A security firm "took over those switches, turning them into poltergeists that could turn on heaters and irons—a fire hazard and electricity-waster." Hackers taking over household devices are more likely to occur due to the connectivity of billions of everyday devices now connected to the Internet.

Along with homes being controlled, cars have navigated towards smartphone keys. These keyless cars allow hackers to create the software for a key fob and drive the car. A thief could take the car with only a $300 hardware kit and the Vehicle Identification Number found on windshield of most cars.

Andy Greenberg, *This Bluetooth Attack Can Steal a Tesla Model X in Minutes*, WIRED (November 23, 2020).

The *Chicago Tribune* reported how a cybercriminal assumed secret control of a family's smart home devices:

> Arjun and Jessica Sud routinely use a baby monitor to keep tabs on their 7-month-old's bedroom. Last month, they heard something chilling through the monitor: A deep male voice was speaking to their child . . . The couple grabbed their son, now fully awake, and headed downstairs. When they passed their Nest thermostat, normally set around 72 degrees, they noticed it had been turned up to 90. Then, the voice was back, coming through the speaker in a downstairs security camera. And this time, it was talking to them.

Ally Marotti, *'Why Are You Looking at Me? I See You Watching Me.' Smart Devices Like Nest Getting Hacked in Digital Home Invasions*, CHICAGO TRIBUNE (Feb. 10, 2019).

(C) EMERGING CYBERCRIME CATEGORIES

(1) Election Cybercrimes

Russia deploys misinformation campaigns as a general policy to influence elections:

> The U.S. intelligence community has revealed its assessments about which candidates are being supported or opposed by certain foreign malefactors. Russia is working against former Vice President Joe Biden, Democrats' nominee, having supported President Trump's election in 2016.
>
> Russia's military intelligence agency, the GRU, also targeted a number of state election systems in 2016 with malware that could have stolen or altered or sabotaged the way they operate. No votes were changed, but the FBI and Department of Homeland Security and state agencies were put on their guard about the prospect for disruptions or other problems from cyberattacks.

Philip Ewing, *Wray: Russian Interference Heavy On Agitation, Less So State Cyberattacks*, NPR (Sept. 17, 2020).

A study of Facebook posts in the 2016 election found that one in six "suspicious" advertisers originated with Russia's Internet Research Agency. Andrey Rudakov, *How Russian Facebook Ads Divided and Targeted U.S. Voters Before the 2016 Election*, WIRED (Apr. 16, 2018).

The 2020 U.S. Presidential Election had widespread mail-in voting and security worked unlike the 2016 Presidential Election where Russian propaganda groups placed a large number of ads on Facebook to undermine the candidacy of Hillary Clinton. Alan Butler, *Election Cybersecurity amid a Global Pandemic*, 45 HUM. RTS. 9 (2020). Election security in the midst of a global pandemic is an example of a new cybercrime category.

Romania's presidential election was targeted by Russian hackers in December 2024 ahead of their presidential election:

> The Russian hackers launched more than 85,000 attacks against election-related systems. The credentials they stole were later leaked on Russian hacker forums. This activity threatened election integrity and public confidence.
>
> *Trump and Harris campaign phone hack*: Chinese hackers accessed phones used by senior U.S. political figures in October 2024. The FBI launched an investigation into the incident, but it raised election security concerns.

Notable Recent Cyber Attacks. Significant Cyber Attacks That Shaped Cybersecurity, FORTINET.COM (2025).

(2) Darknet Cybercrimes

The dark web is defined broadly as "websites hosted on anonymous networks such as Tor that are not indexed by Google or other search engines. These sites are intentionally hidden and require special software or configurations to access, most commonly the Tor browser." The following Dark Web statistics demonstrate its evolving nature in 2026:

- Tiny but expanding footprint: The dark web accounts for 0.01% of the internet, yet its usage and content continue to grow.
- Daily users rising: Millions of people now access Tor and similar networks each day to reach encrypted services and hidden platforms.
- Dominant underground markets: Drug sales, stolen credentials, and illicit digital services continue to drive most dark web commerce.

What Is the Dark Web? Scale, Trends & Growth DEXPOSE (2026 Report). A 2026 study concluded that the dark web's growth:

- Fraud-as-a-Service 'superstores' expanding to meet huge criminal demand for tools to beat modern anti-fraud systems
- Know your customer (KYC)-ready bank accounts, 'fraud for beginners' tutorials and plug-and-play fraud kits amongst range of available services
- Criminal-on-criminal attacks driving changes to dark web marketplaces as fraudsters grapple with AI challenge
- Social media platforms emerging as a threat to the dark web as criminals value convenience

The Dark Web Revealed: New Study Shows Problems Mounting for Cybercriminals (LEXIS/NEXIS RISK SOLUTIONS, Feb. 10, 2026).

A German court handed down prison sentences from 3 to 9 years to "four men convicted of founding and running a darknet forum for child pornography, with tens of thousands of members swapping illegal pictures and videos." *Operators of Darknet Child Porn Forum Jailed in Germany,* AGENCE FRANCE PRESSE (Mar. 7, 2019).

(3) Dark Market

The Internet enables new crimes—misuse of remote administration tools—as an attack vector; a prominent issue on the rise since mid-late 2016 with the rise of dark markets selling RDP Access [Microsoft Remote Desktop Protocol]:

> Malicious cyber actors have developed methods of identifying and exploiting vulnerable RDP sessions over the Internet to compromise identities, steal login credentials, and ransom other sensitive information. FBI, *Cyber Actors Increasingly Exploit The Remote Desktop Protocol to Conduct Malicious Activity* (Sept. 27, 2018).

Cybercrimes on the dark market often involve the sale of illegal drugs:

- Darknet market activity remains resilient, with aggregate DNM flows reaching $2.6 billion in 2025, underscoring the persistence of crypto-enabled drug markets despite repeated enforcement actions.

- On-chain fentanyl-related flows declined sharply, aligning with a decline in fentanyl interdictions and a meaningful drop in opioid overdose deaths—highlighting blockchain data as a means of measuring strategic and operational impact as well as a potential early warning signal for public health authorities. . . .
- Despite repeated law enforcement takedowns, market exits, and infrastructure disruptions, DNMs continue to facilitate the sale of illicit drugs at scale, while also serving as key hubs for fraud-related services.

From Fentanyl to Fraud: On-Chain Activity Highlights Illicit Market Evolution, CHAINANALYSIS (Feb. 19, 2026).

(4) Cybercrimes on Social Media

Cyberbullying, harassment, identity theft, phishing, and online grooming are examples of cybercrimes on social media. In *Sharpe v. Commonwealth,* 2026 Va. App. LEXIS 142 (Va. Ct. of App. Mar. 10, 2026), a 29-year-old choir teacher, began communicating with A.H., a 17-year-old student, in May 2021 on Snapchat, a social media site. The counselor and student daily texted:

> Their relationship escalated from discussing tennis to daily texting and meeting outside of

school, with Sharpe buying A.H. gifts and making inappropriate comments.

Sharpe solicited explicit photographs from A.H. through Snapchat, beginning on June 15, 2021, and continuing until November 2021. A.H. eventually disclosed the communications to her therapist, who reported the matter to the Department of Social Services, leading to a police investigation and Sharpe's indictment. The court of appeals affirmed the trial court's decision.

In *Gaytan v. State*, 2026 Miss. App. LEXIS 105 (Miss. Ct. of App. Mar. 2026), Gaytan, a 21 year old male communicated with TL, a 15 year old female on Instagram from January 1-23, 2022. They agreed to meet for sex, and Gaytan picked up TL at night and took her to a hotel. Security footage captured Gaytan's car, and Instagram messages confirmed he knew TL's age.

Gaytan was indicted on child exploitation and two sexual battery counts. He pled guilty to one count of sexual battery; other counts were dismissed. The court sentenced him to 8 years imprisonment plus 10 years post-release supervision.

In *People v. Carter-Tucker,* 2026 Ill. App. Unpub. LEXIS 540 (Ill Ct. of App., 5th Dist. Mar. 10, 2026), a family feud escalated on Facebook between Carter-Tucker's family and her aunt's family. A cruel Facebook post mocking Carter-Tucker's deceased infant daughter led Carter-Tucker and sisters to attack 16-year-old Dynasty Craig on May 25, 2023. Carter-Tucker fired 8–10 gunshots from moving vehicle toward crowd, striking Linnell Blount in head. The State argued that the provocation from the Facebook post did not justify the defendant's violent response. The court stated that: the defendant argues that instead of mitigating her sentence based upon the strong provocation caused by the Facebook post about her deceased child, the trial court aggravated her sentence by improperly focusing on the defendant's reaction to that offensive post.

The court acknowledged the cruel Facebook post mocking the death of the defendant's daughter and its emotional impact. The appeals court concluded that trial court did not disregard the provocation factor, nor did it factor in the defendant's emotional reaction to that provocation as aggravating in itself.

(5) Cyberbullying

Cyberbullying is "the use of electronic communication to bully a person, typically by sending messages of an intimidating or threatening nature."

Cyberbullying/Cyber-Harassment; N.J.S.A. 2C:33–4.1. New Jersey's cyber-harassment statute states:

a. A person commits the crime of cyber-harassment if, while making a communication in an online capacity via any electronic device or through a social networking site and with the purpose to harass another, the person:

> (1) threatens to inflict injury or physical harm to any person or the property of any person;
>
> (2) knowingly sends, posts, comments, requests, suggests, or proposes any lewd, indecent, or obscene material to or about a person with the intent to emotionally harm a reasonable person or place a reasonable person in fear of physical or emotional harm to his person; or
>
> (3) threatens to commit any crime against the person or the person's property.
>
> Cyber harassment occurs when someone uses social media, email, text messaging, or any other form of electronic communication to harass and threaten a person.

The 2022 School Crime Supplement to the National Crime Victimization Survey (National Center for Education Statistics and Bureau of Justice) found nationwide:

> among students ages 12–18 in grades 6–12 who reported being bullied during school (19.2% of all students), about 21.6% reported being bullied online or by text, including twice as many girls (27.7%) as boys (14.1%).

Frequency of Cyberbullying, STOPBULLYING.GOV (last reviewed Oct. 7, 2024).

In a Massachusetts cyberbullying case, Phoebe Prince, a 15-year-old high school student, committed suicide after being subject to systematic harassment from her classmates. Phoebe, whose family had recently emigrated from Ireland, dated a senior football player, who previously had been the boyfriend of one of her tormentors.

Her classmates posted insults calling her an "Irish slut" and "whore" in anonymous posts on Twitter, Craigslist, Facebook, and Formspring. Phoebe Prince committed suicide two days before the school's winter cotillion dance. Even after Prince's death, her classmates left vicious messages on a memorial Facebook.

A Massachusetts District Attorney charged six of the instigators of the bullying with violating Prince's civil rights, criminal harassment, and statutory rape. The students accepted plea agreements placing them on probation so it is uncertain whether they would have been convicted on the more serious charges.

In Massachusetts, the question of whether the criminal law was adequate to deal properly with this high-profile school bullying case inspired legislators to enact cyberbullying criminal statutes. Nine years after the antibullying statute was enacted, it has not achieved its purpose.

(6) Revenge Porn

Revenge porn may be broadly defined as nonconsensual pornography created and posted by males to shame their ex-spouse or former partner.

See generally, Danielle Keats Citron & Mary Anne Franks, *Criminalizing Revenge Porn*, 49 WAKE FOREST L. REV. 345, 346 (2014) (making the case for criminalizing involuntary porn or the distribution of sexually graphic images of individuals without their consent).

A 2017 nationwide side of online revenge porn concluded:

1. Victimized or threatened with NCP. (Non-Consensual Porn), 12.8% of all participants reported having been victims of NCP (having had asexually-explicit image of themselves shared without their consent) or having been threatened with NCP.

2. NCP Victims. Eight percent of all participants reported having been victims of NCP (having had a sexually-explicit image of themselves shared without their consent) at some point in their lives.

3. Only threatened with NCP. 4.8% of all participants reported having only been threatened with NCP, without it ever being distributed.

4. NCP Perpetrators. 5.2% of all participants reported having perpetrated NCP (having shared a sexually-explicit image of someone without their consent) at some point in their lives.

CCRI Cyber Civil Rights Initiative, *2017 Nationwide Online Study of Nonconsensual Porn Victimization* (June 2017) at 11.

In 2025, Congress passed S.146, the Tools to Address Known Exploitation by Immobilizing Technological Deepfakes on Websites and Networks (TAKE IT DOWN) Act which has two provisions:

> The first provision criminalizes the nonconsensual distribution of intimate images (NDII), whether authentic (sometimes referred to as "revenge porn") or digitally manipulated (often referred to as "deepfake porn"). The second provision requires covered platforms to remove nonconsensual intimate visual depictions within 48 hours.

CCRI Statement on the Passage of the TAKE IT DOWN Act (S. 146) (April 28, 2025).

(7) AI as a Cyberattack Surface

Artificial Intelligence (AI) enabled cybercrimes are evolving rapidly. In *People v. Lewis*, 2026 N.Y. App. Div. LEXIS 1100 (N.Y. Sup. Jud. Ct. App. Div. Feb. 24, 2026), a 58-year-old man generated morphed images by superimposing his 16-year-old cousin's face onto adult bodies engaged in sexual conduct.

The defendant was convicted under federal morphed child pornography law before New York's July 8, 2025 amendment. Nevertheless, his conduct did not violate pre-amendment Penal Law § 263.15 because no actual child performed sexual acts, requiring that his conviction be vacated.

In a New Hampshire case, the defendant took the faces of "15-year-old girls from some of his camp photos and used Photoshop to morph them onto the bodies of adult women in pornographic pictures."

David Brooks, *'Deepfake' Tech Echoes Old N.H. Ruling on 'Morphed' Child Porn Pictures*, GRANITE GEEK BLOG (June 26, 2019).

The New Hampshire Supreme Court overturned his conviction for child pornography reasoning that:

> the images didn't meet the legal definition of child pornography because they weren't made with actual children and thus weren't illegal—despite the rage and disgust they produced in the girls and their families, not to mention anybody else who learned about them. *Id.*

Following these state supreme court decisions, the state legislatures in Florida and New Hampshire amended their child pornography laws to cover "morphed" images. New York had already amended its child pornography laws to cover morphed images, but it did not apply to the defendant's case.

In *United States v. Wilkerson*, 2025 U.S. Dist. LEXIS 251014 (M.D. Fla. Dec. 5, 2025), Wilkerson was accused of possessing thousands of animated depictions of sexual abuse on children in the style of Japanese animēshon ("anime"). Officers found over 10,000 images of anime, including drawings of torture and bestiality, adults engaged in sexual acts, and minors engaged in sexual acts.

At least one image of a child engaged in a sexual act appears to have been generated by artificial intelligence and is similar to the anime images in that it presented a cartoonish image of a child.

Wilkerson was charged with a violation of 18 U.S.C. § 1466A, which prohibits any person from knowingly possessing a visual depiction of any kind, including a drawing, cartoon, sculpture, or painting, which depicts a minor engaging in sexually explicit conduct and is obscene. The court denied Defendant's motion to dismiss Count One of the indictment on all grounds.

"Criminals used artificial intelligence-based software to impersonate a chief executive's voice and demand a fraudulent transfer of €220,000 ($243,000) in an unusual" cybercrime case. 3A COMPUTER CONTRACTS § 15.01 (Michael L. Rustad ed. 2026).

Artificial intelligence is used fraud schemes deploying deepfake media. Emerging generative artificial intelligence (GenAI) technologies are deployed in crimes against financial institutions and their customers. 1 Bank Secrecy Act and Anti-Money Laundering Service § 9.10 (2026).

The following statistics demonstrate the rapidly evolving role of artificial intelligence (AI) in perpetrating cybercrimes.

- 27 sec: Fastest eCrime breakout time on record.

- Eighty-nine percent increase in attacks by AI-enabled adversaries.

- Forty-two percent increase in zero-day vulnerabilities exploited prior to public disclosure.
- Forty percent of vulnerabilities exploited by China-nexus threat actors targeted edge devices.
- 266% increase in cloud-conscious intrusions by state-nexus threat actors.

Crowdstrike 2026: *Global Threat Report* (2026).

§ 8-2. Computer Fraud & Abuse Act

(A) CRIMINAL PROVISIONS

The most important federal statute used to prosecute cybercrime is the Computer Fraud and Abuse Act (CFAA) which punishes and deters computer hackers, e.g., "electronic trespassers." 18 U.S.C. § 1030. The CFAA prohibits accessing a computer without authorization, or in excess of authorization.

Section 1030(a)(2) of the Computer Fraud and Abuse Act provides that whoever "intentionally accesses a computer without authorization or exceeds authorized access, and thereby obtains. . . information from any protected computer," commits a federal crime. 18 U.S.C. § 1030(a)(2)(C).

To "exceed[ ] authorized access" means "to access a computer with authorization and to use such access to obtain or alter information in the computer that the assessor is not entitled so to obtain or alter." 18 U.S.C. § 1030(e)(6).

Congress amended the CFAA to address Internet-related crimes.

For example, the USA Patriot Act: "addressed situations where an attacker within the United States attacks a computer system located abroad and situations in which individuals in foreign countries route communications through the United States as they hack from one foreign country to another."

U.S. Department of Justice, Computer Crime and Intellectual Property Section Criminal Division, *Prosecuting Computer Crimes* (2017) at 5.

The CFAA penalizes the act of accessing a protected computer to steal national security information. The term "protected computer," 18 U.S.C. § 1030(e)(2), is a statutory term of art that covers computers used in or affecting interstate or foreign commerce and computers used by the federal government and financial institutions.

The computer must be "used in or affecting interstate or foreign commerce or communication." This broad definition covers all computers connected to the Internet.

The CFAA also sanctions the act of accessing a computer to misappropriate national security information. The computer must be "used in or affecting interstate or foreign commerce or communication." The CFAA applies to "protected computers" that in practice is all computers connected to the Internet. Congress amended the CFAA to update the statute responding to evolving cybercrimes:

- Eliminated the requirement in 18 U.S.C. § 1030(a)(2)(C) that information must have been stolen through an interstate or foreign communication, thereby expanding jurisdiction for cases involving theft of information from computers.
- Eliminated the requirement in 18 U.S.C. § 1030(a)(5) that the defendant's action must result in a loss exceeding $5,000 and created a felony offense where the damage affects ten or more computers, closing a gap in the law.
- Expanded 18 U.S.C. § 1030(a)(7) to criminalize not only explicit threats to cause damage to a computer, but also threats to (1) steal data on a victim's computer, (2) publicly disclose stolen data, or (3) not repair damage the offender already caused to the computer.
- Created a criminal offense for conspiring to commit a computer hacking offense under Section 1030.
- Broadened the definition of "protected computer" in 18 U.S.C. § 1030(e)(2) to the full extent of Congress's commerce power by including those computers used in or affecting interstate or foreign commerce or communication.

- Provided a mechanism for civil and criminal forfeiture of property used in or derived from Section 1030 violation.

U.S. Department of Justice, Computer Crime and Intellectual Property Section Criminal Division, *Prosecuting Computer Crimes* (2017) at 5.

Prosecutors in Internet crime cases deploy the CFAA to punish the release of viruses, worms, or malware to penetrate a computer's firewall in order to steal or destroy data. 18 U.S.C. § 1030(a)(5). Subsection 1030(a)(5) criminalizes those who deliberately attack computers or infect data with harmful code. Subsection 1030(a)(7)(B) criminalizes extortion by threats to obtain information without authorization or in excess of authorization.

(1) Obtaining National Security Information

The elements of a Section 1030(a)(1) criminal offense require that a defendant: (1) knowingly accessed computer without or in excess of authorization, (2) obtained national security information, (3) had reason to believe the information could injure the U.S. or benefit a foreign nation, and (4) made a willful communication, delivery, transmission (or attempt) or willfully retained the information. Prosecutors have rarely deployed this section since Congress enacted the CFAA.

(2) Computer Access Without Authorization

The Computer Fraud and Abuse Act (CFAA), 18 U.S.C. § 1030, prohibits accessing a computer "without authorization." 18 U.S.C. § 1030(a)(2).

The CFAA case law suggests that prosecutors find it challenging to prove exceeding authorization. Therefore, employers will also find it difficult to pursue civil actions against ex-employees who have violated the Act.

The *United States v. Drew*, 259 F.R.D. 449 (C.D. Cal. 2009), was a controversial expansion of the Computer Fraud and Abuse Act (CFAA) to cyberbullying. Lori Drew, a homemaker, masqueraded as a teenage boy, stalked a 13-year-old girl, and induced her to commit suicide. The court summarized the facts:

> Drew, a resident of O'Fallon, Missouri, entered into a conspiracy in which its members agreed to intentionally access a computer used in interstate commerce without (and/or in excess of) authorization in order to obtain information for the purpose of committing the tortious act of intentional infliction of emotional distress upon 'M.T.M.,' subsequently identified as Megan Meier Megan was a 13 year old girl living in O'Fallon who had been a classmate of Drew's daughter Sarah. Pursuant to the conspiracy, on or about September 20, 2006, the conspirators registered and set up a profile for a fictitious 16 year old male juvenile named 'Josh Evans' on the www.MySpace.com website ('MySpace'), and

posted a photograph of a boy without that boy's knowledge or consent.

Megan Meier killed herself shortly after receiving a message from Josh that the "world would be a better place without you." Lori Drew deleted her MySpace account after the teenager's suicide. In the indictment, prosecutors charged Drew with "one count of conspiracy in violation of 18 U.S.C. § 371 and three counts of violating a felony portion of the CFAA, 18 U.S.C. §§ 1030(a)(2)(C) and 1030(c)(2)(B)(ii), which prohibit accessing a computer without authorization or in excess of authorization." The jury found Drew guilty of violating the CFAA.

The most controversial aspect of the *U.S. v. Drew* prosecution was whether the intentional breach of My Space's terms of use was tantamount to a trespass constituting a misdemeanor crime for purposes of the CFAA. The California federal court held that stretching the CFAA to apply to a mere violation of the terms of use was unconstitutionally vague, reversing Drew's jury conviction.

(3) Trespassing Against a Government Computer

Trespassing against a government computer and obtaining information is covered by 18 U.S.C. § 1030(a)(3). Under that subsection, the government must prove that the defendant: (1) intentionally accessed, (2) without authorization, (3) a nonpublic computer was exclusively for the use of the U.S. Government, or was used by or affected by the use of a U.S. Government computer. 18 U.S.C. § 1030(a)(3).

(4) Accessing to Defraud

The CFAA provides whoever "knowingly and with intent to defraud, accesses" a computer covered by the Act "without authorization, or exceeds authorized access, and by means of such conduct furthers the intended fraud and obtains anything of value" shall be punished as provided in the Act. 18 U.S.C. § 1030(a)(4).

In an "unauthorized use" or "exceeds authorized use" case, the CFAA requires a defendant to: (1) knowingly and (2) with intent to defraud (3) access a protected computer (4) without authorization or exceeding authorized access (5) in order to further the intended fraud and (6) the defendant obtained something of value, including use of the computer or data that exceeded $5,000 over a one-year period.

(5) Damaging Computers or Data

Damaging a computer or its information is addressed by 18 U.S.C. § 1030(a)(5), which criminalizes multiple offenses. Section 1030(a)(5)(A) makes it a crime to knowingly cause transmission of a program, information, code, or command such as a computer virus that intentionally causes damage.

Similarly, Section 1030(a)(5)(B) criminalizes the intentional access of a computer without authorization resulting in damage. Finally, Section 1030(a)(5)(C) makes it a crime to intentionally access a protected computer without authorization causing damage or loss.

Section 1030(a)(5)'s offenses are felonies if they result in damages or loss of $5,000 during the year, or modify the medical care of a person, cause physical injury, threaten public health or safety, or damage computer systems used for justice, national defense, national security, or civil liability. Finally, it is a felony to affect ten or more protected computers during a year regardless of damages or loss.

In *United States v. Hutchins*, 361 F. Supp. 3d 779 (E.D. Wisc. 2019), an English citizen was charged with having:

> knowingly caused and aided and abetted the transmission of a program, information, code, and command and as a result of such conduct, attempted to cause damage without authorization, to ten or more protected computers during a 1-year period.

The complaint against Hutchins alleged: "violations of the CFAA, which criminalizes actions intended to damage protected computers." The court stated that Hutchins:

> developed UPAS Kit and provided it to Individual A, who subsequently sold it to someone in the Eastern District of Wisconsin. The superseding indictment further alleges that Hutchins developed Kronos and provided it to Individuals A and B, the former of whom advertised, marketed, and sold Kronos in the Eastern District of Wisconsin. It also alleges that Hutchins used a YouTube video to promote the sale of Kronos, and referred interested

purchasers of Kronos to Individual A. . . . However, as stated, the charges sufficiently allege activity in the United States, specifically in the Eastern District of Wisconsin. There is no extraterritorial activity at issue.

The court refused to grant Hutchins motion to suppress or dismiss the indictment.

(6) Trafficking in Passwords

Section 1030(a)(6) prohibits a person from knowingly trafficking in computer passwords and similar information with intent to defraud, when the trafficking affects interstate or foreign commerce, or when the password may be used to access a computer used by or for the U.S. Government without authorization.

The elements of the CFAA for trafficking in passwords include: (1) trafficking, (2) in computer password or similar information, (3) knowingly and with intent to defraud, and (4) trafficking affects interstate or foreign commerce or a computer used by or for the U.S. Government.

The term "trafficking" in Section 1030(a)(6) is defined by reference to the definition of the same term in 18 U.S.C. § 1029, and means "transfer, or otherwise dispose of, to another, or obtain control of with intent to transfer or dispose."

(7) Threatening to Harm a Computer

Section 1030(a)(7) addresses extortion, prohibiting threats to harm a computer or data. Prosecutors must prove that the defendant has: (1) intent to extort money or any other thing of value, (2) transmitted the threat in interstate or foreign commerce, and (3) made a threat to damage a protected computer, reveal confidential information, or demand money in connection with the extortion.

Attempts and conspiracy to commit computer crimes are addressed in amendments to the CFAA. Inchoate offenses such as attempt, conspiracy, and aiding and abetting are commonly covered in federal computer statutes but difficult to prosecute inchoate or attempted cybercrime.

(B) CFAA'S CIVIL LIABILITY

The Computer Fraud and Abuse Act (CFAA) is primarily a criminal statute, recognizes a private cause of action for damages and injunctive relief is permitted. 18 U.S.C. § 1030(g).

Congress amended the Computer Fraud and Abuse Act (CFAA) in 1994 to allow for the victims of computer crime to pursue a private cause of action if they suffered a "damage or loss of at least $5,000" they may have a civil remedy under 18 U.S.C. § 1030(g).

The CFAA's civil provisions allow the victims of cybercrime to recover for damages or losses. For purpose of the CFAA provision imposing civil and criminal liability on anyone who accesses computer without authorization or exceeds authorized access to computer, employee is authorized to access computer when his employer approves or sanctions his admission to that computer. 18 U.S.C. § 1030(a)(2).

To prove that defendant intentionally accessed a protected computer without authorization, in violation of Computer Fraud and Abuse Act (CFAA), government must prove that defendant (1) intentionally (2) accessed without authorization (3) protected computer and (4) thereby obtained information. 18 U.S.C.A. § 1030(a)(2).

The CFAA defines "damage" to include "any impairment to the integrity or availability of data, a system, or information." 18 U.S.C. § 1030(e)(8). "Loss" under the CFAA is defined broadly as:

> any reasonable cost to any victim, including the cost of responding to an offense, conducting a damage assessment, and restoring the data, program, system, or information to its condition prior to the offense, and any revenue lost, cost incurred, or other consequential damages incurred because of interruption of service[.]

18 U.S.C. § 1030(e)(11).

In *Facebook Inc. v. Power Ventures, Inc.*, 844 F.3d 1058 (9th Cir. 2016), Facebook, Inc. sued another social media site, Power Ventures, over a promotional campaign. Power accessed Facebook users' data and initiated form e-mails and other electronic messages promoting its website. Initially, Power had implied permission from Facebook.

But Facebook sent Power a cease and desist letter and blocked Power's IP address; nevertheless Power continued its campaign. In total, more than 60,000 external e-mails promoting Power were sent through the Facebook system. An unknown number of internal Facebook messages were also transmitted.

Facebook contended that Power's actions violated the CFAA, CAN-SPAM, and California Penal Code Section 502. The Ninth Circuit held that Power violated the CFAA and California Penal Code Section 502 only after it received Facebook's cease and desist letter and nonetheless continued to access Facebook's computers without permission.

In *Google LLC v. Does 1–25*, 2025 WL 3451343 (S.D. Dec. 1, 2025), Google LLC filed a Complaint for injunctive and other relief to stop Doe Defendants 1–25, a criminal enterprise (the "Lighthouse Enterprise"), from using a set of software tools called "Lighthouse" to facilitate widespread phishing attacks that have harmed and continue to harm millions of victims and numerous businesses, including Google.

The defendants created fake websites mimicking the New York City government's website and New York E-ZPass website for use in phishing schemes. They successfully phished personal and financial information from victims within this District and New York State. The court found that the defendants:

> used Google's trademarks as part of spoofed websites used to solicit victims' personal and financial information, including their Gmail credentials, within this District and New York

State, and have directed multiple forms of electronic communication to user devices in this district and New York State.

The court concluded that Google has established each of the factors required for a preliminary injunction. The court concluded that:

> Google has shown a likelihood of success on the merits of its claim that Defendants violated and continue to violate the CFAA. Google has demonstrated that Defendants have—knowingly and with intent to defraud—trafficked in passwords or similar information through which a computer may be accessed without authorization in interstate commerce through online forums such as Telegram channels, in violation of 18 U.S.C. § 1030(a)(6). Defendants transfer and sell phished account credentials and authorization codes to other members of the Enterprise and other cybercriminals. Defendants' actions have caused loss to one or more persons in excess of $5,000 in a one-year period, including the costs Google incurred responding to and investigating the Lighthouse Schemes.

§ 8-3. Electronic Communications Privacy Act

(A) OVERVIEW OF THE ECPA

The Electronic Communications Privacy Act (ECPA) of 1986 updated the Federal Wiretap Act of 1968, which addressed interception of conversations using "hard" telephone lines, but did not apply to interception of computer and other digital and electronic communications.

Congress updated the ECPA when it enacted the USA Patriot Act. The statutory purpose was to update the ECPA to keep pace with the evolution of new communications technologies and methods, including easing restrictions on law enforcement access to stored communications in some cases. U.S. Department of Justice, *Electronic Communications Privacy Act of 1986 (ECPA)*, 18 U.S.C. §§ 2510–2523.

The ECPA, as amended, protects wire, oral, and electronic communications while those communications are being made, are in transit, and when they are stored on computers. The Act applies to email, telephone conversations, and data stored electronically.

Title I of the ECPA amended the federal wiretap statute to update the meaning of interception of electronic communications to accommodate innovative technologies. The term "electronic communication" now applies broadly to e-mail or other Internet-related communications.

The ECPA imposes liability on a person who "intentionally intercepts . . . any wire, oral, or electronic communication," 18 U.S.C. § 2511(1)(a), subject to a number of exemptions. 18 U.S.C. § 2511(2)(a)–(h). "Electronic communication" includes communication by radio, 18 U.S.C. § 2510(12), and " 'readily accessible to the general public' means, with respect to a radio communication" that the communication is "not . . . scrambled or encrypted," 18 U.S.C. § 2510(16)(A).

Second, the Act exempts intercepting "radio communication" by "any station for the use of the general public;" by certain governmental communication systems "readily accessible to the general public," including police, fire, and civil defense agencies; by a station operating on an authorized frequency for "amateur, citizens band, or general mobile radio services;" or by a marine or aeronautical communications system. 18 U.S.C. § 2511(2)(g)(ii)(I)–(IV).

Title I of the ECPA criminalizes three types of activities: (1) intercepting or endeavoring to intercept electronic communications, (2) disclosing or endeavoring to disclose unlawfully intercepted information, and (3) using the content of unlawfully intercepted information.

Title II of the ECPA, which is called the Stored Communications Act (SCA), protects the privacy of the contents of files stored by service providers and of records held about the subscriber by service providers, such as subscriber name, billing records, or IP addresses. 18 U.S.C. §§ 2701–12.

Congress enacted the Stored Communications Act (SCA), 18 U.S.C. §§ 2701–2711 in 1986 as Title II of the ECPA, governs the privacy of stored Internet communications. Section 2701(c)(1) exempts from subsection (A) "conduct authorized by the person or entity providing a wire or electronic communications service." 18 U.S.C. § 2701(c)(1).

The U.S. Department of Justice notes that the structure of the SCA reflects a series of classifications that indicate the drafters' judgments about what kinds of information implicate greater or lesser privacy interests:

> For example, the drafters saw greater privacy interests in the content of stored emails than in subscriber account information. Similarly, the drafters believed that computing services available 'to the public' required more strict [sic] regulation than services not available to the public. . .To protect the array of privacy interests identified by its drafters, the [Act] offers varying degrees of legal protection depending on the perceived importance of the privacy interest involved. Some information can be obtained from providers with a subpoena; other information requires a special court order; and still other information requires a search warrant. In addition, some types of legal process require notice to the subscriber, while other types do not.

U.S. Dept. of Justice, *Searching and Seizing Computers and Obtaining Electronic Evidence In Criminal Investigations* (2009).

The ECPA, like the CFAA, recognizes a civil act for private plaintiffs who have been victimized by the unauthorized or unconsented interception or access of electronic communications. The ECPA requires proof the defendant knew or had reason to know the electronic communication had been illegally intercepted.

Under the ECPA, federal courts may order ISPs to disclose stored communications and transaction records. The ECPA requires prosecutors to prove facts capable of articulation by illustrating reasonable grounds relevant to a criminal investigation to support orders for service providers to turn over confidential customer information.

The subscriber whose information is turned over to the government has no reasonable expectation of privacy and is thus not protected under the Fourth Amendment.

The prohibitions enumerated in the ECPA are subject to certain specific exceptions. Providers of wire or electronic communications services may monitor their services to ensure adequacy. The "ordinary course of business" exception allows employers to access stored or electronic communications, which enables them to monitor their employees' e-mail.

To satisfy the "ordinary course of business" exception, the employer must show: (1) the device used to intercept the electronic communication, and (2) the device is used by the employer within the ordinary course of the business.

The employer is only allowed to intercept electronic communications long enough to determine the topic being discussed. If the communication is personal, the employer must cease intercepting the communications any further. The following chart summarizes ECPA's key sections.

ECPA Key Provisions

Intercepting a Communication	18 U.S.C. § 2511(1)(a)
Disclosing an Intercepted Communications	18 U.S.C. § 2511(1)(c)
Using an Intercepted Communications	18 U.S.C. § 2511(1)(d)

Within the ECPA, Congress enacted a private action authorizing plaintiffs to seek monetary damages against a person who "intentionally intercepts, endeavors to intercept, or procures any other person to intercept or endeavor to intercept, any wire, oral, or electronic communication." 18 U.S.C. § 2511(1)(a).

To establish a *prima facie* case for a civil violation of § 2511(1)(a), a plaintiff must prove five elements: that a defendant (1) intentionally (2) intercepted, endeavored to intercept or procured another person to intercept or endeavor to intercept (3) the contents of (4) an electronic communication (5) using a device.

(B) ECPA DEFENSES

The ECPA exempts intercepting "an electronic communication made through an electronic communication system" if the system is configured so that it is "readily accessible to the general public." 18 U.S.C. § 2511(2)(g)(i). As noted above, the ECPA also includes two statutory exceptions: the "ordinary course of business" exception and for activities incidental to rendering services.

The business exception to ECPA provides a provider may intercept electronic communications within its network for incidental activities. The ECPA allows service providers or anyone else to intercept and disclose an electronic communication where either the sender or recipient of the message has effectively consented to disclosure, explicitly or implicitly.

Section 2511(2)(d) of the ECPA prohibits employers from intercepting e-mail messages; however, the ECPA does not apply if an employee consents to e-mail monitoring. Consent, as defined by the ECPA, encompasses implied consent, which in the context of e-mail monitoring, is an employer's prior notice that it will monitor Internet usage and e-mail.

The USA Patriot Act amended the ECPA to list crimes for which investigators may get a wiretap order for wire communications. To combat terrorism, the Act permits federal government agents to intercept e-mail and monitor other Internet activities. In order to investigate terrorism, the FBI can seek National Security Letters (NSL) enabling it to gain access to subscriber information.

A NSL is defined as an administrative subpoena allowing the FBI to gain access to, among other things, subscriber information, or electronic communication transactional records held by Internet service providers when this information is relevant to international terrorism or clandestine intelligence activities.

§ 8-4. Internet-Related Specific Purpose Acts

(A) IDENTITY THEFT

The Identity Theft Penalty Enhancement Act (ITPEA), which took effect of July 15, 2004, established a new offense of aggravated identity theft. 18 U.S.C. § 1028A.

The federal identity theft act states:

> (a) Offenses.—
>
> (1) In general.—Whoever, during and in relation to any felony violation enumerated in subsection (c), knowingly transfers, possesses, or uses, without lawful authority, a means of identification of another person shall, in addition to the punishment provided for such felony, be sentenced to a term of imprisonment of 2 years.
>
> (2) Terrorism offense.—Whoever, during and in relation to any felony violation enumerated in Section 2332b(g)(5)(B), knowingly transfers, possesses, or uses, without lawful authority, a means of identification of another person or a false identification document shall, in addition to the punishment provided for such felony, be sentenced to a term of imprisonment of 5 years.

18 U.S.C.A. § 1028A.

This federal criminal statute has been cited in over 4,000 cases as of March 11, 2026. The identity theft statute is deployed against hackers who misappropriate credit card information or "phishers," who misappropriate trade secrets or other information through fraudulent e-mails. In general, those who violate Section 1028A are subject to a mandatory two-year term of imprisonment. In cases of terrorism related aggravated identity theft, including that related to Section 1030(a)(1).

Aggravated identity theft carries a mandatory, consecutive two-year prison term if "during and in relation to" a predicate offense, a defendant "uses, without lawful authority, a means of identification of another person." 18 U.S.C. § 1028A(a)(1).

H.R.7270, the Stop Identity Fraud and Identity Theft Act of 2026, was introduced in the 119th Congress to establish a comprehensive, government-wide approach to combat identity theft and fraud within the financial services industry.

(B) ACCESS DEVICE FRAUD

Access device fraud is a relatively new cybercrime to address theft using payment devices. 18 U.S.C. § 1029. "Unauthorized" access devices include lost, stolen, or revoked devices, whereas "counterfeit" ones include fictitious, altered, or forged devices. 18 U.S.C. § 1029(e)(2) & (3). Conviction for access device fraud may result in a 10-year prison sentence. 18 U.S.C. § 1029(c)(1)(A)(i).

In *United States v. Carver*, 916 F.3d 398 (4th Cir. 2019), the victim discovered that while he was in Las Vegas, his credit cards were being charged to a hotel room in South Carolina. Upon investigating further, the police determined that the Carver, the defendant, had stolen the plaintiff's credit card and was at the hotel room, with an "overwriter" encoding machine, driver's licenses for various people's names, and banking information.

Despite Carver arguing that the cards in his possession did not work, they did not constitute an "unauthorized access device." In its holding, the Fourth Circuit explained that even though the cards may not work, they could be considered an unauthorized access device under the statutory language of 18 U.S.C. § 1029(e)(2) & (3).

The government only had to prove that each card "was in principle the sort of thing that people use to obtain money (like a credit card or bank number)." The court ruled that if an unauthorized access device is expired, revoked, cancelled, or otherwise incapable of being used to obtain money, it would still be the basis for a federal criminal sentence.

(C) ANTI-STALKING STATUTES

Most states have enacted anti-stalking criminal law statutes that apply to the Internet. However, litigants have been more likely to seek remedy under the available federal anti-stalking statutes. The District of Columbia's anti-stalking law enumerates several mental states and modes of committing the offense of stalking:

> Specifically, it is unlawful to 'engage in a course of conduct' either '[w]ith the intent to cause,' 'knows would cause' or 'should have known would cause a reasonable person' to '[f]ear for his

> or her safety or the safety of another person,' '[f]eel seriously alarmed, disturbed, or frightened,' or '[s]uffer emotional distress.'

D.C. Code § 22–3133(a)(1)–(a)(3) (2012).

The D.C. statute seeks to hold stalkers answerable:

> The Council enacts this stalking statute to permit the criminal justice system to hold stalkers accountable for a wide range of acts, communications, and conduct. The Council recognizes that stalking includes a pattern of following or monitoring the victim, or committing violent or intimidating acts against the victim, regardless of the means.

D.C. Code § 22–3131(b).

The federal anti-stalking statute defines stalking as:

> Whoever . . . with the intent to kill, injure, harass, intimidate, or place under surveillance with intent to kill, injure, harass, or intimidate another person, uses the mail, any interactive computer service or electronic communication service or electronic communication system of interstate commerce, or any other facility of interstate or foreign commerce to engage in a course of conduct that . . . causes, attempts to cause, or would be reasonably expected to cause substantial emotional distress to a person.

18 U.S.C. § 2261A(2)(B) (2013).

Additionally, 18 U.S.C. § 2266(2) defines "course of conduct" as "a pattern of conduct composed of 2 or more acts, evidencing a continuity of purpose." To prove stalking, the government must establish defendants: (1) employed a facility of interstate commerce, (2) to engage in a course of conduct with the intent to place a person in reasonable fear of death or serious bodily injury either to that person or to a partner or immediate family member, and (3) the course of conduct actually put that person in reasonable fear of death or serious bodily injury to himself or his partner or immediate family member.

In *United States v. Yung*, 2020 WL 5946065 (D. Del. Oct. 7, 2020), Yung pled guilty to one count of cyberstalking, in violation of 18 U.S.C. §§ 2261A(2)(B) and 2261(b), a Class D Felony, for which the maximum penalties are not more than five years' imprisonment, three years' supervised release, a $250,000 fine, restitution, and a $100 special assessment.

The *Yung* court awarded damages to one of Yung's victims for a "payment for home security system upgrades was proximately caused by Defendant's cyberstalking campaign, which yielded, inter alia, unsolicited visitors to Victim #1's home under extremely troubling circumstances."

The court also ordered Yung to reimburse Georgetown University for the costs of taking down his Internet posts and securing its computer system. The court concluded: "that Georgetown University's property, namely its security systems, was 'damaged' as a result of Defendant's cyberstalking campaign."

The federal anti-stalking statute is frequently asserted in family court cases where no-contact orders are sought.

In *United States v. Cook*, 472 F. Supp. 3d 326 (N.D. Miss. 2020), the court found that a defendant's online postings were not specific enough to constitute true threats under the federal stalking statute:

> Cook's Facebook posts are not true threats precluding him from First Amendment protection. Cook's posts, when read in context, lack entirely the specificity required to bring them under the umbrella of a true threat. Nowhere in any post does Cook explicitly state that he plans to physically harm Lepicier, or any other named public official. 'God willing I'm going to take them out' is different from telling an FBI agent you have a pistol and you will use it to kill the president or repeatedly and directly telling another person in a chat room that you were going to kill the students in your high school while making references to one of the Columbine shooters.

(D) INTERNET SEX CRIMES TRAFFICKING

The Justice for Victims of Trafficking Act of 2015 (JVTA) established a fund to cover the costs of the programs it authorizes, which is paid for by a $5,000 special penalty assessment for convicted sex offenders, human smugglers, and human traffickers. Section 105 increases restitution to the victims of sex trafficking. The JVTA uses forfeited assets to satisfy restitution orders for victims, thus giving law enforcement a greater number of more effective tools to fight sex trafficking.

(E) THE ECONOMIC ESPIONAGE ACT

The Economic Espionage Act (EEA) signed into law by President Clinton on October 11, 1996, was enacted to punish and deter foreign and domestic spies threatening America's economic well-being. Until 1996, there was no federal criminal statute punishing industrial spying by foreign governments and agents. The prosecution of trade secret theft as a criminal offense is a recent development.

The EEA criminalizes both trade secret misappropriation and the theft of other confidential information. To qualify for trade secret protection, the information must have actual or potential economic value the owner has taken reasonable measures to protect. For domestic economic espionage, individuals can be fined $250,000 and are subject to ten years of imprisonment. For organizations, the maximum fine is $5,000,000. 18 U.S.C. § 1835.

The EEA criminalizes two types of offenses: (1) economic espionage benefiting foreign governments or entities and (2) the theft of trade secrets benefiting any person but the true owner. Most prosecutions were filed under Section 1832 classifying "attempt" and "conspiracy" as distinct offenses from those acts that constitute completed crimes under the statute.

The EEA specifically prohibits the theft of trade secrets for the benefit of a foreign government, instrumentality, or agent. Individuals convicted of this offense are subject to $500,000 fines and a maximum of fifteen years in prison, while organizations face fines of up to $5,000,000. Prosecutors seldom use this provision because the U.S. Attorney General requires that the Assistant Attorney General for the National Security Division approve lawsuits against foreign governments.

In 2016, Congress amended the Economic Espionage Act enacting the Defend Trade Secrets Act of 2016 (DTSA) granting companies victimized by trade secret theft the right to seek injunctive relief and damages. Trade secret owners are now able to conduct discovery and seek monetary and injunctive relief.

Courts can award trade secret owners the greater of either $5,000,000 or three times the value of the stolen trade secret, including expenses for research and design and other costs. The essence of a criminal tort remedy is using private enforcement to supplement public prosecution as with CFAA and ECPA civil lawsuits.

In the first year after the DTSA was enacted, civil litigants filed over one hundred cases, approaching the total number of criminal cases filed by federal prosecutors in the two decades after the EEA became law in 1996. The DTSA is discussed in depth in Chapter 12.

§ 8-5. Global Cybercrime Enforcement

The globalization of cybercrime is evidenced by a U.S. Department of Justice advertisement for a Dark Web and Cryptocurrency International Computer Hacking and Intellectual Property Attorney Advisor. The advisor will aid on a variety of criminal justice projects including:

> (1) developing and delivering technical assistance and programs on criminal investigations involving the Dark Web and cryptocurrency, with particular emphasis on Asia Pacific and Eastern Europe/Central Asia regions where sophisticated TOC threats are located;
>
> (2) identifying gaps in existing law, providing advice to legislative bodies on effective legislation and amendment of existing laws to improve enforcement; and
>
> (3) building capacity of law enforcement agencies on a range of Dark Web and cryptocurrency topics.

Catherine de Bolle, *The Role of Europol in International Interdisciplinary European Cooperation Conference Contribution*, 19 EUR. POLICE SCI. & RES. BULL. 17 (2020).

(A) CYBERCRIME CONVENTION

The Convention on Cybercrime, sponsored by the Council of Europe (COE), was the first international treaty addressing computer crime and Internet-related crime. Concluded in Budapest in 2001, the Cybercrime Convention is an international treaty to improve cooperation between nation states in the fight against cybercrime, harmonize the law, and improve investigative techniques. The United States became a signatory country to the Convention in 2006.

The Cybercrime Convention is an agreement to adopt appropriate legislation and fostering international co-operation. Articles 2–4 requires signatories to enact national legislation addressing computer crimes such as illegal access, illegal interception, and data interference. Article 5 requires signatories to criminalize the creation or transmission of computer viruses or malware and expects states to enact legislation adopting the doctrine of corporate liability for cybercrimes.

Articles 7 and 8 requires signatories to criminalize computer related forgery and fraud. Article 9 is an agreement to criminalize the production and distribution of child pornography. Articles 10 and 11 is an agreement to address copyright infringement and aiding and abetting computer crimes.

Article 17 of the Cybercrime Convention also treats computer crime as an extraditable offense calling for mutual assistance in the investigation and prosecution of computer crimes. Article 24 provides mechanisms for obtaining an "cxpeditious preservation of data" on a computer system or server in another territory.

The President of the Parliamentary Assembly of the Council of Europe (PACE), has urged European governments to do more to crack down on online hate:

> Online hate is getting worse and worse, said the President. The trolls are destroying lives, sowing misery, and feeding acts of real-world violence. In some parts of the internet, there is a daily tide of racism, misogyny or homophobia and it has to stop.
>
> [Governments] need clear and comprehensive laws outlawing hate-crime, without undermining legitimate freedom of expression, and should make sure police have the powers and resources to tackle it effectively in line with the Council of Europe's Cybercrime Convention.

We Must Do More to Stop the Trolls, MENA (Aug. 22, 2020).

(B) UN CONVENTION AGAINST CYBERCRIME

The United Nations Convention against Cybercrime was adopted by the General Assembly of the United Nations on 24 December 2024 in New York by resolution 79/243. This UN Convention is the first global treaty to address cybercrime. The UN's statutory purpose is to enable international cooperation in addressing cybercrime:

> Cybercriminals exploit digital systems using malware, ransomware, and hacking to steal money, data, and other valuable information. Information and communications technology

> (ICT) are also used to facilitate crimes such as drug trafficking, arms smuggling, human trafficking, money laundering and fraud. . .Until now, there has been no globally negotiated convention on cybercrime. The new Convention against Cybercrime will enable faster, better-coordinated, and more effective responses, making both digital and physical worlds safer.

United Nations, *Why the Convention against Cybercrime Matters* (Dec. 24, 2024).

(C) GLOBALIZED CYBERCRIME ENFORCEMENT

Many less developed countries have a weak record in punishing cybercriminals. "Arrests and incarceration are intended to be a deterrent, but the poor track record of convictions for cybercrimes (and the jurisdictional issues) mean that many DDoS service providers are undeterred." Richard Parker, *Playing "Whack a Mole": Law Enforcement Response to DDoS as a Service*, READ/WRITE WEB BLOG (July 18, 2020).

For example, the conviction rate in cybercrimes in Maharashtra India in the three years was "just 56 of the 4,500-plus arrested offenders sentenced to jail." *Maharashtra Women 'Most Unsafe' From Cyber Stalkers, Bullies*, TIMES OF INDIA (Oct. 11, 2020).

An INTERPOL assessment of the impact of COVID-19 on cybercrime makes these key findings:

- *Online Scams and Phishing*—Threat actors have revised their usual online scams and phishing schemes. By deploying COVID-19 themed phishing emails, often impersonating government and health authorities, cybercriminals entice victims into providing their personal data and downloading malicious content. Around two-thirds of member countries which responded to the global cybercrime survey reported a significant use of COVID-19 themes for phishing and online fraud since the outbreak.

- *Disruptive Malware (Ransomware and DDoS)*—Cybercriminals are increasingly using disruptive malware against critical infrastructure and healthcare institutions, due to the potential for high impact and financial benefit. In the first two weeks of April 2020, there was a spike in ransomware attacks by multiple threat groups which had been dormant for the past few months. Law enforcement investigations show the majority of attackers estimated quite accurately the maximum amount of ransom they could demand from targeted organizations.

- *Data Harvesting Malware*—The deployment of data harvesting malware such as Remote Access Trojan, info stealers, spyware and banking Trojans by cybercriminals is on the rise. Using COVID-19 related information as a lure, threat actors infiltrate systems to compromise networks, steal data, divert money and build botnets.

- *Malicious Domains*—Taking advantage of the increased demand for medical supplies and information on COVID-19, there has been a significant increase of cybercriminals registering domain names containing keywords, such as 'coronavirus' or 'COVID.' These fraudulent websites underpin a wide variety of malicious activities including C2 servers, malware deployment and phishing. From February to March 2020, a 569 per cent growth in malicious registrations, including malware and phishing and a 788 per cent growth in high-risk registrations were detected and reported to INTERPOL by a private sector partner.

- *Misinformation*—An increasing amount of misinformation and fake news is spreading rapidly among the public. Unverified information, inadequately understood threats, and conspiracy theories have contributed to anxiety in communities and in some cases facilitated the execution of cyberattacks. Nearly 30 per cent of countries which responded to the global cybercrime survey confirmed the circulation of false information related to COVID-19. Within a one-month period, one country reported 290 postings with the majority containing concealed malware. There are also reports of misinformation being linked to the illegal

> trade of fraudulent medical commodities. Other cases of misinformation involved scams via mobile text-messages containing 'too good to be true' offers such as free food, special benefits, or large discounts in supermarkets.

INTERPOL, *INTERPOL Report Shows Alarming Rate of Cyberattacks During COVID-19* (Aug. 4, 2020).

Given the cross-border nature of cybercrime, law enforcement agencies are continually requesting strengthened statutes and additional mutual law enforcement treaties (MLATs). The Cybercrime Convention requires that signatories recognize computer crime. What is needed is further development of global cybercrime cooperation to address the problem of cross-border criminal activity.

CHAPTER 9
CONTENT REGULATION ON THE INTERNET

§ 9-1. Overview of Internet Regulations

This chapter covers content regulation on the Internet. Section 9-1 is an overview of content regulation. Section 9-2 critically examines U.S. federal content regulation. Section 9-3 covers U.S. state regulation of the Internet.

Section 9-4 explains how U.S. content regulation is subject to the First Amendment and addresses constitutional constraints such as vagueness and overbreadth, as well as unprotected speech.

Section 9-5 critically examines U.S. content controls on pornography and adult entertainment. Finally, cross-border content regulation is covered in Section 9-6.

By definition, the Internet is a cross-border legal environment linking hundreds of countries. Billions of Internet users around the world interact in cyberspace. An effective response to content regulation requires a comprehensive approach considering differences in legal cultures. Significant gaps and differences in countries' laws of content regulation will complicate the issue of harmonization.

The options for content regulations are: (1) regional or international regulation, (2) Federal or national regulation, (3) State or local regulation, or

(4) online platform self-regulation. The EU's approach is for online platforms to work directly with the European Commission and individual national states. Content regulation on the Internet is best addressed by regional or international cooperation such as the EU approach, which will be highlighted later in this chapter.

§ 9-2. U.S. Regulation of Internet Content

(A) COMMUNICATIONS DECENCY ACT

Section 230 of the Communications Decency Act. Section 230 generally protects providers of "interactive computer service[s]" from being held liable for publishing third-party information on their platforms. 47 U.S.C. § 230(c)(1). The CDA makes clear that "[n]o provider or user of an interactive computer service shall be treated as the publisher or speaker of any information provided by another information content provider."

CDA Section 230 provides immunity to providers of interactive computer services from being treated as publishers of information provided by another information content provider.

A defendant is immune from state law liability under CDA Section 230 if it is (1) a provider or user of an interactive computer service (2) whom a plaintiff seeks to treat, under state law cause of action, as a publisher or speaker (3) of information provided by another information content provider. 47 U.S.C. § 230(b)(1).

To establish immunity, a defendant must show: (1) it provides an "interactive computer service"; (2) the plaintiff's claim treats it as the publisher or speaker of information; and (3) the information at issue was created by a third party—"information provided by another information content provider."

Doe for Doe v. Snap, Inc., 2025 WL 2926161 (Del. Super. Ct. Oct. 15, 2015).

Senator J. James Exon proposed the Communications Decency Act (CDA) that was the first content regulation proposed for the Internet. He stated: "[t]he information superhighway should not become a red-light district. [The CDA] will keep that from happening and extend the standards of decency which have protected telephone users to new telecommunications devices." 141 Cong. Rec. S1953 (daily ed. Feb. 1, 1995) (statement of Rep. Exon).

The CDA included two provisions intended to regulate content: "the 'indecent transmission' provision," 47 U.S.C. § 223(a)(1), and "the 'patently offensive display' provision," 47 U.S.C. § 223(d).

In *Reno v. ACLU*, 521 U.S. 844 (1997), the Supreme Court held the Communications Decency Act (CDA) violated the First Amendment because the CDA prohibited Internet users from using the Internet to communicate material deemed patently offensive to minors.

The *Reno* Court explained the statute, granting expedited review, which prevented the Court from converting the case into an as-applied challenge. The Court also noted the "vast array of plaintiffs, the range of their expressive activities, and the vagueness of the statute" made it impractical to consider an as-applied challenge.

Content-based law is constitutional only if it survives strict scrutiny. *Reed v. Town of Gilbert*, 576 U.S. 155 (2015).

Strict scrutiny requires that the law "furthers a compelling interest and is narrowly tailored to achieve that interest." "A statute is narrowly tailored if it targets and eliminates no more than the exact source of the 'evil' it seeks to remedy." *Frisby v. Schultz*, 487 U.S. 474 (1988). "[I]t is the rare case in which a State demonstrates that a speech restriction is narrowly tailored to serve a compelling interest." *Williams-Yulee v. Fla. Bar*, 575 U.S. 433 (2015).

Section 230 generally immunizes websites, search engines, and other Internet service providers for liability arising out of third-party content. In recent years, courts have begun to strictly scrutinize claims of CDA Section 230 immunity. Members of Congress have frequently called for reforming or revoking this broad liability shield:

> The same law, however, has also famously played a factor in the proliferation of harmful content. Despite bipartisan support to amend the CDA and a renewed appetite of late to regulate technology, the myriad attempts to reform the CDA in Congress have largely sputtered. . .Yet the bipartisan critics of the CDA have not given up. More recently, those critics have become more vocal in blaming

> Section 230 for enabling the worst of the internet (e.g., hate speech, revenge porn, disinformation and other objectionable content) and for giving large tech platforms too much leeway in moderating or presenting content.

A Final Bow for Section 230? Latest Plea for Reform Calls for Sunset of Immunity Law, JD SUPRA (JUNE 12, 2024).

Courts are increasingly recognizing exceptions to CDA Section 230 where the service provider is content creator not just an intermediary.

THOMAS H. KOENIG & MICHAEL L. RUSTAD, GLOBAL INFORMATION TECHNOLOGIES: ETHICS AND THE LAW (2d ed. 2023) at 169 (stating that courts are chipping away at the Section 230 shield recognizing exceptions).

In *TikTok, et al. v. State of Nevada*, 578 P.3d 640 (Nev. 2025), the State filed a lawsuit against Tik alleging violations of Nevada Deceptive Trade Practices Act (NDTPA) based on allegations that operator knowingly designed platform to keep young users on the platform as long as possible to maximize revenue and made misrepresentations and omissions about platform's safety for young users.

TikTok defended on the grounds of no personal jurisdiction, the First Amendment and CDA Section 230, The Nevada district court concluded that CDA Section 230 did not shield TikTok's misrepresentations:

the district court concluded that § 230 of the CDA did not immunize TikTok because the State's complaint did not seek to place TikTok in the shoes of third-party content creators, but rather their own content:

> [TikTok's] liability in this case does not depend on any of the third-party content posted or distributed by [its] platform, but rather the harmful design features of the platform itself. To comply with the duties alleged in the Complaint, [TikTok] would not need to alter any third-party content or otherwise engage in publication activities. Instead, [it] would need to change only its own misstatements, omissions, marketing, platform development, and design decisions.

The Nevada Supreme Court found a sufficient basis for personal jurisdiction and that CDA Section 230 did not foreclose the State's unfair and deceptive trade practices act. Second, the CDA § 230 and the First Amendment do not bar the State's NDTPA claims as pleaded.

The Nevada Supreme Court held that TikTok's own alleged misrepresentations and misleading omissions and did violate the "First Amendment or invoke TikTok's traditional editorial functions immunized under the CDA § 230." The state supreme court affirmed the lower court's decision that Tik Tok was not shielded by Section 230:

> On its face, the State's complaint does not seek to hold TikTok liable for any third-party content

> that it publishes. The state . . .targets TikTok's alleged own knowingly false statements and omissions to regulators and the public about young users' safety on the platform. Though the State references problematic third-party content in its complaint—such as TikTok "challenge" trends and videos depicting drugs, sex, and suicide—it does so to support its claims that (1) TikTok made misrepresentations about its enforcement of the platform's community guidelines and the safety measures that TikTok implements and (2) TikTok knows that young users experience mental, physical, and privacy harms due to their compulsive TikTok use.

The Nevada Supreme Court concluded that this claim: does not trigger CDA § 230 immunity because the State seeks to hold TikTok liable for its own statements and omissions and resulting duties to users with only a tangential relationship to third-party content. among users and guardians of young users, thus generat[ing] a legal duty distinct from the conduct at hand.

In *United States v. EZ Lynk*, 149 F.4th 190 (2d Cir. 2025), EZ Lynk manufactures and sells the EZ Lynk System, a three-part system that allows car owners to download and install software that alters the functioning of the computer systems in their cars.

The EZ Lynk Auto Agent, an electronic device plugs into a vehicle's [on-board diagnostics] port to access, override, or reprogram the vehicle's computer system. The EZ Lynk system also includes a smartphone application called the 'Auto Agent App,' which connects the EZ Lynk Auto Agent to EZ Lynk's Internet-based service called the 'EZ Lynk Cloud.'

Once connected to the Cloud, drivers can "send and receive data and software relating to their vehicles' computer systems," allowing them to share, record, and reprogram their vehicle from their smartphones.

The EZ Lynk System allows drivers to obtain and install software called "tunes" to reprogram their vehicles. These "tunes" created by third parties, are accessed and installed through the EZ Lynk System. EZ Lynk also provides "storage space" in the Cloud where the third-party technicians can upload and store their tunes. Drivers can access and download tunes stored in the EZ Lynk Cloud through the Auto Agent App. Z Lynk,

This is a "defeat device[,]" 40 C.F.R. § 1068.101(b)(2), that disables vehicle emissions controls in violation of the Clean Air Act, EZ Lynk and other defendants argue that they have no liability for this defeat device because they qualify for immunity under Section 230 of the Communications Decency Act.

The Second Circuit affirmed the district court that the defendants "directly and materially contributed to" the creation of delete tunes, which made them ineligible for CDA Section 230 immunity.

After the U.S. Supreme Court's decision in *Ashcroft v. Free Speech Coalition*, 535 U.S. 234 (2002), Congress enacted the "Prosecutorial Remedies and Other Tools to end the Exploitation of Children Today" (Protect Act of 2003). The Protect

Act criminally sanctions the following: (1) the advertising, (2) promotion, (3) presentation, (4) distribution, and (5) solicitation of child pornography.

The Protect Act of 2003 classifies "primary producers" to include anyone who creates a visual representation of actual sexually explicit conduct, through videotaping, photography, or computer manipulation. The Protect Act of 2003 criminalizes speech accompanying, or seeking the transfer of child pornography via the reproduction or physical delivery from one person to another. 18 U.S.C. § 2252A(a)(3)(B).

Secondary producers either upload these images to a third-party website or manage the content of the website directly. The producer must inspect the depicted individual's government issued picture identification card and determine his or her name as well as date of birth. 18 U.S.C. § 2257(b)(1).

The U.S. Justice Department explains the purpose of the Protect Act of 2003:

> Problem #1: Law Enforcement Had Inadequate Tools to Help Locate Missing Children and Prosecute Offenders.
>
> Solution #1: The Act Establishes the AMBER Alert Program, and Provides Significant New Investigative Tools. AMBER Alert programs are a proven tool to help recover abducted children.
>
> Establishing a national AMBER Alert Program. Building on the steps already taken by the Bush

Administration to support AMBER Alert programs, this bill allows for national coordination of state and local AMBER Alert programs, including the appointment of a national AMBER Alert Coordinator and the development of guidance for issuance and dissemination of AMBER Alerts, which includes:

- Enhanced tools to protect children:

- This bill allows law enforcement to use existing legal tools for the full range of serious sexual crimes against children. Under prior law, wiretaps are authorized for a range of crimes, but not for many of the various crimes associated with using the internet to lure children for purposes of sexual abuse and sex trafficking.

- This bill makes clear there is no statute of limitations for crimes involving the abduction or physical or sexual abuse of a child, in virtually all cases. Under previous law, the statute of limitations expired when the child turned 25, potentially allowing child rapists to go free if law enforcement could not solve the crime in time.

- Under current law, defendants who commit crimes against children are often released on bail. The bill makes it more difficult for defendants accused of serious crimes against children to obtain bail. This is similar to other existing provisions for some drug, firearms, and violent crimes.

Problem #2: Federal Law Did Not Ensure Adequate or Consistent Punishment for Those Who Committed Crimes Against Children.

Solution #2: The PROTECT Act Provides Appropriately Severe Penalties for Those Who Would Harm Children.

Increased penalties for non-family member child abduction: the minimum prison sentence is now 20 years.

Increased penalties for sexual exploitation of children and child pornography: a first offense of using a child to produce child pornography is now 15 to 30 years.

"Two Strikes" provision that requires life imprisonment for offenders who commit two serious sexual abuse offenses against a child.

Provisions to address the rates of "downward departures"—when judges sentence criminal defendants to less time in jail than the Sentencing Guidelines state.

For years, downward departures in child pornography possession cases have ranged between 25% and 29% nationwide.

One judge, for example, granted a 50% downward departure to a 5'11," 190-lb. child pornography defendant—who had accessed over 1,300 child pornography pictures and begun an Internet correspondence with a 15-year-old girl in another state—in part due to his concern that the defendant would be "unusually susceptible to abuse in prison." *United States v. Parish,* 308 F.3d 1025 (9th Cir. 2002) (rejecting Government's appeal and affirming the sentence).

The bill provides the judiciary with less authority to give reduced prison sentences, by eliminating much-abused grounds of departure such as diminished capacity, aberrant behavior, and family and community ties

In one recent child pornography case, a judge departed downward in part on the ground that the defendant had a "diminished capacity" due to the fact that he "was extremely addicted to child pornography." The bill ensures that pedophiles will not be able to get reduced sentences just because they are pedophiles.

- Prior to this Act, the length of post-release supervision of sex offenders was capped at five years, which is plainly inadequate in light of the high rate of recidivism for such offenders. The Act would allow a term of supervised release of any terms of years or for life.

Problem #3: Past Legal Obstacles Have Made Prosecuting Child Pornography Cases Very Difficult. Last year, the Supreme Court declared unconstitutional a federal law that criminalized the possession of "virtual" child pornography, i.e., materials whose production may not have involved the use of real children. This decision has made it immeasurably more difficult to eliminate the traffic in real child pornography.

Child pornography takes place largely over the Internet, so most of the child pornography cases that are brought involve computer files of images. Defendants now routinely seek to escape conviction by claiming that there is a "reasonable doubt" as to whether the computer image is that of a real child.

As computer imaging advances, this problem will worsen. Some experts already claim that it is impossible to tell whether a particular image was made using a real child. Future prosecutions will become battles of experts that will confuse juries and harm our ability to protect our nation's children.

Solution #3: Strengthen the Laws Against Child Pornography in Ways that Can Survive Constitutional Review. Among other provisions, the bill will:

- Revise and strengthen the prohibition on 'virtual' child pornography.
- Prohibit any obscene materials that depict children, and provided tougher penalties compared to existing obscenity law.
- Encourage greater voluntary reporting of suspected child pornography found by internet service providers on their systems.

In *United States v. Williams*, 553 U.S. 285 (2008), the U.S. Supreme Court upheld the Pandering Provision of the Protect Act. This statute makes it illegal to send material, or purported material, in a manner that "reflects the belief, or is intended to cause another to believe," that the material being sent contains illegal child pornography. 18 U.S.C. § 2252A(a)(3)(B). The *Williams* Court found offers to provide or obtain child pornography to be categorically excluded from the First Amendment.

In *Williams*, the defendant used a sexually explicit screen name and conversed with a Secret Service agent masquerading as the mother of a young child on a public chat room. Defendant offered to trade the agent sexually explicit images depicting his four-year-old daughter in a sexualized manner in exchange for similar photos. His chat room message said, "[d]ad of toddler has 'good' pics of her an [sic] me for swap of your toddler pics, or live cam."

The court described the further evidence that Williams was creating and distributing child pornography:

> Soon thereafter, Williams messaged that he had photographs of men molesting his 4-year-old daughter. Suspicious that 'Lisa n Miami' was a law-enforcement agent, before proceeding further Williams demanded that the agent produce additional pictures. When he did not, Williams posted the following public message in the chat room: 'HERE ROOM; I CAN PUT UPLINK CUZ IM FOR REAL—SHE CANT.' Appended to this declaration was a hyperlink that, when clicked, led to seven pictures of actual children, aged approximately 5 to 15, engaging in sexually explicit conduct and displaying their genitals. The Secret Service

then obtained a search warrant for Williams's home, where agents seized two hard drives containing at least 22 images of real children engaged in sexually explicit conduct, some of it sadomasochistic.

The prosecutors charged the defendant with one count of promoting, or "pandering," material intended to cause another to believe the material contained illegal child pornography and carries a sixty-month mandatory minimum sentence.

Williams challenged the constitutionality of the Protect Act's pandering provision. The Eleventh Circuit found the pandering provision of the Act to be both substantially overbroad and vague, and as a result found this provision to be facially unconstitutional.

In a 7–2 opinion, the U.S. Supreme Court reversed the Eleventh Circuit. Justice Scalia's majority opinion concluded that the federal anti-child pornography statute did not violate the First Amendment's right to free speech thereby upholding William's conviction.

(B) FIGHT ONLINE SEX TRAFFICKING ACT (FOSTA)

On April 11, 2018, President Donald J. Trump signed FOSTA, formally known as the "Allow States and Victims to Fight Online Sex Trafficking Act of 2017." In 2018, Congress amended Section 230 by passing FOSTA. Pub. L. No. 115–164, 132 Stat. 1253. Among other things, FOSTA provides that Section

230 immunity does not apply to certain sex trafficking claims.

> Pursuant to 47 U.S.C. § 230(e)(5)(A), "[n]othing in [Section 230] . . . shall be construed to impair or limit . . . any claim in a civil action brought under Section 1595 of title 18, if the conduct underlying the claim constitutes a violation of Section 1591 of that title."

In *Does 1–6,* the court described FOSTA as follows:

> In turn, this provision of FOSTA incorporates two sections of the Trafficking Victims Protection Reauthorization Act (TVPRA), 18 U.S.C. § 1589 et seq. First, Section 1595 of the TVPRA provides a civil cause of action for violations of the federal trafficking laws. 18 U.S.C. § 1595(a). It permits trafficking victims to sue the perpetrators of their trafficking as well as anyone who "knowingly benefits . . . from participation in a venture which that person knew or should have known" was engaged in sex trafficking.

Does 1–6 v. Reddit, Inc., 51 F.4th 1137, 1140–41 (9th Cir. 2022).

For a plaintiff to invoke Allow States and Victims to Fight Online Sex Trafficking Act (FOSTA) bypassing publisher immunity under Communications Decency Act (CDA) for civil actions brought under statute providing civil remedy for sex trafficking of children, she must plausibly allege that website's own conduct—not third party's—violated the federal criminal child sex trafficking statute.

Does 1–6 v. Reddit, Inc., 51 F.4th 1137, 1141 (9th Cir. 2022).

In *Does 1–6*, users of the social media platform Reddit posted and circulated sexually explicit images and videos of minors online.

In response, the victims, or their parents, sued Reddit pursuant to 18 U.S.C. § 1595. The district court dismissed the claim, holding that Section 230 of the Communications Decency Act (CDA), 47 U.S.C. § 230(c)(1), shielded Reddit from liability. The district court concluded that because Reddit was an "interactive computer services" provider, it generally enjoys immunity from liability for user-posted content under § 230(c)(1), or "Section 230 immunity."

Congress enacted the Allow States and Victims to Fight Online Sex Trafficking Act of 2018 (FOSTA) to make it clear that CDA Section 230 immunity does not apply to child sex trafficking claims—if the "conduct underlying the claim" also violates 18 U.S.C. § 1591, the criminal child sex trafficking statute. 47 U.S.C. § 230(e)(5)(A).

In *Does 1–6*, the issue was whether the availability of FOSTA's immunity exception is contingent upon a plaintiff proving that a defendant-website's own conduct—rather than its users' conduct—resulted in a violation of 18 U.S.C. § 1591.

The plaintiffs argued that:

> the presence of child pornography on Reddit is blatant, but Reddit has done little to remove the unlawful content or prevent it from being

posted, because it drives user traffic and revenue. As of April 2021, when this suit was filed, Reddit hosted many subreddits that openly and explicitly marketed themselves as fora for child pornography, with names like /r/Bestof YoungNSFW, /r/teensdirtie, /r/TeenBeauties, and /r/YoungGirlsGoneWild. Users publicly "trade" and solicit child pornography on these pages, and advocacy groups and the press have repeatedly reported this activity to Reddit.

The plaintiffs also contended that Reddit earned substantial revenue for hosting child pornography on its service:

> Plaintiffs allege that Reddit earns substantial advertising revenue from subreddits that feature child pornography because they generate controversy and attract viewers. Indeed, third-party advertising tools have listed several subreddits dedicated to child pornography as some of the most popular pages on the platform, which encourages advertisers to buy ad space on those pages. As such, the plaintiffs contend that Reddit financially benefits from openly hosting child pornography. The plaintiffs further contend that, because it enjoys the revenue generated by child pornography, Reddit has taken little action to block it from the platform.

The parents filed a class action against Reddit predicated upon the federal civil sex trafficking statute, 18 U.S.C. § 1595. They contended that:

"Reddit is liable as a beneficiary of child sex trafficking, among other causes of action."

Reddit filed a motion to dismiss for failure to state a claim, which the district court granted. The district court held that, to avoid Section 230 immunity under FOSTA, the plaintiffs were required to plead that Reddit's own conduct violated the criminal sex trafficking statute, 18 U.S.C. § 1591, and they failed to do so. Plaintiffs filed an appeal in the Ninth Circuit. The Ninth Circuit affirmed the lower court's dismissal on CDA Section 230 grounds reasoning:

> Taken as true, these allegations suggest only that Reddit "turned a blind eye" to the unlawful content posted on its platform, not that it actively participated in sex trafficking. Moreover, the plaintiffs have not alleged a connection between the child pornography posted on Reddit and the revenue Reddit generates, other than the fact that Reddit makes money from advertising on all popular subreddits. As such, the plaintiffs have failed to state a claim that Reddit violated 18 U.S.C. § 1591.

The court affirmed on the grounds that the plaintiffs failed to plead and prove that Reddit's own conduct violated the federal child pornography statute:

> For claims based on beneficiary liability, this requires that the defendant knowingly benefited from knowingly facilitating sex trafficking. Because the plaintiffs have not

plead that Reddit has done so in this case, we affirm.

§ 9-3. State Regulation of the Internet

(A) DORMANT COMMERCE CLAUSE

The Dormant Commerce Clause (Article I, Section 8) of the United States Constitution provides, "Congress shall have power . . . [t]o regulate commerce . . . among the several states[.]" U.S. Constitution, art. I, § 8, cl. 3. State laws intruding upon the federal government's exclusive authority to regulate interstate commerce are invalid under the Dormant Commerce Clause.

A state law may burden interstate commerce when it "has the practical effect of requiring out-of-state commerce to be conducted at the regulating state's direction." *Am. Booksellers Found. v. Dean*, 342 F.3d 96 (2d Cir. 2003). The Commerce Clause entrusts Congress with the authority "[t]o regulate Commerce with foreign Nations, and among the several States, and with the Indian Tribes." U.S. Constitution, art. I, § 8, cl. 3.

The U.S. Supreme Court "has long recognized that this affirmative grant of authority to Congress also encompasses an implicit or 'dormant' limitation on the authority of the States to enact legislation affecting interstate commerce." *Healy v. Beer Inst.*, 491 U.S. 324 (1989).

In a Dormant Commerce Clause analysis, the Court asks whether a challenged law discriminates against interstate commerce. A discriminatory law will survive only if it "advances a legitimate local purpose that cannot be adequately served by reasonable nondiscriminatory alternatives." *Or. Waste Sys. Inc. v. Dep't of Envtl. Quality*, 511 U.S. 93 (1994).

Absent *per se* discrimination a statute "will be upheld unless the burden imposed on [interstate] commerce is clearly excessive in relation to the putative local benefits." *Pike v. Bruce Church, Inc.*, 397 U.S. 137 (1970). In *American Libraries Ass'n v. Pataki*, 969 F. Supp. 160 (S.D.N.Y. 1997), the federal court struck down a content regulation on the grounds it violated the Dormant Commerce Clause. The statute invalidated amended N.Y. Penal Law § 235.21 through the addition of a new subdivision. The amendment criminalized simulating sex with minors:

> Knowing the character and content of the communication which, in whole or in part, depicts actual or simulated nudity, sexual conduct or sado-masochistic abuse, and which is harmful to minors, [to] intentionally use[ ] any computer communication system allowing the input, output, examination or transfer, of computer data or computer programs from one computer to another, to initiate or engage in such communication with a person who is a minor.

Pataki concluded the New York statute violated the Dormant Commerce Clause because, the nature of the Internet requires a "cohesive national scheme of regulation so that users are reasonably able to determine their obligations" regarding the kind of material that may be permissibly disseminated thereby.

Without national regulations, Internet users will be subject to inconsistent local statutes regulating the content of their communications, i.e., the various states may not have a uniform definition of "harmful to minors."

As the *Pataki* court observed, New York could realistically prosecute violations of New York Penal Law Section 235.22(2), which, like Section 288.2, subdivision (b), prohibits adults from luring minors into sexual contact via Internet communication of harmful material, without violating the commerce clause.

The *Pataki* court concluded that, in regard to the statute at issue, New York had "deliberately imposed its legislation on the Internet and, by doing so, projected its law into other states whose citizens use the Net."

(B) ANTI-SPAM REGULATIONS

The Controlling the Assault of Non-Solicited Pornography and Marketing Act of 2003 (CAN-SPAM Act), 15 U.S.C. §§ 7701 to 7713; 18 U.S.C. § 1037. The CAN-SPAM Act regulates commercial emails. It prohibits the use of false or misleading 'transmission information,' including deceptive subject headings and domain names, for any commercial email sent to

> a protected user, 15 U.S.C. § 7704(a)(1); and it requires the inclusion of 'a valid physical postal address of the sender,' § 7704(a)(5)(iii). The Act creates a cause of action for ISPs to enforce its provisions. *See* § 7706(g)(1). Statutory damages and attorney fees can be awarded to prevailing ISPs.

XMission, L.C. v. Fluent LLC, 955 F.3d 833, 837 (10th Cir. 2020).

The CAN-SPAM Act took effect on January 1, 2004. "In general, the CAN-SPAM Act, 15 U.S.C. § 7701 et seq., prohibits the transmission of commercial electronic mail messages to a protected computer which include header information or subject headings that are materially misleading." *Bullseye Restaurant, Inc. v. James River Insurance Company*, 387 F. Supp. 3d 273, 282 (E.D. N.Y. 2019).

In *United States v. Kilbride*, 584 F.3d 1240 (9th Cir. 2009), an e-mail spammer was indicted under an eight-count complaint including the CAN-SPAM Act, for distributing pornographic e-mail spam messages. The spammers were convicted of transmitting e-mails with materially false header information. The spammers used fictitious e-mail addresses and registered domain names using a false contact name and phone number.

The court also found Kilbride materially falsified information under meaning of Section 1037, because he had a third party alter headings. The federal appeals court affirmed the defendants' convictions and sentences for CAN-SPAM, fraud, and conspiracy to commit fraud in connection with electronic mail, both interstate transportation and interstate transportation for sale of obscene materials, and conspiracy to commit money laundering.

The Commerce Clause entrusts Congress with the authority "[t]o regulate Commerce with foreign Nations, and among the several States, and with the Indian Tribes." U.S. Constitution, art. I, § 8, cl. 3. States enact many content regulations challenged on the ground that they these regulations violate the Dormant Commerce Clause, which is a " 'dormant' limitation on the authority of the States to enact legislation affecting interstate commerce."

CAN-SPAM Act's express preemption clause preserves Congress's intended purpose—i.e., to regulate commercial e-mail "on a nationwide basis," 15 U.S.C. § 7701(b)(1). As of April 29, 2021, 121 federal court decisions have decided CAN-SPAM Act issues.

§ 9-4. First Amendment Limitations

The federal Constitution places limits on states' authority to regulate the content of Internet websites owned by parties located outside the states' borders. In *Yahoo! Inc. v. La Ligue Contre Le Racisme et L'Antisemitisme,* 169 F. Supp. 2d 1181 (N.D. Cal. 2001), Yahoo!, hosted auction sites, message boards, and chat rooms primarily for U.S. users. A Paris court ruled both messages about Nazis and the sale of Third-Reich memorabilia violated the French Criminal Code.

Even though Yahoo!'s French subsidiary removed Nazi-related material and images, French users could still access this material by using the American Yahoo! website. The French court issued an order, fining Yahoo! 100,000 Francs per day until they removed "all Nazi-related messages, images, and text stored on its server, particularly any Nazi relics, objects, insignia, emblems, and flags on its auction site[.]" *Yahoo! Inc. v. La Ligue Contre Le Racisme Et L'Antisemitisme*, 379 F.3d 1120, 1122 (9th Cir. 2004).

Yahoo! refused to honor the French court's order, filing a complaint in the Northern District of California requesting a declaration the French court's order was unenforceable since it was in conflict with the First Amendment of the U.S. Constitution. The court stated that:

> [t]he French court's determination that Yahoo! was in violation of French law may not be reviewed by any U.S. court. Yahoo!, however, contends that enforcement of the French court's judgment in the United States would violate Yahoo!'s First Amendment rights.

A federal court refused to enforce the French order instead requiring the American website to remove Nazi-related materials. The U.S. federal court ruled the judgment violated U.S. public policy that was protected by the First Amendment. The Ninth Circuit reversed the federal district court's declaratory judgment ruling the court had no personal jurisdiction over the French authorities.

In *Herrick v. Quigley*, 756 Fed. Appx. 726 (9th Cir. 2019), Herrick, a pre-adjudication civil detainee at the Washington State Special Commitment Center, filed a pro se action alleging policies denying him Internet access violated his First and Fourteenth Amendment rights. The district court granted summary judgment on all claims in favor of all defendants.

The Ninth Circuit affirmed, finding "the State has valid security interests in managing Internet and computer access for detainees in a total confinement facility of this nature, and the challenged policies are reasonably related to that interest." The court found Herrick's facial challenges to be unpersuasive stating:

> To the extent that Herrick asserts a facial challenge to the SCC's policies, we find his argument even less persuasive because the SCC clearly has valid therapeutic reasons for denying internet and computer access to detainees based on their treatment requirements. To prevail in a facial challenge based on the First Amendment, a plaintiff must either demonstrate that 'no set of circumstances exists under which [the regulation] would be valid,' or that 'a substantial number of its applications are unconstitutional, judged in relation to the statute's plainly legitimate sweep.'

United States v. Stevens, 559 U.S. 460 (2010).

(A) CONTENT-NEUTRAL REGULATIONS

To be content neutral, the government regulation of expressive activity must be justified without referencing the content of the regulated speech. In the case of the First Amendment:

> a content neutral regulation with an incidental effect on speech component must serve a substantial governmental interest, the interest must be unrelated to the suppression of free expression, and the incidental restriction on speech must not burden substantially more speech than is necessary to further that interest.

Geoffrey R. Stone, *Content Regulation and the First Amendment,* 25 WM. & MARY L. REV. 189 (1983).

A content neutral regulation need not employ the least restrictive means. However the proposed regulation must avoid burdening substantially more speech than is necessary to further the government's legitimate interests. Courts will uphold content neutral restrictions so long as the government narrowly tailors the regulation to serve a significant governmental interest.

Courts use the following factors to determination whether a regulation is narrowly tailored: (1) the time, (2) the place, or (3) the manner of protected speech. *City of Renton v. Playtime Theatre*, 475 U.S. 41 (1986).

(B) CONTENT SPECIFIC REGULATIONS

Regulation of speech or expression based on the substance of the message is content specific regulation as opposed to the manner or method in which the message being expressed, which is content-neutral. Content-based laws are presumptively unconstitutional and subject to strict scrutiny, the highest form of judicial review, as opposed to content-neutral laws where the standard is intermediate scrutiny.

In *Ex Parte Dennis Lee Odom*, 570 S.W.3d 900 (Tex. App. 2018), the court upheld a content-specific regulation requiring convicted sex offenders to report online identifiers:

> Dennis Lee Odom, a convicted sex offender charged with failing to report online identifiers, appeals the denial of his pretrial application for writ of habeas corpus challenging Article 62.0551(a)'s reporting requirements as a facially unconstitutional violation of the First Amendment right to freedom of speech.

Odom argued that "Article 62.0551 is unconstitutional on its face because '[i]t results in an impermissible prior restraint on speech and is overbroad when considering the State's interest in preventing crime.' " The court ruled that the registration program statute requiring registered sex offenders to disclose online identifiers implicated the First Amendment right to anonymous Internet speech but found it to be content neutral regulation of speech thus subject to intermediate scrutiny.

The court found the Texas sex offender-reporting requirement to be narrowly tailored in meeting a substantial and compelling state interest, as required to survive intermediate scrutiny review under the First Amendment, thereby affirming the lower court.

The court applied a three-part test. First, do the Internet reporting requirements implicate First Amendment rights? If First Amendment rights are implicated, what level of scrutiny should be applied? And third, do the challenged provisions pass muster under the proper level of scrutiny?

To survive intermediate scrutiny, a content-neutral regulation of protected speech must (1) serve or advance a substantial governmental interest unrelated to the suppression of free speech and (2) be narrowly tailored to serve that interest without unnecessarily interfering with free speech. The court upheld the statute as a legitimate way to regulate the use of the Internet by sex offenders "because it is a powerful tool that can be used to commit sex crimes."

The Texas Appeals Court held the Sex Offender Registration Statute did not burden substantially more speech than is necessary in furthering the State's legitimate interests. "Accordingly, Odom fails to establish that the statute is facially unconstitutional as substantially overbroad in violation of the First Amendment."

(C) FACIAL CHALLENGES

With a facial challenge, the plaintiff contends that a statute is unconstitutional at all times and under all circumstances. Facial challenges are disfavored for several reasons. Claims of facial invalidity often rest on speculation. Consequently, they raise the risk of premature interpretation of statutes.

Facial challenges also run contrary to the fundamental principle of judicial restraint that courts should neither " 'anticipate a question of constitutional law in advance of the necessity of deciding it' " nor " 'formulate a rule of constitutional law broader than is required by the precise facts to which it is to be applied.' " *Ashwander v. TVA*, 297 U.S. 288 (1936) (Brandeis, J., concurring).

> Finally, facial challenges threaten to short circuit the democratic process by preventing laws embodying the will of the people from being implemented in a manner consistent with the Constitution. . . . The overbreadth doctrine, under which a statute is facially invalid if it prohibits a substantial amount of protected speech, is strong medicine that should be employed with hesitation, and then only as a last resort; accordingly, courts vigorously enforce the requirement that a statute's overbreadth be substantial, not only in an absolute sense, but also relative to the statute's plainly legitimate sweep.

Center for Individual Freedom v. Madigan, 697 F.3d 464 (7th Cir. 2012).

In *Madigan*, a nonprofit organization made a facial challenge to invalidate Illinois campaign finance disclosure requirements on the grounds were facially vague and overbroad restrictions of speech, thereby violating both the First and Fourteenth Amendments.

The Illinois disclosure requirements (1) cover election activity relating to ballot initiatives, which have no federal analog; (2) do not exempt from regulation those groups that lack the "major purpose" of influencing electoral campaigns; and (3) cover campaign-related advertisements that appear on the Internet.

The court held Illinois's regulation of expenditures for contributions to and electioneering communications concerning ballot initiative campaigns are not facially overbroad or vague. The court rejected the facial challenge, ruling the statute will not "restrict or chill a substantial amount of protected speech because it treats certain Internet speech as electioneering communications." The court found that "this element of the statute is neither vague nor overbroad."

(D) VAGUENESS

A federal or state statute or regulation is "void for vagueness" when it is so ambiguous; a person cannot know with certainty what acts are proscribed. Plaintiffs may challenge content-based restrictions of speech on vagueness grounds. The vagueness doctrine is an outgrowth of the Due Process Clause of the Fifth Amendment.

In *Reno v. American Civil Liberties Union*, 521 U.S. 844 (1997), the Court struck down a part of the Communications Decency Act (CDA) on the grounds of vagueness and over breadth. The Court reasoned the CDA's use of the undefined terms "indecent" and "patently offensive" would have a chilling effect on speakers and therefore, raised special First Amendment concerns. The CDA's vagueness undermined the likelihood it had been carefully tailored to the congressional goal of protecting minors from potentially harmful materials.

(E) OVERBREADTH

The First Amendment's "overbreadth doctrine" is a tool for striking down Internet-related content regulations deemed facially invalid if the content prohibits a substantial amount of protected speech:

> The Supreme Court has recognized a particular type of facial challenge in the First Amendment context under which a law may be struck down entirely as impermissibly overbroad. Under this overbreadth doctrine, 'a statute is facially invalid if it prohibits a substantial amount of protected speech.'

Center for Individual Freedom, 697 F.3d at 476 (citing *United States v. Williams*, 553 U.S. 285 (2008)).

The scope of this content-based speech imposes a heavy burden on the Government to explain why a less restrictive provision would fail. *Reno v. ACLU*, 521 U.S. 844 (1997). The Communication Decency

Act's expansive coverage of unprecedented content and as a result of this finding, acknowledged the breadth of the content-based restriction, therefore, placing a heavy burden on the government to explain why they could not enact a less restrictive provision.

(F) UNPROTECTED SPEECH

The Virginia Supreme Court struck down a spammer's criminal conviction on First Amendment overbreadth grounds. In *Jaynes v. Commonwealth of Virginia*, 666 S.E.2d 303 (Va. 2008), the court upheld the conviction of a defendant who violated Virginia's Computer Crime Act by sending over 10,000 commercial e-mails within a 24-hour period to subscribers of America Online, Inc. (AOL) on three separate occasions. The spammer used routing and transmission information thereby bypassing AOL's security controls, and as a result, trespassed on AOL's proprietary network.

Jaynes intentionally falsified both the header information and sender domain names before sending the e-mails to the recipients. The *Jaynes* court found Virginia's statute criminalizing the falsification of IP addresses as overly broad and unacceptably burdensome to the right to engage in anonymous speech.

The court also found the Virginia statute to be prohibiting communications containing political, religious, or other speech. The court applied the strict scrutiny standard, requiring the state computer crime statute to be narrowly tailored.

In *State v. Williams*, 2018 WL 3569309 (Ariz. Ct. of App. July 24, 2018), Williams was charged with aggravated harassment of young woman, KS who he "first met in October 2014 at a charity event." Williams, an aspiring photographer, attended to take pictures alongside a photographer K.S.'s modeling group had invited to the event.

At one point, another model's breasts became accidentally exposed and Williams captured the mishap in his photographs. The pattern of harassment began when K.S. requested that William turn over the photos to her and asked him not to photograph her in the future.

Williams followed K.S. on social media, announced his presence on social media when he was in her vicinity, and ignored her requests not to photograph her. Williams also frequently "tagged" K.S.'s personal Facebook page or public pages associated with or operated by her. K.S. attempted to block Williams's access to the pages and profiles she controlled, however, he "got around the block" and continued tagging her.

> Additionally, within an hour of K.S.'s vehicle being vandalized with pink paint, Williams tagged her in a post saying, '[her] color was going to be orange and his was going to be pink.' K.S. testified she was upset by this post, as it demonstrated '[Williams] had found [her] home.'
>
> In August 2015, K.S. applied for a protective order against Williams in the Pima County Consolidated Justice Court. Following a hearing

> in which Williams and one witness testified on his behalf, Williams was enjoined from coming within 1,000 feet of K.S. and was ordered to have 'no contact' with her. Only four days after the injunction was served, Williams posted to a local radio station's Facebook page that K.S., a recurring radio personality on the station, was a 'fraud' and a 'real porno actress,' tagging one of K.S.'s pages in the process. That same day, Williams tagged K.S. in at least two more posts on his own Facebook page, accusing her and the judge who had granted the injunction of ethical violations and stating, 'I can't wait to see you in orange and your judge will be your cell mate. I guarant[ee].' The following morning, he replied to comments on his post to the radio station's page, again tagging K.S.'s pages.
>
> Williams was charged with aggravated harassment for the posts on August 25, 2015, and the morning of August 26, 2015. He was convicted and sentenced.

Williams asserts he 'had a constitutionally protected right to use social media as long as he did not contact [K.S.] or engage in unprotected speech.' The court upheld the jury verdict against Williams finding his First Amendment defense of his right to post on social media to be without merit.

In *State v. Muccio*, 881 N.W.2d 149 (Minn. Ct. of App. 2016), a father reported to law enforcement that he had found inappropriate images on his 15-year-old child's iPad. The photographs depicted a close-up of a female's genitals, a close-up of a female's buttocks covered by a thong, and a female naked from the waist to the neck. Muccio sent the images on her Instagram account via direct message.

A search warrant revealed Muccio and the child had sexually explicit conversations and had exchanged sexually explicit photographs. The State of Minnesota charged Muccio with one count of felony communication with a minor on the grounds of sexual conduct. A lower court concluded the statute was facially overbroad and unconstitutional under the First Amendment and dismissed count one.

The Minnesota Appeals Court affirmed, finding that the statute was overly broad and did not just proscribe unprotected speech.

§ 9-5. Adult Entertainment & Pornography

To determine whether an Internet-related work is subject to regulation as obscenity, many federal courts apply the standard of *Miller v. California*, 413 U.S. 15 (1973).

The *Miller* test has three prongs: (1) whether the average person, applying contemporary community standards would find that the work, taken as a whole, appeals to the prurient interest; (2) whether the work depicts or describes, in a patently offensive way, sexual conduct specifically defined; and (3) whether the work, taken as a whole, lacks serious literary, artistic, political, or scientific value.

Federal criminal statutes also address Internet pornography. Section 2252A(a)(2) prohibits any person from knowingly receiving or distributing child pornography that has traveled in interstate or foreign commerce. The statute requires proof the defendants knowingly possessed and distributed photographs of minors. The statute requires publishers of pornographic material to verify the age of models. Section 2257 applies equally well to cyberspace.

In *Breitfeller v. Playboy*, 2007 WL 294233 (M.D. Fla. Jan. 29, 2007), some 17-year-old girls filed suit against several defendants for distributing a video of them that was taken when the girls were participating in a wet t-shirt contest. The court ruled Playboy knew or should have known that there was a risk the images contained minors, and that its decision to remain ignorant as to the plaintiffs' ages therefore satisfied the statute's *knowingly* requirement.

Underage minors have been charged with violating 18 U.S.C. § 2252A, by taking sexually explicit photos of themselves and sending them to friends. In *Clark v. Roccanova*, 772 F. Supp. 2d 844 (E.D. Ky. 2011), the court ruled sexting by a 14 year old girl to other minors could constitute a violation of 18 U.S.C. § 2252A. Criminal prosecutions of online pornography often turn on whether a community standard has been violated. Courts differ as to whether there should be a national or a local community standard in Internet-related obscenity cases.

§ 9-6. Cross-Border Content Regulation

The global Internet's legal environment makes it inevitable there will be conflict as one country's content regulation will clash with another country's content regulations. Deplorable Internet-content protected as free expression in the U.S. is criminalized in the Middle East and many other countries.

(A) EUROPEAN UNION (EU) CONTENT REGULATION

The EU's Juncker Commission took several actions to protect Europeans online—be it from terrorist content, illegal hate speech, or fake news. The Commission works with major Internet companies such as Google and Facebook as well as EU Member States and EU Agencies to improve the battle fight against illegal content online. European Commission, *A Europe That Protects: Countering Illegal Content Online* (2020).

(1) Terrorist Content

Europol's EU Internet Referral Unit seeks to identify and root out terrorist's abuse of online platforms. "The Unit scans the web, identifies and flags terrorist content to the hosting companies, and provides operational support and analysis to EU Member States."

The IRU has made 40,000 content referrals to 80 platforms in more than 10 languages since 2015. They have assembled a database of over 50,000 hashes of known terrorist images and videos. Automatic "detection tools are deployed on some platforms remove 83% to 98% of identified terrorist content."

(2) Online Racist & Xenophobic Hate Speech

Under the EU's Code of Conduct on Countering Illegal Hate Speech Online, Internet companies "remove on average 70% of illegal hate speech notified to them and in more than 80% of these cases, the removals took place within 24 hours." The EU's Framework Decision on Combatting Racism and Xenophobia by means of criminal law requires Member States to criminalize:

> The public incitement to violence or hatred directed against a group of persons or a member of such a group defined by reference to race, colour, religion, descent or national or ethnic origin. This is the legal basis for defining illegal online content.

(3) Content Constituting Child Sexual Abuse

Europeans will also be better protected from harmful content, including pornography and violence, under the EU's Audiovisual Media Services Directive. "Age verification and parental control mechanism will more effectively deny children access to this content."

(B) EUROPEAN MEMBER STATES INITIATIVES

The twenty-seven countries of the European Union enjoy free expression as the European Commission states:

> Everyone has the right to freedom of expression. This right shall include freedom to hold opinions and to receive and impart information and ideas without interference by public authority and regardless of frontiers. . . . This right is enshrined in article 11 of the Charter of Fundamental Rights.

European Commission, *Freedom of Expression and Information* (2021).

"Censorship creep" is undermining free speech norms on the Internet:

> In the wake of terrorist attacks in late 2015, European Union (EU) regulators warned tech companies that they would face prohibitively expensive fines and potential criminal penalties unless extremist and hateful content was swiftly removed. . . . Already, European lawmakers have pressed companies to ban 'fake news' to help combat extremist expression.

Danielle Keats Citron, *What to Do About the Emerging Threat of Censorship Creep on the Internet*, CATO INSTITUTE (Nov. 28, 2017).

"Many other countries operate on a completely different level when it comes to protecting rights that, in America, we consider to be the most basic."

ALLI KOLLICK ET AL., COUNTRIES WITHOUT FIRST AMENDMENT RIGHTS (Ames Iowa: Iowa State University, 2012). South Korea's National Security Law, for example, "makes it illegal to share sympathies or beliefs with North Korea, however much more of the censorship is focused towards the media."

While China formally has a constitutional provision guaranteeing free expression, censorship is widespread. "Chinese citizen's freedom of press and religion are treated similarly as the government tries to censor the Chinese people from the different ways of life in the world." Many other countries have no tradition of free expression. Ellen Cranley, *The 57 Nations in the World That Aren't 'Free,'* BUSINESS INSIDER (June 11, 2019).

How should the line be drawn between free expression and offensive deplorable content?

> In the wake of the advent of social media, the debate has gotten even louder. People saying what they want gives the bosses of Facebook, Twitter and other social media sites a big headache. But saying what you like is more accepted in the United States than anywhere else, according to recent research. The Pew Research Center polled 38 countries around the world in 2015 and found that Americans are more tolerant of free speech than other nationalities. They are also the most supportive of freedom of the press and the right to use the internet without government censorship.

Alex Gray, *Freedom of Speech: Which Country Has the Most?*, WORLD ECONOMIC FORUM (Nov. 8, 2016).

Perhaps, the most challenging issue is how to handle content regulation in a cross-border legal environment where there are very different views of the value of free expression. Many of the most important content creators such as Google are not subject to the First Amendment. Google creates, transmits, and distributes content in hundreds of countries.

Despite the dominance of civil codes derived from Roman law, in all the continental European countries there are many national differences. Sweden and Norway have a well-established ombudsman tradition for resolving consumer complaints considered a stark contrast to the U.S. tradition of a strong civil justice system.

"Sweden's consumer ombudsman, responsible for enforcing the country's ban, said he would welcome a Europe-wide ban in order to thwart children's advertising being beamed into the country via satellite." John Tylee, *Sweden Declares Plans to Extend Kid's Ad Ban Campaign* (Nov. 26, 1999).

Such a ban would conflict with the U.S. First Amendment. Christine Wade, *Consumer Enforcers Clean Up Web in Worldwide Sweeps*, OFFICE OF FAIR TRADING, HERMES DATABASE (Oct. 8, 2004) (discussing role of Norwegian ombudsman in resolving consumer complaints).

Perhaps the biggest difference between U.S. and European law is their approaches to intermediary liability. Chapter 6 explained the U.S. approach that Internet intermediaries have no liability for content supplied by third parties. CDA Section 230 gives all platforms a safe harbor for liability for any content posted on Internet sites. In contrast, EU countries make intermediaries liable for illegal content if it is not disabled or taken down:

> In recent years, national legislators in EU Member States have been pushing for new laws to combat negative societal phenomena such as hateful or terrorist content online. These regulatory efforts have one common denominator: they shift the focus from conditional intermediary liability to holding intermediaries directly responsible for the dissemination of illegal content on their platforms.

Eliska Pirkova, *EU Content Regulation: What's the (Online) Harm?*, ACCESSNOW.ORG (Oct. 10, 2019).

(C) NON-EU COUNTRIES

A large number of countries connected to the Internet do not traditionally follow the right of expression. A traditional Islamic jurist would likely find an unveiled female face on a social media site to be shameful however; blasphemy laws are not strictly limited to Islamic republics. The Republic of Ireland outlawed cyberspace incitement including "blasphemous Internet statements in defiance of the law." DAVID NASH, BLASPHEMY IN THE CHRISTIAN WORLD (2012).

(D) CHINA'S AUTHORITARIAN STATE

On August 7, 2014, China's state Internet Information Office issued regulation on instant messaging apps. This regulation requires real name registration similar to the "Microblogging Rules." To date, it is unclear when the real name registration will be fully implemented by social media providers. Enacted in 2011, the Beijing Municipal Law on microblogging specifically addresses the conduct on social media violates national security.

(E) AFRICAN CENSORSHIP

In Africa, which is known for having the lowest Internet connection of any continent, the Internet Governance Forum identified a troubling trend:

> An emerging trend in most African countries is the formulation of policies and regulations that sharply target online platforms with aim of curtailing the freedom of expression and infringe on the right to privacy. An introduction of arbitrary laws and policies that may affect not only democracy within states but also affect the running of business within these countries. Authorities are over stepping their regulatory mandate with aim of playing the role of communication regulator in the respective countries. The trend is spreading fast like a bush fire.

Internet Forum Governance, *IGF 2018 WS #331* (2018).

CHAPTER 10
COPYRIGHTS IN CYBERSPACE

Copyright protects original works of authorship, while a patent protects inventions or discoveries. Ideas and discoveries are not protected by the copyright law, although the way in which they are expressed may be.

Copyright protects creative works (books, drawings, videos, and other forms of communication). Copyright protection occurs automatically upon fixation in a tangible medium. The World Wide Web continues to enable copyright infringement on a scale unfathomable in the 1980s and 1990s.

This chapter on global copyright law is divided into six sections. Section 10-1 presents and overview including a brief history of copyright law, while Section 10-2 covers basic concepts and methods for obtaining copyright protection. This section covers fair use and First Amendment limitations as well as database protection.

Section 10-3 examines the types of copyright infringement: direct and secondary infringement. Section 10-4 covers the online copyright issue of peer-to-peer sharing.

Section 10-5 is a study of the Digital Millennium Copyright Act (DMCA) of 1998, which updated copyright law for the Internet. For the first time, Congress addressed provider liability. The DMCA allows creators to issue "takedown notices" for infringing content, provides "safe harbor" to platforms that remove such content, and prohibits bypassing digital locks (Section 1201).

Finally, Section 10-6 addresses international copyright issues such as the extraterritorial impact of copyright law, and moral rights. Moral rights (droit moral) in European copyright law protect the personal, non-economic connection between creators and their works, ensuring the right of attribution and integrity. Moral Rights in U.S. Copyright Law are limited to certain works of visual art.

§ 10-1. The Path of Copyright Law

(A) A SHORT HISTORY OF COPYRIGHT LAW

The path of the law of copyright law begins in 1710 with the Statute of Anne. Following the American Revolution, most of the states enacted copyright laws patterned after this English act.

The U.S. Constitution provides that Congress shall have the power "[t]o promote the progress of science and useful arts, by securing for limited times to authors . . . the exclusive right to their . . . writings[.]" U.S. Const., art. I, § 8, cl. 8. The Copyright Statute of 1790 protected works of authorship including "maps, charts, and books." Authors had the right to "print, publish, and vend" their works.

The U.S. Copyright Office's history of copyright law states:

> The first federal copyright statute was enacted in 1790 and covered maps, charts, and books.

> This statute granted to authors and proprietors a term of 14 years with the privilege of renewal for a second term of 14 years. There were general revisions of the copyright law in 1831, 1870 and 1909. The law under which we have been operating for the past 68 years is the Act of March 4, 1909. This act is based on the printing press as the prime disseminator of information. Significant changes in technology have resulted in a wide range of new communications techniques that were unknown in 1909—for example, radio, television, communications satellites, cable television, computers, photocopying machines, videotape recorders, etc., and there are promises of even greater changes in the future. This growth in technology made revision of the Act of 1909 imperative.

U.S. Copyright Office, *A Brief History of Copyright in the United States* at Chapter 1, 1:1.

The Copyright Act of 1976 constitutes the basis of copyright law in the United States today. "It took effect on January 1, 1978, implementing fundamental and sweeping changes in many aspects of copyright law. Copyright protection extends to all 'original works of authorship' to consider new kinds of media." *Copyright Act of 1976*, THE FIRST AMENDMENT ENCYCLOPEDIA (2020).

The Copyright Term Extension Act (CTEA) provisions extending copyright terms for both existing and future copyrighted works by 20 years was rational exercise of legislative authority conferred by Copyright Clause; change brought

United States law into line with international norms, and there was evidence that extension would encourage copyright holders to invest in restoration and public distribution of their works. U.S. Const. Art. 1, § 8, cl. 8; 17 U.S.C. § 302(a). *Eldred v. Ashcroft*, 537 U.S. 186 (1986).

Congress's power to "protect the 'Writings' of 'Authors' " is "broad," such that "writings" is not "limited to script or printed material," but rather encompasses "any physical rendering of the fruits of creative intellectual or aesthetic labor." *Burrow-Giles Lithographic Co. v. Sarony*, 111 U.S. 53, 58 (1884)

Under the U.S. Copyright Act of 1976, copyright protection attaches "immediately" upon the creation of "original works of authorship fixed in any tangible medium of expression," provided those works meet certain requirements.

The Copyright Act of 1976 provides copyright protection to "original works of authorship fixed in any tangible medium of expression, now known or later developed, from which they can be perceived, reproduced, or otherwise communicated, either directly or with the aid of a machine or device." 17 U.S.C. § 102(a).

The "fixing" of the work in the tangible medium must be done is "by or under the authority of the author." *Thaler v. Perlmutter*, 687 F. Supp. 3d 140, 146–47 (D.D.C. 2023).

A copyright claimant can also register the work with the Register of Copyrights. Upon concluding that the work is indeed copyrightable, the Register will issue a certificate of registration, which, among other advantages, allows the claimant to pursue infringement claims in court. 17 U.S.C. §§ 410(a), 411(a).

§ 10-2. Obtaining Copyright Law Protection

Copyright is the branch of intellectual property law that protects the owner of rights in artistic works against those who 'copy' works without permission. Copyright is a form of protection provided by many legal systems to the authors of "original works of authorship," including literary, dramatic, musical, artistic, and other creations of the mind. It is well settled that copyright protection is available to works stored on computer servers.

Courts have interpreted the Copyright Act to protect software, websites, and other Internet-related intellectual property. *Perfect 10, Inc. v. Amazon.com, Inc.*, 508 F.3d 1146, 1160 (9th Cir. 2007) (discussing copyright protections available to works "embodied (i.e., stored) in a computer's server . . . or hard disk, or other storage device . . ."). Copyright covers:

- HTML
- Deposits and trade secrets
- Derivative computer programs
- CD-ROMs
- Computer screen displays
- User manuals

- Video games
- Object code

The U.S. Copyright Office treats each version of a new software program containing new, copyrightable authorship to be a separate work, requiring a separate application, filing fee and deposit for each version of the program:

> Submit the source code for the specific version of the computer program you want to register. Source code is the set of statements and instructions authored using a programming language (e.g., C++, PERL, and Java). Source code is comprehensible to a person familiar with programming language but requires conversion into object code before it is comprehensible to a computer or other electronic device.

U.S. Copyright Office, *Copyright Registration of Computer Programs*, CIRCULAR 61.

Copyright law is malleable to cover new information technologies. Nevertheless, the court in *Thaler v. Perlmutter*, 687 F. Supp. 3d 140, 146–47 (D.D.C. 2023) must unwilling to stretch copyright law to works created by artificial intelligence. The court reasoned that human authors create copyright:

> Copyright has never stretched so far, however, as to protect works generated by new forms of technology operating absent any guiding human hand, as plaintiff urges here. Human authorship is a bedrock requirement of copyright. Undoubtedly, we are approaching new frontiers

in copyright as artists put AI in their toolbox to be used in the generation of new visual and other artistic works. The increased attenuation of human creativity from the actual generation of the final work will prompt challenging questions regarding how much human input is necessary to qualify the user of an AI system as an "author" of a generated work, the scope of the protection obtained over the resultant image, how to assess the originality of AI-generated works where the systems may have been trained on unknown pre-existing works, how copyright might best be used to incentivize creative works involving AI, and more.

The court answered this complex question in the negative concluding that completely AI-generated works were not works of authors, since there was no human author. Protection arises automatically during creation of a work of authorship—even if the author does not include a copyright notice or fails to register the work with the U.S. Copyright Office.

An Internet website is protectable by copyright as soon as it is posted as is all postings including those by third parties. Nevertheless, it is advisable to include a copyright notice—i.e., the letter c in a circle: ©, or the word "Copyright" and the first year of a publication of a work (e.g., Copyright 2026, Michael L. Rustad)—because registration and notice confer benefits to the copyright owner.

Electronic copyright registration is inexpensive (costing between $45 and $65) and includes three essential elements: (1) a completed application form,

(2) a nonrefundable filing fee, and (3) a nonreturnable deposit. Section 407 of the Copyright Act requires the copyright applicant to provide two copies of published works and one copy of unpublished works. 17 U.S.C. § 407.

Copyright arises automatically during creation of a work of authorship—even if the author does not include a copyright notice or fails to register the work with the U.S. Copyright Office.

The deposit requirement is that the applicant sends a copy or copies of the work being registered that is "deposited" with the U.S. Copyright Office. For computer programs, there are special rules to comply with the registration requirement. 37 C.F.R. § 202.20. A Certificate of Registration constitutes *prima facie* evidence of the validity of a copyright, but only if it was obtained within five years of the first publication of the work.

A copyright registration certificate is evidence of the validity of the copyright so the holder of the registration certificate need not put on evidence of ownership or originality in the copyrighted work.

A copyright owner's exclusive rights or any subdivision of those rights may be transferred, but the transfer of exclusive rights is not valid unless that transfer is in writing and signed by the owner of the rights conveyed or such owner's duly authorized agent.

Copyright applicants can search on-line for registrations filed since January 1, 1978, using the search engines of the U.S. Copyright website.

Copyrights can be registered online through the electronic Copyright Office (eCO), which:

> is the preferred way to register basic claims for literary works; visual arts works; performing arts works, including motion pictures; sound recordings; and single serial issues. Electronic registration is also required for group registration of serials. Benefits of electronic registration include faster processing times, status tracking, online payment, and the option to upload certain categories of works or to send a physical copy of a work. The standard filing fee for electronic registration is $65 for basic claims. However, the filing fee [for online registrations] is $45 if you register one work by a single author who is also the claimant and the work is not made for hire.

U.S. Copyright Office, *Copyright Office Fees*, COPYRIGHT.GOV (Mar. 3, 2020).

If there is a proper copyright notice affixed to a work, a defendant in a copyright infringement suit cannot use an "innocent infringer" defense to mitigate actual or statutory damages. 17 U.S.C. § 401(d). Registration serves as notice to the public that material is protected by copyright and shows the year of first publication.

A copyright lasts for the life of the author plus 70 years, or 95 years from first publication in the case of anonymous works, pseudonymous works, works made for hire (or 120 years from the year of creation, whichever occurs first). For works created after January 1, 1978, the copyright term is:

- One author—life of the author plus 70 years.
- Joint works—life of last surviving author plus 70 years.
- Anonymous & works made for hire—95 years from publication, or
- 120 years from creation whichever is first.

Because of the U.S. entering the Berne Convention in 1988, an author's copyright protection is automatic, beginning as soon as a work is created. For works first published on or after March 1, 1989, use of the copyright notice is optional.

Before 1978, statutory copyright was secured by the act of publishing a work with a notice of copyright physically on the work. If a work remained unpublished, statutory copyright could only be secured by the act of registration.

If a work was published without a copyright notice, the work may enter the public domain and as a result does not have copyright protection. Any work that was in the public domain on or before January 1, 1978, remains in the public domain. Notice of copyright is required on all works published prior to 1989.

Registration of a copyright is not required for its validity, but U.S. authors needs this to institute an infringement suit. Deposit of copies of the work is required to obtain registration of copyright. Registration of copyright requires:

(1) A properly completed application form.

(2) A nonrefundable filing fee of $45 for a single author, one work (effective through March 20, 2020) for each application.

(3) A nonreturnable deposit of the work being registered.

Whether on a website, social media, or any other Internet-related medium, copyright protection applies only if a work satisfies two criteria: originality and fixation.

An author receives copyright protection the moment it is created and fixed in a tangible form perceptible either directly or with the aid of a machine or device. The U.S. Copyright Act grants copyright holders a bundle of exclusive rights, including the rights to "reproduce . . . in copies," "prepare derivative works," "distribute copies," "perform," and "display" their works. 17 U.S.C. § 106.

(A) ORIGINALITY

Copyright requires two elements, originality, and fixation. Originality means independent creation and a minimal spark of creativity. A work of authorship is original even if it contains nonoriginal content.

Originality is satisfied if something non-trivial is added to extant works. A device such as a camera may be used to create a work of authorship, which was settled in an 1884 U.S. Supreme case where the author sought protection in a photography of Oscar Wilde.

The question before the Court was whether the photograph of Wilde was copyrightable subject matter. The defendant argued, among other things, that the work was not copyrightable because it was a mere mechanical process and was therefore not creative.

The Court disagreed finding that the plaintiff's own original mental conception was protectable. The Court noted that the photographer gave visible form by posing the said Oscar Wilde in front of the camera, selecting, and arranging the costume, draperies, and other various accessories. After this case, courts have extended copyright protection to other technologies including software. *Burrow-Giles Lithographic Co. v. Sarony*, 111 U.S. 53 (1884).

Mere copying such as reproducing software or a toy does not satisfy originality. Copyright protects only author's original creative expression and others are free to copy nonoriginal elements.

In 2014, the United States Copyright Office published an opinion to clarify that "only works created by a human can be copyrighted under United States law, which excludes photographs and artwork created by animals or by machines without human intervention. The U.S. Copyright Office will not register works produced by nature, animals, or plants." U.S. Copyright Office, *Copyrightable Authorship: What Can Be Registered* at § 313.2 (Jan. 28, 2021). The Ninth Circuit denied authorship to a monkey's selfie. *Naruto v. Slater*, 888 F.3d 418 (9th Cir. 2018).

(B) FIXATION

An author must fix a work of authorship in a tangible medium of expression to satisfy the fixation requirement. A work is "fixed" in a tangible medium of expression when it is "sufficiently permanent or stable to permit it to be perceived, reproduced, or otherwise communicated for a period of more than transitory duration." 17 U.S.C. § 101.

The rise of Internet-related copyright infringement lawsuits threatens the continued "expansion and upgrading of the Internet." 144 Cong. Rec. 24465–66 (1998). In the context of cyberspace, the acts of transmitting an e-mail or viewing a web page—both of which store copies in the user's computer RAM—qualify as copies for purposes of the Copyright Act.

However, it remains unclear whether something in dynamic RAM is fixed for establishing a copyright. However, the Ninth Circuit, in *MAI Systems Corp. v. Peak Computer*, 991 F.2d 511 (9th Cir. 2003), held that simply loading a computer operating system into RAM, which is accomplished by turning the computer on, created a fixed copy for purposes of the Copyright Act.

(C) WHAT IS NOT PROTECTABLE

Works that have not been fixed in a tangible form of expression or lack a modicum of originality are not protectable. Protection does not extend to any part of a work that uses infringing material. Titles, names, familiar symbols, designs, variations of lettering, and a list of ingredients or contents are not protectable either. Idea, procedures, concepts, or principles are outside copyright law's sphere of application along with works consisting entirely of public domain material.

(1) Idea/Expression

Copyright protects expression, not ideas. In *Baker v. Selden*, 101 U.S. 99 (1880), the U.S. Supreme Court first conceptualized the "idea/expression" dichotomy. Selden copyrighted a book in which he described a method of bookkeeping and sued Baker when Baker published a book on bookkeeping with functionally equivalent methods, but with different columns and headings.

The Court ruled Selden could not copyright his method of accounting because it was an idea however could copyright the forms used to implement his system of bookkeeping, which was expression. In practice, it is difficult to separate functionality from expression. Courts hold mannequins and Halloween costumes are entitled to copyright protection, even though the aesthetic aspects of those works are inseparable from their functionality.

(2) Governmental Works

Works of the U.S. government, or its employees acting within the scope of their professional duties, are not protectable by copyright. Copyright may not be secured in works prepared by federal employee in official duties.

(3) Functionality or Utility

The functionality or utility of any work of authorship is not protectable. Thus, a website, protocol, or programming language's utility does not qualify for copyright protection but patent law may cover this work. Copyright protection can only be secured if the functional aspects are separable from the aesthetic aspects.

(4) Public Domain Information

Copyright law does not encompass information in the public domain. A code writing organization could not enjoin a website operator from posting the text of a city's model building code because the code was in the public domain and not protected by copyright, notwithstanding software licensing agreement and a copyright notice prohibiting copying and distribution.

Under Section 106, authors receive a bundle of rights including the right: (1) to reproduce the copyrighted work in copies or phonorecords, (2) to prepare derivative works based upon the copyrighted work, (3) to distribute copies or phonorecords of the copyrighted work to the public by sale or other transfer or ownership, or by rental, lease, or lending, (4) in the case of literary, musical, dramatic, and choreographic works, pantomimes, motion pictures, and other audiovisual works, to perform the copyrighted work publicly, (5) in the case of literary, musical, dramatic, and choreographic works, pantomimes and pictorial, graphic, or sculptural works—including the individual images of a motion picture or other audiovisual work—to display the copyrighted work publicly, and (6) in the case of sound recordings, to perform the copyrighted work publicly by means of a digital audio transmission. 17 U.S.C. § 106.

In *Georgia v. Public.Resource.Org*, 140 S.Ct. 1498 (2020), the U.S. Supreme Court cautioned against the overextension of copyrights. The Court ruled that the State of Georgia could not claim a copyright in its annotated law code. Chief Justice Roberts wrote:

> Officials empowered to speak with the force of law cannot be the authors—and therefore cannot copyright—the works they create in the course of their official duties.
>
> The 1976 Copyright Act gave author's exclusive rights including 'reproduction' and 'distribution.' The 1976 Copyright Act codified the doctrines of 'fair use' and 'first sale.' The U.S. doctrine of fair use is consistent with the Berne Convention as well as TRIPs.

JOHN T. CROSS ET AL., GLOBAL ISSUES IN INTELLECTUAL PROPERTY LAW 140 (2010).

(5) First Sale Doctrine

The right to distribute ends once the owner has sold that particular copy. 17 U.S.C. § 109(a) & (c). The first sale doctrine provides that an individual who knowingly purchases a copy of a copyrighted work from the copyright holder receives the right to sell, display or otherwise dispose of that particular copy, notwithstanding the interests of the copyright owner. 17 U.S.C. § 109.

Since the first sale doctrine never protects a defendant who makes unauthorized reproductions of a copyrighted work, it is never a defense to copyright infringement. Most computer software producers distribute code through licensing agreements. With a license, the copyright holder remains the "owner" of all distributed copies.

Licensing is a contractual device that side steps the first sale doctrine and permits licensors to commodify digital products such as software and databases. The U.S. Department of Justice explain the indeterminacy of the first sale doctrine in criminal prosecutions:

> Few issues have created greater confusion in criminal copyright prosecutions than the 'first sale doctrine.' The doctrine is one of the specific statutory restrictions which Congress has placed on the exclusive rights of copyright owners. Criminal defendants frequently resist prosecution by claiming that they believed that the works they were selling had been the subject of a legitimate first sale. Moreover, several criminal copyright convictions have been overturned because of inadequacies in the government's proof on this issue. For this reason, a federal prosecutor should have a clear understanding of the first sale doctrine when

considering whether to bring a criminal copyright case.

U.S. Department of Justice, *Copyright Infringement-First Sale* (2020).

(6) Fair Use Doctrine

"To create Android, which was released in 2007, Google wrote millions of lines of new computer code. But it also used 11,330 lines of code and an organization that's part of Oracle's Java platform." *High Court Sides with Google in Copyright Fight With Oracle*, THE ASSOCIATED PRESS (Apr. 5, 2021). On April 5, 2021, the U.S. Supreme Court held that Google's reimplementation of Java APIs was fair use as a matter of law.

"The court ruled that Google's use of Java code, which was developed by Oracle, 'did not violate the copyright law' and was done under 'fair use' provisions." William Daniel, *Google Extends its 5-day Streak to 10% After US Supreme Court Hands the Tech Giant Victory in $9 Billion Battle With Oracle,* BUSINESS INSIDER (Apr. 5, 2021).

The fair use doctrine now codified as Section 107 of the Copyright Act evolved from a common law doctrine. "Fair use" is a statutory exception to the copyright owner's exclusive right "to reproduce the copyrighted work in copies." 17 U.S.C. § 106(1). See 17 U.S.C. § 107 ("[T]he fair use of a copyrighted work . . . is not an infringement of copyright."). The Copyright Act's four statutory factors used to determine whether a given copyrighted work constitutes fair use are:

- The purpose and character of the use including whether such use is of a commercial nature or is for nonprofit educational purposes;
- The nature of the copyrighted work;
- The amount and substantiality of the portion used in relation to the copyrighted work as a whole; and
- The effect of the use upon the potential market for or value of the copyrighted work.

17 U.S.C. § 107.

To date, no court has addressed how fair use applies to Twitter and hundreds of other social networking sites.

> If Pinterest users post or pin another's work without permission, have they violated copyright law? Does it matter if the work posted or pinned by a user was originally posted to Pinterest by the author or creator of the work? If users impermissibly post or pin a copyrighted work, are they then contributing to infringement when another user in turn re-posts it or pins it on their own page? There is a surplus of questions but is a shortage of answers.

Mary Ann L. Wymore, *Social Media and Fair Use: Pinterest as a Case Study*, BLOOMBERG LAW (2013).

A meme is an image, video, or text that goes viral. In *Philpot v. AlterNet Media Inc.*, 2018 WL 6267876 (N.D. Cal. Nov. 30, 2018), the court addressed whether a meme containing Philpot's copyrighted photograph of singer Willie Nelson was infringing. Philpot filed a complaint:

> alleging that AlterNet violated the Copyright Act, 17 U.S.C. § 501 et seq., and the Digital Millennium Copyright Act ('DMCA'), 17 U.S.C. § 1202 et seq., when it posted Philpot's copyrighted image of Willie Nelson with a superimposed quote on its Facebook page.

The court summarized the dispute as follows: Philpot took a photograph of Willie Nelson in performance at Farm Aid 2009 in Saint Louis and registered it with the United States Copyright Office.

He made the photograph of the famous singer "available through the website Wikimedia for reproduction, distribution, public display, public performance, and public digital performance of the photograph and derivative works, solely under and pursuant to the terms of the Creative Commons Attribution 2.0 Generic license."

AlterNet's Internet meme incorporated Nelson's picture without a license or Philpot's permission. The court noted further that:

> The AlterNet posting on Facebook was introduced with the comment, 'We need more values like this,' and the following quote superimposed on the Nelson photograph: 'Rednecks, hippies, misfits—we're all the same.

> Gay or straight? So what? It doesn't matter to me. We have to be concerned about other people, regardless. I don't like seeing anybody treated unfairly. It sticks in my craw. I hold on to the values from my childhood.'

The court concluded that AlterNet's posting of Philpot's photograph was not protected by fair use: "First of all, there are almost no allegations concerning Philpot's purpose in taking the photo. Second, it is not clear as a matter of law what AlterNet's purpose was in reproducing the photo."

The court found the second factor on the nature of the copyrighted work was not proven at this stage in the litigation: "[i]n order to make a determination as to the image's unique creativity, the Court requires a factual inquiry that is inappropriate at this stage, weighing this factor against dismissal."

Similarly, the third factor for the amount and substantiality of the portion of the work was also unsuitable to be determined on the pleadings. Finally, the fourth factor—the effect of the use on the potential market for or value of the work could not be determined on the pleadings. The court denied AlterNet's motion to dismiss Philpot's copyright infringement claim.

Google LLC v. Oracle America, Inc., 140 S.Ct. 520 (2020), the U.S. Supreme Court will decide whether copyright protection extends to a software interface. This case stemmed from the development of Google's Android platform, which incorporated part of Java programming code. Oracle purchased the overarching company and therefore obtained the Java source code.

Oracle filed suit against Google for copyright and patent infringement after the sale. Google contends that its use of the Java source code in its platform constitutes fair use. This is likely to be a landmark case on the contours of copyright law in its treatment of source code.

(7) First Amendment Limitations

Section 106 of the Copyright Act grants "a bundle of exclusive rights to the owner of the copyright," including the rights "to publish, copy, and distribute the author's work." *Harper & Row Publishers, Inc. v. Nation Enters.,* 471 U.S. 539, 546–547 (1985) (citing 17 U.S.C. § 106). The U.S. Supreme Court noted that the U.S. Copyright Act of 1976:

> represents the culmination of a major legislative reexamination of copyright doctrine . . . Among its other innovations, it eliminated publication 'as a dividing line between common law and statutory protection.' . . . It also recognized for the first time a distinct statutory right of first publication, which had previously been an element of the common-law protections afforded unpublished works . . . Though the right of first publication, like the other rights enumerated in § 106, is expressly made subject to the fair use provision of § 107, fair use analysis must always be tailored to the individual case.

The U.S. Supreme Court ruled that the Nation Magazine's publication of an excerpt of President Gerald Ford's memoirs did not constitute fair use:

> The Nation conceded that its verbatim copying of some 300 words of direct quotation from the Ford manuscript would constitute an infringement unless excused as a fair use. Because we find that The Nation's use of these verbatim excerpts from the unpublished manuscript was not a fair use.

The rights of copyright owners are not absolute, subject to a list of statutory exceptions, including the exception for fair use provided in 17 U.S.C. § 107. If fair use, or another statutory exception, is established, then the use of the copyrighted work does not infringe on the copyright owner's exclusive rights. *See* 17 U.S.C. § 107.

The fair use doctrine recognizes First Amendment constraints on copyright protection. For purposes of determining whether parody of copyrighted work is "fair use," inquiry focuses on whether new work merely supersedes object of original creation or whether and to what extent it is "transformative" and alters original work with new expression, meaning or message. *Campbell v. Acuff-Rose Music, Inc.*, 510 U.S. 569 (1994).

In *Acuff-Rose Music*, the plaintiff contended that the rap group, 2 Live Crew and their record company song "Pretty Woman" infringed their copyright in Roy Orbison's "Oh, Pretty Woman." 17 U.S.C. §§ 101, 107. The U.S. District Court granted summary judgment for 2 Live Crew, holding that its song was a parody that made fair use of the original song. See Copyright Act of 1976, 17 U.S.C. § 107.

The Sixth Circuit Court of Appeals reversed and remanded, holding that the commercial nature of the parody rendered it unfair under the first of four factors relevant under § 107. They reasoned that the rappers took the "heart" of the original and making it the "heart" of a new work.

The appeals court concluded that 2 Live Crew had, qualitatively, taken too much under the third § 107 factor; and that market harm for purposes of the fourth § 107 factor had been established by a presumption attaching to commercial uses.

The U.S. Supreme Court reversed holding that the Sixth Circuit erred in holding that, as a matter of law, 2 Live Crew copied excessively from the Orbison original under the third fair use factor, which asks whether "the amount and substantiality of the portion used in relation to the copyrighted work as a whole" are reasonable in relation to the copying's purpose. 17 U.S.C. § 107. The Court reasoned that:

> Where we part company with the court below is in applying these guides to parody, and in particular to parody in the song before us. Parody presents a difficult case. Parody's humor, or in any event its comment, necessarily springs from recognizable allusion to its object through distorted imitation. Its art lies in the tension between a known original and its parodic twin.

When parody takes aim at a particular original work, the parody must be able to 'conjure up' at least enough of that original to make the object of its critical wit recognizable. *See, e.g., Elsmere Music,* 623 F.2d, at 253, n. 1; *Fisher v. Dees,* 794 F.2d, at 438–439. What makes for this recognition is quotation of the original's most distinctive or memorable features, which the parodist can be sure the audience will know. Once enough has been taken to assure identification, how much more is reasonable will depend, say, on the extent to which the song's overriding purpose and character is to parody the original or, in contrast, the likelihood that the parody may serve as a market substitute for the original. But using some characteristic features cannot be avoided. Even if 2 Live Crew's copying of the original's first line of lyrics and characteristic opening bass riff may be said to go to the original's 'heart,' that heart is what most readily conjures up the song for parody, and it is the heart at which parody takes aim. Moreover, 2 Live Crew thereafter departed markedly from the Orbison lyrics and produced otherwise distinctive music.

Parodies are protectable as they are "transformative," altering the original with new expression, meaning, or message. If the new work is transformative, it is protectable as fair use. Examples of parodies include:

- *Austin Powers* (parody of James Bond movies).

- *Spaceballs* (parody of Star Wars movies).
- *Robin Hood: Men in Tights* (parody of Robin Hood movies).

(8) Databases

Copyright inheres in original works of authorship fixed in a tangible medium. Copyright Act protects the contents of a database as a special kind of literary copyright work, but only it constitutes the author's own intellectual creation. A merely factual compilation is not sufficiently "original" as it is not an author's intellectual product. In the U.S. databases are protected by licensing them as opposed to copyright.

TRIPS (trade-related intellectual property) includes compilations whose selection or arrangement "constitute intellectual creations," but does not extend copyright protection to the underlying data.

In 1996, the EU adopted the database directive concluding that databases not sufficiently protected by contract law. Database owners have a copyright law right: to prevent extraction and/or re-utilization of the whole or of a substantial part evaluated qualitatively and/or quantitatively, of the contents of that database.

The Database Directive says that member states may allow the free "extraction" of database contents if used "for the purposes of illustration for teaching or scientific research."

Database owner must have substantially invested in the "obtaining, verification and presentation" of the contents, rather than in the creation of the content itself. Database rights last under the Directive for fifteen years from the end of the year that the database was made available to the public, or from the end of the year of completion for private databases.

The European Union's Database Directive calls it the *sui generis* right, meaning "of its own kind," in order to distinguish it from copyright. The European Commission describes the directive as follows:

> The Directive protects databases by copyright if they are original. Non-original databases such as compilations of legal cases and laws, listings of advertisements or databases of scientific publications can also be protected if the investment in obtaining, verifying, and presenting the data was substantial. This protection is known as the '*sui generis*' right, i.e., a specific property right for databases that is unrelated to other forms of protection such as copyright.

European Commission, *Protection of Databases* (2020).

The EU Commission enacted this directive to encourage and protect investment in databases which did not qualify for copyright protection.

(D) DERIVATIVE WORKS

A "derivative work" is a work based upon one or more preexisting works such as "a translation, musical arrangement, dramatization, fictionalization, motion picture version, sound recording, art reproduction, abridgment, condensation, or any other form in which a work may be recast, transformed, or adapted." 17 U.S.C. § 101. Section 103 of the U.S. Copyright Act provides that compilations and derivative works fall within the subject matter of copyright. 17 U.S.C. § 103.

Films based upon books are classifiable as derivative works. Editorial revisions, annotations, elaborations, or other modifications such as an altered or updated website, may qualify as a derivative work. A translation, musical arrangement, or abridgment of a work may be "recast, transformed, or adapted" into a derivative work. 17 U.S.C. § 101.

A "derivative work" is a work based upon one or more preexisting works such as a translation or film version of a novel, or any other recasting of an original copyrighted work. "Paradigmatic examples of derivative works include the translation of a novel into another language, the adaptation of a novel into a movie or a play, or the recasting of a novel as an e-book or an audiobook." *Author's Guild v. Hathi Trust*, 755 F.3d 87, 99 (2d Cir. 2019).

Examples of derivative works include "a motion picture that is based on a literary work, a three-dimensional costume based upon two-dimensional cartoon characters, or three-dimensional figurines based on cartoon characters." *Andreas Carlsson Production A.B. v. Barnes*, 2016 WL 11499656 at *5 (C.D. Cal. Nov. 11, 2016).

(E) WORK MADE FOR HIRE

Under federal copyright law, a work made for hire is a work whose copyright is initially owned by an entity other than the actual creator. In the case of "works made for hire," the employer and not the original creator is considered the author and the owner of the work. The "work for hire" doctrine is an exception to this general rule.

This doctrine makes an employer the copyright owner for works prepared by their employee within the scope of employment—even if the employer does nothing more than hire the employee who creates the work.

§ 10-3. Litigating Copyright Infringement Cases

To establish a claim of copyright infringement, a plaintiff must show that it owns the copyright and that the defendant himself violated one or more of the plaintiff's exclusive rights under the Copyright Act. Copyright registration made before or within five years after the first publication of the work shall constitute *prima facie* evidence of the validity of the copyright. 17 U.S.C. § 410(c).

U.S. copyright law recognizes three principal kinds of copyright infringement: (1) primary copyright infringement, (2) contributory copyright infringement, and (3) vicarious copyright infringement as depicted below.

Primary or direct infringement is copying by the primary wrongdoer without authorization. This involves direct infringement of exclusive rights granted to the copyright holder, such as the right to reproduce, distribute, display, or perform the protected work, or to grant permission for the making of derivative works. Infringement claims can be filed against "anyone who violates any of the exclusive rights of the copyright owner." 17 U.S.C. § 501.

"Copyright trolls are in the business of acquiring the right to bring lawsuits against alleged infringers and threatening to file copyright infringement claims in order to induce rapid settlements against large groups of defendants." Jonathan Bick, *Brave New World of Copyright Trolls*, CONNECTICUT LAW TRIBUNE (Oct. 20, 2014).

(A) DIRECT INFRINGEMENT

In a direct infringement case, the copyright holder must prove the defendant had access to the plaintiff's work and copied it without authorization. The plaintiff's burden in a direct infringement action is proof of: (1) direct evidence of infringement or circumstantial evidence of infringement; (2) Access to the plaintiff's copyrighted work; and (3) unlawful copying of the work as evidenced by substantial similarity of original and infringing work.

In a copyright infringement case, a prevailing plaintiff must choose between actual or statutory damages. 17 U.S.C. § 504(a)(1)–(2) (noting that copyright owner has the option of seeking actual or statutory damages).

A defendant in a copyright infringement suit cannot use an "innocent infringer" defense to mitigate actual or statutory damages when the copyright owner attached a proper copyright notice. 17 U.S.C. § 401(d). "The word 'copying' is shorthand for the infringing of any of the copyright owner's five exclusive rights" under 17 U.S.C. § 106.

In *McGucken v. Newsweek LLC,* 464 F. Supp. 3d 594 (S.D.N.Y. 2020), the district court allowed a copyright lawsuit against Newsweek to proceed arising out of an online posting of a photograph without permission of the photographer. The issue was whether an embedded Instagram post gave the new site a license to repost a photographer's copyrighted image.

Media companies treat embedding as an industry practice. The court called this industry practice into question finding no consent. Instagram's policy for posting did not give Newsweek either a license or a sublicense to post the photograph.

(B) SECONDARY COPYRIGHT INFRINGEMENT

Secondary Copyright Liability

Contributory	*Vicarious*	*Inducement*
One who, with knowledge of the infringing activity, induces, causes, or materially contributes to the infringing conduct of another	One who has the right and ability to supervise the infringing activity and also has a direct financial interest	One who distributes a device with the object of promoting its use to infringe copyright, as shown by clear expression or other affirmative steps taken to foster infringement

All three indirect infringement theories turn on a showing of underlying direct infringement. Secondary copyright infringement is analogous to aiding and abetting on the criminal side of the law. Evidence of active steps to induce direct copyright infringement includes activities such as advertising an infringing use or instructing users how to access infringing content.

Until the last few years, nearly all peer-to-peer (P2P) copyright infringement enforcement actions targeted the secondary infringers rather than the primary users.

(1) Contributory Infringement

One infringes contributorily by intentionally inducing or encouraging direct infringement. Contributory infringement exists if the defendant engages in personal conduct that encourages or assists the infringement.

A claim for contributory infringement requires proof that the defendant is one who, with knowledge of the infringing activity, induces, causes, or materially contributes to the infringing conduct of another. *Cobbler Nev., LLC v. Gonzales*, 901 F.3d 1142, 1144 (9th Cir. 2018).

To prevail in a contributory copyright infringement claim, the copyright owner must prove that the defendant is "one who, with knowledge of the infringing activity, induces, causes or materially contributes to the infringing conduct of another."

Three things must be proven by the copyright owner: (1) direct copyright infringement by a third party, (2) knowledge by the defendant, the third party, of direct infringement, and (3) defendant's material contribution to the infringement.

In an Internet-related copyright case, plaintiffs will have a claim for contributory copyright infringement if a third-party website hosts and distributes infringing content while contributing to this infringing conduct. "Liability exists if the defendant engages in personal conduct that encourages or assists the infringement." *A&M Records, Inc. v. Napster, Inc.*, 239 F.3d 1004, 1019 (9th Cir. 2001).

Defendants have no duty to stop infringement until they have "specific knowledge" of infringement, and even then, that "duty only covers specific instances of infringement the defendant knows or has reason to know about." Cf. *Y.Y.G.M. SA v. Redbubble*, 75 F.4th 995, 1002–03 (9th Cir. 2023).

(2) Vicarious Infringement

A defendant is liable for vicarious copyright infringement if the defendant "profit[s] from direct infringement while declining to exercise a right to stop or limit it." *Metro-Goldwyn Mayer Studios v. Grokster*, 545 U.S. 913 (2005).

To state a claim for vicarious copyright infringement, a plaintiff must allege the defendant has: (1) the right and ability to supervise the infringing conduct and (2) a direct financial interest in the infringing activity.

(3) Inducement

A plaintiff must allege four elements to state a claim for inducing copyright infringement: "(1) the distribution of a device or product; (2) acts of infringement; (3) an object of promoting its use to infringe copyright; and (4) causation." *Live Face on Web v. Cremation Society of Illinois*, 2018 WL 4927268 at *2 (E.D. Pa. Oct. 10, 2018) (citation omitted).

In, *Live Face on Web v. Cremation Society of Illinois,* LFOW did not allege facts to demonstrate the defendant took affirmative steps to induce infringement. LFOW further alleges these "acts of vicarious infringement were willful." The court found the allegations failed as "they were merely a formulaic recitation of the claim's elements."

§ 10-4. The Path of Peer-to-Peer File Sharing

Peer-to-peer (P2P) sharing of video and music files is an Internet-related development that has shaped the law of secondary copyright infringement. For example, sharing music or video files on BitTorrent is an infringement of the copyright owner's distribution right if unauthorized.

Once all the pieces have been downloaded, the file is automatically assembled into its original form. In the past fifteen years, the U.S. music and film industry has filed numerous secondary copyright infringement lawsuits against the enablers of infringement as well direct infringement lawsuits against the individuals who share copyrighted files on P2P services.

In *Metro-Goldwin-Mayer Studios, Inc. v. Grokster, Ltd.*, 545 U.S. 913 (2005), the Court unanimously held that defendant P2P file sharing companies Grokster and Streamcast could be sued for inducing copyright infringement for acts taken in the course of marketing file sharing software used for P2P file sharing. The defendants argued that their software was capable of non-infringing uses under the test articulated by the Court in *Sony Corp. of America v. Universal City Studios, Inc.*, 464 U.S. 417 (1984).

Sony addressed the issue of whether distributors of the Betamax video tape recorder were secondarily liable for copyright infringement. There was no evidence that Sony sought to encourage copyright infringement through use of the Betamax or had taken steps to profit from unlawful taping.

The *Grokster* defendants offered evidence that users employed the program to exchange some authorized files. The defendants argued that in the future, users would exchange even more authorized content through Grokster, including academic research, public domain files, and user-created audio and video files.

The *Grokster* Court enunciated an inducement rule imported from patent law providing "one who distributes a device with the object of promoting its use to infringe copyright, as shown by clear expression or other affirmative steps taken to foster infringement, is liable for the resulting acts of infringement by third parties." The Court was unclear in viewing inducement as a subtype of contributory or vicarious infringement or a newly created category of secondary liability.

The Court found that Grokster and Streamcast P2P networks induced infringement by enabling and encouraging the use of their products for file sharing. In the wake of *Grokster*, it remains unclear whether inducement is a separate secondary copyright cause of action or merely a type of contributory copyright infringement.

The U.S. Supreme Court reasoned that "mere knowledge of infringing potential or of actual infringing uses would not be enough here to subject a distributor to liability;" rather, "[t]he inducement rule . . . premises liability on purposeful, culpable expression and conduct, and thus does nothing to compromise legitimate commerce or discourage innovation having a lawful purpose." "The classic instance of inducement is by advertisement or solicitation that broadcasts a message designed to stimulate others to commit violations."

§ 10-5. Digital Millennium Copyright Act

(A) OVERVIEW OF THE DMCA

On October 12, 1998, Congress passed the Digital Millennium Copyright Act (DMCA), 17 U.S.C. § 1201 et seq. to fulfill its obligations under the 1996 World Intellectual Property Organization (WIPO) Copyright treaties. The DMCA's legislative history states that:

> the act of circumventing a technological protection measure put in place by a copyright owner to control access to a copyrighted work is the electronic equivalent of breaking into a locked room in order to obtain a copy of a book.

H.R. Rep. No. 105–551, at 17 (1998).

The DMCA's anti-trafficking rules are the equivalent of "making it illegal to break into a house using a tool, the primary purpose of which is to break into houses." (U.S. Senate Report). The DMCA defines:

> a technological measure as 'effectively controlling access to a work' if the measure, in the ordinary course of its operation, requires the application of information, or a process or a treatment, with the authority of the copyright owner, to gain access to the work.

17 U.S.C. § 1201(a)(3)(B).

The DMCA created both civil remedies, 17 U.S.C. § 1203 and criminal sanctions against circumventing copyright protection or marketing anti-circumvention devices. 17 U.S.C. § 1204. The DMCA specifically authorizes courts to grant temporary and permanent injunctions on such terms, as it deems reasonable to prevent or restrain a violation. 17 U.S.C. § 1203(b)(1).

Title II of the DMCA is the Online Copyright Infringement Liability Limitation Act that created four safe harbors precluding liability on service providers for copyright infringement that occurs as the result of specified activities.

Section 512(c) of the Digital Millennium Copyright Act ("DMCA") establishes a safe harbor, which protects qualifying service providers from liability for infringement when users of the service upload infringing material onto the providers' websites. See 17 U.S.C. § 512(c)(1).

Under 17 U.S.C. § 512(i), a service provider's eligibility for safe harbor only if it:

(A) has adopted and reasonably implemented, and informs subscribers and account holders of the service provider's system or network of, a policy that provides for the termination in appropriate circumstances of subscribers and account holders of the service provider's system or network who are repeat infringers; and

(B) accommodates and does not interfere with standard technical measures.

17 U.S.C. § 512(i)(1).

The anti-circumvention rules found in Section 1201 et seq. of Title 17. Section 1201(a) prohibits (i) circumventing such technological measures and (ii) trafficking in technology designed to circumvent such technological measures.

Congress sought to prohibit certain efforts to unlawfully circumvent protective technologies, while at the same time preserving users' rights of fair use. 17 U.S.C. § 1201(b)(1)(A) & (C). The chief exceptions to the DMCA's anti-circumvention rule are for:

- law enforcement;
- good faith encryption research;
- non-infringing reverse engineering for interoperability;
- enabling filtering of internet content to protect minors; and

- allowing the security testing of computer systems.

A U.S. Senate Subcommittee contended that Facebook, YouTube, and other Tech Giants that they had a duty to do more to prevent copyright piracy. Online copyright infringement results in $29 billion in losses each year. A head of a nonprofit contends that the DMCA is not working as it was intended and the Tech Giants must do more. Britain Eakin, *Tech Giants Must Do More To Tackle Piracy, Sen. Panel Told*, LAW360 (Dec. 15, 2020).

(B) TITLE I PROVISIONS

Title I of the DMCA added Chapter 12, entitled "Copyright Protection and Management Systems," to the U.S. Copyright Act. The DMCA distinguishes between circumvention and trafficking. Trafficking in qualified technology circumventing technological measures controlling either access to a copyrighted work, or protects the author's rights, are both prohibited.

While the actual act of circumvention is only prohibited when a defendant circumvents a technological measure that controls access, not protecting the author's rights.

The DMCA provides legal protection for anti-copying technology as well as anti-access technology. The WIPO Copyright Treaty (WCT), a special agreement under the Berne Convention, deals with the protection of works and the rights of their authors in the digital environment. The WCT requires signatory powers to provide remedies against defendants circumventing digital rights management tools or tampering with copyright management information.

DRM tools restrict the use and copying of digital information. Congress had the statutory purpose of facilitating "the robust development and world-wide expansion of electronic commerce, communications, research, development, and education in the digital age." U.S. Senate, S. Rep. No. 105–190 (1998) at 1–2.

(1) Anti-Circumvention Provisions

Section 1201(a)(1) prohibits the circumvention of any technological measure that "effectively controls access to" a protected work. 17 U.S.C. § 1201(a)(1)(A); To state a claim for violation of § 1201(a), a plaintiff must allege that "(i) the work at issue was protected under the Copyright Act, (ii) the copyrighted work was protected by a 'technological measure,' and (iii) the technological measure was 'circumvented' in order to obtain access to the copyrighted work." *CDK Glob., LLC v. Tekion Corp.*, No. 25-cv-01394-JSC, 2025 WL 1939951, at *8 (N.D. Cal. July 15, 2025).

The DMCA's anti-circumvention rules are set forth in Section 1201 et seq. of Title 17. The DMCA defines a "technological measure that effectively controls access to a work" as a measure that, "in the ordinary course of its operation, requires the application of information, or a process or a treatment, with the authority of the copyright owner, to gain access to the work." 17 U.S.C. § 1201(a)(3)(B). YouTube, for example, used technological measures to published videos that control access to and prevent unauthorized use.

A technological measure "effectively protects a right of a copyright owner under this title if the measure, in the ordinary course of its operation, prevents, restricts, or otherwise limits the exercise of a right of a copyright owner under this title." 17 U.S.C. § 1201(b)(2)(B).

Section 1201 prohibits the circumvention of anti-access technology as well as the making and selling of anti-circumvention devices. To "circumvent a technological measure" means that the defendant has descrambled a scrambled work, decrypted an encrypted work, or bypassed a technological measure protecting a copyrighted work. 17 U.S.C. § 1201(a)(3)(A).

The DMCA makes it a criminal offense for a person to produce or traffic in technologies intended to circumvent Digital Rights Management (DRM), controlling access to copyrighted works, whether or not there is actual infringement of a copyright.

> Software that circumvents 'digital walls' in violation of the DMCA . . . is like a skeleton key that can open a locked door, a combination that can open a safe, a device that can neutralize the security device attached to a store's products, or a digital crowbar.

Universal City Studios v. Corley, 273 F.3d 429, 453 n. 27 (2d Cir. 2001).

> A technological measure 'effectively controls access to a work' if the measure, in the ordinary course of its operation, requires the application of information, or a process, or a treatment, with the authority of the copyright owner, to gain access to the work.

17 U.S.C. § 1201(a)(3)(B).

The DMCA proscribes circumventing anti-access measures; however, it does not prohibit circumventing anti-copying measures. For example, Apple's FairPlay and Microsoft Windows Digital Rights Managers provide controls on the viewing or playing of copyright materials, which is accessing a service.

The DMCA's anti-circumvention prohibitions criminalize picking digital locks that guard access to copyrighted materials. The DMCA's anti-circumvention prohibitions do not, however, prohibit circumvention of technological measures that protect the exclusive rights of an author under § 106 of the Copyright Act, such as copying or distribution, as such infringement may be protected by fair use.

Fair use is affirmative defense to claim of copyright infringement. 17 U.S.C.A. § 107. In *Cardovo v. Huneault*, 2026 WL 184598 (N.D. Calif. Jan. 23, 2026), the operator of channel on video-sharing website brought action against owners of another channel, alleging copyright infringement of two copyrighted videos, misrepresentation in Digital Millennium Copyright Act (DMCA) counternotices, that owners' use of particular video did not qualify as fair use, and unlawful circumvention of technological measures and seeking damages, injunctive relief, declaratory relief, and attorneys' fees and costs.

The owners moved to dismiss second, third, and fourth claims for failure to state claim. Next, the defendants submitted DMCA counter-notices to YouTube, pursuant to 17 U.S.C. § 512(g)(3), seeking reinstatement of nine of the eleven videos.

Mr. Cordova allege that Huneault's counter-notices contained "substantially identical boilerplate language and multiple false statements," including that Huneault was the "original creator" of the videos, that the videos were protected by the fair use doctrine and "were taken down by mistake because they fall under the Fair use act," and that Huneault had already retained counsel "to defend my fair use videos in court."

The Court agreed that Cordova adequately alleged facts from which a reasonable inference may be drawn that defendants' "fair use" representations were false and made in bad faith.

Eric Goldman noted that Section 512(f) claims rarely survive motions to dismiss:

> The facts at issue here are not likely to be found in other cases. First, it's rare to have 512(f) defendants publicly discuss the legal standards that apply to their conduct. Second, using takedown/putback notices as extortive weapons could demonstrate the Rossi-required scienter, but most courts would not consider the exercise of takedown/putback rights as extortive without

significant additional evidence of extortive intent. After all, courts can't penalize defendants for taking advantage of legally enshrined rights.

Eric Goldman, *It Takes a Lot for 512(f) Claims to Survive a Motion to Dismiss—Cordova v. Huneault*, TECHNOLOGY & MARKETING BLOG (Jan. 25, 2026).

(2) Anti-Trafficking Provisions

The DMCA anti-trafficking provision prohibits individuals from providing or otherwise trafficking in any "technology, product, service, device, component, or part thereof, that is . . . designed or produced for the purpose of circumventing a technological measure." 17 U.S.C. § 1201(a)(2)–(b)(1).

In *Dish Network L.L.C. v. World Cable Inc.*, 893 F. Supp. 2d 452 (E.D.N.Y. 2012), the court held to state a claim under the DMCA's anti-trafficking provision, the complaint must allege that "[d]efendants trafficked in a product or service that enabled the circumvention, not access to what has already been obtained."

(C) TITLE II'S SAFE HARBORS

The Online Copyright Infringement Liability Limitation Act (OCILLA) created limitations on liability for network service providers who fulfill specific safe-harbor exemptions. OCILLA creates a conditional safe harbor for online service providers (OSP) including Internet service providers and most Internet intermediaries by shielding them for liability from infringement of third parties on their services.

In the ordinary course of their operations, service providers must engage in all kinds of acts that expose them to potential copyright infringement liability. For example, service providers must make innumerable electronic copies simply to transmit information over the Internet.

Certain electronic copies are made to speed up the delivery of information to users. Other electronic copies are made in order to host World Wide Web sites. U.S. *Senate Report on The Digital Millennium Act* (S. Rept. 105–090) at 8 (1998).

OCILLA placed limitations on liability for network service providers who fulfill specific safe-harbor exemptions. Further, OCILLA developed a mechanism of takedown notices for infringing content on websites.

In response, the service provider must remove the infringing material from its website. Upon receipt of a counter-notice objecting to the takedown, the service provider must replace the subscriber's material on the website.

> Section 512 provides separate safe harbors for each of the four diverse types of services: transitory digital network communications services by so-called 'conduit' Internet service providers (ISPs); caching services; hosting services, which store material at the direction of users, including services such as Facebook, Twitter, and Flickr; and information location

tools, which include search engines, directories, and other linking services.

Guinevere Jobson and Armen Nercessian, *Developments Related to the Safe Harbors Under the Digital Millennium Copyright Act*, 73 BUS. LAW. 243 (2017–2018).

To qualify for the DMCA Section 512 safe harbors, an ISP must satisfy three requirements:

> (i) the service provider must either lack both actual knowledge of the infringing activity and awareness of facts or circumstances from which infringing activity should be apparent, or it must promptly, upon gaining such knowledge move to prevent the use of its service to further such infringing activity; (ii) the service provider must not receive a financial benefit directly attributable to infringing activity it has the ability to control; and (iii) the service provider must expeditiously remove material from its service on receipt of an appropriate written notice in order to qualify for safe harbor protection under the DMCA.

The copyright owner must give the provider's designated agent a written takedown notice which includes: (1) a physical or electronic signature of a person authorized to act on behalf of the copyright owner of the right allegedly infringed, (2) identification of the copyrighted works allegedly infringing, (3) identification of the parts of the copyrighted work that are infringing and thus should be removed, (4) sufficient information to contact copyright owner or complaining party, (5) a statement by the complainant in the good faith belief that the material is infringing, and (6) a statement that the information in the notice is accurate.

Section 512(f)(1)–(2) of the DMCA provides remedies if a person "knowingly materially misrepresents" information "(1) that material or activity is infringing, or (2) that material or activity was removed or disabled by mistake or misidentification." 17 U.S.C. § 512(f)(1)–(2). Those persons who knowingly misrepresent the facts in take-down notices:

> shall be liable for any damages, including costs and attorneys' fees, incurred by the alleged infringer, by any copyright owner or copyright owner's authorized licensee or by a service provider, who is injured by such misrepresentation, as the result of the service provider relying upon such misrepresentation in removing or disabling access to the material or activity claimed to be infringing, or in replacing the removed material or ceasing to disable access to it.

17 U.S.C. § 512(f)(2).

Section 512 of the DMCA gives ISPs such as websites a safe harbor from secondary copyright infringement if these websites respond quickly to takedown requests for infringing third party postings. To be eligible for the DMCA safe harbor, an ISP must "reasonably implement" a termination policy, not just adopt one. 17 U.S.C. § 512(i)(1)(A).

"An ISP has not 'reasonably implemented' a repeat infringer policy if the ISP fails to enforce the terms of its policy in any meaningful fashion." *BMG Rights Mgmt. (U.S.) LLC v. Cox Commc'ns, Inc.*, 881 F.3d 293, 303 (4th Cir. 2018).

The court in *UMG v. Grande Communications Inc.*, 384 F. Supp. 3d 743 (W.D. Tex. 2019) explained that merely adopting a repeat termination policy without enforcing precludes protection from the DMCA liability shield stating:

> Adopting a repeat infringer termination policy that is not 'carried out is not an "implementation" as required by § 512(i).' *In re Aimster Copyright Litig.*, 252 F. Supp. 2d 634, 659 (N.D. Ill. 2002), aff'd, 334 F.3d 643 (7th Cir. 2003). '[T]he relevant question is whether [the ISP] actually terminates the uploading privileges of repeat infringers under appropriate circumstances.' *Capitol Records, LLC v. Escape Media Grp., Inc.*, 2015 WL 1402049 at *12 (S.D.N.Y. Mar. 25, 2015) at 755.

(D) DMCA SUBPOENA TO UNVEIL ANONYMOUS INFRINGERS

The DMCA sets forth a statutory scheme for copyright holders to notify Internet service providers of the existence of allegedly copyrighted material on their servers. 17 U.S.C. § 512(c)(3). A "safe harbor" is provided to service providers who remove or disable access to allegedly infringing material following receipt of a DMCA notice. A valid DMCA notification requires that the infringing materials be present at the time notification is served. *In re DMCA Subpoena to eBay, Inc.*, 2015 WL 3555270 (S.D. Cal. June 5, 2015).

(E) DMCA LITIGATION

DMCA remedies include injunctions, damages, impoundment and destruction of offending devices or products. Treble damages are available against repeat offenders. 17 U.S.C. § 1203. The DMCA provides for criminal penalties including a $500,000 fine and up to 5 years imprisonment for first offense; $1,000,000 and up to 10 years imprisonment for subsequent offense. 17 U.S.C. § 1204.

In *Riot Games v. Argote*, No. 16-cv-5871 (C.D. Cal. March 3, 2017), a California court awarded Riot Games a $10 million award for copyright infringement against a game-cheating bot maker. The product circumvented Riot's technological measures, which controlled access to games such as Leaguesharp and League of Legends.

Riot used anti-circumvention protection to prevent players from hacking, running automated software programs, cheating, or using unlicensed copies of Riot's games. Riot alleged that the German defendants and their Peruvian shell company with selling game-breaking software bypassing Riot's access controls.

The court ordered the defendants to halt their sales of game-breaking software and to destroy all copies of their illegal software. The defendants were also prohibited from reverse engineering or decompiling Riot's games in the future. The latest digital rights management (DRM) systems use forensic watermarking to augment traditional controls.

In *Design Basics, LLC v. WK Olson Architects, Inc.*, 2019 WL 527535 (N.D. Ill. Feb. 11, 2019), since 2009, Design Basics created over 350 new home design plans and have an inventory of over 2,800 plans, which they have registered with the United States Copyright Office. Design filed suit against Olson for copying eleven of Design Basics' architecture plans. The federal district court dismissed Design Basic's DMCA claim. Finally, the court addressed the Plaintiffs' DMCA claim.

The DMCA makes it illegal for a person to knowingly falsify, remove, or alter copyright management information (CMI). 17 U.S.C. § 1202. To establish a violation of the statutory prohibition against modifying or removing copyright management information (CMI) without authorization, a plaintiff must prove: (1) the existence of CMI in connection with a copyrighted work; and (2) that a defendant distributed works or copies of works; (3) while knowing that CMI has been removed or altered without authority of the copyright owner or the law; and (4) while knowing, or having reasonable grounds to know that such distribution will induce, enable, facilitate, or conceal an infringement. 17 U.S.C. § 1202(b).

This provision defines CMI as the information conveyed in connection with copies of a work, including its title, author, copyright owner, the terms and conditions for use of the work, and identifying numbers or symbols referring to the work's copyright information. 17 U.S.C. § 1202(c).

In *Farrington v. Fingerlakes1.com*, 2020 WL 7350336 (W.D.N.Y. Dec. 15, 2020), Farrington alleged that Fingerlakes violated the DMCA by removing copyright management information (CMI) from photograph posted on its website and published a *New York Po*st article using the photograph.

The court found that the defendant's default establishes that its removal of the gutter credit was intentional. Further, it had reason to know that removing the gutter credit would conceal an infringement—namely, its own—because doing so would hide the authorship of the photograph. The court found these actions established that the defendant violated the DMCA.

Under 17 U.S.C. § 1202(a), it is unlawful to "(1) provide copyright management information that is false, or (2) distribute or import for distribution copyright management information that is false."

In *McGucken v. Shuttershock, Inc.*, 166 F.4th 361 (2d Cir. 2024), McGucken, a professional photographer. Between 2018 and 2022, hundreds of McGucken's photographs began appearing on the platform of an online stock photo marketplace called Shutterstock, Inc. without his knowledge or consent. Shutterstock operates an online marketplace for photographs, video footage, music, and other digital content.

The Shutterstock platform contains over 424 million images and twenty-six million video clips. Every day, Shutterstock adds approximately 200,000 images and an average of 75,000 video clips to the market. s case arose after 337 of McGucken's original photographs were uploaded by three of Shutterstock's contributors and were made available for license through the website.

Shutterstock licensed 165 of McGucken's images to its customers, generating $2,131.60 in revenue that was shared between Shutterstock and the contributors who uploaded the images.

McGucken sued Shutterstock for false copyright management information ("CMI") under 17 U.S.C. § 1202 and copyright infringement under 17 U.S.C. § 106. The District Court granted Shutterstock's motion for summary judgment on all counts, concluding that Shutterstock could avoid liability for copyright infringement through a safe harbor provision of the Digital Millennium Copyright Act ("DMCA"), and that its removal of metadata from some of McGucken's images did not violate § 1202.

The Second Circuit concluded that McGucken failed to introduce any evidence that Shutterstock had the requisite scienter to be liable for false CMI under 17 U.S.C. § 1202. The federal appeals court affirmed affirm the federal district court's grant of summary judgment to Shutterstock on those claims.

The court noted that Shutterstock satisfied most of the requirements to qualify for safe harbor immunity under the DMCA. The court ruled that there remained two issues of fact that preclude summary judgment:

(1) whether the infringing activity alleged by McGucken occurred "by reason of the storage at the direction of a user of material that resides on" Shutterstock's online marketplace;

(2) whether Shutterstock has the "right and ability to control" the infringing activity at issue here.

The court remand the case to the district court.

In *McGucken v. Shuttershock, Inc.*, 166 F.4th 361 (2d Cir. 2026), the court stated that:

> [t]o be liable under § 1202(a), a party must engage in one of these two acts "knowingly and with the intent to induce, enable, facilitate, or conceal infringement." In other words, § 1202(a) contains a pair of scienter elements: to be liable, a party must both have actual knowledge that the CMI at issue is false and have acted with the intent to induce, enable, facilitate, or conceal infringement.

The Second Circuit found that McGucken's § 1202(b) claim failed:

> While Shutterstock concededly knows that it removes CMI from every image ingested into its system, Shutterstock explained—and McGucken failed to refute—that it removes metadata from all images primarily to avoid computer viruses and the dissemination of

personally identifiable information, and not for any reasons related to infringement. Nothing in the record suggests that Shutterstock removed McGucken's CMI or distributed his work knowing that the CMI had been removed without his consent. Nor is there evidence demonstrating that Shutterstock removed CMI from McGucken's images "knowing, or, with respect to civil remedies under Section 1203 [which are sought here], having reasonable grounds to know, that it will induce, enable, facilitate, or conceal an infringement of any right under this title [i.e., copyright]." 17 U.S.C. § 1202(b)(3).

(F) U.S. COPYRIGHT OFFICE STUDY OF SECTION 512

The U.S. Copyright Office issued its report on the DMCA recommendations for how Congress might amend the statute if the initial balance was no longer working for all concerned. The Report made the following recommendations electing not to recommend wholesale changes to Section 512 deferring to Congress. U.S. Copyright Office, *Section 512 of Title 17: A Report of the Register of Copyright* (May 2020).

Over the decades, the shift in the balance of the benefits and obligations for copyright owners and OSPs under Section 512 has resulted in an increasing burden on rights holders to adequately monitor and enforce their rights online, while providing enhanced protections for OSPs in circumstances beyond those originally anticipated by Congress.

§ 10-6. International Issues

International copyright protection is challenging because of different intellectual property regimes and different traditions of enforcing these regimes. Software licensors market products in a global marketplace and therefore must protect their own intellectual property rights, while avoiding infringing the rights of others.

Before launching a new software product globally, a software maker needs to conduct an audit to determine copyright protected materials and avoid violating the copyrights of others, thus complying with the copyright law of each country where they do business.

(A) EXTRATERRITORIALITY

Takedown disputes will increasingly involve parties in different countries raising extraterritoriality issues. In general, intellectual property rights are left to each nation to enforce. A copyright infringement claim may not be brought in U.S. courts for conduct committed entirely outside the territorial boundaries of the United States.

(B) MORAL RIGHTS

The heirs of famous French author Victor Hugo sued to block a sequel to Les Misérables in which the original ending of the book had been changed. Hugo's heirs contended that the alternative version of his work corrupted his original vision. In the U.S., the current owners of any copyrighted work are allowed to change it in any way they want, even if the changes harmed the reputation or were e counter to the identity of an author like Victor Hugo.

In *Huston v. Turner Ent. Co.*, Cour De Cassation [1992] E.C.C. 334, Cour De Cassation, *The Asphalt Jungle* was originally a black and white film by a US director.

Ted Turner colorized the film and a French television station planned to broadcast the updated version, which the Cour De Cassation found to be an infringement of the moral rights of the authors under French law. The Cour De Cassation court reasoned:

> the fact that the black and white movie was made at the time when color was available to the artist, and therefore, the motion picture in question was filmed in black and white (and not in color) following a deliberate aesthetic choice, which the author considered to be the best for the work. The French court held that Ted Turner's colorization of a John Huston film, *Asphalt Jungle,* violated the Huston estate's moral rights. Under American Law, moral rights receive protection through judicial interpretation of several copyright, trademark, privacy, and defamation statutes, and through 17 U.S.C. § 106A, known as the Visual Artists Rights Act of 1990 (VARA). VARA applies exclusively to visual art.

Roberta Kwall in JOHN T. CROSS ET AL., GLOBAL ISSUES IN INTELLECTUAL PROPERTY LAW 127 (2010).

Roberta Kwall proposes amending the 1976 Copyright Act to implement an American version of the moral rights doctrine that would balance all the competing interests concerned in extending protection to the personal rights of creators.

Visual artists possess an attribution right in their works as well as rights to prevent intentional distortion, mutilation, or other modification of their work, and to block destruction of works of "recognized stature," subject to several limitations. For example, a sculptor has the right to prevent the destruction of her statute.

The U.S. is a Berne Convention signatory, which explicitly recognizes moral rights. Article 6b provides that independent of the author's economic rights, and even after the transfer of the said rights, the author shall have the right to claim authorship of the work and to object to any distortion, mutilation, or other modification of, or other derogatory action in relation to the said work, which would be prejudicial to the author's honor or reputation.

> The term 'moral rights' is taken from the French phrase droit moral and refers to certain noneconomic rights that are considered personal to an author. Chief among these rights are the right of an author to be credited as the author of his or her work (the right of attribution) and the right to prevent prejudicial distortions of the

> work (the right of integrity). These rights have a long history in international copyright law.

U.S. Copyright Office, *Study on the Moral Rights of Attribution and Integrity* (2019).

The United States has historically not adopted moral rights because the US endorses a market-based approach to copyright law. Annemarie Bridy, *The Evolution of Authorship: Work Made by Code*, 39 COLUM. J.L. & ARTS 395, 401 (2016).

The United States enacted the Visual Artists Rights Act of 1990 (VARA) to implement the Berne Convention. Regardless of assignment or ownership of rights, VARA protects the expectation that a visual work will not be revised, altered, or distorted. VARA has little application to the Internet since it only protects works of visual art that have attained the status of "recognized stature."

"The Internet raises the potential for infringement of an author's *moral rights*. Issues raised specifically by the internet include the circumstances"—where their creations are presented when a website links to another site. MAREE SANSBURY, MORAL RIGHTS AND THEIR APPLICATION IN AUSTRALIA (Sydney Australia: Federation Press, 2003) at 147.

The right to false attribution could be extended to computer programs or website creations. Similarly, manipulating an electronic or digitalized photograph could violate the right not to have an artist's work distorted, mutilated, or modified. A French court ruled the moral rights of movie director John Huston were violated when Ted Turner colorized *The Asphalt Jungle*.

The French court concluded that the deceased director had deliberately chosen to film in black and white as an aesthetic choice. If this case had been filed in the U.S., it would have been dismissed because moral rights in the U.S. are only protected in the specific area of visual arts. Any "assignment of economic rights is not accompanied by assignment of moral rights . . . French rights, may provide a remedy where infringement relating to a digital work is disseminated over the Internet." CATHERINE COLSTON & JONATHAN GALLOWAY, MODERN INTELLECTUAL PROPERTY (New York, New York: Routledge, 2010) at 450.

(C) EXTRATERRITORIAL REACH

"If a web server located outside the United States hosts video content that can be viewed by Internet users located in the United States, does a public performance result under U.S. copyright law?" John Delaney & Monica Cai, Morrison & Foerster LLP—Social Media, *Copyright's Long Arm: Foreign Website Found to Infringe U.S. Copyright Law*, JD SUPRA (BLOG) (July 23, 2018).

In *Spanski Enters. v. Telewizja Polska, S.A.*, 883 F.3d 904 (2018), the D.C. Circuit Court affirmed a district court ruling that Polska, which uploaded and digitally formatted TV episodes in Poland, was nevertheless liable for copyright infringement as "the infringing performances" (and relevant conduct) "occurred on the computer screens in the United

States" and were thus actionable in the United States.

Neither the automated nature of appellant foreign broadcaster's video-on-demand system, nor the role of U.S. end-users in selecting content originating out of Poland insulated the broadcaster from liability to appellee copyright holder because the performances occurred within the U.S. and, under the Morrison "focus" test, the Copyright Act's focus was to protect a copyright holder's exclusive right to perform a copyrighted work publicly by prohibiting infringement under 17 U.S.C. § 501.

The D.C. Circuit federal appeals court concluded that "the district court's factual findings clearly supported that the broadcaster deliberately removed geoblocking from fifty-one episodes, was aware of the holder's exclusive U.S. rights, and purposefully hid its conduct; therefore, both the liability and damage findings were justified." The appeals court summarized its holding as follows:

> To sum up, then, we hold that where a foreign broadcaster uploads copyrighted content to its website and directs that content onto a computer screen in the United States at a user's request, the broadcaster commits an actionable domestic violation of the Copyright Act. Consistent with this view of the law, the district court, based on its supportable factual findings, found TV Polska liable for infringing Spanski's copyrights in the fifty-one episodes and concluded that damages of $60,000 per episode were appropriate in light of the circumstances. Seeing

no basis for upsetting these considered judgments, we affirm as to both liability and damages.

Copyright law is territorial while the is cross-border by its very nature. U.S. courts have been more receptive to expanding the extraterritorial reach of copyright law. Each advance in digital interconnectivity brings new types of intellectual property concerns and novel ways to infringe property rights on a worldwide basis. What is required is an international copyright law to protect the rights of owners against infringing acts posted on websites, social media, and other Internet forums.

CHAPTER 11

TRADEMARKS ON THE GLOBAL INTERNET

A trademark is generally a word, phrase, symbol, or design, or a combination thereof, that identifies and distinguishes the source of the goods of one party from those of others. A service mark is the same as a trademark, except that it identifies and distinguishes the source of a service rather than goods.

Courts protect trademarks against imitation or unauthorized use because they represent creative or inventive leaps of the mind. Apple Inc.'s various apple-shaped logos, for instance, signify to consumers a single source of a product and carry a certain level of recognizable consistency and quality.

The term "trademark" also extends to trade dress, which has come to include not only a product's packaging, but also the items total image and overall appearance. Trade dress is the long and feels of a product or services. Trade dress also refer to the visual, non-functional, and distinctive overall look of businesses such as Staples, Target, or Burger King.

Today, even sound can create a mental association in the minds of consumers, and thus be protected under trademark law. For example, "Intel Inside" logo and sound are well-known computer-related trademarks, recognized worldwide.

Apple is the world's most valuable brand with an estimated value of $608 billion, followed by Microsoft ($565B) and Google ($433B). "Nvidia's four-place jump since 2025 is particularly notable. As demand for AI chips and data center infrastructure accelerates, the company's brand has strengthened alongside its financial performance."

Ranked: The World's Most Valuable Brands in 2026, VISUAL CAPITALIST (Mar. 6, 2026).

§ 11-1. Trademark Basics

This chapter on global trademark law is divided into nine sections. Section 11-1 is an overview covering topics such as how to obtain trademark protection, the spectrum of distinctiveness, and limits on what can be trademarked.

Section 11-2 is an overview of trademark claims, while Section 11-3 examines direct and secondary trademark infringement. Section 11-4 covers the federal anti-dilution act, while Section 11-5 covers cybersquatting and the Anticybersquatting Act of 1999. Section 11-6 covers trademark law defenses including nominative fair use, the First Amendment, trademark parodies and laches.

Section 11-7 covers the intersection between trademarks and domain names, covering topics like domain name hijacking and reverse hijacking. Next, Section 11-8 covers the Uniform Dispute Resolution Procedure for resolving the conflict between trademarks and domain names. Finally, 11-9 examines global trademark law issues. A trademark is defined in the Lanham Act as any word, name, symbol, or device or any combination thereof adopted and used by a manufacturer or merchant to identify his goods and distinguish them from those manufactured or sold by others. 15 U.S.C. § 1127. The federal Lanham Act that governs trademarks, requires that a defendant's use of the plaintiff's mark constitutes "use in commerce." 15 U.S.C. § 1114(1).

"Use in commerce" is a broad term that is satisfied whenever "the trademark has been displayed to customers in connection with a commercial transaction." *Kelly-Brown v. Winfrey*, 717 F.3d 295, 306 (2d Cir. 2013).

The Lanham Act recognizes actual use as well as "intent to use" applications:

> [A]ny word, name, symbol, or device, or any combination therefore is a service mark or trademark if it is "used by a person, or . . . a person has a bona fide intention to use in commerce and applies to register" the mark in the federal register established by the Lanham Act. 15 U.S.C. § 1127.
>
> A trademark distinguishes the source of the goods of one party from those of others. A trademark must distinguish products to be registrable. This requirement prevents consumer confusion and allows for brand recognition.

The distinctiveness of the trademark determines its relative strength or weakness and will, accordingly, define the scope of protection to be accorded the mark against the confusing similarity of others. Apple, Nike, Amazon, Google, Coca Cola, and Starbucks are extremely well-known.

A mark is strong if it is conspicuously distinctive; it is distinctive if the public has already been educated to accept it as the hallmark of a particular source. Then, too, a mark can be distinctive either because it is unique, that is, distinctive in itself, because it has been the subject of wide and intensive advertisement, or because of a combination of both.

Trademarks must be sufficiently distinctive to be protectable. Chick-fil-A is a federally registered trademark as is its slogan, "EAT MOR CHIKIN." Apple (Computers) as is the Nutshell Series and logo. West Academic and West Academic publishing, which publishes *Global Internet Law in a Nutshell* are also trademarked. A trademark is always connected to the specific goods or services sold to customers with that trademark.

The USPTO states that the following marks satisfy the requirement of distinctive marks:

> Strong trademarks are typically creative or unique, setting you apart from your competitors. These trademarks include fanciful, arbitrary, or suggestive trademarks.
>
> Fanciful trademarks are invented words. They only have meaning in relation to their goods or services. For example, Exxon® for petroleum or Pepsi® for soft drinks.
>
> Arbitrary trademarks are actual words that have no association with the underlying goods or services. Think of the term "apple." If an apple orchard tried to register the word "apple" as a trademark for the type of apples they grow, that

trademark wouldn't be registerable. But, Apple® has been registered as a trademark for computers. Apple® for computers is unique.

Suggestive trademarks are words that suggest some quality of the goods or services, but don't state that quality of the goods or services outright. Consider Coppertone® for sun-tanning products. The trademark gives the impression that using Coppertone® suntan oil will make your skin shimmer like copper.

Owners of trademarks obtain rights through use. The owners of these trademarks have built up their strength through advertising, or demonstrate use over many years in their business. Consumers purchasing an Apple iPhone 12 are often willing to pay a premium because they know that they can expect a degree of quality consistent with the Apple brand. Apple has hundreds of trademarks including:

3D Touch®, interfaces; AirDrop®, software feature; AirMac®, wireless hardware/software solution; AirPlay®, software feature; AirPods®, wireless headphones; AirPods Pro®, wireless headphones, AirPort®, wireless hardware/ software solution; AirPort Express®, wireless hardware/software solution; AirPort Time Capsule®, wireless hard drive/Wi-Fi base station; AirPower®, charging devices; charging devices; AirPrint®, software feature; AirTunes™, application program; Animoji®, messaging feature; Aperture®, application program; and Apple®, computers, computer software, computer peripherals, etc.

Apple Legal, *Apple Trademark List* (2021).

The Apple® iPhone® mobile digital device comes with the Multi-Touch™ touchscreen interface. Apple and iPhone are trademarks of Apple Inc., registered in the U.S. and many other countries. Multi-Touch is a trademark of Apple Inc. Apple is a trade name, meaning that it is a designation used by a company to distinguish itself from others in the same field. Trademarks are source identifiers for goods and services. The following are some examples of source identifiers.

Trademark	*Source Identifiers*
Mercedes, Volvo, Ford, Chevrolet	For automobiles
Domino's Pizza, Pizza Hut, Papa John's, Little Caesars, and California Pizza Kitchen.	For pizzas
Apple, Dell, Lenovo, Microsoft, and HP,	For personal computer and laptops.
Coca Cola, Pepsi-Cola, Red Bull, Fanta, and Sprite	For soft drink makers
Louis Vuitton, Chanel, Nike, Gucci, and Hermès	For clothing brands.

Rolex, Seiko, Citizen, Omega, Casio, and Citizen	For watches
Boston Celtics, Dallas Cowboys star, NY Yankees "NY", and Chicago Bulls	Trademarks for sports teams
Meta (Facebook), Instagram, TikTok, and X.	Trademarks for social media.

A service mark, as its name suggests, identifies the source of services as opposed to a source of goods. E*Trade, for example, is a service mark for online investing. McDonald's Golden Arches, and brand names like Google and FedEx are well-known service marks.

Servicemarks	*Source Identifier*
Nike's "Just Do It":	Marketing and athletic services
FedEx	Express delivery
Google	Search engines and online services
Disney	Entertainment services
Walmart	Retail store services

(A) TRADEMARK REGISTRATION

Trademark applications may be based on either (1) a bona fide intent-to-use the mark in commerce or (2) actual use of the mark in commerce.

(1) Actual Use Trademark Applications

The trademark applicant specifies the date of first use. The applicant will typically show how the mark appears on labels or packaging of goods sold in the stream of commerce. To register a trademark, the applicant needs to prove use in commerce, which means that Use in commerce means the applicant has been using their trademark in selling or transporting goods out of state or in providing services to customers who live outside your state.

Trademark applicants need to submit a specimen showing how they use trademark. Use in commerce may be shown by a trademark placed on the label, packing or display of goods sold or transported in interstate commerce.

Applicants also need to provide the date they first used your trademark in commerce and the date they first used it anywhere.

The term "use in commerce" originated when trademarks where affixed on goods or containers. In the digital website world, the first party who either uses a mark in commerce or files an application in the U.S. Trademark Office generally holds the first right to register that mark.

The U.S. Trademark Office may accept evidence an applicant has used a mark "in commerce" for five years as prima facie evidence of distinctiveness. 15 U.S.C. § 1054. An owner will typically use trademarks on its product and packaging, while service marks advertise services.

(2) Intent to Use Applications

If an applicant has not used a trademark in commerce yet, they can file an intent to use application if they have a good faith intention to do so in the future. Trademarks or service marks can be registered on an intent-to-use (ITU) filing basis.

Intent-to-use applications are filed pursuant to 15 U.S.C. § 1051(b), which states:

> that a person who has a bona fide intention, under circumstances showing the good faith of such person, to use a trademark in commerce may request registration of its trademark on the principal register. 15 U.S.C.S. § 1051(b)(1). At the time of application, the applicant must aver that they have a bona fide intention to use the mark in commerce, 15 U.S.C.S. § 1051(b)(3)(B), though actual use of the mark is not required at the time of application.

Intent to use means that the applicant has not begun using their trademark in commerce, but they have a bona fide intent to do so within the next three to four years.

(3) Lanham Act's Federal Registration

The federal Lanham Act of 1946 established a federal system for registering, protecting, and regulating trademarks. An applicant files a trademark regulation (either actual use or intent to use) with the USPTO and paying the required fees.

A trademark owner may not use the federal registration symbol "TM" until the mark is actually registered in the U.S. Patent and Trademark Office. Both registered and unregistered trade names and trademarks are protected under the Lanham Act, § 1 et seq., 15 U.S.C. § 1051 et seq.

When proving ownership, federal registration of a trademark constitutes *prima facie* evidence of the validity of the registered mark and of the registrant's exclusive right to use the mark in commerce.

Registration with the Trademark Office gives the owner exclusive rights only in the United States. However, marks may be registered in different countries; a practice that is recommended for companies selling goods and rendering services on the Internet to foreign countries.

The registration of trademarks signals constructive notice of mark ownership, and creates a legal presumption in favor of ownership. Trademark registrants have the right to bring infringement or dilution actions in federal court. However, the

USPTO explains the advantages of owning a federal trademark registration on the Principal Register:

- Public notice of your claim of ownership of the mark;
- A legal presumption of your ownership of the mark and your exclusive right to use the mark nationwide on or in connection with the goods/services listed in the registration;
- The ability to bring an action concerning the mark in federal court;
- The use of the U.S. registration as a basis to obtain registration in foreign countries;
- The ability to record the U.S. registration with the U.S. Customs and Border Protection (CBP) Service to prevent importation of infringing foreign goods;
- The right to use the federal registration symbol ®; and
- Listing in the United States Patent and Trademark Office's online databases.

USPTO, *Trademark FAQs, What Are the Benefits of Federal Trademark Registration?*

Trademark applicants need to consider (1) the mark they want to register, (2) the goods and/or services in connection with which you wish to register the mark, and (3) whether they will be filing the application based on actual existing use of the mark or a *bona fide* intention to use the mark in the future. The USPTO describes the basis for filing as follows:

A trademark application must specify the proper "basis" for filing, and whether there is current use of the mark in commerce or on intent to use the mark in commerce in the future.

In a trademark or service mark application based on use in commerce under § 1(a) of the Trademark Act, 15 U.S.C. § 1051(a), the mark must be in use in commerce on or in connection with all the goods and services listed in the application as of the application filing date. 37 C.F.R. §§ 2.2(k)(1), 2.34(a)(1)(i).

Trademark applications, filed in the USPTO, must include: (1) the name of the applicant, (2) a name and address for correspondence, (3) a clear drawing of the mark, (4) a listing of the goods or services, and (5) the filing fee for at least one class of goods or services.

The federal trademark application must include a statement that the mark is in use in commerce, verified in an affidavit or declaration under 37 C.F.R. § 2.20. If this verified statement is not filed with the original application, it must also allege that the mark was in use in commerce on or in connection with the goods or services listed in the application as of the application filing date. 37 C.F.R. § 2.34(a)(1)(i).

In a trademark or service mark application based on "intent-to-use" under § 1(b) of the Trademark Act, 15 U.S.C. § 1051(b), the applicant typically begins use in commerce after the filing date. The application must include a verified statement that the applicant has a bona fide intention to use the mark in commerce on or in connection with the goods or services listed in the application as of the application filing date. 37 C.F.R. § 2.2(k)(1), § 2.32(a)(5), and § 2.34(a)(2).

The date of first use anywhere is either the date when the goods were first sold or transported or the date when the services were first rendered under the mark, if such use is *bona fide* and in the ordinary course of trade. 15 U.S.C. § 1127.

Under U.S. trademark law, the first person to use a mark in interstate commerce, rather than the first person to register it, has priority. The factors in determining first use include looking to which party: 1) first affixed the mark to a product, 2) name appeared with the trademark, 3) maintained the quality and uniformity of the product, or 4) created the good will associated with a product.

The U.S. Trademark Office publishes approved trademarks on the Principal Register of the United States Patent and Trademark Office (USPTO). A trademark is a brand name. The Trademark Office defines:

> a trademark or service mark includes any word, name, symbol, device, or any combination, used or intended to be used to identify and distinguish the goods/services of one seller or provider from those of others, and to indicate the source of the goods/services.

USPTO, *What Is a Trademark or Service Mark and How Do They Differ From Patents and Copyrights?* (2021).

The Trademark Office permits a company to use the "TM" (trademark) or "SM" (service mark) designation, which signals rights even if it has not registered its marks. However, a company may not use the federal registration symbol "®" while an examination is pending, and must wait until the Trademark Office of the USPTO actually registers the mark.

The term of a federal trademark registration is 10 years and can be renewed indefinitely for 10-year periods. Trademark owners must file an affidavit, or a declaration of continued use, with the USPTO to keep the registration alive between the fifth and sixth year after the date of initial registration. Failure of the registrant to provide the affidavit results in cancellation of the trademark registration. Trademarks may be established by using a mark in commerce, without a federal registration.

Famous trademarks like Coca-Cola will have trademark protection in perpetuity as long as they continue to renew their registration with the USPTO. The two principal rights in a trademark are a federal trademark registration and the right to use the mark. In general, the first party who either uses a mark in commerce or files an application in the trademark office has the ultimate right to register that mark.

(B) THE SPECTRUM OF DISTINCTIVENESS

To qualify as a trademark, the mark must be distinctive; the stronger a mark the more the public remembers it and associates it with the trademark owner's goods and services. J. THOMAS MCCARTHY, 2

MCCARTHY ON TRADEMARKS & UNFAIR COMPETITION § 11:2 (2012).

The strength of the protected mark, "is evaluated in terms of its conceptual strength and commercial strength." *GoTo.com, Inc. v. Walt Disney Co.*, 202 F.3d 1199, 1207 (9th Cir. 2000) "From weakest to strongest, marks are categorized as generic, descriptive, suggestive, and arbitrary or fanciful."

The most distinctive marks—i.e., arbitrary and fanciful marks—receive the most trademark protection, whereas the least distinctive marks—i.e., generic marks—receive no trademark protection. *Pom Wonderful LLC v. Hubbard*, 775 F.3d 1118 (9th Cir. 2014).

To determine whether a proposed mark is protectable, courts ascertain the strength of the mark by placing it into one of four categories of distinctiveness, in ascending order: (1) generic, (2) descriptive, (3) suggestive, or (4) arbitrary or fanciful *Variety Stores, Inc. v. Wal-Mart Stores, Inc.*, 888 F.3d 651 (4th Cir. 2018).

Marks falling into the latter two categories are deemed inherently distinctive and are entitled to protection because their intrinsic nature serves to identify the particular source of a product. In contrast, descriptive terms may be distinctive only upon certain showings of acquired distinctiveness or secondary meaning, whereas generic terms are never distinctive.

The continuum to measure trademark distinctiveness incorporates the following definitions:

> A generic mark is generally a common description of goods and is ineligible for trademark protection. . . . A descriptive mark describes a product's features, qualities or ingredients in ordinary language, and may be protected only if secondary meaning is established. . . . A suggestive mark employs terms, which do not describe but merely suggest the features of the product, requiring the purchaser to use 'imagination, thought, and perception to reach a conclusion as to the nature of goods. . . .' Fanciful or arbitrary marks are eligible for protection without proof of secondary meaning and 'with ease of establishing infringement.'

W.W.W. Pharm. Co. v. Gillette Co., 984 F.2d 567, 572 (2d Cir. 1993).

(C) IMMORAL OR SCANDALOUS MARKS

The Lanham Act has historically barred the registration of marks that consist of or comprise immoral or scandalous matter, or matter which may disparage persons, institutions, beliefs, or national symbols, or bring them into contempt or disrepute (the disparagement provision). 15 U.S.C. § 1052(a). Decision as to whether marks or scandalous or immoral often lack principled distinctions as illustrated by the following examples.

Scandalous & Immoral	*Not Scandalous or Immoral*
Madonna Wine	BUDDA beachwear
Messias Wine	Big Pecker T-Shirts
Bullshit Briefcases	Black Tail Adult Magazines

A disparaging mark " 'dishonor[s] by comparison with what is inferior, slights, deprecates, degrades, or affects or injures by unjust comparison.' " *Pro-Football, Inc. v. Harjo*, 284 F. Supp. 2d 96, 124 (D.D.C. 2003) (denying cancellation of Washington Redskins trademark). "The most publicized 'disparaging' mark controversy in recent years is the cancellation of the Redskin football team's trademark registration because it considers the name and logo disparaging to Native Americans." Jux Law Firm, *Scandalous or Immoral, Disparaging, or Deceptive Marks: Can They Be Registered?* (2014).

STOP THE ISLAMISATION OF AMERICA, Koran wine, Jesus juice, Buddha beachwear, and wife-beater t-shirts are other examples of disparaging marks that have been denied federal trademark registration.

Although disparaging marks are typically denied federal trademark registration, U.S. courts may sometimes find preserving First Amendment rights outweigh barring of a mark in certain circumstances. The U.S. Supreme Court recently ruled that the name of the Asian-American dance rock band, "THE SLANTS" was not disparaging, striking down the disparagement clause of the Lanham Act because it violated the First Amendment's Free Speech Clause.

The case began in 2010 when Simon Tam, the "front man" for the band sought to register the mark THE SLANTS for "Entertainment, namely, live performances by a musical band." *Matal v. Tam*, 137 S.Ct. 1744 (2017).

In June 2017, in a unanimous decision, the United States Supreme Court ruled that the government may not refuse to register potentially offensive names in the Trademark Office. Justice Alito, writing for the Court, ruled that the disparagement clause violates the Free Speech Clause of the First Amendment reasoning that:

> The clause reaches any trademark that disparages any person, group, or institution. It applies to trademarks like the following: 'Down with racists,' 'Down with sexists,' 'Down with homophobes.' . . . The clause is far too broad in other ways as well. The clause protects every person living or dead as well as every institution. Is it conceivable that a trademark saying would disrupt commerce: 'James Buchanan was a disastrous president' or 'Slavery is an evil institution'?

The Court rejected the argument that trademarks are "commercial speech", stating that even commercial speech is not subject to the government's viewpoint discrimination. The Court also rejected the Government's attempt to classify trademark registrations as government speech, which would afford a speaker less First Amendment protection.

Similarly, in *Iancu v. Brunetti*, 139 S.Ct. 2294 (2019), the United States Supreme Court ruled the government may not refuse to register "immoral" or "scandalous" remarks. Justice Kagan, writing for the majority, ruled the Lanham Act's prohibition on the registration of "immoral" or "scandalous" remarks is unconstitutional because it is viewpoint-based discrimination in violation of the Free Speech Clause of the First Amendment.

The Court rejected the government's argument that the provision was viewpoint neutral and refused to treat rejections based on these criteria as examiners' mistakes. In so doing, the Court explained:

> [T]he Lanham Act allows registration of marks when their messages accord with, but not when their messages defy, society's sense of decency or propriety. Put the pair of overlapping terms together and the statute, on its face, distinguishes between two opposed sets of ideas: those aligned with conventional moral standards and those hostile to them; those inducing societal nods of approval and those provoking offense and condemnation.
>
> The statute favors the former, and disfavors the latter. . . . The facial viewpoint bias in the law results in viewpoint-discriminatory application . . . The PTO, for example, asks whether the public would view the mark as

> 'shocking to the sense of truth, decency, or propriety'; 'calling out for condemnation'; 'offensive'; or 'disreputable.'
>
> Using those guideposts, the PTO has refused to register marks communicating 'immoral' or 'scandalous' views about (among other things) drug use, religion, and terrorism. But all the while, it has approved registration of marks expressing more accepted views on the same topics.

Iancu v. Brunetti, 139 S.Ct. 2294, 2296, 2300 (2019).

(D) FUNCTIONAL LIMITS OF TRADEMARKS

Congress adopted the functionality doctrine by explicitly prohibiting trademark registration or protection under the Lanham Act for a functional product. Section 1052(e)(5) prohibits the registration of a mark, which comprises any matter that, as a whole, is functional—meaning it is essential to the use or purpose of the article or it affects the cost or quality of the article.

This doctrine developed as a common law rule prohibiting trade dress or trademark rights in the functional features of a product or its packaging in order to ensure that the proper boundaries are kept between patent law and trademark law.

In *Rosetta Stone Ltd. v. Google, Inc.*, 676 F.3d 144 (4th Cir. 2012), the Fourth Circuit found the functionality doctrine was inapplicable to keywords, reversing the district court's conclusion that Rosetta Stone's trademarked keywords marks were functional product features "or that Rosetta Stone's *own use* of this phrase was somehow functional when it entered into Google's AdWord program." While the keywords have an indexing function, they served a classic trademark purpose identifying goods or services.

§ 11-2. Internet-Related Trademark Claims

Thousands of domain name/trademark disputes have been decided over the past decade. In a domain name infringement action, a trademark owner could typically have causes of action such as: (1) trademark infringement, (2) state and federal dilution, (3) false designation of origin, (4) false advertising, and (5) Anticybersquatting Act remedies. A Texas federal court explains how trademark priority is determined:

> In trademark law, ownership is determined by priority of use. See *Hana Fin., Inc. v. Hana Bank*, 574 U.S. 418, 419 (2015) ("The party who first uses a mark in commerce is said to have priority over other users."). Generally, the first party to use a trademark becomes the holder of the mark and the "senior" user regardless of whether that party registers the mark first. *Rex Real Est. I, L.P.*, 80 F.4th at 844. This is because ownership of trademarks is established by use, not by registration. The senior user of a trademark is entitled to enjoin "junior" users from using the mark, or one that is deceptively similar to it, subject to certain limits. . . The party seeking to prove prior use must do so by a preponderance of the evidence. *Maida's Belts &*

Buckles, Inc. v. Lasting Designs, LLC, 2026 U.S. Dist. LEXIS 50601 (S.D. Tex. Mar. 10, 2026).

The owner of a federally registered trademark has a protectable ownership interest, as required to prevail on a trademark-infringement claim under the Lanham Act. Lanham Trade-Mark Act §§ 32, 43, 15 U.S.C.A. §§ 1114(1)(a), 1125(a).

To prevail on its trademark-infringement claims, Plaintiff must demonstrate: (1) use and valid ownership of the trademarks, (2) that the defendant used the same or similar marks in commerce, and (3) a likelihood of confusion.

To determine whether a defendant's use of a mark is likely to cause confusion, court considers eight factors: "(1) the strength of the mark; (2) proximity or relatedness of the goods; (3) similarity of the marks; (4) evidence of actual confusion; (5) marketing channels used; (6) type of goods and the degree of care likely to be exercised by the purchaser; (7) the defendant's intent in selecting the mark; and (8) the likelihood of expansion of the product lines." *Baron App Inc. v. OPENAI, Inc.*, 2026 WL 447428 (N.D. Calif. Feb. 16, 2026).

These *Sleekcraft* factors were first articulated by the Ninth Circuit in *AMF, Inc. v. Sleekcraft Boats*, 599 F.2d 341 (9th Cir. Cal. June 28, 1979). The Ninth Circuit reversed the district court, ruling that a likelihood of confusion existed between AMF's "Slickcraft" and the defendant's "Sleekcraft" boat marks. The court found that although the defendant acted in good faith, the high similarity and market proximity caused consumer confusion, requiring an injunction. To succeed on a trademark infringement claim under 15 U.S.C. § 1125(a)(1)(A), a plaintiff must demonstrate: (1) ownership of a trademark, and (2) a likelihood of consumer confusion through a balancing of the eight *Sleekcraft* factors. *The Upper Deck Co. v. Pixels, Inc.*, 2026 WL 637336 (S.D. Calif. Mar. 6, 2026).

No one factor is determinative, as the likelihood of confusion test considers the totality of the facts under the circumstances. However, some courts consider the similarity of the marks and the proximity of the goods to be "particularly probative factors." *Stone Creek, Inc. v. Omnia Italian Design, Inc.*, 875 F.3d 426 (9th Cir. 2017).

Under Section 35 of the Lanham Act, a plaintiff seeking damages for counterfeiting and infringement has the option of seeking either actual or statutory damages—but not both. Stephen W. Feingold & Howard S. Hogan, *Unique Online Trademark Issues*, Chapter 7 in STEPHEN FEINGOLD, INTELLECTUAL PROPERTY IN CYBERSPACE (2d ed. 2011).

Internet Trademark Causes of Action

Cause of Action	*Type of Claim*	*Liability Standard*
Trademark Infringement Act, 15 U.S.C. § 1114(1)	Trademark Infringement by incorporating owner's	With the sale of goods, it is likely to cause consumer confusion as to

	trademark in defendant's mark.	the source of those goods or as to the sponsorship or approval of such goods.
Trademark Dilution Revision Act of 2006 (TDRA): 15 U.S.C. § 1125(c)	Dilution of Famous Trademarks by incorporating mark in domain name.	Impairs the mark's distinctiveness, whether or not the mark is used on a competing product or in a way that is likely to cause customer confusion. Must be a famous mark, meeting statutory standards.
False designation of origin and unfair competition: 15 U.S.C. § 1125(a)(1)(A)	False designation of origin by incorporating an owner's trademark in domain name.	False designation origin, use in commerce, causes confusion, mistake, or deception.

False or misleading description or representation: 15 U.S.C. § 1125(a)(1)(B)	False or misleading description of fact, or false *or* misleading statements.	False or misleading statements in commercial advertising.
ACPA: 15 U.S.C. § 1125(d)	Domain names registered in bad faith identical or confusingly similar to a trademark.	Bad faith intent to profit from the mark and registers, traffics in, or uses a domain name that is (A) identical or confusingly similar to a distinctive mark, or (B) dilutes a famous mark.

§ 11-3. Internet-Related Trademark Infringement

(A) DIRECT INFRINGEMENT

To establish trademark infringement under the Lanham Act, a plaintiff must prove: (1) that it owns a valid mark; (2) that the defendant used the mark in commerce and without plaintiff's authorization; (3) that the defendant used the mark (or an imitation of it) in connection with the sale, offering for sale, distribution, or advertising of goods or services; and

(4) that the defendant's use of the mark is likely to confuse consumers. 15 U.S.C. § 1114(1)(a).

Similar elements are required in claims under 15 U.S.C. § 1125(a) for false designation of origin. To state a claim for false designation of origin and false advertising under the Lanham Act, plaintiff must allege that the defendant's use of the plaintiff's mark in a manner in connection with goods or services used in commerce is likely to confuse consumers about the source or sponsorship of the goods or services. Lanham Act, § 43(a), 15 U.S.C. § 1125(a).

A federal cause of action for unfair competition derives from 15 U.S.C. § 1125(a), commonly known as Section 43(a) of the Lanham Act. Distinct categories of federal unfair competition exist under the Lanham Act including passing off and false advertising. A federal cause of action for unfair competition derives from 15 U.S.C. § 1125(a), commonly known as Section 43(a) of the Lanham Act. False advertising is a category of federal unfair competition.

Whether the court calls the violation infringement, unfair competition, or false designation of origin, the test is identical: is there a likelihood of confusion? In general, the more unique or arbitrary a mark, the more protection a court will afford it.

There are two requirements a plaintiff must allege to survive a Fed. R. Civ. P. 12(b)(1) motion to dismiss for lack of subject matter jurisdiction: (1) the trademark violation was in connection with any goods or services, and (2) the defendant used the trademark in commerce. To prevail in a trademark infringement case, plaintiffs must meet a three-prong test: (1) Did the plaintiff own a valid and enforceable mark? (2) Did the defendant cause confusion? and (3) Did the plaintiff use the mark in commerce? Stephen W. Feingold & Howard S. Hogan, *Unique Online Trademark Issues*, Chapter 7 in G. PETER ALBERT, JR. AIPLA, INTELLECTUAL PROPERTY IN CYBERSPACE (New York, New York: Bloomberg BNA, 2d ed. 2011).

The owner of a mark registered with the Patent and Trademark Office can bring a civil action against a person alleged to have used the mark without the owner's consent. 15 U.S.C. § 1114. The Lanham Act specifically prohibits person from reproducing, counterfeiting, copying, or colorably indicating a registered mark, which is likely to cause confusion. A plaintiff claiming infringement of an incontestable mark must show likelihood of consumer confusion as part of the *prima facie* case. 15 U.S.C. § 1115(b).

In *Tiffany v. eBay, Inc.*, 600 F.3d 93 (2d Cir. 2017), the Second Circuit concluded that eBay did not directly infringe on Tiffany's trademark where it resold genuine Tiffany goods. Tiffany argued that some of the goods being sold on eBay were counterfeit, which the Second Circuit explained:

> is not a basis for a claim of direct trademark infringement against eBay, especially inasmuch as it is undisputed that eBay promptly removed all listings that Tiffany challenged as counterfeit and took affirmative steps to identify and remove illegitimate Tiffany goods.

The Second Circuit declined to impose liability on eBay because it reasoned that "eBay cannot guarantee the genuineness of all of the purported Tiffany products offered on its website" and this "would unduly inhibit the lawful resale of genuine Tiffany goods."

In *RVG Holdings LLC v. Hangzhou Taohaowu Tech. Co.*, 2026 WL 685952 (S.D.N.Y. Mar. 11, 2026), RVRG contended that AllChinaBuy defendants operated a website that allowed consumers to purchase counterfeit versions of RVRG's products. RVRG alleged that their actions constitute direct trademark infringement and false designation of origin in violation of the Lanham Act. The court dissolved the preliminary injunction it issued concluding that RVRG was not likely to succeed on the merits of its claims.

The New York federal court concluded that it was not likely that RVRG would be successful in proving that AllChinaBuy was liable for direct infringement. Since like eBay and Amazon, they merely facilitated sales for independent vendors and thus escaped Lanham Act liability. The court followed another court decision, *King Spider LLC v. Panda (Hong Kong) Technology Co.*, 24-CV-2668, 2025 WL 89123 (S.D.N.Y. Jan. 14, 2025):

> [A]nother court in this District was asked to answer the same "use in commerce" question, in the same posture, concerning a very similar defendant. King Spider involved trademark infringement claims brought by a clothing company against a Chinese company,

Pandabuy, with the same business model as AllChinaBuy. Judge Clark entered a preliminary injunction against the defendants, finding that the plaintiffs had demonstrated a likelihood of success on the merits of their claims. However, following the defendant's appearance, Judge Clarke granted a motion to dissolve the preliminary injunction. Central to that decision was Judge Clarke's finding that Pandabuy did not "exercise sufficient control over the creation, manufacture, or sale of offending goods to be considered akin to a 'seller' or 'manufacturer' to whom Lanham Act liability applies." Judge Clarke based that finding on the facts that Pandabuy did not manufacture any products, maintain any inventory, or otherwise hold itself out to consumers as the seller of the goods at issue. Instead, Pandabuy acted more like a "passive facilitator" by connecting "consumers with third-party products" that consumers then purchased and received via third-party purchasing agents and warehouses with whom Pandabuy contracted.

The New York federal court concluded that AllChinaBuy's role in the distribution process is indistinguishable from that played by Pandabuy:

> First, it is undisputed that AllChinaBuy does not create or manufacture any of the offending goods. The goods are manufactured and marketed by third parties over whom AllChinaBuy has no control. Additionally, like Pandabuy, AllChinaBuy maintains no inventory

and collects money only via a fee on shipping, contrary to the general practices of a seller, who would typically adjust prices in relation to the value of the goods in question.

The court dissolved the preliminary injunction because AllChinaBuy was not akin to a seller.

In *Louis Vuitton Malletier S.A. v. Sunny Merchandise Corp.* 97 F. Supp. 3d 485 (S.D. N.Y. 2024), Louis Vuitton brought a lawsuit against Sunny Merchandise Corp and other defendants asserting various federal and state trademark claims.

Louis Vuitton challenged Sunny's use of the marks "LOUIS VALENTIN" and "LOUIS•V" on its sunglasses, as well as Sunny's use of several designs that Louis Vuitton believes are confusingly similar to its Damier, LV, and Flower Marks. Sunny, which was founded by Gene Tsai and his wife, imports and sells inexpensive sunglasses made in China. The court Sunny and other Chinese defendants violated Louis Vuitton's trademarks:

When viewed holistically in light of the ultimate question of confusion, the analysis comes out even more strongly in favor of granting Louis Vuitton's partial motion for summary judgment on its infringement claims.

Of particular importance to the Court in reaching this conclusion was the strength of Louis Vuitton's mark, the likelihood of confusion due to the apparent similarity between the two marks, and, underlying all this, Sunny's apparent bad faith in adopting the

LOUIS VALENTIN and LOUIS • V marks. Summary judgment in favor of Louis Vuitton is appropriate on the strength of these factors alone.

Moreover, other factors, including the degree of similarity between the two marks, the competitive proximity of the products or services, and the likelihood that Louis Vuitton will "bridge the gap," also favor Louis Vuitton. The court concluded that the evidence demonstrated "that Sunny intentionally attempted to appropriate the ubiquitous LOUIS VUITTON mark through the use of its confusingly similar LOUIS • V and LOUIS VALENTIN marks."

(B) SECONDARY TRADEMARK INFRINGEMENT

(1) Contributory Infringement

Contributory infringement occurs where a service provider "continue[s] to supply its services to one who it knew or had reason to know was engaging in trademark infringement" and has "direct control and monitoring of the instrumentality used by a third party to infringe." *Louis Vuitton Malletier, S.A. v. Akanoc Solutions, Inc.*, 658 F.3d 936, 942 (9th Cir. 2011)

To be liable for contributory trademark infringement, a defendant must have (1) "intentionally induced" the primary infringer to infringe, or (2) continued to supply an infringing product to an infringer with knowledge that the infringer is mislabeling the particular product supplied. "The tests for secondary trademark infringement are even more difficult to satisfy than those required to find secondary copyright infringement." *Perfect 10, Inc. v. Visa Int'l Serv. Ass'n,* 494 F.3d 788, 806 (9th Cir. 2007).

To support a contributory trademark dilution claim, plaintiff must show that defendants either encouraged others to dilute plaintiff's trademark, or continued to supply their product to one whom it knows or has reason to know is engaging in trademark infringement. Lanham Act, § 43(c), 15 U.S.C. § 1125(c).

When the primary infringer supplies a service rather than a product, a court must consider the extent of control exercised by the defendant over the third party's means of infringement. The knowledge requirement is objective and is satisfied where the defendant knows or has reason to know of the infringing activity. *Lockheed Martin Corp. v. Network Solutions, Inc.*, 194 F.3d 980 (9th Cir. 1999).

Any liability for contributory infringement will depend upon whether or not the contributing party intended to participate in the infringement, or actually knew about the infringing activities. *Inwood Labs., LLC,* 456 U.S. 844 (1982). There can be no contributory infringement as a matter of law where a plaintiff's direct claim of trademark infringement fails. *Antares Pharma Inc. v. Gordon Silver, Inc.*, 2025 WL 3012736 (D. Del. Oct. 28, 2025).

(2) Vicarious Liability

Vicarious liability occurs where "the defendant and the infringer have an apparent or actual partnership . . . or exercise joint ownership or control over the infringing product." *Perfect 10, Inc. v. Visa Intern. Service Ass'n*, 494 F.3d 788, 807 (9th Cir. 2007). Vicarious liability for trademark infringement requires a finding that the defendant and the infringer have an apparent or actual partnership, have authority to bind one another in transactions with third parties or exercise joint ownership or control over the infringing product.

In *Perfect 10, Inc.*, 494 F.3d 788 (9th Cir. 2007), the Ninth Circuit refused to find Visa vicariously liable for its role in enabling payment for website access to content violating the copyrights and trademarks of a third party magazine publisher. The appeals court uncovered no affirmative acts by the defendants suggesting to third parties that they should infringe the publisher's trademarks.

The Ninth Circuit reasoned that even if the defendants allowed the infringing merchants to use their logos, trade name, or trademarks, they would not be liable for false advertising because they had no duty to investigate the truth of the statements made by others. Moreover, the court found Visa did not encourage the improper conduct at issue; they merely processed credit card payments.

§ 11-4. Trademark Dilution Revision Act of 2006

Federal dilution claims only extend to famous marks, those marks with such powerful consumer associations that even non-competing uses can impinge on their value. Under the statute, "a mark is famous if it is widely recognized by the general consuming public of the United States as a designation of source of the goods or services of the mark's owner." 15 U.S.C. § 1125(c)(2)(A).

Federal dilution claims require the plaintiff to show that its mark is famous and distinctive, that the defendant began using its mark in commerce after the plaintiff's mark became famous and distinctive, and that the defendant's mark is likely to dilute the plaintiff's mark.

Congress enacted the Trademark Dilution Revision Act of 2006 that displaced the FTDA of 1996. For § 1125(c)(1) to apply, the defendant must have "commence[d]" a diluting use of the plaintiff's mark *after* the point at which the mark became famous.

The TDRA amended the Lanham Act to render one liable to the owner of a trademark who, with "a bad faith intent to profit from that mark," "registers, traffics in or uses a domain name" that is either identical or confusingly similar to a "distinctive" mark or is identical, confusingly similar or dilutive of a "famous mark." 15 U.S.C. § 1125(c).

To state a *prima facie* dilution claim under the TDRA, the plaintiff must show the following:

(1) that the plaintiff owns a famous mark that is distinctive;

(2) that the defendant has commenced using a mark in commerce that allegedly is diluting the famous mark;

(3) that a similarity between the defendant's mark and the famous mark gives rise to an association between the marks; and

(4) that the association is likely to impair the distinctiveness of the famous mark or likely to harm the reputation of the famous mark.

15 U.S.C. § 1125(c).

(A) BASICS OF FEDERAL DILUTION CLAIMS

To prevail on a trademark dilution claim under the Trademark Dilution Revision Act (TDRA) of 2006, 15 U.S.C. § 1125(c), a plaintiff must show that: (1) the mark is famous and distinctive; (2) the defendant is making use of the mark in commerce; (3) the defendant's use began after the mark became famous; and (4) the defendant's use of the mark is likely to cause dilution by blurring or dilution by tarnishment.

In *River Light V., L.P. v. Tanaka*, 2018 WL 5778234 (S.D. Fla. Nov. 2, 2018), the court found that a counterfeiter diluted Tory Burch's famous trademarked purses, selling fakes on the Internet.

The court described the difference between blurring and tarnishment:

> Dilution causes harm by removing the reputation of the trademark owner from the owner's control. Thus, a trademark owner can prove dilution of the distinctive quality of its mark through use of an identical or similar mark by another.

(1) Dilution by Tarnishment

Tarnishment in the trademark sense occurs when a famous mark is linked to products of poor quality or is portrayed in an unwholesome manner. "Dilution by tarnishment" is defined as the "association arising from the similarity between a mark or trade name and a famous mark that harms the reputation of the famous mark." 15 U.S.C. § 1125(c)(2)(C).

The Trademark Dilution Revision Act of 2006 (TDRA) applies when a website tarnishes a famous trademark by incorporating the mark in a domain name. 15 U.S.C. § 1125(c).

A domain name can tarnish a famous trademark, as in *Mattel, Inc. v. Jcom, Inc.*, 1998 WL 766711 (S.D.N.Y. Sept. 11 1996), where the court held that the use of the Barbie trademark by an adult entertainment web site, combined with particular fonts and color schemes, tarnished the mark.

The TDRA amended the Trademark Act of 1946 to describe the factors determining whether a mark is "distinctive and famous," 15 U.S.C. § 1125(c)(1), and defines "dilution" as "the lessening of the capacity of a famous mark to identify and distinguish goods or services," 15 U.S.C. § 1127. The TDRA amended Section 43(c) of the Lanham Act to enable trademark owners of famous trademarks to file a federal anti-dilution action.

This 2006 amendment to the Lanham Act overrules the Supreme Court's ruling in *Moseley v. Victoria Secret Catalogue, Inc.*, 537 U.S. 418 (2003), which interpreted the prior federal Anti-Dilution Act to require prevailing plaintiffs to prove actual dilution.

In *Moseley*, the Court settled a circuit court split as to whether plaintiffs had to prove actual dilution in a federal dilution action. The TDRA overturned *Moseley* when it provided relief for "likely," as opposed to actual, dilution. 15 U.S.C. § 1125(c)(1).

To prevail on a trademark dilution claim under the TDRA, 15 U.S.C. § 1125(c) a plaintiff must show:

> (1) the mark is famous and distinctive; (2) the defendant is making use of the mark in commerce; (3) the defendant's use began after the mark became famous; and (4) the defendant's use of the mark is likely to cause dilution by blurring or dilution by tarnishment.

UPS filed suit against the United Pot Smokers for federal trademark dilution and other federal and state trademark claims. UPS alleges the group along with UPS420, THCPLant, and Does 1–10 is using the UPS logo to deceptively brand and market its own company, a marijuana delivery business. UPS said the "intentional use of marketing and branding elements confusingly similar to UPS's trademarks." *Today's Pickup: UPS Sues Pot Delivery Company; War On Detention Announced*, FREIGHTWAVES (Feb. 21, 2019).

Dilution by tarnishment occurs where the plaintiff's mark is linked with something unsavory or degrading. This category includes things like X-rated movies, hard-core pornography, revenge porn websites, crude humor, and pirated goods.

(2) Dilution by Blurring

Blurring weakens the mark's ability to evoke the first product in the minds of consumers. Many courts describe blurring as a whittling away of a mark's distinctiveness. The TDRA defines "dilution by blurring" as the association arising from the similarity between a mark or trade name and a famous mark that impairs the distinctiveness of the famous mark.

Blurring weakens the mark's ability to evoke the first product in the minds of consumers. Many courts describe blurring as a whittling away of a mark's distinctiveness. In determining whether a mark or trade name is likely to cause dilution by blurring, the court may consider all relevant factors, including the following:

(i) The degree of similarity between the mark or trade name and the famous mark.

(ii) The degree of inherent or acquired distinctiveness of the famous mark.

> (iii) The extent to which the owner of the famous mark is engaging in substantially exclusive use of the mark.
>
> (iv) The degree of recognition of the famous mark.
>
> (v) Whether the user of the mark or trade name intended to create an association with the famous mark.
>
> (vi) Any actual association between the mark or trade name and the famous mark.

15 U.S.C. § 1125(c)(2)(B).

The Ninth Circuit explains the essence of blurring as the weakening of the ability of a trademark:

> to evoke the first product in the minds of consumers. 'For example, Tylenol snowboards, Netscape sex shops, and Harry Potter dry cleaners would all weaken the 'commercial magnetism' of these marks and diminish their ability to evoke their original associations.'

Levi Strauss & Co. v. Abercrombie & Fitch Trading Co., 633 F.3d 1158 (9th Cir. 2011).

In *H-D U.S.A., LLC v. SunFrog, LLC*, 311 F. Supp. 3d 1000 (W.D. Wisc. 2018), court found that SunFrog was liable for dilution by blurring:

> 'Dilution by blurring' is the 'association arising from the similarity between a mark or trade name and a famous mark that impairs the distinctiveness of the famous mark.' 15 U.S.C. § 1125(c)(2)(B). It occurs when consumers see

> the plaintiff's mark used on a plethora of different goods and services, raising the possibility that the mark will lose its ability to serve as a unique identifier of the plaintiff's product The Lanham Act sets out a non-exclusive list of factors for courts to consider to determine whether dilution by blurring is likely to occur: (1) the similarities between the marks; (2) the degree of inherent or acquired distinctiveness of the famous mark; (3) the extent to which the plaintiff is engaging in substantially exclusive use of the famous mark; (4) the degree of recognition of the famous mark; (5) the defendant's intent to create association with the famous mark; and (6) any actual association between the marks. 15 U.S.C. § 1125(c)(2)(B).
>
> Here, SunFrog used identical or materially indistinguishable variations of the Famous Marks, those marks are distinctiveness and famous, and SunFrog intended to create an association with the Famous Marks to trade on Harley-Davidson's fame and goodwill.

In their analysis, the federal court found Harley-Davidson's trademarks to be famous and diluted by a website selling counterfeit products:

> To be famous, a mark must be widely recognized by the general consuming public of the United States as a designation of source of the goods or services of the mark's owner. 15 U.S.C. § 1125(c)(2)(A). Courts may consider all relevant factors in determining fame, including: (1) the

> duration, extent, and geographic reach of advertising and publicity of the mark; (2) the amount, volume, and geographic extent of sales of goods and services offered under the mark; (3) the extent of actual recognition of the mark; and (4) whether the mark is registered. Importantly, fame for purposes of dilution is considered in relation to the American general public, not a potential niche market for a product.

The court found Harley-Davidson marks to be famous observing:

> Harley-Davidson has owned some of the Famous Marks for over 100 years and has earned billions in sales after spending millions in promotional efforts. In short, the two cases are not in the same league. Instead, this case is far closer to *Visa Int'l Serv. Ass'n v. JSL Corp.*, 590 F. Supp. 2d 1306, 1315 (D. Nev. 2008), where the court found that decades of worldwide promotion and over a trillion dollars in sales volume rendered the VISA mark famous. Thus, the Court finds that the Famous Marks are famous as a matter of law.

The court found that SunFrog's cheap knock-offs tarnished Harley-Davidson's marks:

> Here, tarnishment has occurred in several ways. First, SunFrog's cheaply made, knockoff products fall well below the quality standards that Harley-Davidson has long set for its licensees, harming its reputation with the purchasing public. . . . As the Seventh Circuit

> has explained, '[i]f [a] seller provides an inconsistent level of quality, or reduces quality below what consumers expect from earlier experience, that reduces the value of the trademark.'
>
> Second, even if SunFrog's products met Harley-Davidson's quality control standards, many of them would not meet its content criteria. Many of the offending products include vulgar, political, or religious content that Harley-Davidson would not have approved to appear on licensed products. Others modify or mutilate the H-D Marks, or display marks that Harley-Davidson does not license, which again Harley-Davidson would not have approved of. There is perhaps no greater tarnishment of a famous brand than using it in an unauthorized way that likely will offend potential purchasers of genuine goods.

(B) TDRA REMEDIES

The remedy under the TDRA is limited to an injunction, "unless the person against whom the injunction is sought willfully intended to trade on the owner's reputation or to cause dilution of the famous mark." 15 U.S.C. § 1125(c)(2). Under the FTDA, the owner of a famous mark may obtain injunctive relief against any "person who, *at any time after* the owner's mark has become famous, *commences use* of a mark . . . in commerce that is likely to cause dilution." 15 U.S.C. § 1125(c)(1).

(C) TDRA DEFENSES

In response to First Amendment, or associational policy concerns, the TDRA exempts certain uses of a famous mark. TDRA defenses include the following: (1) the mark is not famous, (2) the use is classified as a parody, (3) noncommercial use of the mark, (4) fair use of a famous mark is permitted in comparative advertisements, and (5) dilution is not likely.

The TDRA expressly excludes from its reach "[a]ny fair use, including a nominative or descriptive fair use, or facilitation of such fair use, of a famous mark by another person other than as a designation of source for the person's own goods or services." 15 U.S.C. § 1125(c)(3)(A).

In *Hormel Foods Corp. v. Jim Henson Prods.*, 73 F.3d 497 (2d Cir. 1996), the Second Circuit observed that a successful parody "tends to increase public identification" of the famous mark with its source. In Jim Henson's film, *Muppet Treasure Island*, the Spa'am is the high priest of a tribe of wild boars that worships Miss Piggy as its Queen Sha Ka La Ka La.

The court observed that, "[a]lthough the name 'Spa'am' is mentioned only once in the entire movie, Henson hopes to poke a little fun at Hormel's famous luncheon meat by associating its processed, gelatinous block with a humorously wild beast." Hormel contended, "Even comic association with an unclean 'grotesque' boar will call into question the purity and high quality of its meat product." The Second Circuit noted that the district court:

> found no evidence that Spa'am was unhygienic. At worst, he might be described as 'untidy.' Moreover, by now Hormel should be inured to any such ridicule. Although SPAM is in fact made from pork shoulder and ham meat, and the name itself supposedly is a portmanteau word for spiced ham, countless jokes have played off the public's unfounded suspicion that SPAM is a product of less than savory ingredients.

The federal anti-dilution statute specifically provides comparative advertising and parody as examples of non-dilutive fair uses. 15 U.S.C. § 1125(c)(3)(A)(i) & (ii). Just as with any trademark action, a defendant may assert a right to use a trademark in a news commentary or a comparative advertisement. Fair use is a statutory defense under the FTDA.

§ 11-5. Anticybersquatting Act of 1999

The Anticybersquatting Consumer Protection Act (ACPA) is the principal tool used by trademark owners to reclaim domain names containing their trademarks or trade names from cybersquatters. The ACPA, 15 U.S.C. § 1125(d), creates civil liability for someone who registers, traffics in, or uses a domain name with a bad faith intent to profit from the protected mark of another party.

The ACPA, which amended the Lanham Act, addresses the: (1) registration, use, or trafficking in, a domain name, (2) that is identical or confusingly similar to a distinctive or famous trademark, (3) with a bad-faith intent to profit from the mark.

Under the ACPA, a person is liable for "cybersquatting":

> if, without regard to the goods or services of the parties, that person: (i) has a bad faith intent to profit from that mark; and (ii) registers, traffics in, or uses a domain name that—(I) in the case of a mark that is distinctive at the time of registration of the domain name, is identical or confusingly similar to that mark.

15 U.S.C. § 1125(d)(1)(A).

The ACPA provides a remedy for cybersquatting when:

> a person other than the trademark holder registers the domain name of a well-known trademark and then attempts to profit from this by either ransoming the domain name back to the trademark holder or by using the domain name to divert business from the trademark holder to the domain name holder.

beIN Media Group LLC v. bein.ae et al., 2019 WL 1129153 (S.D. Cal. Mar. 11, 2019).

> The elements to bring a cybersquatting claim, as defined by the ACPA, are (1) the registration, use, or trafficking in, a domain name, (2) that is identical or confusingly similar to a distinctive or famous trademark, (3) with a bad faith intent

to profit from the mark. 15 U.S.C. § 1125(d)(1)(A)(ii).

In *beIN Media,* the court found that the trademark owner was entitled to default judgment reasoning:

> Here, Plaintiff alleged and established that it holds several U.S. Trademarks to the word 'BEIN' in different classes of goods and services . . . Registration of a trademark with the PTO is *prima facie* evidence that the mark is distinctive and enforceable. Thus, the Court finds that Plaintiff has sufficiently alleged that its marks is distinctive. . . . Further, it was alleged that the BEIN and beIN marks are used in the offending <bein._> domain names.
>
> It also alleged that each of the offending <bein._> domain names are registered to Zicha, incorporate Plaintiff's trademarked name in its entirety, they do not contain any variation of Zicha's full name, Honza Jan Zicha. Although it not clear that the <bein._> domain names have ever been used for any bona fide commercial or noncommercial uses, the FAC alleges the domain pages have no substantive uses, with some featuring the words 'beIN.com will be back soon' and 'something new and awesome coming soon.' Finally, Zicha's offer to sell the <bein._> domain names to Plaintiff is itself, 'the hallmark of a violation of the ACPA and a criterion expressly . . .' Therefore, the Court finds these allegations sufficient for a finding of bad faith.

Therefore, accepting Plaintiff's allegations as true, the Court finds that Plaintiff has sufficiently alleged a substantive claim for cybersquatting under 15 U.S.C. § 1125(d).

In *Chanel, Inc. v. bestaaachanel.com*, 2019 WL 451174 (S.D. Fla. Feb. 5, 2019), Chanel established a cause of action for cybersquatting, pursuant to the ACPA, 15 U.S.C. § 1125(d), in a default judgment against counterfeiters. The court stated:

> As admitted by default, and established by the evidence submitted, at least one Defendant has acted with the bad-faith intent to profit from at least one of the Chanel Marks and the goodwill associated with the Chanel Marks by registering the Subject Domain Name identified on Schedule 'B' attached to Plaintiff's Motion (the 'Cybersquatted Subject Domain Name'). The Cybersquatted Subject Domain Name incorporates at least one of the Chanel Marks in its entirety, surrounded by descriptive or generic terms, rendering the domain name nearly identical to at least one of the Chanel Marks.

The *Chanel* court also noted that the:

> ACPA expressly empowers the Court to order the forfeiture or cancellation of the domain name or the transfer of the domain name to the owner of the mark. 15 U.S.C. § 1125(d)(1)(C); *Victoria's Cyber Secret Ltd. P'ship v. Secret Catalogue, Inc.*, 161 F. Supp. 2d 1339, 1356 (S.D. Fla. 2001). Accordingly, Plaintiff is entitled to the transfer and ownership of Defendant's Cybersquatted

Subject Domain Name because it is confusingly similar to at least one of the Chanel Marks.

The ACPA gave Chanel the right to elect "to recover actual damages or statutory damages of not less than $1,000.00 and not more than $100,000.00 per domain name, as the court considers just. 15 U.S.C. § 1117(d)." The Plaintiff elected statutory damages, and respectfully requested an award in the amount of $10,000.00. The court found this amount reasonable and awarded statutory damages.

(A) ELEMENTS OF ACPA CLAIMS

The Anticybersquatting Consumer Protection Act (ACPA) prohibits "cybersquatters" from registering Internet domain names that are identical or confusingly similar to registered service marks and trademarks. 15 U.S.C. § 1125(d)(1). The prohibition contained in § 1125(d)(1) applies when a domain name is identical or confusingly similar to a mark that is distinctive "at the time of registration of the domain name."

To prevail on an ACPA claim, a plaintiff must prove the following:

(1) The defendant registered, trafficked in, or used a domain name;

(2) The domain name is identical or confusingly similar to a protected mark owned by the plaintiff; and

(3) The defendant acted 'with bad faith intent to profit from that mark.'

Gizmo Beverages, Inc. v. Park, 2019 WL 141461 (C.D. Cal. Jan. 9, 2019).

The court in Gizmo Beverages noted that a finding of bad faith is an essential element to find an ACPA violation:

> The ACPA enumerates nine nonexclusive factors for courts to consider in determining whether bad faith exists. 15 U.S.C. § 1125(d)(1)(B)(i). The use of the listed criteria is permissive, *Virtual Works, Inc. v. Volkswagen of Am., Inc.*, 238 F.3d 264, 269 (4th Cir. 2001), and 'the most important grounds for finding bad faith are the unique circumstances of the case,' *Interstellar Starship,* 304 F.3d at 946 (quotation omitted). 'Bad faith intent . . . shall not be found in any case in which the court determines that the person believed and had reasonable grounds to believe that the use of the domain name was a fair use or otherwise lawful.' 15 U.S.C. § 1125(d)(1)(B)(ii).

The *Gizzo Beverage* court found the defendant was not liable for an ACPA violation stating:

> Here, Plaintiff argued that the 'bad faith' prong was met by Defendants' filing a claim for arbitration, which Plaintiff infers was an attempt to use the domain names as leverage.
>
> . . . The Court finds Defendants did not use control over the domains here to gain leverage over Plaintiffs in a business dispute and did not otherwise act in bad faith. As a result, Plaintiff has not met its burden under the ACPA.

Gizmo Beverages, Inc. v. Park, 2019 WL 141461 at *9 (C.D. Cal. Jan. 9, 2019).

(B) ACPA SAFE HARBOR

The ACPA recognizes a safe harbor provision for a defendant who acted in good faith. If "the court determines that the person believed and had reasonable grounds to believe that the use of the domain name was a fair use or otherwise lawful," then the defendant will not be held liable under the ACPA. 15 U.S.C. § 1125(d)(1)(B)(ii).

> Both the Anticybersquatting Consumer Protection Act (ACPA) and the Uniform Domain Name Resolution Policy, paragraph 4(c)(i–iii) (UDRP) prescribe safe harbor defenses, but the ACPA provides a defense not expressly found in the UDRP: bad faith 'shall not be found in any case in which the court determines that the person believed and had reasonable grounds to believe that the use of the domain name was a fair use or otherwise lawful.'

15 U.S.C. § 1125(d)(1)(B)(ii). UDRP Commentaries, *Safe Harbor Under the ACPA: Reasonable Grounds for Believing Use Not Unlawful* (Mar. 12, 2013).

In *ZP No. 314, LLC v. ILM Capital, LLC,* 335 F. Supp. 3d 1242 (S.D. Ala. 2018), the court found that the defendant did not qualify for the ACPA provision because the defendants' re-registration of the subject domain names in March 2017 and May 2018 constitutes an actionable offense under the ACPA.

In *McAllister Olivarius v. Mermel*, 298 F. Supp. 3d 661 (S.D.N.Y. 2018), a disgruntled client of a law firm registered the domain name mcallisterolivariustruth.com in order to divert potential clients and others seeking information about the firm. The former client threatened to publish allegedly damaging documents about plaintiff on the website. The law firm filed an ACPA action and the court found that the safe harbor was not available to the former client:

> Mermel argues that because he 'believed that he had the right to speak the truth,' . . . his use of plaintiff's mark is protected by the ACPA's safe harbor provision and the First Amendment. . . . However, this defense is not intended to create a loophole that could swallow the Act by allowing a domain name holder to evade liability merely by putting up a seemingly innocent site under an infringing domain name.

J. THOMAS MCCARTHY, MCCARTHY ON TRADEMARKS § 25:78 (4th ed. 2004).

"A defendant who acts even partially in bad faith in registering a domain name is not, as a matter of law, entitled to benefit from the Act's safe harbor provision." *Mermel*, 298 F. Supp. 3d at 675–76. The court also noted that:

> even if Mermel's blackmail did warrant First Amendment protection, courts have held that the First Amendment does not protect the use of a trademark in a domain name that creates a

likelihood of confusion as to the source or sponsorship of the attached website.

(C) *IN REM* JURISDICTION

The ACPA allows a trademark owner to file an *in rem* civil action against a domain name and provides instructions on how to provide sufficient notice of such an action. Specifically, the ACPA provides that service of process in an *in rem* action may be accomplished by sending notice of the alleged violation and intent to proceed under the ACPA to the registrant of the domain name at the postal and e-mail addresses provided by the registrant to the registrar, and by publishing notice of the action as the court may direct promptly after filing the action. 15 U.S.C. § 1125(d)(2)(A) and (B).

In *Blackshore Properties Inc. v. EQN.com*, 2019 WL 338884 (E.D. Va. Jan. 28, 2019), Blackshore filed an *in rem* action against two defendants: John Doe (Doe), an unknown individual who is alleged to have unlawfully hijacked plaintiff's domain name; and EQN.com, the domain name in question. The court entered a default judgment against EQN.com and ordered that the domain name EQN.com be returned to plaintiff.

Blackshore acquired the domain name EQN.com in May 2011 and transferred the domain name to the registrar Enom, Inc. While plaintiff's Enom account was protected by a user name and password, Doe managed to gain unauthorized access to the account and transferred the registration for EQN.com to 22.cn, a registrar commonly used in domain name theft schemes. Plaintiff did not authorize or know of the transfer that gave Doe control over the domain name.

Blackshore filed suit against Doe and EQN.com (together, "defendants") in October 2018, asserting *in rem* claims against EQN.com under the ACPA, a state-law quiet title action, as well as other individual claims against Doe under state and federal law.

Neither EQN.com nor Doe filed a responsive pleading within the 21-day deadline, nor to date neither of the defendants have entered an appearance. The court entered judgments against them, ordering the transfer of the domain name back to Blackshore, the rightful owner.

In *9349–9176 Quebec Inc. v. manyvids.to,* 2019 WL 1095821 (N.D. Cal. Jan 14, 2019), a Canadian corporation, used the "MANYVIDS" trademark in connection with selling pornography online. The defendant "www.manyvids.to" was an X-rated website owned by an unknown person or entity, registered through the nation of Tonga's domain name registry services located in the Northern District of California.

The defendant's website displayed content owned or licensed by MANYVIDS, including videos containing its watermark. The court found the defendant liable for bad faith cybersquatting:

> Plaintiff alleges that it owns the domain names 'www.manyvids.com' and 'www.manyvids.net' which it runs as online adult content sites

> featuring its copyrighted videos. The domain name 'www.manyvids.to,' which is not affiliated with Plaintiff, was registered after Plaintiff registered its sites, and is used to run an adult content website that looks and operates like Plaintiff's site, and even includes Plaintiff's copyrighted videos.
>
> Thus, Plaintiff sufficiently pleads facts to establish that the infringing domain names are confusingly similar to Plaintiff's lawfully owned marks. Plaintiff also sufficiently pleads facts to establish bad faith, based on the website's apparent design to divert Plaintiff's customers.
>
> There are no facts in the complaint suggesting that the owner of 'www.manyvids.to' had intellectual property rights in the domain name, that the owner had a prior use of the name in connection with a bona fide offering of goods, or that the owner had reasonable grounds to believe that the use of the domain name was a fair use or otherwise lawful. Accordingly, the second and third factors weigh in favor of entry of default judgment.

The court ordered the Tonga registrar of the domain name "www.manyvids.to" to transfer that domain name to the plaintiff immediately. The court granted the plaintiff's motion for default judgment, along with an injunction requiring the domain name "www.manyvids.to" to be transferred to MANYVIDS, but denied its request for attorney's fees.

(D) ACPA REMEDIES

The ACPA provides, in lieu of actual damages and lost profits, for the award of statutory damages of a "just" amount, ranging from $1,000 to $100,000 per violation. 15 U.S.C. § 1117(d).

§ 11-6. Trademark Law Defenses

(A) NOMINATIVE FAIR USE

In order to assert a successful fair use defense to a trademark infringement claim, the defendant must prove three elements: that the use was made (1) other than as a mark, (2) in a descriptive sense, and (3) in good faith. 15 U.S.C. § 1115(b)(4). To qualify under nominative fair use, there are three requirements. First, the product or service in question must not be readily identifiable without use of the trademark.

Second, the defendant may only use as much of the mark as is reasonably necessary to identify the product or service. Third, the defendant must not do anything in conjunction with the mark that would suggest sponsorship or endorsement by the trademark holder.

The nominative fair use analysis allows a defendant to use the plaintiff's mark to describe the plaintiff's product, so long as the goal is for the defendant to describe her own product.

A computer repair shop, for example, can advertise that it fixes Dell laptops even though "Dell" is a registered trademark. In *New Kids On The Block v. News America Publishing, Inc.*, 971 F.2d 302 (9th

Cir. 1992), the Ninth Circuit adopted a nominative fair use test:

> First, the product or service in question must be one not readily identifiable without use of the trademark, second, only so much of the mark or marks may be used as is reasonably necessary to identify the product or service, and third, the user must do nothing that would, in conjunction with the mark, suggest sponsorship or endorsement by the trademark holder.

Fair use also enables comparative advertising and the use of another's trademark in a manner such as the Pepsi Challenge, which featured taste tests between Coca-Cola and Pepsi in malls around the country in the 1980s.

(B) FIRST AMENDMENT IN CYBERSPACE

Fan Sites, rogue sites, or gripe sites that mention trademarks in the course of criticizing companies are generally protected by the First Amendment unless a court finds that those sites are deceptive or create consumer confusion. Gripe sites must make it clear that they are not affiliated with trademarks.

In *Bihari v. Gross*, 119 F. Supp. 2d 309 (S.D.N.Y. 2000), the court found a "Gripe Site" that was critical of the plaintiff's interior design work did not violate Marianne Bihari's trademark because no reasonable consumer would believe that the plaintiff or her company, Bihari Interiors, sponsored the site.

The court also found that the "Gripe Site" was not diverting users from the Bihari Interior site.

Companies will find it difficult to enjoin websites critical of their goods and services that have become ubiquitous on the Internet.

In the early years of the Internet, trademark owners often won lawsuits against domain name registrants who incorporated their trade names or marks. An early example of such a complaint occurs in, *Bally Total Fitness Holding Corp. v. Faber*, 29 F. Supp. 2d 1161 (C.D. Cal. 1998), where a critic of the chain of health clubs set up an anti-Bally website entitled, "Bally's sucks."

Bally filed suit for trademark dilution, stating that the defendant was using its trademarks in an unauthorized manner. The federal court in California granted summary judgment in favor of Faber, reasoning, "no reasonable person would think Bally's is affiliated with or endorses [the anti-Bally site]." The court also found "fair use" in the anti-Bally site's use of Bally's intellectual property.

(C) TRADEMARK PARODIES

A parody is a "simple form of entertainment conveyed by juxtaposing the irreverent representation of the trademark with the idealized image created by the mark's owners." *L.L. Bean, Inc. v. Drake Publishers, Inc.*, 811 F.2d 26 (1st Cir. 1987).

In *Lyons Partnership v. Giannoulas*, 179 F.3d 384 (5th Cir. 1999), the Fifth Circuit ruled that the Ted Giannoulas creation of the sports mascot a parody. The Famous Chicken stepping on a Barney the dinosaur lookalike constituted a parody protectable by the First Amendment of the U.S. Constitution. A parody makes a trademark the brunt of its joke, or satirical message, and therefore does not infringe upon the trademark.

In *Louis Vuitton Mallettier S.A. v. My Other Bag, Inc.*, the Second Circuit ruled that a simple tote bag was a successful parody of the French manufacturer's luxury handbags. The *Louis Vuitton* court reasoned the tote bags were "obviously a joke" based on the "my other car" trope. The *Louis Vuitton* court reasoned further the totes were not an "idealized image" of a mark created by the manufacturer.

Rather, the totes' utilitarian nature conveyed a joking and amusing parody based on their utilitarian nature that starkly contrasted with the actual designer bags designed to be handled with "reverent care and display to communicate a certain status," not to "be stuffed with produce at the supermarket, sweaty clothes at the gym, or towels at the beach." *Louis Vuitton Malletier S.A. v. My Other Bag, Inc.*, 156 F. Supp. 3d 425 (2d Cir. 2016).

(D) TRADEMARK LACHES

Laches is an equitable defense consisting of three elements (1) delay in asserting one's trademark rights, (2) lack of excuse for the delay, and (3) undue prejudice to the alleged infringer caused by the delay. To avoid the equitable defense of laches, or "sleeping on your rights," trademark owners should conduct public searches of social media and other websites.

Non-generic, non-misleading, genuine, and continuous use of trademarks is necessary for continuous protection. In cybersquatting cases, the trademark owner should not wait too many years to file a complaint either in federal court or in a UDRP dispute-resolution proceeding.

§ 11-7. Domain Name Hijacking & Reverse Hijacking

Trademark hijacking is when a cybersquatter registers a domain name that is identical or confusingly similar to a plaintiff's trade name or trademark. In contrast, a "reverse domain name hijacking" occurs when a cybersquatter or person with no legitimate interest in a mark files a complaint against the domain name registrant who does have a legitimate interest in the mark. Reverse cybersquatting lawsuits are filed in order to extract a nuisance settlement.

Under the Lanham Act, "a domain name registrant who is aggrieved by an overreaching trademark owner may commence an action to declare that the domain name registration or use by the registrant is not unlawful under the Lanham Act." 15 U.S.C. § 1114(2)(D)(v).

To prevail on a reverse domain name hijacking claim under the Anti-Cybersquatting Consumer Protection Act (ACPA), the plaintiff must show: (1) that it is a domain name registrant; (2) that its domain name was suspended, disabled, or transferred under a policy established by a registrar; (3) that the owner of the mark that prompted the domain name to be suspended, disabled, or transferred has notice of the action by service or otherwise; and (4) that the plaintiff's registration or use of the domain name is not unlawful under the Act. 15 U.S.C. § 1114(2)(D)(v).

In *Telemedia Network Inc. v. Sunshine Films, Inc.*, 2002 WL 31518870 (Cal. Ct. App. 2d Dist. Nov. 13, 2002), an adult entertainment company modified a domain name to redirect traffic of a rival to its own website, a practice known as "domain name hijacking." The diversion of traffic occurred when customers who were trying to access Sexnet found a website operated by Sunshine with no content. Sunshine's purpose was to raise revenue through deceptive means.

§ 11-8. Uniform Domain Name Resolution Policy

(A) OVERVIEW OF UDRP PROCEEDINGS

The World Intellectual Property Organization (WIPO) developed the Uniform Domain Name Resolution Policy (UDRP) for the arbitration of domain name disputes. WIPO is an agency of the United Nations that administers many international treaties. For example, WIPO entered into a cooperative agreement with the World Trade Organization (WTO) in 1996.

WIPO's UDRP policy and rules play a role in harmonizing IP law by providing uniform remedies for trademark owners against cybersquatters and other abusive domain name practices. In 2012 alone, trademark holders filed 2,884 cybersquatting cases covering 5,084 Internet domain names under procedures based on the Uniform Domain Name Dispute Resolution Policy (UDRP). WIPO, *WIPO Arbitration and Mediation Center—2012 Review* (2012).

UDRP arbitral panels have the power to cancel or transfer domain name registration. ICANN can also order such relief upon receipt of an order from a court or arbitral tribunal. Nevertheless, UDRP panels have no arbitral authority to award monetary damages, statutory damages, or any other remedies typically other than the power to cancel or transfer domain names.

The Lanham Act gives domain name registrants the right to challenge Uniform Dispute Resolution Policy decisions that resulted in the suspension, cancellation, or transfer of their domain names.

Section 1114(2)(D)(iv) provides that if a registrar transfers a domain name based on a "knowing and material misrepresentation" that a domain name is identical to, confusingly similar to, or dilutive of a mark, the person making the misrepresentation shall be liable for damages. 15 U.S.C. § 1114(2)(D)(iv).

(B) UDRP PROVIDERS

Under the UDRP, most types of trademark-based domain-name disputes are resolvable by agreement, court action, or arbitration before a registrar will cancel, suspend, or transfer a domain name. The UDRP arbitration panel decides cases arising out of abusive registrations of domain names such as cybersquatting. Under the UDRP's expedited proceedings, the owner of trademark rights files a complaint with an approved dispute-resolution service provider.

UDRP panels are limited in what remedies they may impose. Panels may order that a registrar cancel, transfer, or change a domain name registration but have no authority to award monetary damages or attorney's fees.

The UDRP rules have been adopted by ICANN and are incorporated by reference in every new domain name registration. Jurisdiction is not an issue because the domain name registrant has agreed in advance to submit to UDRP should a trademark dispute arise.

(C) HOW THE UDRP WORKS

(1) Domain Name Registration

The year 1999 marked the release of the WIPO's Uniform Dispute Resolution Policy (UDRP). All ICANN-accredited registrars have adopted the UDRP. Certain managers of country-code top-level domains (e.g., .nu, .tv, .ws) have also adopted it.

The UDRP policy provides trademark owners with an expedited administrative procedure to resolve disputes over abusive practices such as "cybersquatting," "reverse cybersquatting", and other abusive domain name registration abuses.

A federal court described the three principal UDRP institutions key to understanding the management of domain names:

> First, companies called 'registries' operate a database (or 'registry') for all domain names within the scope of their authority. Second, companies called 'registrars' register domain names with registries on behalf of those who own the names. Registrars maintain an ownership record for each domain name they have registered with a registry. Action by a registrar is needed to transfer ownership of a domain name from one registrant to another. Third, individuals and companies called 'registrants' own the domain names. Registrants interact with the registrars, who in turn interact with the registries.

Office Depot Inc. v. Zuccarini, 596 F.3d 696, 699 (9th Cir. 2010).

Under the Domain Name System, the registrant is the company or individual to whom the domain name actually belongs. A website operator must signify an administrative contact—a person authorized by the registrant to make changes in the domain name—at the point of registration. For example, the administrative contact may transfer, cancel, or assign rights to the domain name.

Registrars are companies that register domain names and accredited by ICANN. During the accreditation process, registrars agree to adhere to the Uniform Domain Name Dispute Resolution

Policy. ICANN posts a list of Approved Dispute-Resolution Service Providers.

In addition, to this Policy, there are Rules for Uniform Domain Name Dispute Resolution Policy. Dispute-Resolution service providers do the administrative work of processing complaints, vetting arbitrators, and overseeing cases. Charges for domain name registration are competitive, being as little as $10.

Domain name registrants agree to UDRP proceedings arising from alleged abusive registrations of domain names. For example, a cybersquatting claim may be initiated by a holder of trademark rights.

In 2013, the ICANN will significantly expand the domain name space with internationalized domain names (IDNs) and non-Latin characters such as Chinese, Cyrillic, and Arabic characters. BLOOMBERG BNA, ELECTRONIC COMMERCE & LAW REPORT, *Keeping Up With the Domain Name Explosion* (Dec. 28, 2012).

Domain name registrants agree to UDRP proceedings arising from alleged abusive registrations of domain names—for example, cybersquatting—may be initiated by a holder of trademark rights. In 2013, the ICANN will significantly expand domain name space with internationalized domain names (IDNs) and non-Latin characters such as Chinese, Cyrillic, and Arabic characters.

Trademark owners will generally prevail under the UDRP if they can prove a domain name is either identical or confusingly similar to their trademark or service mark. Bad faith registrations may have their registration cancelled or transferred to the true owner.

The emblem of bad faith is when a registrant obtains a domain name for the sole purpose of selling, renting, or transferring the registration to the true owner for a profit, which is the classic test for cybersquatting. Another test for bad faith is whether the registrant registers the domain name to prevent the true owners from using it.

(2) Liability of the Domain Name Registrars

The ACPA provides an immunity to domain name authorities, which includes registrars, from damages claims "for the registration or maintenance of a domain name for another absent a showing of bad faith intent to profit from such registration or maintenance of the domain name." 15 U.S.C. § 1114(2)(D)(iii).

A federal court in 1999 became the first to rule that a domain name registrar was not liable for direct infringement or liable for dilution if it had not made commercial use of the mark in its capacity as the sole and exclusive domain name registrar.

Domain name registrars generally have no liability for direct, contributory, or vicarious trademark infringement for accepting the registration of an Internet domain name that is confusingly similar to a plaintiff's service mark or trademark. Domain name registries may not face liability for intellectual property infringement, but may be liable for negligence, conversion, or other torts, where they do not act reasonably.

In *Academy of Motion Pictures Arts and Sciences v. GoDaddy.com*, 2013 WL 12122803 (C.D. Cal. June 21, 2013), a federal district court held that an accredited domain name registrar was not entitled to ACPA immunity for its "parked pages program."

The ad program enabled GoDaddy to share revenue with its registrants. The court distinguished the "parked pages program" from GoDaddy's registrar function, finding that the registrar was not entitled to immunity because it used and trafficked in domain names.

(3) Appealing UDRP Decisions

The Lanham Act expressly permits registrants to challenge Uniform Dispute Resolution Policy decisions that resulted in the suspension, cancellation or transfer of their domain names. Section 1114(2)(D)(iv) provides that if a registrar transfers a domain name based on a "knowing and material misrepresentation" that a domain name is identical to, confusingly similar to, or dilutive of a mark, the person making the misrepresentation shall be liable for damages.

§ 11-9. Global Trademark Issues

(A) GLOBAL E-BUSINESS CONCERNS

It is now difficult to imagine the contours of trademark infringement without considering new methods of infringement enabled by bandwidth, browsers, and digital data. Beginning in the mid-1990s, entrepreneurs registered thousands of domain names containing the trademarks of famous companies in the hopes of selling them back for a ransom price. In the past two decades, global trademark law has been reworked to address challenges posed by domain names and cybersquatting.

The UDRP rules for deciding domain name disputes are drafted to bridge disparate legal cultures, thus helping to resolve disputes that cross national borders. Without Internet websites, no court would need to decide issues such as whether a pop-up ad infringed a company's trademark or constituted an unfair business practice in cyberspace.

Lawyers representing information-based companies must make difficult decisions to determine where to seek protection. Trademarks, by their very nature, are symbols and often language-based signifiers. U.S. companies targeting customers in foreign countries must comply with trademark regimes in each country where they do business.

Lawyers seeking trademark protection in foreign countries must consider translation challenges "particularly where multiple language may be spoken within a particular nation." JOHN T. CROSS ET AL., GLOBAL ISSUES IN INTELLECTUAL PROPERTY LAW 162 (2010).

Trademark law has been harmonized but there are still differences in how a company obtains trademark rights. U.S. trademark protection tends to be broader than in Europe giving protection to "nontraditional marks such as colors, smells, sounds, and taste." European countries are more hesitant than the U.S. to approve non-traditional trademarks.

The U.S. recognizes nontraditional marks such as odor, color or movement not recognized in other countries. Sounds, colors, designs and other nontraditional marks have already been registered in the USPTO.

The European Court of Justice upheld the German Patent and Trademark Office refusal to register an olfactory mark with services including advertising, education, and food or drink.

The Office of Harmonization for the Internal Market also upheld the refusal to register a gustatory trademark for a pharmaceutical product. The mark consisted of the taste of artificial strawberry flavor. These EU decisions illustrate the reluctance to recognize nontraditional marks that would be recognized by the USPTO. Another U.S./EU difference is in so-called marks that are immoral. An examiner rejected registration of SCREW YOU as a Community Trademark.

The Office of Harmonization allowed registration of the mark for artificial breasts and breast pumps sold exclusively in sex shops. The Office of Harmonization reasoned that someone buying goods in a sex shop would unlikely be offended by a trademark with sexually charged language.

In May 2017, for example, the Chancellor of the High Court of Justice in London ruled that the dark and light purple colors on Glaxo Group Ltd.'s asthma inhaler did not qualify for trademark protection in the European Union.

The European Community Trade Mark was for the terms "SCREW YOU" (inter alia for contraceptives), FUCKIN ISLAND (goods from Class 25) and FUCK OF THE YEAR (inter alia for services in the field of broadcasting).

The Court of Appeal of Milan, ended with the judgement by the Court of Cassation, which confirmed the invalidity in Italy of the trademark "Buddha Café," due to the lack of distinctiveness and contrariety to public policy, as it offended the Buddhist religious sentiment.

In Japan, Yakuza and other gang names are not registrable as trademarks because they were "scandalous or contrary to public policy or accepted principles of morality." John Cross states that Canada has ruled that T-shirts, blouses, slacks and a beauty pageant with the mark "Miss Nude Universe" was not scandalous, obscene or immoral. But in *Scranage's Trade Mark Application*, the UK Trademarks Registry reversed denial of registration of the mark: "There is no 'effing' used in connection with T-shirts and caps as contrary to accepted principles of morality."

JOHN CROSS, et al., GLOBAL ISSUES IN INTELLECTUAL PROPERTY LAW (2010) at 176, n. 5 & 6.

Scranage's Application to register FOOK was refused because in some regional UK accents the word was phonetically indistinguishable from "fuck." The 2005 ruling stated that it would not be appropriate to register "fuck" because it is "a swear word and deeply offensive and insulting to many people . . . [and] likely to cause justifiable outrage amongst a significant section of the public."

CHAPTER 12
TRADE SECRETS IN CYBERSPACE

This chapter on global trade secrets is divided into four sections. Section 12-1 is an overview of the law of trade secrets. Section 12-2 covers the state law of secrets, with an emphasis on the Uniform Trade Secrets Act, adopted by most states. Section 12-3 examines the Defend Trade Secrets Act and the federalization of trade secrets followed by Section 12-4, global trade secret issues.

In general, trade secrets are confidential information not generally known among, or accessible because the owner of this information takes reasonable measures to protect it in the relevant business sector. The World Intellectual Property Organization notes that trade secrets are commercially valuable only because they are kept secret. Trade secrets need to take preventative measures:

> subject to reasonable steps taken by the rightful holder of the information to keep it secret, such as the use of confidentiality agreements for business partners. Oftentimes, they are key components of an IP portfolio that strengthen the business's competitive edge. Like other IP assets, they may be sold or licensed. In principle, unauthorized acquisition, use or disclosure of a trade secret by others in a manner contrary to honest commercial practices is considered misappropriation of the trade secret.

World Intellectual Property Organization (WIPO), *Part III: Basics of Trade Secret Protection* (2026).

The law of trade secrets is the only branch of the law of intellectual property where there is no registration requirement. As WIPO notes: "No registration is necessary to obtain trade secret protection. As long as the information qualifies as a trade secret, it is protected indefinitely."

This chapter examines Internet-related trade secret issues. Trade secrets are perilous in a networked world where intangible assets may be lost at the click of a mouse information technology companies are vulnerable to trade secret theft because of the widespread use of consultants, contractors, and increased outsourcing.

§ 12-1. Overview of the Law of Trade Secrets

(A) BASIC CONCEPTS OF TRADE SECRETS

To qualify as a trade secret, the plaintiff must prove: that confidential information has potential or actual value from not being generally known. Trade secrets protect financial information, technical and scientific information, commercial information, and even negative information. Negative information, information about what will not work when it is used to avoid unworkable methods, can be a trade secret APJI 48.02 Used or Intended for Use—Defined.

The policies underlying trade secret protection are to:

- Prevent free-riding

- Encourage competition
- Competition must have limits
- Encourage innovation over copying
- Importance of private property rights
- Limitations on property rights can exist

Trade secret misappropriation claims may arise out of the law of contracts such as when the defendant breaches a nondisclosure agreement. The following clause is an example of a clause defining confidential information in a nondisclosure agreement:

> Confidential Information as information, technical data, or know-how, including, but not limited to, research, products, software, services, development, inventions, ideas, processes, designs, drawings, engineering, marketing, or finances, disclosed either directly or indirectly in writing, orally or by drawings or inspection of parts or equipment.

Misappropriation may also arise as a tort action when the defendant uses improper means such as theft to acquire a trade secret. Factors determining whether information is a trade secret include:

(1) The extent to which the information is known outside of the business;

(2) The extent to which it is known by employees and those involved in the business;

(3) The extent of measures taken to guard the secrecy of the information;

(4) The value of the information to the owner of the secret and his competitors;

(5) The amount of effort or money expended by him in developing the information; and

(6) The ease or difficulty with which the information could be properly acquired or duplicated by others.

A software company's trade secrets includes proprietary algorithms, source code, unreleased product roadmaps, customer lists, and database structures. Formulas, data flow charts, and specific procedures implemented in the software or website are trade secrets if reasonable measures are implemented to keep this information secret.

In *Luminate Home Loans Inc. v. Better Mortgage Co.*, 2025 WL 3265817 (S.D. Cal. Nov. 21, 2025), the plaintiff claimed the defendant misappropriated the following trade secret information:

(1) operational procedures and training materials;

(2) loan data showing types of loans offered, pricing information for each loan, and revenue;

(3) branch leases, performance, and revenue data;

(4) company cost allocation information for corporate and branch expenses and revenue splits;

(5) organizational documents and employment contracts for Plaintiff's company structure and specifically its NEO division both as a subdivision and its preparations for creating NEO as a standalone wholly owned entity of Plaintiff;

(6) employee data showing each of Plaintiff's employees' compensation, production history, profitability, and contact information;

(7) economic forecasting models for Plaintiff;

(8) records for secondary market sales of loans including who Plaintiff contracts with, the amount they are paid per loan and loan type

(9) loan lead lists;

(10) individual customer lead information;

(11) historical records for Plaintiff-closed loans;

(12) marketing strategies.

Trade secret owners have rights so long as the owner of the trade secret has taken reasonable measures to keep the information secret. To qualify as a trade secret, the information must have actual or potential economic value. This information must not be readily ascertainable through proper means. The key aspects of trade secrets is that they are not generally known nor accessible.

The World Intellectual Property Organization (WIPO) describes the broad scope of trade secrets:

> The subject matter of trade secrets is usually defined in broad terms and includes sales methods, distribution methods, consumer profiles, advertising strategies, lists of suppliers and clients, and manufacturing processes. While a final determination of what information constitutes a trade secret will depend on the circumstances of each individual case, clearly unfair practices in respect of secret information include industrial or commercial espionage, breach of contract and breach of confidence.

WIPO, *How Are Trade Secrets Protected?* (2017).

Trade secret law mandates that trade secret holders take reasonable measures to protect their confidential and proprietary information. The "reasonableness" of the steps taken is determined on a case-by-case basis and depends on the circumstances—for example, a large corporation with in-house legal and IT departments would generally need to have taken more stringent measures to sufficiently protect confidential and proprietary information than smaller entities and startups. Thomas McNulty, *Practical Guidance on Protecting Trade Secrets While Working Remotely*, HIGHLIGHT PRESS (Dec. 3, 2020).

Disclosure is the death knell for a trade secret, destroying its emblematic feature of secrecy. Courts consider six factors in determining whether confidential information constitutes a trade secret:

> (1) the extent to which the information is known outside the business, (2) the extent to which it is known to those inside the business, i.e., by the employees, (3) the precautions taken by the holder of the trade secret to guard the secrecy of the information, (4) the savings affected, and the value to the holder, in having the information as against competitors, (5) the amount of effort or money expended in obtaining and developing the information, and (6) the amount of time and expense it would take for others to acquire and duplicate the information.

Daniels Health Scis., L.L.C. v. Vascular Health Scis., L.L.C., 710 F.3d 579, 583 (5th Cir. 2013).

§ 12-2. The State Law of Trade Secrets

(A) THE UNIFORM TRADE SECRETS ACT

The Uniform Trade Secrets Act (UTSA) is a model law drafted by the National Conference of Commissioners on Uniform State Laws (NCCUSL) enacted in 49 states, the District of Columbia and the U.S. Virgin Islands. New York is the only state that has not adopted UTSA.

UTSA preempts all other state laws providing civil remedies for misappropriation of a trade secret, including claims for civil conspiracy.

The UTSA provides a cause of action for trade secret misappropriation and:

- Defines the types of information eligible for trade secret protection.
- Sets out a private cause of action for trade secret misappropriation.
- Provides remedies for misappropriation, including injunctions, damages and, in certain cases, attorneys' fees.

Thomson-Reuters, *Glossary: Uniform Trade Secrets Act (UTSA)* (2026).

UTSA updated and harmonized the state law of trade secrets.

New York courts adopted the definition of trade secret from Section 757 of the Restatement of Torts: "A trade secret consists of a formula, process, device, or compilation which one uses in his business and which gives him an opportunity to obtain an advantage over competitors who do not know or use it." UTSA provides that a trade secret includes:

> a formula, pattern, compilation, program, device, method, technique, or process, that: (1) derives independent economic value, actual or potential, from not being generally known to the public or to other persons who can obtain economic value from its disclosure or use, and (2) is the subject of efforts that are reasonable under the circumstances to maintain its secrecy.

(B) UTSA'S DEFINITION OF SECRECY

Secrecy is the principal issue in most trade secret litigation. Courts consider six factors in determining whether confidential information constitutes a trade secret: (1) the extent to which the information is known outside the business, (2) the extent to which it is known to those inside the business, i.e., by the employees, (3) the precautions taken by the holder of the trade secret to guard the secrecy of the information, (4) the savings effected and the value to the holder in having the information as against competitors, (5) the amount of effort or money expended in obtaining and developing the information, and (6) the amount of time and expense it would take for others to acquire and duplicate the information. *Daniels Health Scis., L.L.C. v. Vascular Health Scis., L.L.C.*, 710 F.3d 579 (5th Cir. 2013).

(C) TRADE SECRET MISAPPROPRIATION ACTIONS

The tort of misappropriation of trade secrets requires the plaintiff to prove: (1) the existence of a trade secret, (2) the acquisition of the secret because of a confidential relationship, and (3) the defendant's unauthorized use of the secret. A plaintiff bringing a claim of misappropriation of a trade secret must allege (1) it possessed a trade secret, and (2) defendant is using that trade secret in breach of an agreement, confidence, or duty, or as a result of discovery by improper means.

Companies must implement reasonable security measures in order for information to be protectable as trade secrets. At a minimum, an Internet company must label source code, plans, and other documents with a legend that these materials are confidential and proprietary.

Section 1(2) of UTSA states that:

> (2) "Misappropriation" means: (i) acquisition of a trade secret of another by a person who knows or has reason to know that the trade secret was acquired by improper means; or (ii) disclosure or use of a trade secret of another without express or implied consent by a person who (A) used improper means to acquire knowledge of the trade secret; or (B) at the time of disclosure or use knew or had reason to know that his knowledge of the trade secret was (I) derived from or through a person who has utilized improper means to acquire it; (II) acquired under circumstances giving rise to a duty to maintain its secrecy or limit its use; or (III) derived from or through a person who owed a duty to the person seeking relief to maintain its secrecy or limit its use; or (C) before a material change of his position, knew or had reason to know that it was a trade secret and that knowledge of it had been acquired by accident or mistake.

The Uniform Trade Secrets Act (UTSA) states that misappropriation is the acquisition of a trade secret of another by a person who knows or has reason to know that the trade secret was acquired by improper means. Improper means' includes theft, bribery, misrepresentation, breach or inducement of a breach of a duty to maintain secrecy, or espionage through electronic or other means. UTSA sec. 1(1).

To prevail on a misappropriation claim, a plaintiff must show that (1) the information was a trade secret (i.e., not generally known in the industry), (2) it was misappropriated (i.e., stolen, rather than developed independently or obtained from a third party), or (3) it was used in the defendant's business.

In *Appian Corp. v. Pegasystems, Inc.*, 924 S.E.2d 621 (Va. 2026), Appian filed a lawsuit against Pegasystems, a software industry competitor for misappropriation of trade secrets under Virginia's Uniform Trade Secrets Act (VUTSA).

Appian's VUTSA claim was based on an allegation that Pegasystems hired a "spy" to obtain Appian's confidential information and software. After jury found in favor of company and awarded it over $2 billion in damages. The Virginia Supreme Court affirmed the Virginia Court of Appeals decision that reversed the $2 billion trade secrets misappropriation award, the largest trade secret verdict in history.

The Virginia high court found sufficient evidence finding that competitor misappropriated software company's trade secrets consisting of information regarding functions and weaknesses of company's business process management platform and of documentation such as user manual for platform, in violation of VUTSA.

The court concluded that Appian took reasonable efforts to protect such information, but Pegasystems engaged in elaborate and improper methods to access it, including hiring what it described as a "spy" with access to company's platform to share information regarding platform for competitor's own financial benefit.

Once the spy lost his access to platform, Pegasystems engaged in efforts to trick Appian into granting it access through use of aliases and credentials from outside competitor's organization.

The court described Pegasystems' efforts to misappropriate Appian's software architecture:

> Zou provided intelligence to Pega in three primary ways: (1) preparing video tutorials of himself building applications in Appian to assist Pega in "find[ing] weaknesses [Pega] can exploit" and strengths to incorporate in its products; (2) participating in live presentations with Pega employees to the same effect; and (3) downloading and sharing confidential Appian documentation saved in Appian Forum with Pega.
>
> Appian identified numerous tutorial videos created by Zou to assist Pega. Zou's video presentations to Pega employees were geared toward demonstrating user experience and answering Pega employee questions, including by describing the architecture of Appian's social interface. Zou's presentations also involved visiting Pega's headquarters in Massachusetts twice to meet with senior leadership and other employees.

Pega went to great lengths to conceal Zou's identity during his presentations to Pega employees. Pega leadership "spent hours and hours removing (blurring) [Zou's] name from the videos" he had prepared and requested that he "change his name on the screen and the ownership of the assets (within Appian)" ahead of a presentation to keep *628 himself anonymous. In fact, Pega employees often referred to Zou as "Matt" or "the other 'Matt' " internally—a tongue-in-cheek reference to Matt Calkins, Appian's CEO—to keep him from being "outed" as Pega's "spy."

Appian's expert identified five illustrative improvements Pega's platform traced back to information supplied to the company by Zou:

(1) "smart services"—an invention that allows ordinary users to automatically carry out "complex, dynamic actions" without needing to know how to code;

(2) "ease of editing"—a feature that allows programmers who make a mistake to "go straight back into the editing environment without having to go back through complex series of navigations";

(3) "custom data types"—a feature allowing developers to group related pieces of data together;

(4) "out-of-the-box" social—an "innovative single interface" that brings "collaboration into

> the work context" and gives centralized access to work lists and tasks all in the same place; and
>
> (5) "out-of-the-box" mobile—a feature allowing applications to run on both desktop and mobile devices without additional coding or effort.

The Virginia Supreme Court upheld the court of appeals reversing the trial court because of a number of defective jury instructions and the trial court's exclusion of evidence on sales linked to the misappropriation.

The Holland and Knight law firm stated this was an important case in clarifying:

> the appropriate burden of proof on a VUTSA claim to establish misappropriation damages based on the unjust enrichment of the defendant. But the VSC also addressed other critical aspects of trade secret litigation, reinforcing a somewhat broad interpretation of what can constitute a trade secret under Virginia law and elaborating that whether a company sufficiently protects its trade secrets via implication is a fact-intensive analysis unique to the circumstances of each case.

Holland & Knight, *Virginia High Court Upholds Reversal of $2 Billion Trade Secret Damages Award* (Jan. 13, 2026). Misappropriation means using "improper means" or acquiring it from someone who has acquired it through "improper means."

To state a claim for misappropriation of trade secrets under the Uniform Trade Secrets Act, a plaintiff must allege that: (1) the plaintiff owned a trade secret, (2) the defendant misappropriated the trade secret, and (3) the defendant's actions damaged the plaintiff.

For a plaintiff to recover for misappropriation of a trade secret, they must prove that they used the proprietary information in question for some commercial use. The owner must also demonstrate that the defendant wrongfully acquired the information or data.

Wrongful acquisition occurs when there is a breach of duty of trust, implied or imposed by law, against employees, corporate attorneys, or fiduciaries, such as outside counsel. Economic espionage, interception of electronic communications, or computer hacking are often key in demonstrating wrongful acquisition of trade secrets.

(D) REASONABLE MEANS TO PROTECT SECRETS

Trade secret laws require companies to take reasonable steps to prevent public disclosure. Accidental or other means of public disclosure destroys the status of a trade secret. Trade secrets, in software especially, derive their economic values from their secrecy. For example, trade secret protection lasts indefinitely so long as the software vendor can keep its source code secret. A trade owner must employ reasonable methods to protect trade secrets.

"Reasonable efforts" can include advising employees of the existence of a trade secret, limiting access to information on a "need to know basis," and requiring employees to sign confidentiality agreements. When trade secrets are disclosed, it can be devastating to a company's livelihood. For example, files that are disclosed in public court or via the Internet destroy the data's trade secret status.

(1) Nondisclosure Agreements

Licensors will typically enter into nondisclosure agreements (NDAs) with their employees, consultants, and joint ventures, as a reasonable means of protecting software code. An NDA is a contractual arrangement that requires a recipient of confidential information to keep that information secret.

When the software maker is developing customized software or building a specialized company website, counsel will typically, draft NDA's that bind any employee, consultant, customer, or any relevant third-party privy to sensitive information.

Typically, the nondisclosure agreement will stipulate that the customers, without the developer's prior written consent, cannot disclose trade secrets. Therefore, software developers and their customers will enter into mutual nondisclosure agreements because the developer will typically have access to its customer's intellectual property when configuring or customizing software. Courts will typically determine the enforceability of nondisclosure agreements by asking a series of questions:

> (1) Is the restraint, from the standpoint of the employer, reasonable in the sense that it is no greater than is necessary to protect the employer in some legitimate business interest? (2) From the standpoint of the employee, is the restraint reasonable in the sense that it is not unduly harsh and oppressive in curtailing his legitimate efforts to earn a livelihood? (3) Is the restraint reasonable from the standpoint of a sound public policy?

JTH Tax, Inc. v. Sawhney, 2019 WL 3051760 (S.D.N.Y. July 11, 2019).

(2) Idea Submission Policies

Florida joins the growing number of states that recognize a common law action for idea misappropriation, but it requires a showing of confidentiality and novelty. Information-based businesses will often adopt idea submission policies to avoid conflicts concerning ownership or interests in intellectual property rights.

Idea submission policies are terms of service when customers, employees, or third parties submit ideas to the company. One of the chief purposes of an idea submission policy is to avoid disputes over whether the company misappropriated or disclosed a trade secret.

For example, Apple's Idea Submission Policy notes that it "does not accept or consider unsolicited ideas, including ideas for new advertising campaigns, new promotions, new or improved products or technologies, product enhancements, processes, materials, marketing plans or new product names." Apple's prohibition against the submission of unauthorized ideas seeks to prevent litigation over the source of ideas about Apple's products or marketing strategies.

(E) TRADE SECRET ACT REMEDIES

The UTSA provides a broad range of remedies, including preliminary injunctive relief, monetary damages, lost profits, consequential damages, lost royalties, attorney's fees, and punitive damages. A plaintiff will often seek injunctive relief if they suspect that former employees are violating, or about to violate, NDAs.

Courts may enjoin actual or threatened misappropriation of trade secrets. However, injunctions will be struck down as vague if they do not specify what counts as a trade secret.

In *Bernhard MCC, LLC v. Zeringue*, 266 So.3d 537 (La. App. 5th Cir. 2019), the Louisiana Appeals Court vacated an overly broad and vague injunction that "prohibited Defendants from seeking, requesting, soliciting from any person, or utilizing for any purpose, any confidential and/or proprietary business information of Bernhard."

> The judgment further ordered Defendants to return all of Bernhard's confidential and proprietary business information and any other

material constituting a trade secret and to comply with their respective obligations to Bernhard regarding the confidentiality and non-disclosure of confidential and proprietary business information.

The defendants contended, "[t]he judgment granting injunctive relief fails to describe the prohibited acts with reasonable detail and, thus, is fatally defective." The court vacated the judgment because it failed "to describe with specificity the prohibited conduct. La. C.C.P. art. 3605 states a preliminary injunction 'shall describe in reasonable detail, and not by mere reference to the petition or other documents, the act or acts sought to be restrained.' "

Trade secret owners may claim a reasonable royalty for the loss of revenue attributable to the misappropriation of a trade secret. UTSA § 4 states attorney's fees may be recoverable where a claim of misappropriation is made in bad faith, a motion to terminate an injunction is made or resisted in bad faith, or willful and malicious misappropriation exists.

Section 3 of UTSA also gives the court the power to award "exemplary damages in an amount not exceeding twice any award," upon a finding of "willful and malicious misappropriation." Section 6 of the UTSA statute of limitations states aggrieved parties may seek relief within three years after the owner discovers the misappropriation, or should have discovered it.

(F) DEFENSES IN UTSA LITIGATION

(1) Reverse Engineering

In the anti-reverse engineering clause, a customer will be in breach of the license agreement if it discloses, decompiles, disassembles, or reverse engineers licensed software. In *Mid-Michigan Computer Sys. v. Marc Glassman Inc.*, 416 F.3d 505 (6th Cir. 2005), the Sixth Circuit upheld a $2 million compensatory damages award and a $5 million punitive damages award against a licensee that secretly copied source code from its licensor.

The licensor entered into a license agreement with the defendant to maintain prescription and billing records for customers. The parties also entered into a Source Code Agreement, which provided that defendant would access the escrowed source code only in certain specified emergencies.

The evidence at trial showed that defendant secretly copied software that was then used to reconstruct the plaintiff's source code. Such activity helped save research and manufacturing resources in developing the software that would ultimately replace the plaintiff's pharmacy software. Thus, while reverse engineering is proper, the acquisition of the known product must, of course, also be by fair and honest means to be lawful. UTSA § 1, cmt. 2.

The Reporters for the ALI's Principles of the Law of Software Contracts, discussed in Chapter 4, acknowledge that anti-reverse engineering clauses are "troublesome terms." European courts would not likely enforce clauses that prohibited reverse engineering to achieve interoperability because of the Software Directive. In Europe, all users of software have a right to reverse engineer code to achieve interoperability of computer programs under the Software Directive adopted in 1991.

(2) First Amendment Defenses

"Trade secret protection may be outweighed by First Amendment concerns where the matter at issue is of public concern and the defendant did not participate in the tortious act by which the material was originally obtained." 3 CALLMANN ON UNFAIR COMP., TR. & MONO. § 14:2 (Toronto, Ontario: Thomson-Reuters, 4th ed. 2026) at Chapter 14 on Trade Secrets (ed. Louis Altmann & Malla Pollack).

In recent years, U.S. courts have ruled that the tort of misappropriation must give way to the First Amendment. For example, the First Amendment of the U.S. Constitution protected a website operator's posting of DeCSS, which enabled users to evade the "content scramble system" that both encrypts DVDs and prevents their unauthorized use and duplication.

The California appellate court ruled that because what the DeCSS website operator posted was already public knowledge, the defendant could not be liable for misappropriation since there was no trade secret. *DVD Copy Control Ass'n, Inc. v. Bunner*, 10 Cal.Rptr. 3d 185 (Cal. Ct. of App. 2004).

In *Ford Motor Co. v. Lane*, 67 F. Supp. 2d 745 (E.D. Mich. 1999), the federal court denied a motion for a preliminary injunction to prevent Lane from disclosing alleged trade secrets on the Internet because the proposed injunction would constitute an invalid prior restraint of free speech in violation of the First Amendment.

§ 12-3. Federal Trade Secret Law

In 2016, Congress enacted the Defend Trade Secrets Act (DTSA), giving trade secret owners a private cause of action under the Economic Espionage Act (EEA). The DTSA confers a federal cause of action on an owner of a trade secret that has been misappropriated, so long as the trade secret owner has (1) taken reasonable measures to keep such information secret and (2) the information derives independent economic value. 18 U.S.C. §§ 1836(b)(1) and 1839(3).

The DTSA provides the owner of a trade secret with a civil remedy for misappropriation of that trade secret. 18 U.S.C. § 1836(b)(1). Under the DTSA, a "trade secret" is a form or type of business or technical information that the owner has taken "reasonable measures" to keep secret. 18 U.S.C. § 1839(3).

The information must have "independent economic value" by virtue of its status as unknown or unascertainable information. Misappropriation of a trade secret is the acquisition, disclosure, or unauthorized use of that information by improper means. 18 U.S.C. § 1839(5).

> The DTSA then defines 'misappropriation' as the: disclosure or use of a trade secret of another without express or implied consent by a person who . . . at the time of disclosure or use, knew or had reason to know that the knowledge of the trade secret was . . . acquired under circumstances giving rise to a duty to maintain the secrecy of the trade secret or limit the use of the trade secret.

Unlike the other branches of intellectual property that are based upon federal law, trade secrets were based upon state law. This changed in 2016 when The *Defend Trade Secrets Act* (DTSA) was enacted, codified at 18 U.S.C. § 1836, et seq.

The DTSA allows an owner of a trade secret to sue in federal court when its trade secrets have been misappropriated. The DTSA provides that "[a]ii owner of a trade secret that is misappropriated may bring a civil action under this subsection if the trade secret is related to a product or service used in, or intended for use in, interstate or foreign commerce." 18 U.S.C. § 1836(b).

To state a claim of trade secret misappropriation under the DTSA, a plaintiff must plausibly allege both that: (1) it possessed a trade secret, and (2) the defendant misappropriated the trade secret.

The DTSA created a federal cause of action for trade secrets that:

> preserves a single tort cause of action under state law for misappropriation of trade secrets and eliminate[s] other tort causes of action

> founded on allegations of trade secret misappropriation.

Overdrive, Inc. v. Baker & Taylor, Inc., 2011 WL 2448209 at *4 (Del. Ch. June 17, 2011).

Section 1839(3) of the Defend Trade Secrets Act defines a "trade secret" as:

> all forms and types of financial, business, scientific, technical, economic, or engineering information, including patterns, plans, compilations, program devices, formulas, designs, prototypes, methods, techniques, processes, procedures, programs, or codes, whether tangible or intangible, and whether or how stored, compiled, or memorialized physically, electronically, graphically, photographically, or in writing if—
>
> (A) the owner thereof has taken reasonable measures to keep such information secret; and
>
> (B) the information derives independent economic value, actual or potential, from not being generally known to, and not being readily ascertainable through proper means by, another person who can obtain economic value from the disclosure or use of the information.

The federal trade secrets act "preserves a single tort cause of action under state law for misappropriation of trade secrets and 'eliminate[s] other tort causes of action founded on allegations of trade secret misappropriation.' " *Overdrive, Inc. v. Baker & Taylor, Inc.*, 2011 WL 2448209 (Del. Ch. June 17, 2011).

§ 12-4. Trade Secrets in a Global Internet

Increasingly, trade secrets are federalized with the enactment of federal statutes such as the DTSA and the Economic Espionage Act. Congress enacted the Economic Espionage Act (EEA) in 1996 to criminalize the misappropriation of trade secrets. In 2015,

Congress considered federalizing trade secret law by recognizing civil liability for the EEA. By allowing the victims of trade secret misappropriation to seek civil damages, amendments to the EEA would create a federal civil cause of action for trade secret theft.

An empirical study of all EEA prosecutions from the federal criminal statute's enactment from 1996 to August 1, 2005, uncovered fewer than fifty economic or espionage prosecutions filed in federal courts. Few cases involved foreign defendants. Michael L. Rustad, *The Negligent Enablement of Trade Secrets*, 22 SANTA CLARA COMPUTER & HIGH TECH J. 455 (2006).

In the first decade of EEA prosecutions, the Department of Justice did not file a single case against a hacker stealing trade secrets by "exploiting known software defects" during an Internet transmission.

The impact of the EEA has been underwhelming in the face of growing cross-border espionage.

> Cyberspace—where most business activity and development of new ideas now takes place—amplifies these threats by making it possible for malicious actors, whether they are corrupted insiders or foreign intelligence services (FIS), to quickly steal and transfer massive quantities of data while remaining anonymous and hard to detect.

The Office of the National Counterintelligence Executive (ONCIX), *Foreign Spies Stealing U.S. Economic Secrets in Cyberspace*, November 2011, at Executive Summary.

Cyberspace is a unique complement to the espionage environment because it provides foreign collectors with relative anonymity, facilitates the transfer of a vast amount of information, and makes it more difficult for victims and governments to assign blame by masking geographic locations.

The ONCIX Report explains how the digital environment makes trade secret theft more likely:

> Today, nearly all business records, research results, and other sensitive economic data are digitized and accessible on networks worldwide. Cyber collection can take many forms, including: simple visits to a US company's website for the collection of openly available information; a corporate insider's downloading of proprietary information onto a thumb drive at the behest of a foreign rival; or intrusions launched by FIS (foreign intelligence service) or other actors

against the computer networks of a private company, federal agency, or an individual.

In a highly publicized trade secret case, Huawei, a Chinese tech giant, was charged with the misappropriation of Apples trade secrets:

> According to the report, a Huawei engineer in charge of the smartwatch project tracked down a supplier that makes the heart rate sensor for Apple Watch that has approval from the US Food and Drug Administration (FDA). The engineer arranged a meeting and questioned the supplier about the Apple Watch.

Huawei Involved in Stealing Apple Trade Secrets: Report, BGR: YOUR MOBILE LIFE (BLOG) (Feb. 19, 2019).

The U.S. Justice Department found:

> Huawei is said to have a formal program that rewards employees for stealing information, including bonuses that increase based on the confidential value of the information gathered. The Department has filed a host of criminal charges, including bank fraud, obstruction of justice and theft of technology against Huawei and its detained Chief Financial Officer Meng Wanzhou. Both Huawei and Meng have denied the allegations.
>
> In February 2019, Huawei Technologies Co. pleaded not guilty to U.S. charges of trade-secret theft, a day before the company learns if Canada

> will start extradition proceedings for its chief financial officer.

Huawei Pleads Not Guilty in U.S. Case; Canada CFO Decision Looms, BLOOMBERG NEWS: IP (Feb. 28, 2019).

Huawei is charged with the theft of "trade secrets from T-Mobile US Inc. and also committed wire fraud and obstruction of justice."

Similarly, in 2019, the U.S. charged Jinhua, a Chinese state-owned memory chipmaker, with "conspiring to steal intellectual property from Micron Technology Inc." As a result, the Trump Administration now prohibits U.S. companies from selling products or rendering services to Jinhua. *Chinese Chipmaker to Appeal U.S. Ban Over Alleged Secrets Theft*, BLOOMBERG NEWS: IP (Jan. 25, 2019).

The ONCIX Report notes that the EEA distinguishes between economic espionage (foreign actor defendant) and industrial espionage (domestic defendant):

> The Economic Espionage Act defines *economic espionage* when an actor, knowing or intending that his or her actions will benefit any foreign government, instrumentality or agent, knowingly: (1) steals, or without authorization appropriates, carries away, conceals, or obtains by deception or fraud a trade secret; (2) copies, duplicates, reproduces, destroys, uploads, downloads, or transmits that trade secret without authorization; or (3) receives a trade secret knowing that the trade secret had been

> stolen, appropriated, obtained or converted without authorization. 18 U.S.C. § 1831.
>
> Industrial espionage, or theft of trade secrets, occurs when an actor, intending or knowing that his or her offense will injure the owner of a trade secret of a product produced for, or placed in interstate or foreign commerce, acts with the intent to convert that trade secret to the economic benefit of anyone other than the owner by: (1) stealing, or without authorization appropriating, carrying away, concealing, or obtaining by deception or fraud information related to that secret; (2) copying, duplicating, reproducing, destroying, uploading, downloading, or otherwise transmitting that information without authorization; or (3) receiving that information knowing that that information had been stolen, appropriated, obtained or converted without authorization (Section 101 of the EEA, 18 U.S.C. § 1832).
>
> Thirty-five companies working in robotics, semiconductors, online games, and other emerging technologies filed thirty-five DTSA Act civil actions in California during the first months of 2017.

Alexis Kramer, *Trade Secret Cases Surge as Race for New Tech, Top Talent Heats Up*, ELECTRONIC COMMERCE & LAW REPORT (May 17, 2017).

In 2025, the U.S. House of Representatives passed the Economic Espionage Prevention Act (H.R. 1486), as bipartisan legislation designed to combat the theft of American intellectual property by foreign adversaries:

> This bill authorizes the President to impose visa- and property-blocking sanctions on foreign adversary entities that knowingly engage in (1) economic and industrial espionage with respect to trade secrets and proprietary information owned by U.S. persons, (2) the provision of material support or services to a foreign adversaries' national security entities, or (3) the violation of U.S. export control laws. The bill cites regulations that define China, Russia, Iran, North Korea, Cuba, and the Maduro regime of Venezuela as foreign adversaries.

This proposed statute will give the U.S. government authority to sanction foreign entities:

> that support Russia's military, violate U.S. export controls, or steal American intellectual property. It will also require a report to assess China's support for Russia's military and update the International Emergency Economic Powers Act (IEEPA) to allow stronger actions against China and other foreign adversaries.

U.S. House of Representatives, Economic Espionage Prevention Act (May 6, 2025).

Increasingly, trade secret litigation is cross-border. The U.S. Department of Justice stated that an Illinois federal district court imposed a $50 million fine for a criminal conspiracy to steal proprietary technology from Illinois-based Motorola Solutions, Inc.:

> Beginning in 2006, China-based HYTERA COMMUNICATIONS CORP. LTD. recruited and hired Motorola employees and directed them to take proprietary and trade secret information from Motorola without authorization. The stolen information related to Motorola's digital mobile radio technology, which Motorola had developed through years of research and design. The engineers used the stolen information, including source code, to develop products for Hytera—at a fraction of the cost that it took Motorola to develop the exclusive technology—and competed with Motorola in the digital radio market through 2020.
>
> . . . Seven Hytera employees were indicted in 2021 in federal court in Chicago for their alleged roles in the thefts from Motorola. One of them—GEE SIONG KOK—pleaded guilty in 2022 to a federal charge of conspiracy to steal trade secrets. As part of a plea agreement, Kok agreed to cooperate with the government in its investigation. Kok is awaiting sentencing. Warrants have been issued for the arrests of the six other defendants.

U.S. Department of Justice, *Chinese Telecommunications Company Fined $50 Million for Conspiring To Steal Technology From Motorola Solutions* (Mar. 9, 2026).

In addition to the $50 million fine, Hysteria was sentenced to a five year period of probation, which includes conditions for maintaining an effective compliance program and annual reporting of the program to the government. Motorola also filed a civil suit and received $214 million in restitution for lost profits caused by Hysteria's misappropriation of their technology.

In 2025, two U.S. citizens and two nationals of the People's Republic of China (PRC) were charged with a conspiracy to illegally export cutting-edge NVIDIA Graphics Processing Units (GPUs), which have artificial intelligence (AI) applications, to the People's Republic of China:

> The indictment. . . alleges a deliberate and deceptive effort to transship controlled NVIDIA GPUs to China by falsifying paperwork, creating fake contracts, and misleading U.S. authorities. According to the indictment, the PRC seeks to become the world leader in AI by 2030 and seeks to use AI for its military modernization efforts and in connection with the design and testing of weapons of mass destruction and deployment of advanced AI surveillance tools. The PRC seeks cutting-edge U.S. technology in furtherance of that goal, including NVIDIA GPUs.

U.S. Department of Justice, *U.S. Citizens and Chinese Nationals Arrested for Exporting Artificial Intelligence Technology to China* (Nov. 30, 2025).

Cross-border trade secret misappropriation is a significant national security theft. In 2025, The U.S.

Department of Justice reported a scheme where Chinese front companies exported U.S. technologies to Iraq insurgency groups to evade trade controls:

> Beginning as early as May 2007, Liu and her associates allegedly utilized an array of front companies in the People's Republic of China (PRC) to send dual-use U.S.-origin electronic components to IRGC-linked companies that could be used in the production of UAVs, ballistic missile systems, and other military end uses.
>
> The named individuals allegedly misrepresented the end users of dual-use U.S.-origin electronic components, leading U.S. companies to export goods to PRC-based front companies under the guise that the ultimate destination of these products was China rather than Iran. As a result, a vast amount of dual-use U.S.-origin products with military capabilities have been exported from the United States to IRGC-linked companies Shiraz Electronics Industries (SEI), Rayan Roshd Afzar, and their affiliates, in violation of U.S. sanctions and export control laws and regulations.

U.S. Department of Justice, *Rewards for Justice—Reward Offer for Information Disrupting Chinese Nationals Supplying Technology to Iran's Islamic Revolutionary Guard Corps, a Foreign Terrorist Organization* (Mar. 19, 2025).

The result is that Iran was able to use U.S.-controlled technology to develop and manufacture arms and weapons systems, including UAVs sold to governments and groups in allied countries such as Russia, Sudan, and Yemen.

In February 2026, a federal grand jury has indicted three Silicon Valley engineers on charges of conspiring to commit trade secret theft from Google and other leading technology companies, theft and attempted theft of trade secrets, and obstruction of justice. The U.S. Department of Justice described the indictment:

> According to the indictment filed yesterday and unsealed today, the defendants gained employment at leading technology companies in the area of mobile computer processors. Samaneh Ghandali and Soroor Ghandali, who are sisters, worked at Google before going on to work for another technology company identified as Company 3, and Khosravi, who is married to Samaneh Ghandali, worked at a technology company identified as Company 2. As part of the alleged scheme to commit trade secret theft, the defendants used their employment to obtain access to confidential and sensitive information. The defendants then exfiltrated confidential and sensitive documents, including trade secrets related to processor security and cryptography and other technologies, from Google and other technology companies to unauthorized third-party and personal locations, including to work devices associated with each other's employers, and to Iran. As alleged, the defendants exploited

their positions to steal confidential trade secrets from their employers.

Cross-border civil actions for protecting trade secrets is addressed by the World Trade Organization (WTO) Agreement on Trade-Related Aspects of Intellectual Property Rights (TRIPS). Article 39 of the TRIPS agreement mandates that members protect undisclosed information stating:

> (1) In the course of ensuring effective protection against unfair competition as provided in Article 10bis of the Paris Convention (1967), Members shall protect undisclosed information in accordance with paragraph 2 and data submitted to governments or governmental agencies in accordance with paragraph 3.
>
> (2) Natural and legal persons shall have the possibility of preventing information lawfully within their control from being disclosed to, acquired by, or used by others without their consent in a manner contrary to honest commercial practices (10) so long as such information:
>
> (a) is secret in the sense that it is not, as a body or in the precise configuration and assembly of its components, generally known among or readily accessible to persons within the circles that normally deal with the kind of information in question;
>
> (b) has commercial value because it is secret; and

(c) has been subject to reasonable steps under the circumstances, by the person lawfully in control of the information, to keep it secret.

(3) Members, when requiring, as a condition of approving the marketing of pharmaceutical or of agricultural chemical products which utilize new chemical entities, the submission of undisclosed test or other data, the origination of which involves a considerable effort, shall protect such data against unfair commercial use. In addition, Members shall protect such data against disclosure, except where necessary to protect the public, or unless steps are taken to ensure that the data are protected against unfair commercial use.

World Trade Organization, Art II—Standards Concerning the Availability, Scope and Use of Intellectual Property Rights, Section 7.

TRIPS Article 39 establishes minimum standards, requiring information to be secret, commercially valuable, and subject to reasonable means to protect confidential information.

As of 2026, there is no international convention covering misappropriation. There is a wide variation in how countries protect trade secrets. John Cross and his co-authors note that the tort of misappropriation is strongest in France and others have less rigorous trade secrets protection, whereas Switzerland and Germany "take a cautious approach to misappropriation." JOHN CROSS, ET AL., GLOBAL

ISSUES IN INTELLECTUAL PROPERTY LAW (2010) at 249–250.

Some countries do not recognize trade secret misappropriation at all. Prior to the 1990 Amendments to the Japanese Unfair Competition Law, Japan had no law of trade secrets.

CHAPTER 13
PATENT LAW & THE INTERNET

§ 13-1. Overview of Internet-Related Patents

(A) WHY INTERNET PATENTS

The goal of this chapter is to present the basic concepts and methods of Internet-related patent law. This chapter will explore the foundations of patent protection, patentability, and the patenting process. A patent grants the patent holder the right to exclude others from making, using, or commercially exploiting an invention.

This chapter is divided into six parts. Section 13-1 is an overview of Internet patents covering its constitutional and statutory basis. It examines The Leahy-Smith America Invents Act (AIA), signed in 2011, that changed the U.S. patent system from a "first-to-invent" to a "first inventor-to-file" system for applications filed on/after March 16, 2013.

The AIA harmonized U.S. law with international standards, broadened prior art definitions, and established new post-grant review mechanisms (IPR, PGR) via the Patent Trial and Appeal Board (PTAB), which will reduce litigation costs and improve patent quality.

Section 13-2 examines patentable subject matter, whereas 13-3 covers the concepts and methods of patentability, the elements of a patent, patent invalidity and terms of a patent.

Section 13-4 focuses on Internet-related patents: software patents, e-business methods including the State Street case and post-State Street developments. In *State Street Bank & Trust Co. v. Signature Financial Group, Inc.*, 149 F.3d 1368, 1370–71 (1998), the Federal Circuit determined that software programs that transform data are patentable subject matter under Section 101 of the Patent Act even when there is no physical transformation of an article.

The *State Street* court emphasized that software or other processes that yield a useful, concrete and tangible result should be considered patentable. Before the *State Street* case, many courts assumed that business methods (like ways of doing business, accounting, or investing) were not eligible for patents, This was a landmark case is establishing the patentability of software.

Next, Section 13-5 examines the U.S. Supreme Court's most significant patent cases impacting Internet-related patents. Section 13-6 examines global patent developments. America's information-based economy is increasingly built on a foundation of patents defined as limited duration property rights. An estimated 11,000 patents cover Internet-related business methods. JAMES BESSEN & MICHAEL J. MEURER, PATENT FAILURE (Princeton, New Jersey: Princeton University Press, 2005) at 8–9.

Section 13-7 concludes that Internet Law is a moving stream, not a frozen pond and continues to evolve.

Internet patents deploy software and other computer-related technologies to perform various tasks. Critics of Internet-related business method patents contend that these innovations would develop more efficiently without patent protection.

Internet-related business methods give the holder the right to control the use of the technology. The level and extent of the control depends upon the business method. All patents balance antitrust concerns against market dominance. Patent holders who obtain a patent to discourage competitors has a chilling impact on e-commerce.

Though patent law is somewhat coordinated amongst those countries connected to the Internet, there are still variations in practices from country to country. Since the last edition, the U.S. Supreme Court and the USPTO have limited the scope of business method patents.

(B) CONSTITUTIONAL & STATUTORY BASIS

Article I, Section 8 of the U.S. Constitution gave Congress the power to "promote the Progress of Science and [the] useful Arts, by securing for limited Times to Authors and inventors the exclusive Right to their respective Writings and Discoveries." Patent law, like copyright law, arises out of federal statutes. Congress enacted the first Patent Act in 1790, with the Patent Act of 1793 following soon after. *The Leahy-Smith America Invents Act (AIA) of 2011* displaced the Patent Act of 1952.

(C) AMERICA INVENTS ACT

On September 16, 2011, President Obama signed into law the Leahy-Smith America Invents Act (AIA), which represents a sea change in U.S. patent law. The United States now aligns its law with the rest of the world in adopting the first-to-file (FITF) system, which jettisons the older U.S. rule of awarding patents to the first-to-invent (FI) system.

Under the FI system, applicants got a patent "after disclosing the invention as long as a patent is filed within one year of the disclosure." MARK V. CAMPAGNA, UNDERSTANDING PATENT REFORMS IN THE CONTEXT OF LITIGATION 9 (2009).

The newly aligned FITF system is equivalent to UCC Article 9's chief rule that the first-to-file or perfect obtains protection under the law. Claimants that win the race to registry will prevail over the first to invent rule that the U.S. previously followed.

(D) TYPES OF PATENTS

The U.S. Patent Act provides that "[w]hoever invents or discovers any new and useful process, machine, manufacture, or composition of matter, or any new and useful improvement thereof, may obtain a patent therefor, subject to the conditions and requirements of this title." 35 U.S.C. § 101.

The Act defines a "process" as a "process, art or method, and includes a new use of a known process, machine, manufacture, composition of matter, or material." The USPTO Director noted that patent protection is not given for mere lines of code that do not qualify as processes and apparatuses. Patents are not granted for abstract ideas but to protect innovation:

> Because many breathtaking software-implemented innovations power our modern world, at levels of efficiency and performance unthinkable even just a few years ago, patent protection is every bit as well-deserved for software-implemented innovation as for the innovations that enabled man to fly, and before that for the innovations that enabled man to light the dark with electricity, and before that for the innovations that enabled the industrial revolution.

David Kappos, Under Secretary of Commerce for IP & Director of the USPTO, *An Examination of Software Patents*, Keynote Address: Center for American Progress (November 12, 2012).

A patent lasts for a specific period, usually twenty years, and represents a bargain made between the government and the inventor. Patent protection is available for the invention of "any new and useful process, machine, manufacture, or composition of matter, or any new and useful improvement thereof." 35 U.S.C. § 101.

Federal patent law recognizes three ideal types of patent protection: (1) utility patents, (2) design patents, and (3) plant patents. Utility patents, as their name connotes, are any new or useful process. Design patents protect the ornamental design of products. Plant patents cover the invention and discovery of new plants. 35 U.S.C. § 161.

(1) Utility Patents

Greater than ninety percent of all patents are utility patents, issued for four general types of inventions/discoveries: machines, human made products, compositions of matter, and processes. 35 U.S.C. § 101. Utility patents protect the way an article is used and works (35 U.S.C. § 101), while a "design patent" protects the way an article looks or its appearance.

Internet-related patents are typically utility patents, subcategorized as process patents if they qualify as new and useful. Internet utility patent disputes, like design lawsuits, can result in awards of hundreds of millions of dollars to patent owners. Microsoft concluded that "the number of Internet of Things litigated patents in the U.S. saw an increase of over 400 percent between 2013 and 2018." *Microsoft Expands its Azure Program for IoT Startups*, ICT MONITOR WORLDWIDE (Apr. 4, 2019).

A California jury decided that Apple must pay Qualcomm $31 million for infringing three of its patents that help mobile phones' battery life. Stephen Nellis, *Apple Infringed Three Qualcomm Patents, Jury Finds*, REUTERS (Mar. 15, 2019).

The jury "found that a number of iPhone models—the iPhone 7, iPhone 7 Plus, iPhone 8, iPhone 8 Plus, and iPhone X—infringed in varying degrees on three Qualcomm patents." Brandon Hill, *Qualcomm*

Awarded $31 Million After Apple Found Guilty Of Violating 3 Patents, HOT HARDWARE (Mar. 16, 2019).

In *Smartflash LLC v. Apple, Inc.,* 2015 WL 13649455 (E.D. Tex., Jul. 7, 2015), the Texas-based plaintiff was a holder of several U.S. patents, three of which were integral to storing and providing access to data through electronic payment systems. Smartflash asserted that the defendant, Apple Inc., infringed those patents through their iTunes software.

The jury returned a verdict in favor of Smartflash, finding that Apple infringed all of the asserted claims, that Apple willfully infringed the asserted claims, and that all of the asserted claims were valid. The jury also awarded Smartflash $532,900,000 in damages.

The jury determined that the three patents were valid, and that the iPhone, iPod touch, and iPad devices that used certain functionality in the App Store and the iTunes store infringed the asserted claims.

DivX LLC filed suit against Netflix for "infringing eight of its patents covering foundational internet video streaming technologies." Brian Flood, *Netflix Accused of Infringing Video Streaming Patents,* BLOOMBERG NEWS: IP (Mar. 6, 2019).

The DivX complaint stated:

> The patents allegedly disclose technologies for high-quality video streaming without stalls, digital rights management, and several video

playback features. These technologies are 'necessary for Netflix to deliver the viewing experience that its users expect,' DivX claims. Without DivX's innovations, 'Netflix would not enjoy the success that it does today,' the company said. *Id.*

(2) Design Patents

Design patents, with a term of fourteen years, protect the ornamental, exterior appearance of an object and that appearance must be non-functional. Articles of manufacture may possess both functional and ornamental characteristics. "Both design and utility patents may be obtained on an article if invention resides both in its utility and ornamental appearance." 35 U.S.C. § 171.

Design patents are relevant to Internet inventions because the USPTO considers computer-generated icons, including full screen images and type fonts, to constitute surface ornamentation. Design patents must be original and must not offend any race, religion, sex, ethnic group, or nationality. 35 U.S.C. § 171 and 37 CFR § 1.3.

On May 18, 2015, the United States Court of Appeals for the Federal Circuit affirmed the district court findings that Samsung had infringed Apple's design and utility patents, while also reversing on the infringement of trade dress. *Apple Inc. v. Samsung Electronics*, 786 F.3d 983 (Fed. Cir. 2015).

Samsung argued on appeal that the district court erred in not excluding the functional elements of

Apple's design patents in considering the alleged infringement. The Federal Circuit rejected the argument and found the district court reasoning was proper.

Regarding the issue of infringement of Apple's utility patents, Samsung attempted to argue that the term "substantially centered" is vague and uncertain.

The Federal Circuit credited Apple's expert with providing evidence to demonstrate that one skilled in the art would understand its meaning. The court affirmed the district court's denial of Samsung's motion for judgment as a matter of law on the invalidity of claim 50 of the '163 patent and claim 8 of the '915 patent, as well as the damages awarded for utility patent infringement.

The court denied Samsung's motion for a new trial and remanded for immediate entry of final judgment on all damages awards not predicated on Apple's trade dress claims.

(E) PATENT LAW TERMS

Generally, the term of a new utility patent, which accounts for most Internet-related patents, is 20 years from the date on which the patent application was filed. Plant patents also have a 20-year term, while design patents only have a term of 14 years from the issue date.

Utility or plant patents issued on applications filed before June 8, 1995, have a term of 17 years from the issuance of the patent or 20 years from the filing, whichever is greater.

§ 13-2. Section 101 Patentable Subject Matter

Under § 101 of the Patent Act, the scope of patentable subject matter encompasses "any new and useful process, machine, manufacture, or composition of matter, or any new and useful improvement thereof." 35 U.S.C. § 101.

Congress used "expansive terms" in defining the four categories of inventions eligible for patent protection under § 101: processes, machines, manufactures, and compositions of matter.

Section 101 "contains an important implicit exception: Laws of nature, natural phenomena, and abstract ideas are not patentable." *Alice Corp. Pty. Ltd. v. CLS Bank Intern.,* 573 U.S. 208, 216 (2014). These three categories of subject matter are excepted from patent-eligibility because "they are the basic tools of scientific and technological work," which are "free to all men and reserved exclusively to none." *Mayo Collaborative Servs. v. Prometheus Labs., Inc.*, 566 U.S. 66, 70 (2012).

Internet-related patents are often challenged as ineligible for protection. See, e.g., *Dealertrack, Inc. v. Huber*, 674 F.3d 1315 (Fed. Cir. 2012) ("computer aided" method for processing credit applications is § 101 ineligible); *CyberSource Corp. v. Retail Decisions, Inc.*, 654 F.3d 1366 (Fed. Cir. 2011) (method for detecting fraud in credit card transactions over Internet is § 101 ineligible).

The USPTO cites the following examples of patentable concepts:

> (1) Basic economic practices or theories (e.g., hedging, insurance, financial transactions, marketing); (2) Basic legal theories (e.g., contracts, dispute resolution, rules of law); (3) Mathematical concepts (e.g., algorithms, spatial relationships, geometry); (4) Mental activity (e.g., forming a judgment, observation, evaluation, or opinion); (5) Interpersonal interactions or relationships (e.g., conversing, dating); (6) Teaching concepts (e.g., memorization, repetition); (7) Human behavior (e.g., exercising, wearing clothing, following rules or instructions); and (8) Instructing how business should be conducted.

United States Trademark & Patent Office, *Patent Subject Matter Eligibility* (2012).

In *Express Mobile, Inc. v. Code and Theory LLC,* 2019 WL 477639 (N.D. Calif. Jan. 29, 2019), the defendant actions move to dismiss patent infringement claims contending the patent claims are drawn only to abstract ideas, ineligible for protection under Section 101 of the Patent Act, as elucidated in *Alice Corp. Pty. Ltd. v. CLS Bank Int'l*, 573 U.S. 208 (2014) and its progeny.

The court denied the motion to dismiss because the patents purport to describe a novel technological approach to creating websites on the Internet that was not an abstract idea. Express Mobile argued that the patents "bring together a number of disparate ideas and concepts, to create a new paradigm for creating, storing, and building web pages." *Id.*

According to Express Mobile, prior to the invention of the patents, web pages were created, stored, and rendered in a fundamentally different manner. Individual web pages were typically created by either programming directly in HTML or JavaScript code, or by using a visual editor that output HTML formatted files. These approaches allegedly were cumbersome and inflexible, in various respects. *Id.*

The inventive methodology described in the patents involves building a web page by defining it as a set of user-selected "objects" and/or "settings." The result is not a markup language code file for the web page, but instead a collection of user selected objects and object attributes. These can be saved in a database, for ease of access and efficient storage. *Id.*

Express Mobile explained that because complete code files for each page do not need to be stored, the page structure—the full HTML code itself—is created on the fly each time the page is loaded in a user's Web browser. This is achieved in part through a browser-appropriate "run time engine" and related files. The court agreed with Express Mobile rejecting the invalidity argument based upon an abstract idea:

> The patents here are directed at a purportedly revolutionary technological solution to a technological problem—how to create web pages for the Internet in a manner that permits 'what you see is what you get' editing, and a number of other alleged improvements over the then-existing methodologies. . . . Finally, to the extent that defendants are arguing that any potentially patent-eligible technological improvements set

> out in the specification are not reflected in the actual claims, dismissal under *Alice* is not appropriate, at least at this juncture. Although some claim construction has taken place, it simply cannot be said on the present record that the claims are drawn so broadly as to be divorced from the potentially patent-eligible purported technological improvements described in the specification.

The USPTO issued inventorship guidance for AI-assisted inventions. The USPTO's position is:

> The same legal standard for determining inventorship applies to all inventions, regardless of whether AI systems were used in the inventive process. There is no separate or modified standard for AI-assisted inventions. . . artificial intelligence systems, regardless of their sophistication, cannot be named as inventors or joint inventors on a patent application as they are not natural persons. . . AI systems, including generative AI and other computational models, are instruments used by human inventors. They are analogous to laboratory equipment, computer software, research databases, or any other tool that assists in the inventive process.

U.S. Department of Commerce, United States Patent and Trademark Office, *Examination Guidance* (Nov. 28, 2025) (rescinding the February 13, 2024 guidance on AI patents).

§ 13-3. Essentials of Patentability

The four statutory categories of patentability in Section 101 are (1) processes, (2) machines, (3) manufactures, and (4) compositions of matter. These categories fill out the meaning of "useful arts" in constitutional reference to patents. The federal patent statute requires a claim to have some utility (§ 101), be novel (not anticipated prior to the invention) (§ 102), and be nonobvious (§ 103).

Patentability Demystified

Issues Defined	*Section in Patent Act*
Novelty, Utility Statutory Bar	Section 101
Novelty, Anticipation	Section 102
Nonobviousness	Section 103

(A) PATENTABILITY: NOVELTY

A "claimed invention" is the invention as defined in the application for legal protection. Claims must demonstrate novelty as well as utility. What destroys novelty? Section 102(a)(1) states there is no novelty "if before filing date the patented or claimed invention as patented, was described in a printed publication, or in public use, on sale, or otherwise available to the public."

Section 102(a)(2) also finds no novelty when there is an issued patent or published application filed before the application. Novelty means that a patent claim was not anticipated by technology disclosed in the prior art. 35 U.S.C. § 102.

(1) Anticipation

For on-sale bar to render patent invalid, the device sold must fully anticipate the claimed invention or render it obvious. 35 U.S.C. § 102(b). To show that a patent claim is invalid as anticipated, the accused infringer must show by clear and convincing evidence that a single prior art reference discloses each and every element of a claimed invention; every element of the claimed invention must be described, either expressly or inherently, such that a person of ordinary skill in the art could practice the invention without undue experimentation. 35 U.S.C. § 102. When determining whether patent is invalid as anticipated, the court construes claims and compares them against the prior art. 35 U.S.C. § 102.

A patent examiner rejects a claim as anticipated under 35 U.S.C. § 102 when a single prior art reference discloses every element of the claim. If an invention was anticipated by prior art, it is not patentable. A person shall be entitled to a patent:

> unless—(1) the claimed invention was patented, described in a printed publication, or in public use, on sale, or otherwise available to the public before the effective filing date of the claimed invention; or (2) the claimed invention was described in a patent issued under Section 151, or in application for patent published or deemed published under Section 122(b), in which the patent or application, as the case may be, names

another inventor and was effectively filed before the effective filing date of the claimed invention.

35 U.S.C. § 102(a).

Anticipation includes evidence that the patent application was filed after any of the following events: (1) invention known by others, (2) invention used by others, (3) invention patented in the U.S. or abroad, and (4) invention described in a printed publication in the U.S. or abroad. 35 U.S.C. § 102(a). Section 102(b) allows for a one-year grace period for disclosures that originated, directly or indirectly, from the inventor or a joint inventor. 35 U.S.C. § 102(b).

Anticipation of a patent claim occurs if a single prior art reference discloses every limitation of the claim, either expressly or inherently. See, e.g., *Orion IP, LLC v. Hyundai Motor Am.*, 605 F.3d 967 (Fed. Cir. 2010). Anticipation challenges under § 102 must focus only on the limitations actually recited in the claims.

(2) Statutory Bar

Section 102(a) is a statutory bar if "the claimed invention was patented, described in a printed publication, or in public use, on sale, or otherwise available to the public before the effective filing date of the claimed invention." 35 U.S.C. § 102(a). A party alleging that a patent is invalid for public use is required to prove that, before the critical date, the method was shown or known to work for its intended purpose. 35 U.S.C. § 102(b).

(B) PATENTABILITY: NONOBVIOUSNESS

In determining whether a patent claim is invalid as obvious, a court is required to consider secondary considerations, or objective indicia of nonobviousness, before reaching an obviousness determination, as a check against hindsight bias; such secondary considerations as commercial success, long felt but unsolved needs, failure of others, etc., might be utilized to give light to the circumstances surrounding the origin of the subject matter sought to be patented. 35 U.S.C. § 103.

The obviousness requirement is the most difficult obstacle to overcome. Section 103 requires the claim to be nonobvious when measured against prior art. The test is whether the subject matter as a whole would have been obvious at the time of invention to a person having ordinary skill in the art.

An invention must also not be the functional equivalent of an invention covered by a previously issued patent. An invention is not patentable if someone disclosed the claimed subject matter before the date of filing or before the date of priority. An invention is not patentable if it would have been obvious to one of ordinary skill in the art.

(C) PATENTABILITY: UTILITY

Utility is the requirement that a patentable invention be useful. To satisfy the utility requirement, the invention must be operable or have the capacity to serve as either a product or process. Section 101 of Title 35 requires inventions to have novelty and utility. The utility requirement is seldom a significant barrier against patent seekers. The examiner must reject a patent if it does not achieve a useful result.

"Cold fusion is not patentable because of the lack of enablement under 112 and as inoperative and lacking utility under § 101." J. THOMAS MCCARTHY, MCCARTHY'S DESK ENCYCLOPEDIA OF INTELLECTUAL PROPERTY (3rd ed. 2004).

An invention is "ready for patenting," as required for the on-sale bar to patent's validity based on sale of invention before critical date, if invention has been reduced to practice, i.e., made and working as intended, or depicted in drawings or described in writings of sufficient nature to enable a person of ordinary skill in the art to practice the invention prior to the critical date.

(D) PATENT INVALIDITY

The U.S. Patent Act provides that "[a] patent shall be presumed valid" and that "[t]he burden of establishing invalidity of a patent or any claim thereof shall rest on the party asserting such invalidity." 35 U.S.C. § 282. During prosecution, patent examiners give claims the broadest reasonable interpretation that is still consistent with the specification. Section 132 requires examiners to cite reasons for rejection and rights for reexamination.

(E) PATENT TERMS

The term of a utility patent filed prior to June 8, 1995, is the later of (1) 17 years from the date of issuance of the patent, or (2) 20 years from the first U.S. filing date for the patent. The term for utility patent applications filed after June 8, 1995, is 20 years from the first U.S. filing date.

As recently as the 1980s, it was unclear whether software was patentable which had implications for relatively contemporary Internet-related patents. Today, software patents are primarily utility patents, which include compilers, application programs, and protection for process or method performed by a computer game.

§ 13-4. Internet Related Patents

(A) SOFTWARE PATENTS

Software-implemented inventions are treated in the same manner under the law as any other inventions: (1) Patentable subject matter, (2) Novelty, (3) Inventive Step, (4) Utility, and (5) sufficient disclosure.

No single development has spurred the growth of Internet-related patents more than *State Street Bank & Trust Co. v. Signature Financial Group, Inc.*, 149 F.3d 1368, 1373 (Fed. Cir. 1998). For the first time, a federal court recognized the validity of a business method. The business method at issue in *State Street* was predicated upon mathematical algorithms.

The Federal Circuit's validation of computer-related patents for doing business has had a profound impact on the Internet economy. In the immediate aftermath of the July 1998 decision, there was a 45% increase in the number of computer-related patents issued during the patent office's fiscal year ending on September 30, 1998. John T. Aquino, *Patently Permissive: USPTO Filings Up After Ruling Expands Protection for Business and Net Software*, A.B.A. J. (May 1999).

Since the *State Street Bank* case, the filing of so-called Internet business method patents has skyrocketed. MICHAEL L. RUSTAD & CYRUS DAFTARY, E-BUSINESS LEGAL HANDBOOK § 4.05[F] at 4–187 (2003).

Jonathan Masur documented the growth of business method patents:

> Thousands of patents on business methods and other intangible processes are granted each year, even though the Supreme Court had never before passed on their validity. Moreover, many scholars now believe that these types of patents are counterproductive: By increasing transaction costs and creating anticommons problems, they might well discourage innovation more than they encourage it.

Jonathan S. Masur, *Regulating Patents*, 2010 SUP. CT. REV. 275, 277–78 (2010).

Business methods patents are particularly vulnerable to challenge because of their abstract nature and their lack of clear boundaries. Most of the high-profile cases against information technology companies are for patent infringement.

Eolas successfully sued Microsoft for $521 million for the "browser plugin patent" in 1998. British Telecommunications claimed it owned the patent for web hyperlinks and sued Prodigy for patent infringement in 1989.

The Southern District for New York ruled in favor of Prodigy, finding that no reasonable jury could find that British Telecom's patent covered web hyperlinks. The plaintiff has the difficult burden of not only proving that the infringer had access to the protected work, but that the similarities must be due to copying rather than such factors as independent creation, a common source for both programs, or simple coincidence. The *Eolas* case was stayed on appeal and the parties entered into a confidential settlement in 2007.

In the early software industry, lawyers used trade secrets or copyright law, assuming that software was not patentable. The U.S. Court of Appeals, Federal Circuit, however, in *In re Alappat,* 33 F.3d 1526 (Fed. Cir. 1994), ruled that virtually all computer programs are patentable.

The USPTO has granted software patents for such diverse Internet-related activities as hyperlinking, audio software, file formats, and search engines. A software patent application must clearly describe what the computer does when it performs the steps dictated by software code. Many countries do not recognize software patents.

Software patents are frequently challenged. In *Trustees of Columbia University v. Gen Digital, Inc.*, 2026 WL 680960 (Fed. Cir. Mar. 11, 2026), the Federal Circuit Court of Appeals reversed a $481 million ruling that Columbia University was awarded against Gen Digital in a patent infringement case involving cybersecurity software.

Columbia University filed suit against Gen Digital Inc. markets the Norton software brand, asserting infringement of several patent claims related primarily to protecting computer systems from viruses. Norton filed a motion for judgment on the pleadings arguing that Columbia University's asserted claims were ineligible under 35 U.S.C. § 101. The federal district court denied the motion.

After trial, the jury returned a verdict of willful infringement and awarded $185,112,727 in damages. The Federal Circuit Court of Appeals vacated the verdict concluding that the asserted claims were abstract and not protectable by patent law.

(B) E-BUSINESS METHODS

In the United States, business methods qualify as "patentable eligible subject matter" if they are a new and useful process. At a bare minimum, the process must produce a useful, concrete, and tangible result to qualify as a business method. Software was unpatentable subject matter until the 1980s because it incorporated algorithms.

In *Akamai Technologies, Inc. v. Limelight Networks, Inc.*, 2008 WL 364401 (D. Mass. Feb. 8,

2008), a jury found Limelight infringed an Internet content delivery patent asserted by Akamai Technologies, and handed down a verdict of $45.5 million. In *Akamai,* the patent claim covered software for delivering the embedded objects of a web page. Limelight argued that a reasonable jury could conclude the company believed it did not infringe or cause others to infringe Akamai's patents because of Akamai's prior history of suing infringers.

Limelight appealed and the Supreme Court reversed and remanded back to the Federal Circuit. *Limelight Networks, Inc. v. Akamai Technologies, Inc.,* 572 U.S. 915 (2014).

The U.S. Supreme Court reasoned that because Limelight did not infringe on every step claimed in the method patent, they were not liable for infringement.

Courts accepted this business method exception for nearly a century until 1998 when the Federal Circuit reversed course in *State Street Bank & Trust Co. v. Signature Fin. Group, Inc.*, 149 F.3d 1368 (Fed. Cir. 1998). In *State Street,* Judge Giles Rich, writing for the panel, accepted a patent held by Signature Financial Group for a "hub and spoke" method of computing interest payments.

This method made it possible for mutual fund managers to pool their assets into a partnership, allowing tax advantages and administrative savings. The mere presence of a mathematical algorithm does not preordain that USPTO will reject a patent claim. The Federal Circuit held a programmed computer using this mathematical algorithm was patentable so long as it produced a useful, concrete, and tangible result.

In *State Street*, the court found an algorithm or formula that produced a "concrete and tangible result." Namely, it calculated a final share price for each mutual fund within the partnership as determined by their contributions to the pool, and because of its practical application, it was thus patentable.

The validation of business methods patents was extended in *AT&T Corp. v. Excel Communications, Inc.*, 172 F.3d 1352 (Fed. Cir. 1999), where the Federal Circuit approved a patent that incorporated Boolean algebra to determine the long-distance carriers involved in a telephone call, which in turn created a switching signal for billing purposes.

The *AT&T* Court reasoned that this was not an attempt to patent the Boolean principle, but rather a patent for the process to create the discrete switching signal. The method created a concrete and tangible result, and was therefore patentable. After *State Street* and *AT&T*, USPTO required business method patents to advance the technological arts.

(C) POST-STATE STREET CASES

Businesses filed tens of thousands of business method patent applications since State Street opened the floodgates. In 2000, "Amazon.com was granted a patent on its affiliates' program, which allows 'owners of other Websites to refer customers to

Amazon in exchange for a fee.'" Geneva Sapp, *E-Businesses vie for Technology Ownership*, NETWORK WORLD (Mar. 6, 2000).

The USPTO granted a patent for Amazon.com's "1-click" technology for online shopping. Amazon.com's 1-Click, a "method, and system for placing a purchase order via a communications network" sparked one of the most famous Internet patent debates. The patent permitted customers to make online purchases with a single click, using a pre-defined address and credit card number.

A federal court granted Amazon an injunction, enjoining Barnes & Noble from using a single-click Express Checkout on their online store. The parties settled before trial to determine the validity of the one-click method. Amazon and Barnes & Noble settled their patent infringement dispute in 2000, with Barnes & Noble licensing the 1-Click patent. *Amazon.com, Inc. v. Barnesandnoble.com, Inc.*, 239 F.3d 1343 (Fed. Cir. 2001).

§ 13-5. The Supreme Court's Patent Cases

(A) *MERCEXCHANGE*

The injunctive remedy is often more important than monetary damages in Internet-related patent cases. An injunction is an equitable remedy routinely used to order defendants to refrain from infringing patents. In *eBay Inc. v. MercExchange L.L.C.*, 547 U.S. 388 (2006), the Supreme Court unanimously determined that a federal court should not automatically issue an injunction simply because it has found patent infringement.

The case arose out of dispute between eBay, the Internet's largest auction site, and MercExchange, which owned U.S. Patent 5,845,265 that covers eBay's "Buy It Now" function. In 2000, eBay initiated negotiations with MercExchange to purchase its online auction patent portfolio.

When eBay abandoned the negotiations to purchase the patent, MercExchange filed suit against eBay for patent infringement. MercExchange prevailed in a 2003 Virginia jury trial that found eBay had willfully infringed the patent incorporated in its "Buy It Now" function. MercExchange sought an injunction to prevent eBay's continual use of the patent, but the federal trial court denied its request.

The Federal Circuit Court of Appeals reversed the trial court, reasoning that its decision was consistent with its long-standing practice of issuing permanent injunctions against patent infringement absent exceptional circumstances.

The long-standing rule in the Federal Circuit was to issue injunctions liberally in patent infringement cases so long as the plaintiff could prove an ongoing infringement. To put it bluntly, the Federal Court of Appeals did not require patent owners to demonstrate irreparable harm.

In *MercExchange*, the lower court refused to enjoin the online auction house, finding that damages were adequate. The Federal Circuit Court of Appeals reversed, ruling that in patent infringement cases an injunction is issued absent exceptional circumstances.

The *MercExchange* Court ruled that the Federal Circuit improperly applied a presumed irreparable injury test as opposed to the traditional four-factor test for the issuance of a permanent injunction. Eventually, the Supreme Court intervened, which reversed the Federal Circuit's traditional practice of liberally issuing injunctions in patent infringement cases.

The U.S. Supreme Court ruled that federal courts must now weigh four factors before issuing an injunction: (1) that the plaintiff has suffered an irreparable injury, (2) that remedies available at law are inadequate to compensate for that injury, (3) that considering the balance of hardships between the plaintiff and defendant, a remedy in equity is warranted, and (4) that the public interest would not be disserved by a permanent injunction.

The finding that permanent injunctions are subject to the ordinary rules governing equitable relief means that relief is discretionary, as opposed to relief issued routinely. Injunctive relief is critically imperative in Internet-related patent litigation because of the rapidity with which online businesses can attain or lose market share. In the Internet-based economy, the earliest mover has enormous advantages. Some businesses use patent law strategically as a method for excluding potential rivals.

(B) *BILSKI V. KAPPOS*

In *Bilski v. Kappos*, 561 U.S. 593 (2010), the U.S. Supreme Court unanimously upheld the Federal Circuit's decision that the application for a method of hedging risk was "an unpatentable abstract idea" that was outside the scope of the U.S. Patent Act, § 101. The patent application in *Bilski* was for a procedure that helped buyers and sellers protect against price fluctuations in the volatile energy market by hedging against price changes.

The patent examiner rejected the application, explaining that it was a mere manipulation of an abstract idea and solves a mathematical problem without sufficient practical application. The Board of Patent Appeals and Interferences affirmed, concluding that the application only involved mental steps that transformed physical matter directed to an abstract idea.

The Federal Circuit Court heard the case *en banc* and affirmed, reasoning that the machine-or-transformation test was the sole test for determining the patentability of a process under Section 101. The Federal Circuit Court's view was that an invention is a "process" only if (1) tied to a particular machine or apparatus, or (2) it transforms a particular article into a different state or thing. The U.S. Supreme Court granted certiorari to determine whether patentable subject matter should exclude the process patent.

The Court held that the Federal Circuit incorrectly endorsed the machine-or-transformation test for a process as the only valid criteria. The Court reasoned that the Federal Circuit test was a useful tool but not the sole method of deciding whether an invention is a patent-eligible process.

The Court decided that the process patent for hedging was unpatentable as an abstract idea. In *Bilski*, the Court was concerned that to allow patent risk hedging would pre-empt use of this approach in all fields. The *Bilski* decision limits the availability of process patents. *Bilski* also calls for a rigorous review of software, business method, and many Internet-related process claims.

(C) *MAYO COLLABORATIVE SERVICES*

In *Mayo Collaborative Servs. v. Prometheus Laboratories, Inc.*, 566 U.S. 66, 71 (2012), the U.S. Supreme Court set forth an analytical framework under § 101 to distinguish patents that claim patent-ineligible laws of nature, natural phenomena, and abstract ideas or are ineligible subject matter. First, given the nature of the invention in this case, the court determines whether the claims at issue are directed to a patent-ineligible abstract idea.

In *Prometheus Laboratories,* the applicant's claim was for optimizing the therapeutic efficiency of a drug. Justice Beyer acknowledged that the "administering," "determining," and "wherein" steps were not natural laws, the claim added too little to the law of nature and thus was not patentable.

If the court does find that the claims are patent eligible subject matter, they then consider the elements of each claim—both individually and as an ordered combination—to determine whether the additional elements transform the nature of the claim into a patent-eligible application of that abstract idea.

This second step is the search for an "inventive concept," or some element or combination of elements sufficient to ensure that the claim in practice amounts to "significantly more" than a patent on an ineligible concept.

§ 13-6. Global Patent Developments

The World Intellectual Property Organization (WIPO) World Intellectual Property Indicators (2025) concluded that 3.7 million patent applications were filed worldwide in 2024, a 4.9% increase from 2023 and a fifth consecutive year of expansion. WIPO noted the following about global patent law developments:

- In 2024, innovators around the world filed 3.7 million patent applications, marking a 4.9% increase over 2023 and the fastest year-on-year growth since 2018.
- A substantial increase in filings by applicants residing in China (at least 153,072 additional applications in 2024 compared to 2023), India (+12,274), the Republic of Korea (+7,523) and Japan (+4,533) was the main driver of growth in 2024. Furthermore, over the past five years, China, India and the Republic of Korea have

consistently been the main contributors to the overall growth in patent filings.

- The worldwide filing of 3.7 million applications in 2024 comprised 2.7 million resident filings (72.6% of the total) and 1 million non-resident filings (27.4%).

- Resident filings grew by 6.8% in 2024—the fastest rate of growth since 2016—while non-resident filings remained stable. Over the past decade, resident filings have grown at a faster pace than non-resident filings, with average annual growth rates of 4.1% and 1.6%, respectively.

- The long-term trend in global patent applications has been consistently upward, reflecting the accelerating pace of innovation worldwide. Between 2010 and 2024, filings have nearly doubled, rising 1.9-fold from just under 2 million to 3.7 million.

WIPO, *World Intellectual Property Indicators* (2025) at 8.

WIPO's 2025 study concluded that:

- Patent rights are territorial in nature. In order to protect an invention in several countries, applicants often file patent an application for the same invention in multiple jurisdictions. This being the case, adding patent data from different jurisdictions would inflate the number of new inventions.

- Patent family data are therefore frequently used i order to eliminate (or at least minimize) double counting. The basic idea behind a patent family is to group together all applications—original and subsequent filings—related to each other via priority filing(s).
- WIPO has developed indicators for patent families with the aim of capturing the actual number of unique inventions by excluding double counting so far as possible. The drawback of such data is the consequent time lag, which can be up to three years.
- In 2022, applicants from China accounted for nearly 70% of all patent families, followed by Japan (8.1%), the Republic of Korea (6.9%), the US (6.8%) and Germany (2.1%). Together, these five origins represented 93.8% of the global total.

In a 2019 study, WIPO found that:

The top five IP offices receive around 85.3% of the 3.3 million patent applications filed worldwide in 2019, a considerable share (46.4%) was filed in China alone, primarily by Chinese residents. The next largest shares went to the offices of the U.S., Japan, the Republic of Korea and the European Patent Office (EPO).

WIPO IP Facts and Figures (2019) at 11.

WIPO data confirmed the growth of patent filings:

> There were 14 million patents in force worldwide in 2018, of which around 3.1 million were in force in the United States of America (U.S.), 2.4 million in China and 2.1 million in Japan. Of the 49.3 million active trademark registrations worldwide, 19.6 million were in China alone, followed by 2.4 million in the U.S., 1.9 million in India, and 1.9 million in Japan. The total number of industrial designs in force worldwide grew by 5% to reach 3.75 million. While China accounted for 40.4% of the world total of industrial designs in force—under half—it accounted for nearly all of the utility models in force (93%).

In December 2018, the Chinese Patent Office (CNIPA) suspended subsidies to patent applications for the province of Guandong to cut down on the large number of abnormal patent applications:

> Specifically, all of 13 cities in Guangdong province (including Guangzhou city and Shenzhen city) successively announced to stop offering any kind of patent subsidization to any type of patent (i.e., invention, utility model, and design). Even if the patent is granted, the subsidy will not be awarded to a large extent. Further, the patent subsidy for outbound cases (such as PCT international applications that enter other countries or regions) is also suspended in most cities of Guangdong province.

Mr. Haoyu Zhou, *Guangdong Province Fully Suspend Patent Subsidization*, MONDAQ (Mar. 7, 2019).

The European Patent Convention does not define inventions but only requires that they shall have a "technical character." Business methods and computer program are expressly excluded from patentable subject matter. WIPO notes that computer software must have technical character to be patentable:

> Programs for computers are a form of "computer-implemented invention," an expression intended to cover claims which involve computers, computer networks or other programmable apparatus whereby prima facie one or more of the features of the claimed invention are realised by means of a program or programs. Such claims may e.g., take the form of a method of operating said apparatus, the apparatus set up to execute the method, a readable medium carrying a program (see T 424/03) or, following T 1173/97, the program itself. The examiner should disregard the claim category and concentrate on its content in order to determine whether the claimed subject-matter, considered as a whole, has a technical character.

Moreover, insofar as the scheme for examination is concerned, no distinctions are made on the basis of the overall purpose of the invention, i.e., whether it is intended to fill a business niche, to provide some new entertainment, etc. Technical character should be assessed without regard to the prior art (see T 1173/97, confirmed by G 3/08).

GUIDELINES FOR THE EXAMINATION OF THE EPO, Part G, Chapter II-5, Rule 3.6 Programs for computers.

The Trade-Related Intellectual Property Agreement sets minimum standards for patents for signatory states. The TRIPS Agreement sets the following rules for patents:

- The TRIPS Agreement requires Member countries to make patents available for any inventions, whether products or processes, in all fields of technology without discrimination, subject to the normal tests of novelty, inventiveness and industrial applicability.

- It is also required that patents be available and patent rights enjoyable without discrimination as to the place of invention and whether products are imported or locally produced (Article 27.1).

- There are three permissible exceptions to the basic rule on patentability.

- One is for inventions contrary to *ordre public* or morality; this explicitly includes inventions dangerous to human, animal or plant life or health or seriously prejudicial to the environment. The use of this exception is subject to the condition that the commercial exploitation of the invention must also be prevented and this prevention must be necessary for the protection of *ordre public* or morality (Article 27.2).

- The second exception is that Members may exclude from patentability diagnostic, therapeutic and surgical methods for the treatment of humans or animals (Article 27.3(a)).

- The third is that Members may exclude plants and animals other than micro-organisms and essentially biological processes for the production of plants or animals other than non-biological and microbiological processes. However, any country excluding plant varieties from patent protection must provide an effective sui generis system of protection. Moreover, the whole provision is subject to review four years after entry into force of the Agreement (Article 27.3(b)).

- The exclusive rights that must be conferred by a product patent are the ones of making, using, offering for sale, selling, and importing for these purposes. Process patent protection must give rights not only over use of the process but also over products obtained directly by the process.

- Patent owners shall also have the right to assign, or transfer by succession, the patent and to conclude licensing contracts (Article 28).

- Members may provide limited exceptions to the exclusive rights conferred by a patent, provided that such exceptions do not unreasonably conflict with a normal exploitation of the patent and do not unreasonably prejudice the legitimate interests of the patent owner, taking account of the legitimate interests of third parties (Article 30).

- The term of protection available shall not end before the expiration of a period of 20 years counted from the filing date (Article 33).

- Members shall require that an applicant for a patent shall disclose the invention in a manner sufficiently clear and complete for the invention to be carried out by a person skilled in the art and may require the applicant to indicate the best mode for carrying out the invention known to the inventor at the filing date or, where priority is claimed, at the priority date of the application (Article 29.1).

- If the subject-matter of a patent is a process for obtaining a product, the judicial authorities shall have the authority to order the defendant to prove that the process to obtain an identical product is different from the patented process, where certain conditions indicating a likelihood that the protected process was used are met (Article 34).

- Compulsory licensing and government use without the authorization of the right holder are allowed, but are made subject to conditions aimed at protecting the legitimate interests of the right holder. The conditions are mainly contained in Article 31.

- These include the obligation, as a general rule, to grant such licences only if an unsuccessful attempt has been made to acquire a voluntary licence on reasonable terms and conditions within a reasonable period of time; the requirement to pay adequate remuneration in the circumstances of each case, considering the economic value of the licence; and a requirement that decisions be subject to judicial or other independent review by a distinct higher authority.
- Certain of these conditions are relaxed where compulsory licences are employed to remedy practices that have been established as anticompetitive by a legal process. These conditions should be read together with the related provisions of Article 27.1, which require that patent rights shall be enjoyable without discrimination as to the field of technology, and whether products are imported or locally produced.

World Trade Organization, *Overview: the TRIPS Agreement: Patents* (2026).

The TRIPS Agreement has broadened the sphere of application for what can be patented. All countries need to grant a patent for a minimum of 20 years. TRIPS requires patents to be assessed for non-obviousness and utility. The Agreement gives patent owners the right to block the importation of infringing products. TRIPS limits when governments can order compulsory licensing of patents. The Agreement creates transitional provisions for less developed countries.

Michael L. Rustad, 1A COMPUTER CONTRACTS § 3A.05 (updated 2026).

§ 13-7. Conclusion

Patent law, like the other branches of the law, is constantly evolving in response to the development of the Internet. Justice Holmes's classic essay on the path of the law drew upon six centuries of case reports and statutes. The Internet offers a global marketplace open 24 hours a day, 365 days a year. During the past two decades, social networks evolved as interactive platforms enabling hundreds of millions of users to create, manage, and share their interests online.

The Internet transforms basic assumptions about the nature of communication, knowledge, invention, information, sovereignty, identity, commerce, human rights, and community. This information technology is reshaping intellectual property law as it shatters existing precedent by redefining distance, time, privacy, and the meaning of territoriality. The phenomenal growth in traffic on the World Wide Web requires established legal principles for all branches of the law be adapted to cyberspace.

Global Internet law must continually evolve to meet the new risks and dangers in the twenty-first century's age of information. Further global coordination is essential to surmount the growing substantive and procedural barriers to cross-border Internet-related development.

Travelers on the World Wide Web require uniform procedural and substantive remedies for cross-border civil rights and wrongs, a very difficult achievement because of national rivalries and cultural differences.

INDEX

References are to Pages